DIRECTORY OF STATISTICAL MICROCOMPUTER SOFTWARE

DIRECTORY OF STATISTICAL MICROCOMPUTER SOFTWARE

1988 EDITION

Wayne A. Woodward
Southern Methodist University, Dallas, Texas

Alan. C. Elliot
University of Texas Health Science Center, Dallas, Texas

Henry L. Gray
Douglas C. Matlock
Southern Methodist University, Dallas, Texas

MARCEL DEKKER, INC. • NEW YORK AND BASEL

The Library of Congress has cataloged this work as follows:

Directory of statistical microcomputer software. — 1985 ed.-
New York ; Basel : Dekker, c1985-

v.;23 cm.

Annual.
Compilers: Wayne A. Woodward, Alan C. Elliot, H. L. Gray.

1. Statistics—Computer programs—Directories. 2. Mathematical statistics—Computer programs—Directories. 3. Microcomputers—Programming—Periodicals. 4. Microcomputers—Computer programs—Directories. I. Woodward, Wayne A. II. Elliot, Alan C. III. Gray, Henry L.
QA276.4.D57 519.5'028'55369—dc19 86-642997
ISBN 0-8247-7846-4

MARCEL DEKKER, INC.
270 Madison Avenue, New York, New York 10016

Current printing (last digit):
10 9 8 7 6 5 4 3 2 1

PRINTED IN THE UNITED STATES OF AMERICA

Contents

Preface

The age of microcomputing is now 10 years old. With it has come a new battery of scientific tools. This book is a directory of statistical programs which are currently available on the microcomputer. The first edition, 1985, described 140 such programs. In the current edition, over 200 programs are described. Although many of the programs described in the first edition are no longer being produced, replacements are appearing in the marketplace faster than others are being withdrawn. With such a changing market, a directory such as this is a valuable tool in locating specific programs to provide the kinds of tools users need.

The authors have been collecting information on microcomputer statistical programs since 1980, when an initial survey found only a "handful" of packages. As statistical consultants, the authors became aware of the fact that researchers in many fields were beginning to buy and use these packages. Once it was evident that a boom in these packages was about to begin, the authors developed a questionnaire to gather information on the packages as they surfaced in the marketplace. Initial findings were published in statistical periodicals and drew a quick response for more information.

The 1985 directory was the result of a comprehensive search to identify as many packages as possible. The directory was very well received, but is dated. The authors have carefully updated information from the original book, and added many new products. Many products which are no longer produced were dropped.

Information from questionnaires has been organized with the dBASE III plus program from Ashton-Tate, and was printed using the VersaText word processor from TexaSoft, Inc. Special thanks go to Beverly Woodward for her help in entering and editing the information.

Wayne A. Woodward
Alan C. Elliott
Henry L. Gray
Douglas C. Matlock

Introduction

Statistical software has been around for many years. Specifically, mainframe users may be familiar with products such as SAS, SPSS, BMDP and IMSL. When the microcomputer began to offer inexpensive computing, it was natural for statistical programs to be written for this new medium. At first, microcomputers did not have the memory or power to operate packages with the complexity of those mentioned above. This gave rise to a new generation of statistical software packages. Although the new packages were smaller, they did offer some advantages over their mainframe counterparts. Graphics were often of higher quality, and the microcomputer offered color and more sophisticated interactive capabilities.

How Good Are Microcomputer Packages?

The mainframe packages that have been around for many years have undergone the scrutiny of professional statisticians. This has not guaranteed that they are free of error, but errors have often been found and corrected. Several of the statistical and computational periodicals contain reviews of microcomputer statistical software. However, with over 200 viable microcomputer statistical packages available in the marketplace, such close examination of individual programs is not as feasible as it once was on the handful of mainframe programs. In talks, papers, and discussions, many "horror" stories have been told about microcomputer statistical packages. These include cases where the program gives a wrong degree of freedom, uses the height of the normal curve as if it were a probability, and reports negative sums of squares in an example printed in the manual. Such problems were inevitable in this infant market. This directory does not try to directly evaluate the packages listed. However, references are given when possible concerning published reviews of the products.

One Potential Problem Is Precision

Precision is a potential problem in all mathematical computation. On the microcomputer, many calculations are performed with a limited number of significant digits, often 7 or 8. Some fractions, small numbers and large numbers cannot be stored exactly, and the computer rounds them off. When these rounded numbers are used in further calculations, small errors may be magnified. This same problem existed on the early mainframe computers and can be addressed by special computer algorithms, the use of math co-processors and supporting software, and by performing calculations in higher precision. Some programs have implemented these techniques, and others have not.

What Statistical Procedure to Use

Statistical programs can be made to perform the wrong tests on the right data. In other words, the results obtained from the program are only as good as the decision about which procedure to use. The easy availability of statistical programs make it easy for the statistical layman to perform tests that may or may not be appropriate. An article in CIRCULATION (Glantz, 1980) reported that published reviewed medical research papers used statistical decision making inappropriately 57% of the time -- and this covered a time period before the availability of statistical packages on the microcomputer. Thus, there are two basic concerns with using microcomputer statistical software. One is the possibility that the package itself may not give correct answers, and the second is that the user may be performing the wrong procedure. One can only hope that the emergence of readily available statistical packages will make researchers more conscious of the need to use statistics properly rather than produce more misuse.

What Computer Will It Run On?

Not all microcomputer software will run on all microcomputers. It is important for the potential buyer to be aware of compatibility issues. Statistical software, as with other microcomputer software, is usually targeted to a specific microcomputer, or a family of microcomputers. Most people will be familiar with the major microcomputers of Apple and IBM. It is important to realize that programs written for the IBM PC will not run on the Apple II (unless a different version of the software is available). The exchange of data from one computer to another is not readily performed without special communications software and hardware. This is also true of exchanging data with a mini- or mainframe computer. There are some compatibilities across brands of microcomputers. For example, many computers now adhere to the "IBM standard." Another area of compatibility that the user must examine is the use of peripherals such as monitors, printers and plotters. Many programs support only a selected subset of these devices.

In the preparation of this directory, we have tried to provide you with much of the information you need to match software to your machine. If you have not yet purchased a computer, it is often helpful to decide what software you require first, then find the computer to run the software.

Many producers claim that their package will run on certain major brands of computer "and compatibles." Compatible machines are somewhat mysterious because there are levels of compatibility. Some computers that claim compatibility with the IBM PC, for example, may not actually be 100% compatible. Some compatible machines may be able to read data, but not run programs for the IBM PC. Some programs require the IBM PC BASIC interpreter, which may not be available on a compatible machine without extra costs. If you own a compatible machine, make sure you are able to try out the package on your machine before actually purchasing it.

Disclaimers

While every effort has been made to collect true information on the computer programs described in this book, we are sure that errors do exist. It is incumbent on the reader to realize that the vast majority of the data including the brief textual description was provided by the manufacturer of the product.

Of course, prices and capabilities are subject to change, so before ordering any of these products, we suggest that you write or contact the company. Some publishers offer educational, quantity and site-license discounts.

The Contents of the Directory

Programs in the directory are listed in alphabetical order by product name. An address, phone number and contact person is usually provided. A description of configurations is provided, listing the computer(s), operating systems, amount of memory, storage medium, and price. Under "Number of Drives," the abbreviation TP means cassette tape, and HD means a hard disk is required. A history of the product is given including the date it was first released, and the date of the most current version, along with the number of products currently in use. The textual description and list of reviews were provided by the software publisher.

The purpose and style of the program are described including a brief description of the documentation and the type of graphic output available.

Statistical Features

A list of statistical features is divided into major categories such as descriptive statistics, t-tests, correlation and regression, etc. Many programs which are special purpose in nature may have features in only one of these areas. Other, more general packages may support a wide variety of statistical features.

Reviews

Each publisher was asked to provide a list of published product reviews. These are included just below the product description. Unfortunately, some responders gave incomplete references. Such references were generally not reported in the directory.

Road Maps to Finding What You Want

Several tables in the appendices summarize the features of the programs. For instance, if you are interested in programs which perform analysis of variance, you can look at the "Program Capabilities" under ANOVA to locate which programs claim to provide this function. There is also a table summarizing computer compatibilities. If you are looking for a program for the Macintosh, you will find programs that run on that computer designated in the table.

4CAST/2, 4CAST/2X
Core Analytic, Inc.
674 Rt. 202-206 N
Bridgewater, NJ 08807
(201) 218 - 0900
Contact Person: Fred M. Chalek

CONFIGURATIONS SUPPORTED

Computer	Language	Operating System	RAM	Number Drives	Cost
IBM PC	TURBO PASCAL	DOS	312K	1	$350

NUMBER OF CURRENT USERS 150+
DATE OF FIRST RELEASE May 86
VERSION 1.0 RELEASED May 86

PROGRAM DESCRIPTION

4CaST/2X is a multi-technique, time series forecasting package. 4CaST/2X is oriented toward those users in market research, economics, planning, product management, operations research and forecasting who require a wide variety of techniques (including the Census X-11) coupled with easy to use menus and a powerful graphics capability. This package is designed to provide the user with a base of techniques that can be translated into better forecasts, and then displayed to their best advantage for presentation purposes.

4CaST/2X is a very user oriented PC based package that emphasizes the stepwise approach to good forecasting. The most widely, and currently accepted, techniques for exploratory data analysis, transformations, smoothing techniques, time series decomposition, regression, and trend fitting, all of which are integrated with a hi-res resident graphics capability, are included. The on-line editor is LOTUS-like in function; the commands are menu/function key driven; the calculations are very fast (especially with 8087 support); the user has the ability to create "macros"; the graphics are colorful, easy to use, and can be customized; and the documentation teaches the user how to properly approach time series forecasting as well as how to best use the software.

TYPE OF PROGRAM
Time Series Analysis

PROGRAM DESIGNED FOR
Data Analysis

PROGRAM STYLE
Menu Driven
Integrated System

MISCELLANEOUS PROGRAM FEATURES
Copyable Disk
On Screen Help Function
Optional Support for 8087, 80287 Mathematical Chip

DOCUMENTATION
User's Manual - 350+ pages, 50+ technical references
Table of Contents
Index
Tutorial or Example Lessons
Sample Runs
Formulas Provided

DATA MANAGEMENT
Keyboard Data Entry
Data Manipulations and Transformations

DATA EDITING
Change
Add
Delete

FOREIGN DATA ACCESS
Standard Rectangular ASCII Files
DIF Files
Data Disk
Multiplan
ISX (Statlib)

GRAPHICS FEATURES
Graphics Appear in Color on the Monitor
Graphics can be Output to a Printer
Graphics can be Saved to a File
Titles and/or Labels Available
Uses Pixel Graphics

GRAPHICS
- Histograms
- Scatter (x-y) Plots
- SEE Regression Plots
- SEE Time Series Plots

PRODUCT SUPPORT
- User may call at own Expense
- Classes or Instruction Available

STATISTICAL FEATURES SUPPORTED

DESCRIPTIVE STATISTICS
- Mean
- Standard Deviation or Variance
- Standard Error of the Mean
- Minimum, Maximum
- Median
- Percentiles

t-TESTS
- One Sample t-Test

CORRELATION AND REGRESSION
- Simple Linear Regression
- Multiple Linear Regression
- Stepwise Multiple Linear Regression
- Residuals Calculated
- Weighted Regression
- **REGRESSION PLOTS**
  - Residuals

ANALYSIS OF VARIANCE
- One-Way ANOVA

DISTRIBUTION FUNCTION EVALUATION
- Normal
- t
- F

EXPLORATORY DATA ANALYSIS
- Smoothing Techniques

TIME SERIES ANALYSIS

- Autocorrelations
- Cross Correlations
- Moving Average Smoothing
    - Model Identification
- **TIME SERIES ANALYSIS - FORECASTING**
    - Regression
    - X-11
    - Seasonal
    - Trending
    - Smoothing
- **TIME SERIES ANALYSIS - PLOTS**
    - Data
    - Autocorrelation Function
    - Residuals
    - Forecasts
    - Others

MISCELLANEOUS

- Random Number Generation

A-STAT 83

Rosen Grandon Associates
3106 Edgewater Drive
Greensboro, NC 27403
(919) 292 - 2116
Contact Person: Jane R Rosen-Grandon, M.A.

CONFIGURATIONS SUPPORTED

Computer	Language	Operating System	RAM	Number Drives	Cost
APPLE	BASIC	DOS	48K	1	$ 200
IBM PC	BASIC	DOS	128K	1	$ 175

NUMBER OF CURRENT USERS 1200+
DATE OF FIRST RELEASE Mar 79
VERSION 83.1 RELEASED 1983

PROGRAM DESCRIPTION

A-STAT is a complete database and statistical package including procedures for univariate variable descriptions, continuous and discrete frequency distributions with histograms, cross-tabulation (bi-variate tables) with over 14 measures of association, correlational analysis with pair-wise or list-wise deletion of missing data, multiple regression analysis including Durbin-Watson and residuals and predicted scores, factor analysis, analysis of variance, t-Tests and much more. Routines support missing values and weight variables. Output routed to screen, printer or disk files.

As a Database system, A-STAT supports many forms of data entry, supports full DIF Interfaces, Apple PLOT and FILE Cabinet Interfaces. Routines have access to powerful transformation language. All routines fully compiled Microsoft BASIC. Capacity is an entire disk volume of data (over 2,600 cases).

PRODUCT REVIEWS

Carpenter, James et. al.. "Statistical Software for Microcomputers", BYTE, pp. 234-264, (April 1984).

Collins, T.. "A-STAT 79.6C, a Statistical Package for the Apple II", Infoworld, (April 26, 1982).

Vina, L. de La. "Econometrics Software for Microcomputers", Journal of Business and Economic Statistics, (in press).

Butler, D L and Eamon, D B. "An Evaluation of Statistical Software for Research & Inst.", Behavior Research Methods, Instruments and Computers, pp. 352-358, (1985).

TYPE OF PROGRAM
Statistical Package

PROGRAM DESIGNED FOR
Data Analysis

PROGRAM STYLE
Menu Driven
Integrated System

MISCELLANEOUS PROGRAM FEATURES
Source Code Available
Copyable Disk
On Screen Help Function

DOCUMENTATION
User's Manual - 120 pages, 10 technical references
Table of Contents
Index
Tutorial or Example Lessons
Sample Runs
Formulas Provided
Tutorials and Examples on Disk

DATA MANAGEMENT
Keyboard Data Entry
Data Manipulations and Transformations
Missing Values Allowed in Data

DATA EDITING
Change
Add
Delete

FOREIGN DATA ACCESS
Standard Rectangular ASCII Files
DIF Files

PRODUCT SUPPORT
User may call at own Expense
No Classes or Instruction Available

STATISTICAL FEATURES SUPPORTED

DESCRIPTIVE STATISTICS
Mean
Standard Deviation or Variance
Standard Error of the Mean
Coefficient of Variation
Minimum, Maximum
Median
Percentiles
Skewness
Kurtosis

t-TESTS
One Sample t-Test
Independent Group t-Test/Equal Variance
Independent Group t-Test/Unequal Var
Paired t-Test

CORRELATION AND REGRESSION
Pearson Correlation Coefficient
Simple Linear Regression
Multiple Linear Regression
Residuals Calculated
Estimate Asymptotic Standard Errors

CATEGORICAL DATA ANALYSIS
Chi-Square Contingency Table Analysis
Fisher's Exact Test
Frequencies Can be Entered Directly

ANALYSIS OF VARIANCE
One-Way ANOVA
One-Way with Repeated Measures
Analysis of Covariance
Split Plot

TIME SERIES ANALYSIS
TIME SERIES ANALYSIS - FORECASTING
Linear

MISCELLANEOUS
Random Number Generation
p-Values Given With Tests

ABC STATISTICAL SOFTWARE

Consortium Software
426 Thompson St
Ann Arbor, MI 48106-1248
(313) 763 - 3482
Contact Person: Barb Lohr

CONFIGURATIONS SUPPORTED

Computer	Language	Operating System	RAM	Number Drives	Cost
IBM PC	FORTRAN	PC-DOS	256K	2	$ 200
PRIME 50	FORTRAN	PRIMOS			$1000
DEC VAX/VMS	FORTRAN	VMS			$1000

NUMBER OF CURRENT USERS 559
DATE OF FIRST RELEASE Dec 83
VERSION 2.3 RELEASED Sept 84

PROGRAM DESCRIPTION

ABC is a computer program designed to do basic statistical analysis. ABC was developed in an effort to make data analysis software easy to use for the student, for the instructor who wants to concentrate on teaching, not computing, and for the data analyst whose needs are straightforward but whose time is limited such as administrators, professionals, and business people.

ABC is completly interactive and has an extensive amount of on-line help text, which provides immediate feedback to the user in case of errors or questions. It was written and formatted specifically for video display terminals, and only prints one screenful of information at a time. ABC is menu-oriented, so that the user doesn't need to memorize a large number of commands in order to use the program.

TYPE OF PROGRAM

Statistical Package

PROGRAM DESIGNED FOR
Educational use

PROGRAM STYLE
Menu Driven
Integrated System

MISCELLANEOUS PROGRAM FEATURES
Copyable Disk
On Screen Help Function
Optional Support for 8087 Mathematical Chip

DOCUMENTATION
User's Manual - 186 pages, 0 technical references
Index
Tutorial or Example Lessons
Sample Runs
Formulas Provided
Tutorials and Examples on Disk

DATA MANAGEMENT
Data Manipulations and Transformations
Missing Values Allowed in Data

DATA EDITING
Change
Add
Delete

FOREIGN DATA ACCESS
Standard Rectangular ASCII Files
dBase II Files
Non-rectangular ASCII Files

PRODUCT SUPPORT
User may call at own Expense
No Classes or Instruction Available

STATISTICAL FEATURES SUPPORTED

DESCRIPTIVE STATISTICS
- Mean
- Standard Deviation or Variance
- Minimum, Maximum
- Median
- Mode

CORRELATION AND REGRESSION
- Pearson Correlation Coefficient
- Simple Linear Regression
- Multiple Linear Regression
- Residuals Calculated

CATEGORICAL DATA ANALYSIS
- Chi-Square Contingency Table Analysis
- Multi-Dimensional Tables
- Contingency Coefficient
- Gamma
- Tau C

MISCELLANEOUS
- Transformation of Variables Supported

ABSTAT RELEASE 4

Anderson-Bell Corp.
11479 S. Pine Drive, Suite 424
Parker, CO 80134
(303) 841 - 9755
Contact Person: Joanne Anderson

CONFIGURATIONS SUPPORTED

Computer	Language	Operating System	RAM	Number Drives	Cost
IBM PC	PASCAL	DOS	196K	2	$ 395
TANDY 1000 1200,2000 3000	PASCAL	DOS	196K	2	$ 395
VICTOR 9000	PASCAL	DOS	196K	2	$ 395
XEROX	PASCAL	DOS	196K	2	$ 395

NUMBER OF CURRENT USERS 6000
DATE OF FIRST RELEASE DEC 80
VERSION 4.2 RELEASED Aug 86

PROGRAM DESCRIPTION

ABstat is a general statistics package. It is used by over 6,000 people worldwide. ABstat is an easy-to-use package, takes little effort to learn, and is fast. All the most commonly used statistics are included. Several non-parametric tests make it especially attractive to medical researchers. Users in all fields find ABstat the fastest and easiest way to get the statistical results they need from the data they have.

ABstat's features include descriptive statistics, 4-way analysis of variance, chi-square, correlations, cross-tabulations, multiple linear regression, etc. ABstat can read and write dBase II, III, Lotus 1-2-3 and Symphony or standard ASCII files. ABstat is very fast and NOT copy protected.

PRODUCT REVIEWS

Muhlin, G.. "ABSTAT Statistical Program for CP/M Systems", Infoworld, Vol 5, No. 23, (June 6, 1983).

Linwood, A.S.. "Review: ABSTAT", Apple Orchard, Vol 4, No. 6, (Sept 1983).

Graham, J.D.. "Extenders: Pushing dBase II to the Limit", PC Magazine, Vol 3, No. 2, (Feb 4, 1984).

Infoworld Report Card, Vol 5, No. 48A.

D'Ellis, Chris. "Three Statistical Packages for the VICTOR 9000/SIRIUS", Victor Talk, Vol 2, No. 4, (April 1984).

Creane, J.. "Chomping at the BITS", Personal Computer Age, Vol. 3, No. 4, (April 1984).

Carpenter, James et. al.. "Statistical Software for Microcomputers", BYTE, Vol 9, No. 4, pp. 234-264, (April 1984).

Lima, Anthony K.. "Seven Utilities for dBase II", PC TECH Journal, Vol 1, No. 9, (June 1984).

Siegel, J.. "Econometric Report 83", Quantitative Software Reports, (1983).

"The Book of IBM Software, 1984", The Book Company, Division of Arrays, Inc., (1984).

Pease, J., and Lepage, R.. "An Evaluation of Selected Microcomputer Statistical Programs", Michigan State Univ International Dev Paper #15, (1984).

TYPE OF PROGRAM

Statistical Package

PROGRAM DESIGNED FOR

Data Analysis

PROGRAM STYLE

Command Driven
Integrated System

MISCELLANEOUS PROGRAM FEATURES

Copyable Disk
On Screen Help Function
Optional Support for 8087 Mathematical Chip

DOCUMENTATION

User's Manual - 136 pages, 0 technical references
- Table of Contents
- Index
- Tutorial or Example Lessons
- Sample Runs
- Formulas Provided

Tutorials and Examples on Disk

DATA MANAGEMENT

Keyboard Data Entry
Data Manipulations and Transformations
Missing Values Allowed in Data

DATA EDITING

Change
Add
Delete

FOREIGN DATA ACCESS

Standard Rectangular ASCII Files
dBase II Files
dBase III Files
Symphony Files
Lotus 1-2-3

GRAPHICS FEATURES

Graphics can be Output to a Printer
Graphics can be Saved to a File
Uses Character Graphics

GRAPHICS

Histograms
Scatter (x-y) Plots

PRODUCT SUPPORT

User may call at own Expense
No Classes or Instruction Available

STATISTICAL FEATURES SUPPORTED

DESCRIPTIVE STATISTICS

- Mean
- Standard Deviation or Variance
- Standard Error of the Mean
- Coefficient of Variation
- Minimum, Maximum
- Median
- Skewness
- Kurtosis
- Sum of Values
- Range
- Mode

t-TESTS

- Paired t-Test
- Independent t-Test
- Population t-Test

CORRELATION AND REGRESSION

- Pearson Correlation Coefficient
- Simple Linear Regression
- Multiple Linear Regression
- Residuals Calculated
- Durbin-Watson
- Estimates
- Projections

CATEGORICAL DATA ANALYSIS

- Chi-Square Contingency Table Analysis
- Fisher's Exact Test
- Goodness-of-Fit Tests

ANALYSIS OF VARIANCE

- One-Way ANOVA
- One-Way with Repeated Measures
- Up to 4-Way ANOVA - 1 Repeated Measure
- **MULTIPLE COMPARISONS**
    - Scheffe Post-Hoc Test

NONPARAMETRIC TESTS

- Sign Test (Signed Rank)
- Mann-Whitney U
- Kruskal-Wallis Test
- Spearman or Kendall Correlation
- Kolmogorov-Smirnov 2-Sample Test
- 1-Sample Runs Test
- Wald-Walfowitz 2 Sample Runs Test
- Crosstabs

MISCELLANEOUS

- Date and Time Transformations
- Appending/Merging Files
- Data Sorting

ABTAB, RELEASE 3

BB&A
PO Box 191/425 Main St. Ste 10
Canon City, CO 81212
(303) 275 - 1661
Contact Person: Debbie Johnson

CONFIGURATIONS SUPPORTED

Computer	Language	Operating System	RAM	Number Drives	Cost
IBM PC	TURBO PASCAL	DOS	256K	2	$ 895
NCR DECISION MATE V		DOS	256K	2	$ 895
VICTOR 9000		DOS	256K	2	$ 895

NUMBER OF CURRENT USERS New
DATE OF FIRST RELEASE Mar 84
VERSION 3 RELEASED Sept 85

PROGRAM DESCRIPTION

ABtab is an exceptional software package for survey analysis, market research, sales tracking, trend identification and in fact in any situation where the decision process can be assisted by knowing the relationship between two or more factors.

ABtab is command driven with on screen help. ABtab features include banners up to 10-47 points, 10-way master tabulations, cross-tabs with numerics, contingency tables with statistics, bar graphs and histograms, descriptive statistics, comprehensive data management, etc. ABtab will also read dBase or ASCII files.

PRODUCT REVIEWS

1985 Annual Software Review - PC World (Special Edition), (Winter 1985).

TYPE OF PROGRAM
Categorical Data Analysis

PROGRAM DESIGNED FOR
Data Analysis

PROGRAM STYLE
Command Driven
Integrated System

MISCELLANEOUS PROGRAM FEATURES
Copyable Disk
On Screen Help Function

DOCUMENTATION
User's Manual - 163 pages, 0 technical references
Table of Contents
Index
Tutorial or Example Lessons
Sample Runs
Formulas Provided

DATA MANAGEMENT
Keyboard Data Entry
Data Manipulations and Transformations
Missing Values Allowed in Data

DATA EDITING
Change
Add
Delete

FOREIGN DATA ACCESS
Standard Rectangular ASCII Files
dBASE II and III Files

GRAPHICS FEATURES
Graphics can be Output to a Printer
Graphics can be Saved to a File
Titles and/or Labels Available
Uses Character Graphics

GRAPHICS
Histograms
Scatter (x-y) Plots

PRODUCT SUPPORT
User may call at own Expense
Classes or Instruction Available

STATISTICAL FEATURES SUPPORTED

DESCRIPTIVE STATISTICS

Mean
Standard Deviation or Variance
Standard Error of the Mean
Coefficient of Variation
Minimum, Maximum
Median
Percentiles
Skewness
Kurtosis
Range
Mode
Total

CATEGORICAL DATA ANALYSIS

Chi-Square Contingency Table Analysis
Multi-Dimensional Tables
Fisher's Exact Test
Goodness-of-Fit Tests
Frequencies Can be Entered Directly
Phi Statistic
Cramer's V
Contingency Coefficient
Lambda
Gamma
Tau C
Tau C
Somer's D
Tschuporw's T
Banner and Stub Presentation

MISCELLANEOUS

p-Values Given With Tests
Crosstabs
Two Verification Modes
Categorize Command for Recoding
Two-Way Histograms with Breakdowns
Cells Contain Sum, Mean or SD of Vars
Combine or Eliminate Level of Cell Var.
Multivalue or All-that-Apply Response
Batch or Interactive Mode

ADVANCESTAT 3.0

Ideal Systems
P.O. Box 681
Fairfield, Iowa 52556
(515) 472 - 4507
Contact Person: Christopher Dennen

CONFIGURATIONS SUPPORTED

Computer	Language	Operating System	RAM	Number Drives	Cost
APPLE II	BASIC	DOS	64K	2	$ 195
IBM PC	BASIC	DOS	64K	2	$ 195

NUMBER OF CURRENT USERS ?
DATE OF FIRST RELEASE 1983
VERSION 3.0 RELEASED 1985

PROGRAM DESCRIPTION

ADVANCESTAT is a newly developed product with all the fine features of INTROSTSTAT, yet ADVANCESTAT offers even more power and flexibility. This package can be used easily and effectively in the research lab, in the office and in the classroom. Although it offers a range of tests that could be covered in five different graduate courses, it is still easy and straightforward to use. This program is for the user who wants to concentrate on performing analysis and does not want to waste valuable time learning a software package.

ADVANCESTAT contains statistical procedures that range from simple description to complex multivariate tests. A powerful data file management program complements the statistical tests. This program allows the users to easily edit, view, and record data. New variables can even be calculated using any of the arithmetic operations and functions of BASIC. ADVANCESTAT is a complete program for the serious user. The program includes a full 65 page manual that presents each of the tests in a clear, easy to understand manner. Many examples are given using the Statlab data set that comes with each program. You need to experience this product to appreciate the full range of its capabilities.

TYPE OF PROGRAM
Statistical Package

PROGRAM DESIGNED FOR
Data Analysis
Educational use

PROGRAM STYLE
Menu Driven
Integrated System

MISCELLANEOUS PROGRAM FEATURES
Source Code Available
Copyable Disk

DOCUMENTATION
User's Manual - 65 pages, technical references
Table of Contents
Index
Tutorial or Example Lessons
Sample Runs

DATA MANAGEMENT
Keyboard Data Entry
Data Manipulations and Transformations
Missing Values Allowed in Data

DATA EDITING
Change
Add
Delete

FOREIGN DATA ACCESS
DIF Files

GRAPHICS FEATURES
Uses Pixel Graphics

GRAPHICS
SEE Regression Plots

PRODUCT SUPPORT
User may call at own Expense
No Classes or Instruction Available

STATISTICAL FEATURES SUPPORTED

DESCRIPTIVE STATISTICS
- Mean
- Standard Deviation or Variance
- Standard Error of the Mean
- Minimum, Maximum
- Median
- Frequency Table

t-TESTS
- One Sample t-Test
- Independent Group t-Test/Equal Variance
- Paired t-Test

CORRELATION AND REGRESSION
- Pearson Correlation Coefficient
- Simple Linear Regression
- Multiple Linear Regression
- **REGRESSION PLOTS**
  - Regression Line

ANALYSIS OF VARIANCE
- One-Way ANOVA
- Two-Way ANOVA
- Three-Way ANOVA

NONPARAMETRIC TESTS
- Wilcoxon One Sample Test
- Mann-Whitney U

MISCELLANEOUS
- Crosstabs

ANOVA II

Human Systems Dynamics
9010 Reseda Blvd, Suite 222
Northridge, CA 91324
(818) 993 - 8536
Contact Person: Merideth Wiberg

CONFIGURATIONS SUPPORTED

Computer	Language	Operating System	RAM	Number Drives	Cost
APPLE II APPLE III	BASIC	ADOS 3.3	48K	1	$ 150

NUMBER OF CURRENT USERS 2000
DATE OF FIRST RELEASE Aug 82
VERSION 1.1 RELEASED Sep 83

PROGRAM DESCRIPTION

ANOVA II is a comprehensive analysis of variance package for the Apple II. With it you can analyze a research design as simple as a two-group randomozed design or as complex as a four-factor split-split plot design with a covariate and unequal group sizes. ANOVA II produces a complete analysis of variance summary table as well as descriptive statistics for each cell of an experimental design. The program package also includes separate programs for file creation and review/edit, data transformations, and hi-resolution plots and bar graphs of treatment means.

ANOVA II is very easy to use. For the most part, the specification of experimental designs and the required organization of data closely follow the conventions of standard texts on research designs and analysis of variance. Detailed descriptions of each program and procedure are given in the manual. The user can very quickly learn almost all of the problem definition and data entry requirements of ANOVA II by working through the examples given in the manual.

PRODUCT REVIEWS
"Psychotherapy in Private Practice", Popular Computing, pp. 216, (Oct 1983).

TYPE OF PROGRAM
Statistical Package

PROGRAM DESIGNED FOR
Data Analysis

PROGRAM STYLE
Menu Driven
Integrated System

DOCUMENTATION
User's Manual - 65 pages, 5 technical references
Table of Contents
Index
Tutorial or Example Lessons
Sample Runs

DATA MANAGEMENT
Keyboard Data Entry
Data Manipulations and Transformations

DATA EDITING
Change
Add
Delete

FOREIGN DATA ACCESS
VisiCalc

GRAPHICS FEATURES
Graphics can be Saved to a File
Titles and/or Labels Available
Uses Pixel Graphics

GRAPHICS
Histograms
Bar Charts

PRODUCT SUPPORT
Free Phone Support Available
No Classes or Instruction Available

STATISTICAL FEATURES SUPPORTED

DESCRIPTIVE STATISTICS

- Mean
- Standard Deviation or Variance
- Standard Error of the Mean

ANALYSIS OF VARIANCE

- One-Way ANOVA
- One-Way with Repeated Measures
- Two-Way ANOVA
- Two-Way Unequal Cell Sizes Allowed
- Analysis of Covariance
- Latin Square
- Multiway Factorials
- One to five way ANOVA
- Between - Within Design

ANSTAT - LINEAR MEASUREMENTS

Quality Measurement Systems, Corp.
1675 N. Wayneport Rd.
Macedon, NY 14502
(315) 986 - 5710
Contact Person: Charles Snell

CONFIGURATIONS SUPPORTED

Computer	Language	Operating System	RAM	Number Drives	Cost
IBM PC	BASIC Compiled	DOS	256K	2	
HP 86	BASIC		178K	2	

NUMBER OF CURRENT USERS ?
DATE OF FIRST RELEASE ?
VERSION F 7 RELEASED Aug 86

PROGRAM DESCRIPTION

Anstat(tm) software provides a comprehensive statistical Process Control package which, in combination with the HP 86/87 computer is capable of measuring a wide variety of machined parts using Quality measurment Systems Digital Electronic Gaging Equipment (micrometers, calipers, indicator and height gage). Its applications are numerous and fit a wide range of industries but in no way should ANSTAT(tm) be looked at on a narrow field of applications.

The purpose of Anstat is to process raw data coming from the digital electronic display and supply you with results ranging from a simple printout of actuals all the way to automatic go/nogo decisions and statistical lot evaluations. Anstat operates in 5 alternative modes, Manual, Program, Auto, U-Charts, and A-Charts.

TYPE OF PROGRAM

Quality Control

PROGRAM DESIGNED FOR

Data Analysis

PROGRAM STYLE
Menu Driven
Integrated System

DOCUMENTATION
User's Manual - ? pages, ? technical references
Table of Contents
Index

DATA MANAGEMENT
Keyboard Data Entry

DATA EDITING
Change

GRAPHICS FEATURES
Graphics can be Output to a Printer
Uses Pixel Graphics

GRAPHICS
Histograms
Sigma
Range
X-Bar

PRODUCT SUPPORT
User may call at own Expense
No Classes or Instruction Available

STATISTICAL FEATURES SUPPORTED

DESCRIPTIVE STATISTICS
Mean
Standard Deviation or Variance

CONTROL CHARTS
X-Bar
s
Number of Defects
Number of Defectives
OTHER QUALITY CONTROL PROCEDURES
Acceptance Sampling by Attributes

APP-STAT
Statsoft, Inc.
2832 East 10th Street, Suite 4
Tulsa, OK 74104
(918) 583 - 4149
Contact Person: Sales Office

CONFIGURATIONS SUPPORTED

Computer	Language	Operating System	RAM	Number Drives	Cost
APPLE II	APPLESOFT	DOS	64K	1	$99

NUMBER OF CURRENT USERS 5000
DATE OF FIRST RELEASE 1985
VERSION 1.2 RELEASED 1985

PROGRAM DESCRIPTION

A general purpose statistical package (basic statistics, nonparametrics, multivariate statistics) with graphics and complete database management functions.

Extremely easy to use, even for novices (menu driven), advanced statistics. Very Compact: The entire package fits on one disk including the database management module.

TYPE OF PROGRAM
Statistical Package

PROGRAM DESIGNED FOR
Data Analysis
Educational use

PROGRAM STYLE
Menu Driven
Integrated System

MISCELLANEOUS PROGRAM FEATURES
Source Code Available
Copyable Disk

DOCUMENTATION

User's Manual - 168 pages, 20 technical references

- Table of Contents
- Index
- Tutorial or Example Lessons
- Sample Runs
- Formulas Provided

DATA MANAGEMENT

- Keyboard Data Entry
- Data Manipulations and Transformations
- Missing Values Allowed in Data

DATA EDITING

- Change
- Add
- Delete

FOREIGN DATA ACCESS

- Standard Rectangular ASCII Files
- Any ASCII, i.e by Appleworks

GRAPHICS FEATURES

- Graphics can be Output to a Printer
- Titles and/or Labels Available
- Uses Character Graphics

GRAPHICS

- Histograms
- Scatter (x-y) Plots

PRODUCT SUPPORT

- User may call at own Expense
- No Classes or Instruction Available

STATISTICAL FEATURES SUPPORTED

DESCRIPTIVE STATISTICS
- Mean
- Standard Deviation or Variance
- Standard Error of the Mean
- Coefficient of Variation
- Minimum, Maximum
- Median
- Skewness
- Kurtosis

t-TESTS
- One Sample t-Test
- Independent Group t-Test/Equal Variance
- Independent Group t-Test/Unequal Var
- Paired t-Test

CORRELATION AND REGRESSION
- Pearson Correlation Coefficient
- Simple Linear Regression
- Multiple Linear Regression
- Residuals Calculated
- Durbin-Watson Statistic
- **REGRESSION PLOTS**
  - Residuals

CATEGORICAL DATA ANALYSIS
- Frequencies Can be Entered Directly

ANALYSIS OF VARIANCE
- One-Way ANOVA
- One-Way with Repeated Measures
- Two-Way ANOVA
- Two-Way Unequal Cell Sizes Allowed
- Analysis of Covariance
- Repeated Measures
- Including a Covariate
- Up to 5-Way ANCOVA
- Incomplete Designs
- **MULTIPLE COMPARISONS**
  - Planned Comparisons

NONPARAMETRIC TESTS

Wilcoxon One Sample Test
Mann-Whitney U
Kruskal-Wallis Test
Spearman or Kendall Correlation
Phi-Square
Nu-Square

DISTRIBUTION FUNCTION EVALUATION

Normal
t
Chi Square
F

TIME SERIES ANALYSIS

Autocorrelations of Residuals

MISCELLANEOUS

p-Values Given With Tests

ATLAS
Strategic Locations Planning
4030 Moorpark Ave Ste 123
San Jose, CA 95117
(408) 985 - 7400
Contact Person: Stephen Poizner

CONFIGURATIONS SUPPORTED

Computer	Language	Operating System	RAM	Number Drives	Cost
IBM PC	COMPILED BASIC	DOS	384K	2	$ 449

NUMBER OF CURRENT USERS 1500
DATE OF FIRST RELEASE May 84
VERSION 1.2 RELEASED July 86

PROGRAM DESCRIPTION

ATLAS is an interactive menu driven software package that generates maps and displays data at the state, country, congressional district, ADI or DMA advertising region, zip code or census tract levels. You can also create your own boundaries to be mapped. ATLAS is easy to learn and use. Preset default values permit fast production of high quality maps, and easy to understand menus allow you to quickly customize maps to meet your special needs. ATLAS provides many of the capabilities found in mainframe mapping packages which cost thousands of dollars. ATLAS can overlay two variables on the same map, plot multiple maps on the same page, and pan and zoom in on any geographic area that is of special interest to the user.

Flexibility in map design is a key feature of ATLAS. You may select from 300 modifiable hatching patterns, 16 colors, 3 label sizes, and many options for legend and title placement. Output appears as screen graphics, hardcopy, or overhead transparencies. For each variable ATLAS can create up to 20 data ranges that you may choose as either being equally spaced or having equal data points or you may choose up to 20 arbitrary ranges. To assist in range selection for a variable, ATLAS displays both window and global summary statistics that include max, min, mean, mode, median, standard deviation, and frequency distribution. Hundreds of inexpensive geographic boundary and data files are available for immediate use. Lotus 1-2-3 and Visicalc files can be mapped by ATLAS.

PRODUCT REVIEWS

PC World, (Dec 1984).

American Demographics, (Jan 1985).

Planning Magazine, (Mar 1985).

ICP Business Software Magazine, (Apr 1985).

PC Magazine, (Nov 1985).

Professional Geographer, (Nov 1985).

InfoWorld, (Dec 1985).

Business Software, (Jan 1986).

Journal of Geography, (Feb 1986).

PC Week, (Apr 1986).

TYPE OF PROGRAM

Graphics Package

PROGRAM DESIGNED FOR

Data Analysis

PROGRAM STYLE

Menu Driven
Integrated System

MISCELLANEOUS PROGRAM FEATURES

Copyable Disk
On Screen Help Function

DOCUMENTATION

User's Manual - 0 pages, 0 technical references
- Table of Contents
- Index
- Tutorial or Example Lessons
- Sample Runs
- Formulas Provided

Tutorials and Examples on Disk

DATA MANAGEMENT

Data Manipulations and Transformations
Missing Values Allowed in Data

FOREIGN DATA ACCESS
Standard Rectangular ASCII Files
DIF Files

GRAPHICS FEATURES
Graphics Appear in Color on the Monitor
Graphics can be Output to a Printer
Titles and/or Labels Available
Uses Pixel Graphics

GRAPHICS
Histograms
Maps

PRODUCT SUPPORT
User may call at own Expense
No Classes or Instruction Available

STATISTICAL FEATURES SUPPORTED

DESCRIPTIVE STATISTICS
Mean
Standard Deviation or Variance
Median
Mode

AURORA "STATFLOW"

Great Northern Computer Services Ltd
5 Ashleigh Road, West Park
Leeds, ENGLAND LS16 5AX
(053) 275 - 2629
Contact Person: Mr Paul Rayner

CONFIGURATIONS SUPPORTED

Computer	Language	Operating System	RAM	Number Drives	Cost
CP/M FORMAT		CP/M	64K	1	99
CP/M-86 FORMAT		CP/M-86	64K	1	149
IBM PC		DOS	64K	1	149

NUMBER OF CURRENT USERS 100
DATE OF FIRST RELEASE 1983
CURRENT VERSION RELEASED 1986

PROGRAM DESCRIPTION

STATFLOW is a powerful yet easy to use statistical package for business, commerce, education and research. No previous computer experience is required in order to operate it.

STATFLOW allows the non-technical user to create sets of data, to manipulate them and analyze them using a variety of parametric and nonparametric tests.

TYPE OF PROGRAM

Statistical Package

PROGRAM DESIGNED FOR

Educational use

PROGRAM STYLE

Menu Driven
Integrated System

MISCELLANEOUS PROGRAM FEATURES
Copyable Disk
On Screen Help Function

DOCUMENTATION
User's Manual - 70 pages, 15 technical references
Table of Contents
Index
Tutorial or Example Lessons
Sample Runs
Formulas Provided
Tutorials and Examples on Disk

DATA MANAGEMENT
Keyboard Data Entry
Data Manipulations and Transformations

DATA EDITING
Change
Add
Delete

FOREIGN DATA ACCESS
Standard Rectangular ASCII Files

GRAPHICS FEATURES
Graphics Appear in Color on the Monitor
Graphics can be Output to a Printer
Titles and/or Labels Available

GRAPHICS
Histograms
Scatter (x-y) Plots
Box Plots

PRODUCT SUPPORT
No Classes or Instruction Available

STATISTICAL FEATURES SUPPORTED

DESCRIPTIVE STATISTICS
- Mean
- Standard Deviation or Variance
- Standard Error of the Mean
- Coefficient of Variation
- Minimum, Maximum
- Median

t-TESTS
- One Sample t-Test
- Independent Group t-Test/Equal Variance
- Independent Group t-Test/Unequal Var
- Paired t-Test

CORRELATION AND REGRESSION
- Pearson Correlation Coefficient
- Simple Linear Regression
- Multiple Linear Regression
- Residuals Calculated
- Estimate Asymptotic Standard Errors

CONFIDENCE INTERVALS
- Means
- Difference Between Two Means
- Variances

CATEGORICAL DATA ANALYSIS
- Chi-Square Contingency Table Analysis
- Goodness-of-Fit Tests
- Frequencies Can be Entered Directly

ANALYSIS OF VARIANCE
- One-Way ANOVA
- One-Way with Repeated Measures
- Two-Way ANOVA

NONPARAMETRIC TESTS
- Sign Test (Signed Rank)
- Wilcoxon One Sample Test
- Mann-Whitney U
- Kruskal-Wallis Test
- Spearman or Kendall Correlation

DISTRIBUTION FUNCTION EVALUATION

Normal
Chi Square
Binomial
Poisson

AUTOBJ

Automatic Forecasting Systems Inc.
PO Box 563
Hatboro, PA 19040
(215) 675 - 0652
Contact Person: David P Reilly

CONFIGURATIONS SUPPORTED

Computer	Language	Operating System	RAM	Number Drives	Cost
IBM PC	FORTRAN	DOS	320K	2	$ 595

NUMBER OF CURRENT USERS 60
DATE OF FIRST RELEASE Jul 84
CURRENT VERSION RELEASED Mar 86

PROGRAM DESCRIPTION

AFS'S products for time series analysis were designed to meet all of your software needs pertaining to Box-Jenkins or ARIMA model building. Smart Software allows you to build efficient Box-Jenkins models and produce quality forecasts simply by issuing the AUTOBJ command. This totally automatic univariate model building option is now available separately or as a powerful complement to BOXX.

The complete automatic univariate identification program builds a complete ARIMA model for any given time series. Starting with raw data, the program algorithm follows the exact model building methodology described by Box and Jenkins - that of tentative model identification, parameter estimation and diagnostic checking. While requiring only minimal input by the user, this program is quite flexible in allowing for optional user control. AUTOBJ is the heuristic contained within AUTOBOX to handle univariate modeling. Four levels of output are available. Full output presents the entire model building process along with a brief explanation of each step.

PRODUCT REVIEWS

Pickett, John C.. Science Quarterly, (Winter 1985).

Beaumont, Chris. Journal of Forecasting, (1986).

Shumway, R.H.. American Statistician, (Nov 86).

TYPE OF PROGRAM
Statistical Package

PROGRAM DESIGNED FOR
Data Analysis
Educational use

PROGRAM STYLE
Menu Driven
Integrated System

MISCELLANEOUS PROGRAM FEATURES
On Screen Help Function
Supports 8087 Mathematical Chip

DOCUMENTATION
User's Manual - 40 pages, 3 technical references
Table of Contents
Index
Tutorial or Example Lessons
Sample Runs
Formulas Provided
Tutorials and Examples on Disk

DATA MANAGEMENT
Keyboard Data Entry
Data Manipulations and Transformations

DATA EDITING
Change
Add
Delete

FOREIGN DATA ACCESS
Standard Rectangular ASCII Files
DIF Files
Lotus PRN Files

GRAPHICS FEATURES
Graphics can be Output to a Printer
Graphics can be Saved to a File
Titles and/or Labels Available

GRAPHICS
Scatter (x-y) Plots
SEE Time Series Plots

PRODUCT SUPPORT
- User may call at own Expense
- Classes or Instruction Available

STATISTICAL FEATURES SUPPORTED

DESCRIPTIVE STATISTICS
- Mean
- Standard Deviation or Variance
- Standard Error of the Mean

CORRELATION AND REGRESSION
- Pearson Correlation Coefficient
- Simple Linear Regression
- Multiple Linear Regression
- Stepwise Multiple Linear Regression
- Non-Linear Regression
- Residuals Calculated
- Estimate Asymptotic Standard Errors

TIME SERIES ANALYSIS
- Autocorrelations
- Cross Correlations
- AUTOREGRESSIVE MOVING AVERAGE
  - Model Identification
  - Parameter Estimation
- **TIME SERIES ANALYSIS - PLOTS**
  - Original Data
  - Residuals
  - Forecasts

MISCELLANEOUS
- Test for Normality of Data
- Test for Homogeneity of Error Variance

AUTOBOX

Automatic Forecasting Systems Inc,
PO Box 563
Hatboro, PA 19040
(215) 675 - 0652
Contact Person: David P. Reilly

CONFIGURATIONS SUPPORTED

Computer	Language	Operating System	RAM	Number Drives	Cost
IBM PC	FORTRAN	DOS	320K	2	$995

NUMBER OF CURRENT USERS 130
DATE OF FIRST RELEASE JUL 84
CURRENT VERSION RELEASED MAR 86

PROGRAM DESCRIPTION

AFS's products for time series analysis were designed to meet all of your software needs pertaining to Box-Jenkins or ARIMA model building. AUTOBOX is a valuable, time-efficient forecasting tool when you don't have time to build structural models or when you have to produce forecasts of many items. If you are new to Box-Jenkins modeling, you can use AUTOBOX not only in generating forecasts quickly, but also as a computer-assisted learning device to further your understanding of the modeling process. AUTOBOX is a program that can be used for building models either automatically or not.

AUTOBOX has all features of BOXX, automatic outlier detection and identification, normality and invertibility check, computes good starting values for Transfer Function parameters, allows for Transfer Function Identification via the new and powerful common filter method, automatically deletes non-significant parameters one at a time, suggests the RSB form of the Transfer model for each input series and computes the extended autocorrelation function.

PRODUCT REVIEWS

Pickett, John C.. Science Quarterly, (Winter 1985).

Ord, Keith. OR/MS Today, (Sept 1985).

Beaumont, Chris. Journal of Forecasting, (1986).

Liao, S.. Journal of Business Forecasting, (1986).

Sharda, Ramesh. Computers and Operations Research, (1986).

TYPE OF PROGRAM
Statistical Package

PROGRAM DESIGNED FOR
Data Analysis
Educational use

PROGRAM STYLE
Menu Driven
Integrated System

MISCELLANEOUS PROGRAM FEATURES
Supports 8087 Mathematical Chip

DOCUMENTATION
User's Manual - 80 pages, 3 technical references
Index
Tutorial or Example Lessons
Sample Runs
Formulas Provided
Tutorials and Examples on Disk

DATA MANAGEMENT
Keyboard Data Entry
Data Manipulations and Transformations

DATA EDITING
Change
Add
Delete

FOREIGN DATA ACCESS
Standard Rectangular ASCII Files
DIF Files
Lotus PRN Files

GRAPHICS FEATURES
Graphics can be Output to a Printer
Graphics can be Saved to a File
Titles and/or Labels Available

GRAPHICS
Scatter (x-y) Plots
SEE Time Series Plots

PRODUCT SUPPORT
- User may call at own Expense
- Classes or Instruction Available

STATISTICAL FEATURES SUPPORTED

TIME SERIES ANALYSIS
- Autocorrelations
- Cross Correlations
- AUTOREGRESSIVE MOVING AVERAGE
  - Model Identification
  - Parameter Estimation
- Intervention Models
- Transfer Function Models
- **TIME SERIES ANALYSIS - FORECASTING**
  - Non-linear Least Squares
- **TIME SERIES ANALYSIS - PLOTS**
  - Autocorrelations
  - Partial Autocorrelations
  - Original Data
  - Residuals
  - Forecasts
  - Impulse Response
  - Cross Correlation

MISCELLANEOUS
- Test for Normality of Data
- Test for Homogeneity of Error Variance

AUTOCAST

Core Analytic, Inc.
674 Rt.202-206 N
Bridgewater, NJ 08807
(201) 218 - 0900
Contact Person: Fred M. Chalek

CONFIGURATIONS SUPPORTED

Computer	Language	Operating System	RAM	Number Drives	Cost
IBM PC	TURBO PASCAL	DOS	256K	1	$495

NUMBER OF CURRENT USERS 100
DATE OF FIRST RELEASE Sept 86
VERSION 1.0 RELEASED Sept 86

PROGRAM DESCRIPTION

AUTOCaST is a completely automatic forecasting package designed for the IBM PC/XT/AT and compatibles. It is oriented toward practitioners in the fields of inventory and production control, marketing and product management, operations research, forecasting, finance and financial planning, and market research. AUTOCaST, utilizing the primary technique of exponential smoothing, will quickly, and graphically, analyze and then forecast time series that have different trends, changing seasonal patterns, are erratic, or that have only a few data points.

AUTOCaST is both menu driven and function key oriented for the beginning forecaster, yet still provides full user flexibility for overriding the automatic options. AUTOCaST has fast, high resolution graphics, and supports the 8087 math coprocessor for even faster operation. This package can handle 4 types of trend, 3 types of seasonal patterns, transformations, and confidence limits - all with single keystroke convenience. The automatic parameter search option can be tailored to the users needs by predefining the replacement of outliers, parameter search limits, error type and precision, and simulation (ex post) forecasts.

TYPE OF PROGRAM

Time Series Analysis

PROGRAM DESIGNED FOR
Data Analysis

PROGRAM STYLE
Menu Driven
Integrated System

MISCELLANEOUS PROGRAM FEATURES
Copyable Disk
Optional Support for 8087, 80287 Mathematical Chip

DOCUMENTATION
User's Manual - 200+ pages, ? technical references
Table of Contents
Index
Tutorial or Example Lessons
Sample Runs
Formulas Provided

DATA MANAGEMENT
Keyboard Data Entry
Data Manipulations and Transformations

DATA EDITING
Change
Add
Delete

FOREIGN DATA ACCESS
Standard Rectangular ASCII Files

GRAPHICS FEATURES
Graphics Appear in Color on the Monitor
Graphics can be Output to a Printer
Titles and/or Labels Available
Uses Pixel Graphics

GRAPHICS
SEE Time Series Plots

PRODUCT SUPPORT
User may call at own Expense
Classes or Instruction Available

STATISTICAL FEATURES SUPPORTED

EXPLORATORY DATA ANALYSIS
- Smoothing Techniques

TIME SERIES ANALYSIS
- Autocorrelations
- **TIME SERIES ANALYSIS - FORECASTING**
  - Exponential Smoothing
- **TIME SERIES ANALYSIS - PLOTS**
  - Time Series

BALANCE
Elsevier Scientific Software
P.O. Box 330
1000 AH Amsterdam, NETHERLANDS
(020) 5862828
Contact Person: Keith Foley

CONFIGURATIONS SUPPORTED

Computer	Language	Operating System	RAM	Number Drives	Cost
IBM PC	BASIC	DOS	128K	1	$205
APPLE II	BASIC	DOS	48K	1	$205

NUMBER OF CURRENT USERS 200+
DATE OF FIRST RELEASE 1984
VERSION 1.0 RELEASED 1984

PROGRAM DESCRIPTION

This program compares two series of measurements. Its purpose is to determine whether the two series can be considered to give different results, i.e., whether the means are significantly different. It can be used to compare two medical treatments, two drugs, two analytical methods, etc. This kind of comparison is probably the most frequently used statistical technique and usually Student's t-test is used. It is seldom realised that Student's t-test should be carried out in different ways in different situations and that there are situations where other tests should be carried out. This program is conceived in such a way that it guides the user to the correct kind of test.

BALANCE is a statistical program for the comparison of two series of measurements. The program is conceived in such a way that the user has to make only a small number of decisions in order to obtain a statistically correct conclusion. The program operates in an interactive way and enables the user to manipulate the data, to obtain a histogran of the data and to perform the correct kind of test. The data may be keyed in or they may be read from text files. When data is keyed in during a run of BALANCE, it is advisable to store this data on one of your own diskettes.

TYPE OF PROGRAM
Statistical Package

PROGRAM DESIGNED FOR
Data Analysis

PROGRAM STYLE
Menu Driven
Integrated System

MISCELLANEOUS PROGRAM FEATURES
Source Code Available
Copyable Disk

DOCUMENTATION
User's Manual - ? pages, ? technical references
Table of Contents
Tutorial or Example Lessons
Sample Runs
Formulas Provided

DATA MANAGEMENT
Keyboard Data Entry
Missing Values Allowed in Data

DATA EDITING
Change
Add
Delete

FOREIGN DATA ACCESS
Standard Rectangular ASCII Files

GRAPHICS FEATURES
Graphics Appear in Color on the Monitor
Uses Pixel Graphics

GRAPHICS
Histograms

PRODUCT SUPPORT
Free Phone Support Available
Classes or Instruction Available

STATISTICAL FEATURES SUPPORTED

DESCRIPTIVE STATISTICS
- Mean
- Standard Deviation or Variance

t-TESTS
- Independent Group t-Test/Equal Variance
- Independent Group t-Test/Unequal Var
- Paired t-Test

CONFIDENCE INTERVALS
- Difference Between Two Means
- Variances

NONPARAMETRIC TESTS
- Wilcoxon One Sample Test
- Mann-Whitney U

BASS BASE PRODUCT

Bass Institute Inc
Box 349
Chapel Hill, NC 27514
(919) 489 - 0729
Contact Person: Jeff Bass

CONFIGURATIONS SUPPORTED

Computer	Language	Operating System	RAM	Number Drives	Cost
IBM PC	PASCAL/ ASSEMBLY	DOS	256K	2	$95

NUMBER OF CURRENT USERS 200
DATE OF FIRST RELEASE Feb 86
VERSION 85.32 RELEASED Aug 86

PROGRAM DESCRIPTION

BASS has a complex data structure that stores data values, variable names, formats and variable labels. It is used as a computer language--the user creates a BASS program file with a text editor and then uses BASS to execute the job. The Base module contains data management and statistical abilities and a Advanced Statistic Module is under development. BASS offers substantial source code compatibility with the mainframe program SAS (Reg TM of SAS Institute Inc.). Many SAS programs will run unchanged using BASS on a PC.

BASS offers several enchancements over SAS and similar packages. The data management language can be used with every procedure, not just with a "DATA STEP". Variable which are functions of other variables can be stored as formulas instead of data values for a large space savings. User defined functions and procedures are permitted. Powerful sorts and merges can be performed with many-to-one and by variable capability. BASS is fast and compact, which means that large datasets (up to 32767 observations and 4096 variables) can be processed quickly.

TYPE OF PROGRAM

Statistical Package

PROGRAM DESIGNED FOR
UNKNOWN

PROGRAM STYLE
Command Driven
Integrated System

MISCELLANEOUS PROGRAM FEATURES
Copyable Disk
On Screen Help Function
Optional Support for 8087, 80287 Mathematical Chip

DOCUMENTATION
User's Manual - 172 pages, ? technical references
Table of Contents
Index
Tutorial or Example Lessons
Sample Runs
Tutorials and Examples on Disk

DATA MANAGEMENT
Data Manipulations and Transformations
Missing Values Allowed in Data

DATA EDITING
Change
Add
Delete

FOREIGN DATA ACCESS
Standard Rectangular ASCII Files
DIF Files
SYLK (e.g. Multiplan)

GRAPHICS FEATURES
Graphics can be Output to a Printer
Titles and/or Labels Available
Uses Character Graphics

GRAPHICS
Histograms
Pie Charts
Scatter (x-y) Plots

PRODUCT SUPPORT
User may call at own Expense
No Classes or Instruction Available

STATISTICAL FEATURES SUPPORTED

DESCRIPTIVE STATISTICS
- Mean
- Standard Deviation or Variance
- Standard Error of the Mean
- Minimum, Maximum
- Skewness
- Kurtosis

t-TESTS
- One Sample t-Test
- Independent Group t-Test/Equal Variance
- Independent Group t-Test/Unequal Var
- Paired t-Test

CORRELATION AND REGRESSION
- Pearson Correlation Coefficient
- Simple Linear Regression
- Multiple Linear Regression
- Residuals Calculated

CATEGORICAL DATA ANALYSIS
- Chi-Square Contingency Table Analysis
- Multi-Dimensional Tables
- Fisher's Exact Test
- Goodness-of-Fit Tests
- Frequencies Can be Entered Directly

MISCELLANEOUS
- Random Number Generation
- p-Values Given With Tests

BETASTAT

Belanger Research Associates
541 W. 6th Street
Azusa, CA 91702
(818) 969 - 4112
Contact Person: Robert R Belanger, PhD

CONFIGURATIONS SUPPORTED

Computer	Language	Operating System	RAM	Number Drives	Cost
IBM PC	BASIC	DOS	64K	1	$ 295
CP/M FORMAT	MBASIC	CP/M	64K	1	$ 295
APPLE II	APPLESOFT	DOS	48K	1	$ 295
TRS-80	TANDY BASIC	TRS-DOS	48K	1	$ 295

NUMBER OF CURRENT USERS 2000+
DATE OF FIRST RELEASE Jan 79
CURRENT VERSION RELEASED Jul 84

PROGRAM DESCRIPTION

BetaSTAT is an advanced group of statistics programs for all CP/M and IBM PC compatible microcomputers, Apple II and all TRS-80 models. It is sold as either an integrated package, or any of the seven (eight for IBM) separate modules are available individually.

With a database of up to 192 variables any subset of the data can be run up to 100 variables (for an unlimited number of cases), BetaSTAT is capable of handling from the smallest to the largest research problems possible on a microcomputer. The system of programs is totally menu driven and has advanced data handling features including: permanent disk storage of raw and intermediate data missing data flag; select if function; data transformations; and full review and editing. Other features include: computations in double precision; supports floppy or hard disk drive; raw or intermediate data entry; compatible with other databases (IBM and CP/M only); 8087 support (IBM version). The BetaSTAT modules are: STEPWISE REGRESSION, FACTOR ANALYSIS, DISCRIMINANT FUNCTION, ANALYSIS OF VARIANCE, ANALYSIS OF

COVARIANCE, ANALYSIS OF VARIANCE (W+B) - repeated measures, MATRIX MANIPULATION, and NONPARAMETRICS - for IBM only. All modules are available for practically any microcomputer format(except NONPARAMETRICS which is only on the IBM PC).

PRODUCT REVIEWS
Two/Sixteen + 12, (March 1983).

TYPE OF PROGRAM
Statistical Package

PROGRAM DESIGNED FOR
Data Analysis
Educational use

PROGRAM STYLE
Menu Driven
Integrated System

MISCELLANEOUS PROGRAM FEATURES
Source Code Available
Copyable Disk
Optional Support for 8087 Mathematical Chip

DOCUMENTATION
User's Manual - 83 pages, 11 technical references
Index
Tutorial or Example Lessons
Sample Runs
Formulas Provided

DATA MANAGEMENT
Keyboard Data Entry
Data Manipulations and Transformations
Missing Values Allowed in Data

DATA EDITING
Change
Add
Delete

FOREIGN DATA ACCESS
Standard Rectangular ASCII Files
DIF Files
dBase II Files

GRAPHICS FEATURES
- Graphics can be Output to a Printer
- Titles and/or Labels Available
- Uses Character Graphics

GRAPHICS
- Histograms
- Scatter (x-y) Plots

PRODUCT SUPPORT
- User may call at own Expense
- No Classes or Instruction Available

STATISTICAL FEATURES SUPPORTED

DESCRIPTIVE STATISTICS
- Mean
- Standard Deviation or Variance
- Minimum, Maximum
- Median

t-TESTS
- One Sample t-Test
- Independent Group t-Test/Equal Variance
- Paired t-Test

CORRELATION AND REGRESSION
- Pearson Correlation Coefficient
- Simple Linear Regression
- Multiple Linear Regression
- Stepwise Multiple Linear Regression
- Non-Linear Regression
- Residuals Calculated

CATEGORICAL DATA ANALYSIS
- Chi-Square Contingency Table Analysis
- Multi-Dimensional Tables
- Fisher's Exact Test
- Frequencies Can be Entered Directly

ANALYSIS OF VARIANCE
- One-Way ANOVA
- One-Way with Repeated Measures
- Two-Way ANOVA
- Two-Way Unequal Cell Sizes Allowed
- Analysis of Covariance
- Multi-way ANOVA
- Multiway Factorials

NONPARAMETRIC TESTS

Sign Test (Signed Rank)
Wilcoxon One Sample Test
Mann-Whitney U
Kruskal-Wallis Test
Rank Sum Test

DISTRIBUTION FUNCTION EVALUATION

Normal
t
Chi Square
F

TIME SERIES ANALYSIS

Autocorrelations
Lag Time Analysis
Durbin Watson Statistic

MISCELLANEOUS

Random Number Generation
Linear Discriminant Function Calculation
Sample Size Estimation
Factor Analysis
Matrix Operations

BIOM-PC

Applied Statistics
3 Heritage Lane and Evolution, SUNY
Setauket, NY 11733
(516) 751 - 1203
Contact Person: F. James Rohlf

CONFIGURATIONS SUPPORTED

Computer	Language	Operating System	RAM	Number Drives	Cost
IBM PC	FORTRAN	DOS	256K	1	$ 60

NUMBER OF CURRENT USERS 240
DATE OF FIRST RELEASE 1984
CURRENT VERSION RELEASED 1985

PROGRAM DESCRIPTION

The BIOM package is a collection of FORTRAN programs for performing a variety of basic univariate and bivariate Statistical analyses. They were developed to accompany the second edition of Biometry by Sokal and Rohlf, W. H. Freeman & Co., New York (1981).

The programs have been written in as simple and general a form as possible so that they can be implemented easily, with little reprogramming, on the larger microcomputers (such as IBM-PC) as well as most minicomputers and mainframe computers. Most of the code is compatible with FORTRAN 66, but it is assumed that list-directed (free format) input is available to make input more convenient at a computer terminal and that double precision is available to provide satisfactory accuracy (the programs pass all of the tests outlined by Lachenbruch (1983 Byte 8 (11) 560-570). For compatibility, all input and output is limited to 80-character records. The programs REGR, MULREG, and POLY produce printer plots using standard characters. The programs prompt for all required input and thus can be used conveniently from a terminal. They can also be used in a batch mode, however, since the sequence of input records is predictable (a users manual of 80 pages is furnished). Most of the programs allow a variety of transformations.

PRODUCT REVIEWS
American Statistician, Vol 38, No. 4, pp. 318, (Nov 1984).

TYPE OF PROGRAM
Statistical Package

PROGRAM DESIGNED FOR
Data Analysis

PROGRAM STYLE
Separate Programs for each Procedure

MISCELLANEOUS PROGRAM FEATURES
Source Code Available
Copyable Disk
Supports 8087 Mathematical Chip

DOCUMENTATION
User's Manual - 84 pages, ? technical references
Table of Contents
Sample Runs
Sokal & Rohlf Textbook Explains Methods

DATA MANAGEMENT
Keyboard Data Entry
Data Manipulations and Transformations

FOREIGN DATA ACCESS
Normal Input File Produced by an Editor

GRAPHICS FEATURES
Graphics can be Output to a Printer
Graphics can be Saved to a File
Uses Character Graphics

GRAPHICS
Scatter (x-y) Plots

PRODUCT SUPPORT
User may call at own Expense
No Classes or Instruction Available

STATISTICAL FEATURES SUPPORTED

DESCRIPTIVE STATISTICS
- Mean
- Standard Deviation or Variance
- Standard Error of the Mean
- Coefficient of Variation
- Minimum, Maximum
- Median
- Skewness
- Kurtosis

CORRELATION AND REGRESSION
- Pearson Correlation Coefficient
- Simple Linear Regression
- Multiple Linear Regression
- Non-Linear Regression
- Residuals Calculated
- **REGRESSION PLOTS**
  - Residuals

CONFIDENCE INTERVALS
- Means
- Variances
- Ratio of Variances

CATEGORICAL DATA ANALYSIS
- Multi-Dimensional Tables
- Fisher's Exact Test
- Goodness-of-Fit Tests
- Frequencies Can be Entered Directly

ANALYSIS OF VARIANCE
- One-Way ANOVA
- Two-Way ANOVA
- Analysis of Covariance
- Multiple Regression
- Multi-Way ANOVA
- **MULTIPLE COMPARISONS**
  - Welsch Step-up
  - Tukey
  - t-prime
  - t
  - SS-STP
  - GT2

NONPARAMETRIC TESTS

- Sign Test (Signed Rank)
- Kruskal-Wallis Test
- Jackknife

DISTRIBUTION FUNCTION EVALUATION

- Normal
- Binomial
- Poisson

MISCELLANEOUS

- Test for Normality of Data
- Test for Equality of Variances
- Box-Cox Transformations

BIOMEDICAL RESEARCH CHART TOOL KIT

Sof-ware Tools
P.O. Box 8751
Boise, Idaho 83707
(208) 343 - 1437
Contact Person: Joan Heitzeberg

CONFIGURATIONS SUPPORTED

Computer	Language	Operating System	RAM	Number Drives	Cost
MACINTOSH	BASIC	DOS	512K	1	$99

NUMBER OF CURRENT USERS 15
DATE OF FIRST RELEASE Aug 85
VERSION 1.31 RELEASED May 86

PROGRAM DESCRIPTION

BIOMEDICAL RESEARCH CHART TOOL KIT is an extremely easy-to-use graphics and statistical software package that produces biomedical research charts, graphs and statistics for the needs of scientists, researchers, lab technicians, professors, and students.

The types of charts and graphs provided are: trend charts, scatter plots, histograms, polynomial regression analysis and graph, and bar charts. A Student t Test based on paired or correlated data, mean of single population, and two populations with equal or with unequal variances is included. These biomedical charts and statistical reports are not found in general graphics software. The charts provide optional standard error bar plots, as well as curve fitting capability, all in one easy to use package.

TYPE OF PROGRAM

Regression Analysis

PROGRAM DESIGNED FOR

Data Analysis
Educational use

PROGRAM STYLE

Menu Driven
Integrated System

DOCUMENTATION

User's Manual - 60 pages, ? technical references

- Table of Contents
- Index
- Sample Runs

DATA MANAGEMENT

- Keyboard Data Entry
- Data Manipulations and Transformations

DATA EDITING

- Change
- Add
- Delete

FOREIGN DATA ACCESS

- Standard Rectangular ASCII Files
- Read Clipboard Data - Multiplan, Excel

GRAPHICS FEATURES

- Graphics can be Output to a Printer
- Titles and/or Labels Available
- Uses Pixel Graphics

GRAPHICS

- Histograms
- Scatter (x-y) Plots
- Polynomial

PRODUCT SUPPORT

- User may call at own Expense
- No Classes or Instruction Available

STATISTICAL FEATURES SUPPORTED

DESCRIPTIVE STATISTICS
- Mean
- Standard Deviation or Variance
- Standard Error of the Mean
- Minimum, Maximum
- Skewness
- Kurtosis

t-TESTS
- One Sample t-Test
- Independent Group t-Test/Equal Variance
- Independent Group t-Test/Unequal Var
- Paired t-Test

CORRELATION AND REGRESSION
- Pearson Correlation Coefficient
- Simple Linear Regression

DISTRIBUTION FUNCTION EVALUATION
- t

MISCELLANEOUS
- Random Number Generation
- p-Values Given With Tests

BMDP STATISTICAL SOFTWARE, INC.

BMDP Statistical Software, Inc.
1440 Sepulveda Blvd.
Los Angeles, CA 90025
(213) 479 - 7799
Contact Person: Lynda Glassner

CONFIGURATIONS SUPPORTED

Computer	Language	Operating System	RAM	Number Drives	Cost
IBM PC	FORTRAN	DOS	512K	2	$ 495

NUMBER OF CURRENT USERS 3,000
DATE OF FIRST RELEASE Aug 84
CURRENT VERSION RELEASED Dec 86

PROGRAM DESCRIPTION

BMDP/PC is the microcomputer implementation of BMDP Statistical Software. Each PC program offers the exact features and options available in the corresponding mainframe program. Capabilities range from simple data display and description to the most advanced statistical techniques. The package offers simple statistics, plots, histograms, frequency tables, missing value estimation; regression and nonlinear regression; analysis of variance and covariance; multivariate, factor, cluster and discriminant analysis; time series; nonparametric analysis; survival analysis and life tables. The 1987 release also includes a powerful new Data Manager System for merging and summarizing files, including nonrectangular and hierarchical data. BMDP is used by researchers at most universities and in many government agencies and commercial organizations. The BMDP package is especially well suited for statisticians and others who need flexible and/or advanced methods for data analysis.

PC users may "pick and choose" any combination of programs from the 39 offered. $495 buys a Custom Group of any 4 programs or the Introductory Group which includes 6 programs. Additional programs may be ordered for $50 apiece. Site licenses, quantity discounts, extensive documentation, and 2-day short courses available. Technical support and quarterly newsletter provided free-of-charge for all users.

PRODUCT REVIEWS
The American Statistician, Vol. 39, No. 3, pp. 213-215, (Aug 1985).

TYPE OF PROGRAM
Statistical Package

PROGRAM DESIGNED FOR
Data Analysis

PROGRAM STYLE
Command Driven
Separate Programs for each Procedure

MISCELLANEOUS PROGRAM FEATURES
Copyable Disk

DOCUMENTATION
User's Manual - 766 pages, 215 technical references
- Table of Contents
- Index
- Tutorial or Example Lessons
- Sample Runs
- Formulas Provided

User's Digest

DATA MANAGEMENT
Keyboard Data Entry
Data Manipulations and Transformations
Missing Values Allowed in Data

DATA EDITING
Change
Add
Delete

FOREIGN DATA ACCESS
Standard Rectangular ASCII Files
Non Rectangular ASCII Files

GRAPHICS FEATURES
Graphics Appear in Color on the Monitor
Graphics can be Output to a Printer
Graphics can be Saved to a File
Uses Character Graphics

GRAPHICS
- Histograms
- Scatter (x-y) Plots
- SEE Time Series Plots
- SEE Regression Plots
- SEE EDA Plots

PRODUCT SUPPORT
- Free Phone Support Available
- Classes or Instruction Available

STATISTICAL FEATURES SUPPORTED

DESCRIPTIVE STATISTICS
- Mean
- Standard Deviation or Variance
- Standard Error of the Mean
- Coefficient of Variation
- Minimum, Maximum
- Median
- Percentiles
- Skewness
- Kurtosis
- W Statistic
- Wilks-Shapiro
- Robust Location Estimates
- Winsorized Means
- Interquartile Range

t-TESTS
- One Sample t-Test
- Independent Group t-Test/Equal Variance
- Independent Group t-Test/Unequal Var
- Paired t-Test
- Multivariate T-square (Hotelling's)

CORRELATION AND REGRESSION
- Pearson Correlation Coefficient
- Simple Linear Regression
- Multiple Linear Regression
- Stepwise Multiple Linear Regression
- Non-Linear Regression
- Residuals Calculated
- Polynomial Regression
- Logistic Regression
- Regression Diagnostics
- **REGRESSION PLOTS**
  - Residuals

CONFIDENCE INTERVALS
- Means
- Difference Between Two Means
- Proportions
- Difference Between Two Proportions

CATEGORICAL DATA ANALYSIS
- Chi-Square Contingency Table Analysis
- Multi-Dimensional Tables
- Fisher's Exact Test
- Goodness-of-Fit Tests
- Frequencies Can be Entered Directly
- Full Log-linear Model Fitting

ANALYSIS OF VARIANCE
- One-Way ANOVA
- One-Way with Repeated Measures
- Two-Way ANOVA
- Two-Way Unequal Cell Sizes Allowed
- Analysis of Covariance
- Split Plot
- Latin Square
- Mixed Model ANOVA
- **MULTIPLE COMPARISONS**
    - Duncan's Multiple Range
    - Scheffe
    - Bonferroni
    - Newman-Keuls
    - Tukey
    - Dunnetts

NONPARAMETRIC TESTS
- Sign Test (Signed Rank)
- Wilcoxon One Sample Test
- Mann-Whitney U
- Kruskal-Wallis Test
- Friedman Chi-Square Test
- Spearman or Kendall Correlation
- Goodman Kruskal Gamma
- McNemar Test of Symmetry
- Kappa

EXPLORATORY DATA ANALYSIS
- Stem-and-Leaf Displays
- Biweight
- Hampel Robust Estimation
- Box's Diagnostic Plot
- Trim

TIME SERIES ANALYSIS
- Autocorrelations
- Cross Correlations
- Moving Average Smoothing
- AUTOREGRESSIVE MOVING AVERAGE
  - Model Identification
  - Parameter Estimation
- **TIME SERIES ANALYSIS - FORECASTING**
  - Conditional Least-squares
  - Backcasting
- **TIME SERIES ANALYSIS - PLOTS**
  - Autocorrelations
  - Partial Autocorrelations
  - Original Data
  - Cross Correlation
  - Phase Shift
  - Coherence
- **TIME SERIES ANALYSIS - SPECTRAL ESTIMATE**
  - FFT with Parzen Window

RELIABILITY
- Exponential
- Weibull
- Gamma
- Logistic
- Proportional Hazard

MISCELLANEOUS
- Cluster Analysis
- Life Table Analysis
- Random Number Generation
- Test for Normality of Data
- Test for Equality of Variances
- Linear Discriminant Function Calculation
- Sample Size Estimation
- p-Values Given With Tests
- Principal Components Analysis
- Canonical Correlation
- Boolean Factor Analysis
- Preference Pair
- EM Missing Value Estimation

BOXX

Automatic Forecasting Systems Inc
PO Box 563
Hatboro, PA 19040
(215) 675 - 0652
Contact Person: David P. Reilly

CONFIGURATIONS SUPPORTED

Computer	Language	Operating System	RAM	Number Drives	Cost
IBM PC	FORTRAN	MS-DOS	320K	2	$ 695

NUMBER OF CURRENT USERS 35
DATE OF FIRST RELEASE Jul 84
CURRENT VERSION RELEASED Mar 86

PROGRAM DESCRIPTION

AFS's products for time series analysis were designed to meet all of your software needs pertaining to Box-Jenkins or ARIMA model building. Since the codification of the Box-Jenkins process, more and more time series analysts are agreeing that this technique offers the best solution to the forecasting problem.

BOXX delivers complete non-automatic univariate, transfer function and intervention model capabilities. All algorithms are direct from the Box-Jenkins text. The user simply answers user-friendly prompts with clearly stated defaults. BOXX stores models for easy recall, computes the Pi weights of a univariate model, converts the Transfer Function model to regression form and computes the aggregate forecast and aggregate variance from each forecast origin.

TYPE OF PROGRAM

Statistical Package

PROGRAM DESIGNED FOR

Data Analysis
Educational use

PROGRAM STYLE

Menu Driven
Integrated System

MISCELLANEOUS PROGRAM FEATURES
On Screen Help Function
Supports 8087 Mathematical Chip

DOCUMENTATION
User's Manual - 80 pages, 3 technical references
Table of Contents
Index
Tutorial or Example Lessons
Sample Runs
Formulas Provided
Tutorials and Examples on Disk

DATA MANAGEMENT
Keyboard Data Entry
Data Manipulations and Transformations

DATA EDITING
Change
Add
Delete

FOREIGN DATA ACCESS
Standard Rectangular ASCII Files
DIF Files
Lotus PRN Files

GRAPHICS FEATURES
Graphics can be Output to a Printer
Graphics can be Saved to a File
Titles and/or Labels Available

GRAPHICS
Scatter (x-y) Plots
SEE Time Series Plots

PRODUCT SUPPORT
User may call at own Expense
Classes or Instruction Available

STATISTICAL FEATURES SUPPORTED

TIME SERIES ANALYSIS

- Autocorrelations
- Cross Correlations
- AUTOREGRESSIVE MOVING AVERAGE
  - Model Identification
  - Parameter Estimation
- Transfer Function Models
- Intervention Models
- **TIME SERIES ANALYSIS - FORECASTING**
  - Non-linear Least Squares
- **TIME SERIES ANALYSIS - PLOTS**
  - Autocorrelations
  - Partial Autocorrelations
  - Original Data
  - Residuals
  - Forecasts
  - Cross Correlation
  - Impulse Response

MISCELLANEOUS

- Test for Normality of Data
- Test for Homogeneity of Error Variance

BUSINESS AND ECONOMIC FORECASTING
Lionheart Press, Inc
P.O. Box 379
Alburg, VT 05440
(514) 933 - 4918

CONFIGURATIONS SUPPORTED

Computer	Language	Operating System	RAM	Number Drives	Cost
MS-DOS	COMPILED	DOS	64K	1	
CP/M 5 1/4"	COMPILED	CP/M	64K	1	
APPLE	COMPILED	DOS	64K	1	

NUMBER OF CURRENT USERS 300
DATE OF FIRST RELEASE Mar 84
CURRENT VERSION RELEASED 86

PROGRAM DESCRIPTION

This book with its special programs, shows how to apply forecasting techniques to business problems. A review of demand analysis is given, and the way to make a connection between a company time-series (such as sales) and various general economic time series is reviewed. The various forecasting techniques are used on "real-life" time series, demonstrating which technique is appropriate for which application. Finally it is shown how the development of a forecaster can be related to a market share audit and used in the development of marketing strategy. This is a clear, but sophisticated, exposition written by a forecasting consultant. About 50 monthly and yearly time-series related to the US economy are provided, giving an up-to-date data base for practical forecasting.

TYPE OF PROGRAM

Statistical Package

PROGRAM DESIGNED FOR
Data Analysis

PROGRAM STYLE
Command Driven
Separate Programs for each Procedure

DOCUMENTATION
User's Manual - 0 pages, 0 technical references
Table of Contents
Index
Tutorial or Example Lessons
Sample Runs
Formulas Provided
Tutorials and Examples on Disk

DATA MANAGEMENT
Keyboard Data Entry
Data Manipulations and Transformations

DATA EDITING
Change
Add
Delete

FOREIGN DATA ACCESS
Standard Rectangular ASCII Files

PRODUCT SUPPORT
User may call at own Expense
No Classes or Instruction Available

BUSINESS AND FINANCE MATH

Lionheart Press, Inc.
P. O. Box 379
Alburg, VT 05440
(514) 933 - 4918

CONFIGURATIONS SUPPORTED

Computer	Language	Operating System	RAM	Number Drives	Cost
MS-DOS	COMPILED	DOS	64K	1	
CP/M 5 1/4"	COMPILED	CP/M	64K	1	
APPLE	COMPILED	DOS	64K	1	

NUMBER OF CURRENT USERS 200
DATE OF FIRST RELEASE Mar 84
CURRENT VERSION RELEASED 1986

PROGRAM DESCRIPTION

The Business and Finance Math Program performs all those things about interest and present value and annuities and bond valuation that you know if you could only remember them. The computer programs replace whole books of tables and give accurate calculation for sinking funds, mortgages, compund interests, financial ratio analysis - just about anything you can think of. If you have to manage money, even your own - the book and programs will be an essential addition to your collection.

TYPE OF PROGRAM
Statistical Package

PROGRAM DESIGNED FOR
Data Analysis

PROGRAM STYLE
Command Driven
Separate Programs for each Procedure

DOCUMENTATION
User's Manual - 0 pages, 0 technical references
Table of Contents
Index
Tutorial or Example Lessons
Sample Runs
Formulas Provided
Tutorials and Examples on Disk

DATA MANAGEMENT
Keyboard Data Entry
Data Manipulations and Transformations

DATA EDITING
Change
Add
Delete

FOREIGN DATA ACCESS
Standard Rectangular ASCII Files

PRODUCT SUPPORT
User may call at own Expense
No Classes or Instruction Available

BUSINESS STATISTICS
Lionheart Press, Inc.
P. O. Box 379
Alburg, VT 05440
(514) 933 - 4918

CONFIGURATIONS SUPPORTED

Computer	Language	Operating System	RAM	Number Drives	Cost
MS-DOS	COMPILED	DOS	64K	1	
CP/M 5 1/4"	COMPILED	CP/M	64K	1	
APPLE	COMPILED	DOS	64K	1	

NUMBER OF CURRENT USERS 300
DATE OF FIRST RELEASE Mar 84
CURRENT VERSION RELEASED 1986

PROGRAM DESCRIPTION

A collection of statistical problems that occur in business situations: sampling (including acceptance sampling), how to characterize performance by comparison to some standard mean or variance, quality control, product reliability, waiting line problems, regression techniques, significance testing (parametric and non-parametric), how to design "business experiments". The text consists of a brief review of statistical principles, then continues with a collection of problems or "case studies" that show how to use both the statistical principles and the computer programs.

TYPE OF PROGRAM
Statistical Package

PROGRAM DESIGNED FOR
Data Analysis

PROGRAM STYLE
Command Driven
Separate Programs for each Procedure

DOCUMENTATION
User's Manual - 0 pages, 0 technical references
Table of Contents
Index
Tutorial or Example Lessons
Sample Runs
Formulas Provided
Tutorials and Examples on Disk

DATA MANAGEMENT
Keyboard Data Entry
Data Manipulations and Transformations

DATA EDITING
Change
Add
Delete

FOREIGN DATA ACCESS
Standard Rectangular ASCII Files

PRODUCT SUPPORT
User may call at own Expense
No Classes or Instruction Available

CALCU-PLOT

Human Systems Dynamics
9010 Reseda Blvd, Suite 222
Northridge, CA 91324
(818) 993 - 8536
Contact Person: Merideth Wiberg

CONFIGURATIONS SUPPORTED

Computer	Language	Operating System	RAM	Number Drives	Cost
APPLE II	BASIC	DOS	48K	1	$ 150

NUMBER OF CURRENT USERS 450
DATE OF FIRST RELEASE Aug 83
VERSION 1 RELEASED Jan 85

PROGRAM DESCRIPTION

CALCU-PLOT transforms the most complex equations into graphical displays. It is a package of powerful mathematical utilities. The program solves equations exactly, and plots the graph on the screen. The program then prints the graph on an Epson printer, or saves the graph to disk for printing with another printer.

CALCU-PLOT allows the user to enter own equations or use one of 16 Cartesian, 9 polar standard equations with a choice of constants and limits. The user may enter empirical data on the same graph with an equation curve, or plot empirical data on its own graph. Any three curves can be plotted on one graph. Linear semi-log, log-log, or polar coordinates may be chosen for plotting equations or empirical data.

TYPE OF PROGRAM

Statistical Package

PROGRAM DESIGNED FOR

Data Analysis

PROGRAM STYLE
Menu Driven
Integrated System

DOCUMENTATION
User's Manual - 135 pages, 0 technical references
Table of Contents
Index
Tutorial or Example Lessons
Sample Runs
Formulas Provided
Tutorials and Examples on Disk

DATA MANAGEMENT
Keyboard Data Entry

DATA EDITING
Change

FOREIGN DATA ACCESS
VisiCalc

GRAPHICS FEATURES
Graphics can be Output to a Printer
Graphics can be Saved to a File
Titles and/or Labels Available
Uses Pixel Graphics

GRAPHICS
User Defined Functions

PRODUCT SUPPORT
Free Phone Support Available
No Classes or Instruction Available

CENTS (CENSUS TABULATION SYSTEM)

International Statistical Programs Ctr.
U.S. Bureau of the Census
Washington D.C., 20233
(301) 763 - 4210
Contact Person: Chief, Computer Software Branch

CONFIGURATIONS SUPPORTED

Computer	Language	Operating System	RAM	Number Drives	Cost
IBM PC	Realia COBOL	DOS	256K	1	$500

NUMBER OF CURRENT USERS 100
DATE OF FIRST RELEASE ?
VERSION 4.2 RELEASED Sept 85

PROGRAM DESCRIPTION

The CENSus Tabulation System (CENTS) is an integrated set of computer programs which tabulate, summarize and display statistical tables in publishable form. It was developed originally to facilitate the tabulation of population and housing data from national censuses throughout the world. However, the system can be applied easily to other types of statistical data such as from agriculture censuses, labor force studies or educational surveys.

Features are: A hierarchical structure of tables, for example, various levels of geography can be produced with one pass of the data. The design of the language is such that geographic coding schemes can be easily manipulated to allow the creation of tables or totals and special aggregation. Up to six levels of hierarchy can be produced. CENTS can produce multiple tables in a single pass of the data file. The size of the tabulation programs grow as more tables or CENTS statements are added. Therefore, the limiting factor for the number of tables is the size of the computer memory. There is no limit to the amount of data that can be tabulated using CENTS, making the package appropriate for tabulation of national census data. Data can be tabulated in smaller increments, and the intermediate results saved for aggregation to higher levels of geography.

PRODUCT REVIEWS

Francis, Ivor. Statistical Software--A Comparative Review, Elsevier, (1981).

Dekker, A.L.. Comparing Stat. Software Packages on Tabulation Efficiency, (1984).

TYPE OF PROGRAM

Statistical Analysis

PROGRAM DESIGNED FOR

Data Analysis

PROGRAM STYLE

Command Driven
Integrated System

MISCELLANEOUS PROGRAM FEATURES

Source Code Available
Copyable Disk
On Screen Help Function

DOCUMENTATION

User's Manual - 265 pages, ? technical references
- Table of Contents
- Index
- Tutorial or Example Lessons
- Sample Runs
- Formulas Provided

Tutorials and Examples on Disk

DATA MANAGEMENT

Keyboard Data Entry
Data Manipulations and Transformations
Missing Values Allowed in Data

FOREIGN DATA ACCESS

Standard Rectangular ASCII Files
Hierarchical ASCII File

PRODUCT SUPPORT

User may call at own Expense
Classes or Instruction Available

STATISTICAL FEATURES SUPPORTED

DESCRIPTIVE STATISTICS

- Mean
- Minimum, Maximum
- Median
- Percentiles
- Differences
- Sums

CHART-PAK
Quality Resources
840 McKinley
Plymouth, MI 48170
(313) 453 - 4616
Contact Person: W.A. Loesch

CONFIGURATIONS SUPPORTED

Computer	Language	Operating System	RAM	Number Drives	Cost
IBM PC	BASIC	DOS	64K	2	$100
TANDY	BASIC	DOS	16K	2	$100
KAYPRO	BASIC	CP/M	64K	2	$100

NUMBER OF CURRENT USERS ?
DATE OF FIRST RELEASE Jan 81
VERSION 2.3 RELEASED Jun 86

PROGRAM DESCRIPTION

This program set includes programs for all of the commonly used charting techniques for SPC applications. The programs are user-friendly and utilize tab and line-feed functions of any standard printer - graphics capabilities are not required.

A unique program in this set is the STABILIZED p-CHART. This program uses a data transform method so that straight control limits are formed, regardless of sample size changes.

Program List:
X-Bar & R Chart
Moving Range Chart (For Individuals)
p-Chart
STABILIZED p-Chart
np-Chart
c-CHART
u-CHART
X-Bar & Sigma Chart
Median & Range Chart

TYPE OF PROGRAM
Statistical Package

PROGRAM DESIGNED FOR
Data Analysis

PROGRAM STYLE
Menu Driven
Separate Programs for each Procedure

MISCELLANEOUS PROGRAM FEATURES
Copyable Disk
On Screen Help Function

DOCUMENTATION
User's Manual - 2 pages, 0 technical references
Index
Tutorial or Example Lessons
Sample Runs

DATA MANAGEMENT
Keyboard Data Entry

DATA EDITING
Change
Add
Delete

FOREIGN DATA ACCESS
Standard Rectangular ASCII Files

GRAPHICS FEATURES
Titles and/or Labels Available
Uses Character Graphics

PRODUCT SUPPORT
User may call at own Expense
Classes or Instruction Available

STATISTICAL FEATURES SUPPORTED

DESCRIPTIVE STATISTICS

- Mean
- Standard Deviation or Variance
- Median
- Skewness

CONTROL CHARTS

- X-Bar
- s
- Number of Defects
- Number of Defectives

CLUE
Elsevier Scientific Software
P.O. Box 330
1000 AH Amsterdam, NETHERLANDS
(020) 5862828
Contact Person: Keith Foley

CONFIGURATIONS SUPPORTED

Computer	Language	Operating System	RAM	Number Drives	Cost
IBM PC	BASIC	DOS	128K	1	$405
APPLE II	BASIC	DOS	48K	1	$405

NUMBER OF CURRENT USERS 50
DATE OF FIRST RELEASE 1986
VERSION 1.0 RELEASED 1986

PROGRAM DESCRIPTION

In many chemical and other environoments objects (e.g. foods), these objects can only be characterised by several variables (e.g. inorganic and organic constituents). In these cases, it is not possible to distinguish these objects by simple statistical analysis. Clustering is a mathematical method designed to arrange such objects into groups, based on their mutual similarities and hierarchical relationships. CLUE is a software package designed to perform this clustering task.

With CLUE as many as fifty objects, each determined by fifty variables may be clustered. The package consists of three parts. Part one takes care of the input(from diskette or keyboard) and performs correcting , editing, changing, adding etc. of the data. The second part does the clustering itself. The third part enables you to display or print previously stored clustering results.

TYPE OF PROGRAM

Statistical Package

PROGRAM DESIGNED FOR

Data Analysis

PROGRAM STYLE
Menu Driven
Integrated System

MISCELLANEOUS PROGRAM FEATURES
Source Code Available
Copyable Disk

DOCUMENTATION
User's Manual - 150 pages, ? technical references
Table of Contents
Tutorial or Example Lessons
Sample Runs
Formulas Provided
Tutorials and Examples on Disk

DATA MANAGEMENT
Keyboard Data Entry
Data Manipulations and Transformations
Missing Values Allowed in Data

DATA EDITING
Change
Add
Delete

FOREIGN DATA ACCESS
Standard Rectangular ASCII Files

GRAPHICS FEATURES
Uses Character Graphics

GRAPHICS
Dendrograms

PRODUCT SUPPORT
User may call at own Expense
No Classes or Instruction Available

STATISTICAL FEATURES SUPPORTED

DESCRIPTIVE STATISTICS

Mean

Standard Deviation or Variance

MISCELLANEOUS

Cluster Analysis

COMM-STAT
Statsoft, Inc.
2832 E. 10th Street, Suite 4
Tulsa, OK 74104
(918) 583 - 4149
Contact Person: Diane Cade

CONFIGURATIONS SUPPORTED

Computer	Language	Operating System	RAM	Number Drives	Cost
COMMODORE	BASIC		64K	1	$99
COMMODORE 128	BASIC		128K	1	$99

NUMBER OF CURRENT USERS 5000
DATE OF FIRST RELEASE 1985
VERSION 1.1 RELEASED 1985

PROGRAM DESCRIPTION

A general purpose statistical package (basic statistics, nonparametrics, multivariate statistics) with graphics and statistical database management functions.

Extremely easy to use, even for novices (menu driven), advanced statistics (e.g. 5-way ANCOVA).

TYPE OF PROGRAM
Statistical Package

PROGRAM DESIGNED FOR
Data Analysis
Educational use

PROGRAM STYLE
Menu Driven
Integrated System

MISCELLANEOUS PROGRAM FEATURES
Source Code Available
Copyable Disk

DOCUMENTATION

User's Manual - ? pages, 20 technical references

Table of Contents

Tutorial or Example Lessons

Sample Runs

Tutorials and Examples on Disk

DATA MANAGEMENT

Keyboard Data Entry

Data Manipulations and Transformations

Missing Values Allowed in Data

DATA EDITING

Change

Add

Delete

FOREIGN DATA ACCESS

Standard Rectangular ASCII Files

Any ASCII Data

GRAPHICS FEATURES

Graphics can be Output to a Printer

Titles and/or Labels Available

Uses Character Graphics

GRAPHICS

Histograms

Scatter (x-y) Plots

PRODUCT SUPPORT

User may call at own Expense

No Classes or Instruction Available

STATISTICAL FEATURES SUPPORTED

DESCRIPTIVE STATISTICS
- Mean
- Standard Deviation or Variance
- Standard Error of the Mean
- Coefficient of Variation
- Minimum, Maximum
- Median
- Percentiles
- Skewness
- Kurtosis

t-TESTS
- One Sample t-Test
- Independent Group t-Test/Equal Variance
- Independent Group t-Test/Unequal Var
- Paired t-Test

CORRELATION AND REGRESSION
- Pearson Correlation Coefficient
- Simple Linear Regression
- Multiple Linear Regression
- Residuals Calculated
- **REGRESSION PLOTS**
  - Residuals

CATEGORICAL DATA ANALYSIS
- Chi-Square Contingency Table Analysis
- Frequencies Can be Entered Directly

ANALYSIS OF VARIANCE
- One-Way ANOVA
- One-Way with Repeated Measures
- Two-Way ANOVA
- Two-Way Unequal Cell Sizes Allowed
- Analysis of Covariance
- Repeated Measures
- Incomplete Designs
- Up to 5-Way ANCOVA
- **MULTIPLE COMPARISONS**
  - Planned Comparisons

NONPARAMETRIC TESTS

Wilcoxon One Sample Test
Mann-Whitney U
Kruskal-Wallis Test
Spearman or Kendall Correlation
Phi-Square
Nu-Square

DISTRIBUTION FUNCTION EVALUATION

Normal
t
Chi Square
F

TIME SERIES ANALYSIS

Autocorrelations

MISCELLANEOUS

p-Values Given With Tests

CONCOR (CONSISTENCY AND CORRECTION)

International Statistical Programs Ctr.
U.S. Bureau of the Census
Washington D.C., 20233
(301) 763 - 4210
Contact Person: Chief, Computer Software Branch

CONFIGURATIONS SUPPORTED

Computer	Language	Operating System	RAM	Number Drives	Cost
IBM PC	REALIA COBOL	DOS	256K	HD	$500

NUMBER OF CURRENT USERS 100
DATE OF FIRST RELEASE ?
VERSION 2.4 RELEASED Sept 85

PROGRAM DESCRIPTION

The CONsistency and CORrection system (CONCOR) is an integrated set of computer programs which can identify and correct invalid and inconsistent data being prepared for tabulation and analysis. It was developed to facilitate the editing of population and housing data from national censuses throughout the world as well as other types of statistical data, such as those from agriculture censuses, labor force studies and educational surveys.

CONCOR supports the following editing functions: Structure checks--These checks ascertain that all records that should be present for a particular questionaire are supplied, and that no extra records are included. Range checks--These checks are designed to determine whether a response has a value that is inside or outside the valid limits for that response. These checks are concerned with single responses. Consistency checks--In these checks, two or more responses in a questionaire are compared for their consistency. The responses may be in the same record or in different records within a questionaire. Automatic correction--CONCOR provides the facility for not only finding incorrect or inconsistent data, but also making corrections according to user specifications. The "hot deck" method of correction is one of several methods that are available. Error reports--CONCOR generates comprehensive statistics about the edit tests performed and the number of imputations made. Reports of these statistics are generated at user discretion.

PRODUCT REVIEWS
Francis, Ivor. Statistical Software--A Comparative Review, (1981).

TYPE OF PROGRAM
Editing and Imputation

PROGRAM DESIGNED FOR
Data Analysis

PROGRAM STYLE
Command Driven
Integrated System

MISCELLANEOUS PROGRAM FEATURES
Source Code Available
Copyable Disk
On Screen Help Function

DOCUMENTATION
User's Manual - 180 pages, ? technical references
- Table of Contents
- Index
- Tutorial or Example Lessons
- Sample Runs
- Formulas Provided

Tutorials and Examples on Disk

DATA MANAGEMENT
Keyboard Data Entry
Data Manipulations and Transformations
Missing Values Allowed in Data

DATA EDITING
Change
Delete

FOREIGN DATA ACCESS
Standard Rectangular ASCII Files
Multiple Records Per Case ASCII File

PRODUCT SUPPORT
User may call at own Expense
Classes or Instruction Available

CONSUMER

Gwilym Jenkins & Partners Ltd.
Parkfield, Greaves Rd.
Lancaster, ENGLAND
(0) 524-61831
Contact Person: J. F. Horrel (405) 364-4708

CONFIGURATIONS SUPPORTED

Computer	Language	Operating System	RAM	Number Drives	Cost
IBM PC	FORTRAN	DOS	640K	HD	$3500

NUMBER OF CURRENT USERS 5
DATE OF FIRST RELEASE Nov 86
VERSION 1 RELEASED Nov 86

PROGRAM DESCRIPTION

CONSUMER is designed for the interpretation and forecasting of product demand in the consumer products area. The product is primarily designed for use by non-expert users who wish to interpret and forecast demand under the impact of market factors.

CONSUMER utilizes BOX-JENKINS methods but requires no knowledge of statistics or statistical forecasting.

TYPE OF PROGRAM

Time Series Analysis

PROGRAM DESIGNED FOR

Data Analysis

PROGRAM STYLE

Menu Driven
Integrated System

MISCELLANEOUS PROGRAM FEATURES

Copyable Disk
On Screen Help Function
Optional Support for 8087 Mathematical Chip

DOCUMENTATION

User's Manual - 350 pages, 5 technical references

- Table of Contents
- Index
- Tutorial or Example Lessons
- Sample Runs
- Formulas Provided

Tutorials and Examples on Disk

DATA MANAGEMENT

- Keyboard Data Entry
- Data Manipulations and Transformations
- Missing Values Allowed in Data

DATA EDITING

- Change
- Add
- Delete

FOREIGN DATA ACCESS

- Standard Rectangular ASCII Files
- Lotus

GRAPHICS FEATURES

- Graphics Appear in Color on the Monitor
- Graphics can be Output to a Printer
- Titles and/or Labels Available
- Uses Pixel Graphics
- Uses Character Graphics

GRAPHICS

- Box Plots

PRODUCT SUPPORT

- User may call at own Expense
- No Classes or Instruction Available

STATISTICAL FEATURES SUPPORTED

TIME SERIES ANALYSIS

TIME SERIES ANALYSIS - FORECASTING

Box-Jenkins

CONTOUR - I
Statistical Programs
9941 Rowlett, Suite 6
Houston, TX 77075
(713) 947 - 1551
Contact Person: Bonnie Deming

CONFIGURATIONS SUPPORTED

Computer	Language	Operating System	RAM	Number Drives	Cost
IBM PC	BASIC	DOS	256K	1	$150

NUMBER OF CURRENT USERS ?
DATE OF FIRST RELEASE 1984
CURRENT VERSION RELEASED ?

PROGRAM DESCRIPTION

CONTOUR-I is a computer program aimed at scientists and engineers involved in Research and Development. It is used to draw two-factor response surface contour plots so that data may be visually interpreted.

CONTOUR-I can be readily user-modified to accommodate any response surface model.

TYPE OF PROGRAM

Graphics

PROGRAM DESIGNED FOR

Data Analysis
Educational use

PROGRAM STYLE

Command Driven
Integrated System

MISCELLANEOUS PROGRAM FEATURES

Source Code Available
Copyable Disk

DOCUMENTATION
User's Manual - 25 pages, 0 technical references
Table of Contents
Tutorial or Example Lessons

DATA MANAGEMENT
Keyboard Data Entry

GRAPHICS FEATURES
Graphics can be Output to a Printer
Titles and/or Labels Available
Uses Character Graphics

GRAPHICS
Scatter (x-y) Plots

PRODUCT SUPPORT
User may call at own Expense
No Classes or Instruction Available

STATISTICAL FEATURES SUPPORTED

EXPLORATORY DATA ANALYSIS
Contour Plotting of Functions

CRISP

Crunch Software
2547 22nd Ave
San Francisco, CA 94116
(415) 564 - 7337
Contact Person: Alan Bostrom

CONFIGURATIONS SUPPORTED

Computer	Language	Operating System	RAM	Number Drives	Cost
IBM PC	COMPILED	DOS	256K	2	$ 495

NUMBER OF CURRENT USERS 1500
DATE OF FIRST RELEASE Aug 83
VERSION 3.0 RELEASED Apr 86

ADDITIONAL SOFTWARE REQUIRED
IBM BASRUN.EXE (supplied free)

PROGRAM DESCRIPTION

CRISP is a general purpose set of statistical and utility programs for managing and analyzing data. The interactive, menu-driven nature of the programs allows the user to learn quickly how to carry out a large variety of analyses. Keyboard macros (user defined) and a BATCH utility are also included.

Besides its ease of use, CRISP is unique in providing many powerful utilities for manipulation of data prior to statistical analysis. For example, merging, sorting, transforming data, selecting subsets of data are all easily accomplished. CRISP also handles large problems--up to 252 variables and unlimited cases, and is designed to operate efficiently -- for example, subfile processing and analysis of multiple dependent variables on a single pass through the data. The statistical routines in CRISP offer the kinds of general capabilities found in mainframe packages -- for example a general factorial analysis of variance including repeated measures, principal components on up to 75 variables and flexible specification of regression models. CRISP also offers flexibility in communicating with other programs through ASCII, DIF, dBASE, Rbase files and the ability to integrate your own programs into the CRISP system. CRISP users range from introductory statistics students to PhD statisticians.

PRODUCT REVIEWS

PC World, (Sep 1984).

Goodban, Nancy and Hakuta, Kenji. "Statistical Quintet", PC World, pp. 186-195, (Sep 1984).

Fridlund, Alan J.. "Taking the Numbers Bull by the Horns", Infoworld, pp. 42-48, (Feb 11, 1985).

TYPE OF PROGRAM

Statistical Package

PROGRAM DESIGNED FOR

Data Analysis

PROGRAM STYLE

Menu Driven
Integrated System

MISCELLANEOUS PROGRAM FEATURES

Copyable Disk

DOCUMENTATION

User's Manual - 324 pages, 38 technical references
- Table of Contents
- Index
- Sample Runs

Tutorials and Examples on Disk

DATA MANAGEMENT

Keyboard Data Entry
Data Manipulations and Transformations
Missing Values Allowed in Data

DATA EDITING

Change
Add
Delete

FOREIGN DATA ACCESS

Standard Rectangular ASCII Files
DIF Files
dBase II Files
Rbase 5000 Files
dBASE III Files

GRAPHICS FEATURES
- Graphics Appear in Color on the Monitor
- Graphics can be Output to a Printer
- Graphics can be Saved to a File
- Titles and/or Labels Available
- Uses Character Graphics

GRAPHICS
- Histograms
- Scatter (x-y) Plots

PRODUCT SUPPORT
- User may call at own Expense
- No Classes or Instruction Available

STATISTICAL FEATURES SUPPORTED

DESCRIPTIVE STATISTICS
- Mean
- Standard Deviation or Variance
- Standard Error of the Mean
- Coefficient of Variation
- Minimum, Maximum
- Median
- Skewness
- Kurtosis

t-TESTS
- One Sample t-Test
- Independent Group t-Test/Equal Variance
- Independent Group t-Test/Unequal Var
- Paired t-Test

CORRELATION AND REGRESSION
- Pearson Correlation Coefficient
- Simple Linear Regression
- Multiple Linear Regression
- Stepwise Multiple Linear Regression
- Non-Linear Regression
- Residuals Calculated
- Estimate Asymptotic Standard Errors
- Pair/List-wise Handling of Missing Data
- Rank Correlation
- Studentized Residuals
- Influence Statistics

CATEGORICAL DATA ANALYSIS
- Chi-Square Contingency Table Analysis
- Multi-Dimensional Tables
- Fisher's Exact Test
- Frequencies Can be Entered Directly
- Odds Ratios
- Test of Homogeneity of Odds Ratios
- Kappa Statistic
- Kruskal-Wallis Nominal by Ordinal Table

ANALYSIS OF VARIANCE
- One-Way ANOVA
- One-Way with Repeated Measures
- Two-Way ANOVA
- Two-Way Unequal Cell Sizes Allowed
- Analysis of Covariance
- Nested Factors
- Multiway Factorials
- Crossed Designs - Balanced or Unbalanced
- **MULTIPLE COMPARISONS**
  - Scheffe
  - Bonferroni
  - Newman-Keuls
  - Tukey
  - Dunnetts
  - Sidak
  - Ryan-Einot-Gabriel-Welsch

NONPARAMETRIC TESTS
- Wilcoxon One Sample Test
- Mann-Whitney U
- Kruskal-Wallis Test
- Spearman or Kendall Correlation

MISCELLANEOUS
- Random Number Generation
- p-Values Given With Tests
- Principal Components Analysis
- Cronbach's Alpha Reliability Coefficient

CSS
Statsoft, Inc.
2832 East 10th Street, Suite 4
Tulsa, OK 74104
(918) 583 - 4149
Contact Person: Sales Office

CONFIGURATIONS SUPPORTED

Computer	Language	Operating System	RAM	Number Drives	Cost
IBM PC	FORTRAN/ ASSEMBLER/ C	DOS	384K	2	$495

NUMBER OF CURRENT USERS New
DATE OF FIRST RELEASE Dec 86
VERSION 1.0 RELEASED Dec 86

PROGRAM DESCRIPTION

CSS (Complete Statistical System) ia an advanced statistical package, with graphics, and database management. CSS features comprehensive implementation of basic statistics, nonparametrics, multidimensional tables, regression methods, ANOVA/ANCOVA/MANOVA, contrast analysis, discriminant analysis, factor analysis, time series and forecasting (with complete ARIMA), multidimensional scaling, presentation quality graphics, and complete statistical database management.

CSS combines mainframe level statistical sophistication with a modern user interface (and the flexibility of graphics/data management) setting new standards for the 1987 generation of microcomputer software. The user interface of CSS and all of its input/output routines were developed in Assembler (CSS directly accesses screen, disk, and keyboard bypassing DOS), graphics were developed in C, and statistical routines in optimized Fortran. The program is extremely fast. All output to the screen is instant and handled via Scrollsheets(tm) (i.e., windows in the shape of tables that allow the user to scroll through the output). Graphics and data management were developed in the most flexible manner: the user may either generate predesigned graphics or convert any combination of input/output into presentation quality graphs (drivers provided for most printers, incl. lasers, and plotters). The data management capabilities of CSS are accessed via a superfast spreadsheet (developed in Assembler), and include unlimited transformations, merging, splitting, selecting, sorting, and restructuring of data files, and direct comprehensive import/export facilities to Lotus, Symphony, dBII, dBIII, DIF, SYLK, and other formats.

TYPE OF PROGRAM
- Statistical Package

PROGRAM DESIGNED FOR
- Data Analysis
- Educational use

PROGRAM STYLE
- Menu Driven
- Command Driven
- Integrated System

MISCELLANEOUS PROGRAM FEATURES
- Copyable Disk
- On Screen Help Function
- Optional Support for 8087, 80287 Mathematical Chip

DOCUMENTATION
- User's Manual - 900 pages, 150 technical references
  - Table of Contents
  - Index
  - Tutorial or Example Lessons
  - Sample Runs
  - Formulas Provided
- Quick Reference Card
- Tutorials and Examples on Disk

DATA MANAGEMENT
- Keyboard Data Entry
- Data Manipulations and Transformations
- Missing Values Allowed in Data

DATA EDITING
- Change
- Add
- Delete

FOREIGN DATA ACCESS
- Standard Rectangular ASCII Files
- DIF Files
- Formatted or Free Format ASCII
- DIF Files
- SYLK Files
- Symphony
- dBASE II and III Files
- Lotus

GRAPHICS FEATURES
- Graphics Appear in Color on the Monitor
- Graphics can be Output to a Printer
- Graphics can be Saved to a File
- Titles and/or Labels Available
- Uses Pixel Graphics
- Uses Character Graphics

GRAPHICS
- Histograms
- Pie Charts
- Scatter (x-y) Plots
- Box Plots
- Combination Graphs
- 20 Types of Graphs

PRODUCT SUPPORT
- User may call at own Expense
- Classes or Instruction Available

STATISTICAL FEATURES SUPPORTED

DESCRIPTIVE STATISTICS
- Mean
- Standard Deviation or Variance
- Standard Error of the Mean
- Coefficient of Variation
- Minimum, Maximum
- Median
- Percentiles
- Skewness
- Kurtosis
- Geometric Mean
- Harmonic Mean
- Quartiles
- Many Others

t-TESTS
- One Sample t-Test
- Independent Group t-Test/Equal Variance
- Independent Group t-Test/Unequal Var
- Paired t-Test

CORRELATION AND REGRESSION
- Pearson Correlation Coefficient
- Simple Linear Regression
- Multiple Linear Regression
- Stepwise Multiple Linear Regression
- Non-Linear Regression
- Residuals Calculated
- Durbin Watson
- Cooks Distances
- Mahalanobis Distances
- Ridge Regression
- Regression Through the Orgin
- Many Others
- **REGRESSION PLOTS**
    - Residuals

CONFIDENCE INTERVALS
- Means

CATEGORICAL DATA ANALYSIS
- Chi-Square Contingency Table Analysis
- Multi-Dimensional Tables
- Fisher's Exact Test
- Frequencies Can be Entered Directly
- Numerous Statistics

ANALYSIS OF VARIANCE
- Fixed or Random Effects
- Isolated Control Group
- Unbalanced
- Incomplete
- Nested
- 128 Dependent Measures
- General MANOVA/ANOVA/ANCOVA
- **MULTIPLE COMPARISONS**
    - Fisher's LSD
    - Scheffe
    - Newman-Keuls
    - Tukey
    - Comprehensive Contrast Analysis

NONPARAMETRIC TESTS

- Sign Test (Signed Rank)
- Wilcoxon One Sample Test
- Mann-Whitney U
- Kruskal-Wallis Test
- Friedman Chi-Square Test
- Spearman or Kendall Correlation
- Many Others

DISTRIBUTION FUNCTION EVALUATION

- Normal
- t
- Chi Square
- F

EXPLORATORY DATA ANALYSIS

- Stem-and-Leaf Displays
- Smoothing Techniques
- Median Polish
- 20 Methods

TIME SERIES ANALYSIS

- Autocorrelations
- Cross Correlations
- Moving Average Smoothing
- AUTOREGRESSIVE MOVING AVERAGE
  - Model Identification
  - Parameter Estimation
- **TIME SERIES ANALYSIS - FORECASTING**
  - ARIMA
  - All Simple Standard Methods
  - ARMA
- **TIME SERIES ANALYSIS - PLOTS**
  - Dynamic (Scrollable) Graphs
- **TIME SERIES ANALYSIS - SPECTRAL ESTIMATE**
  - Fourier Decomposition

MISCELLANEOUS

- Test for Normality of Data
- Test for Equality of Variances
- Linear Discriminant Function Calculation
- p-Values Given With Tests
- Factor Analysis
- Principal Component Analysis
- Discriminant Function Analysis
- Multidimensional Scaling
- Many Others

CUSTOM/QC
Stochos,Inc.
14 North College St.
Schenectady, NY 12305
(518) 372 - 5426
Contact Person: Erik M. Roy

CONFIGURATIONS SUPPORTED

Computer	Language	Operating System	RAM	Number Drives	Cost
IBM PC	C	DOS	512K	2	$500

NUMBER OF CURRENT USERS 150
DATE OF FIRST RELEASE Mar 84
VERSION 2.0 RELEASED Sept 86

PROGRAM DESCRIPTION

An easy -to-use menu driven statistical process control program for use by quality assurance professionals. Data input can be from ASCII files, spread sheet programs, manually constructed, or optional automatic data capture. Output is to screen, printer, plotter, or camera. Analysis includes descriptive statistics (mean, standard, deviation, histogram, kurtosis, skewness, pareto, etc.); control charts (x-bar, R, Sigma, P, Cumsum, C, Chi Square, T Square, etc.); statistical estimation (analysis of means, multiple regression, trends); process capability studies;Frequency curve comparison(12 curve table lookup,9 curve data comparison);Sampling plan development and evaluation.

TYPE OF PROGRAM
Quality Control or Reliability

PROGRAM DESIGNED FOR
Data Analysis

PROGRAM STYLE
Menu Driven
Integrated System

MISCELLANEOUS PROGRAM FEATURES
- Copyable Disk
- Optional Support for 8087 Mathematical Chip

DOCUMENTATION
- User's Manual - 300 pages, technical references
  - Table of Contents
  - Tutorial or Example Lessons
  - Sample Runs
- Tutorials and Examples on Disk

DATA MANAGEMENT
- Keyboard Data Entry
- Data Manipulations and Transformations

DATA EDITING
- Change
- Add
- Delete

FOREIGN DATA ACCESS
- Standard Rectangular ASCII Files

GRAPHICS FEATURES
- Graphics Appear in Color on the Monitor
- Graphics can be Output to a Printer
- Titles and/or Labels Available
- Uses Character Graphics

GRAPHICS
- Histograms
- Control Charts

PRODUCT SUPPORT
- Free Phone Support Available
- Classes or Instruction Available

STATISTICAL FEATURES SUPPORTED

DESCRIPTIVE STATISTICS
- Mean
- Standard Deviation or Variance
- Minimum, Maximum
- Median
- Skewness
- Kurtosis
- Standard Error of the Mean

t-TESTS
- One Sample t-Test

CORRELATION AND REGRESSION
- Simple Linear Regression
- Multiple Linear Regression
- Residuals Calculated

CATEGORICAL DATA ANALYSIS
- Fisher's Exact Test
- Goodness-of-Fit Tests
- Frequencies Can be Entered Directly

ANALYSIS OF VARIANCE
- One-Way ANOVA
- One-Way with Repeated Measures
- Two-Way ANOVA

DISTRIBUTION FUNCTION EVALUATION
- Normal
- t
- Chi Square
- F
- Binomial
- Hypergeometric
- Poisson
- Exponential
- Weibull
- Geometric
- Pascal
- Erlang

EXPLORATORY DATA ANALYSIS
- Subgroup Size Exploration for Mean and Variance

TIME SERIES ANALYSIS
- Autocorrelations
- **TIME SERIES ANALYSIS - FORECASTING**
  - Non-linear Least Squares
- **TIME SERIES ANALYSIS - PLOTS**
  - Moving Average with Error Bars

CONTROL CHARTS
- X-Bar
- s
- Proportions
- Number of Defects
- Number of Defectives
- **RELIABILITY**
  - Exponential
  - Weibull
  - Gamma
- **OTHER QUALITY CONTROL PROCEDURES**
  - Acceptance Sampling by Attributes
  - Acceptance Sampling by Variables

MISCELLANEOUS
- Sample Size Estimation
- p-Values Given With Tests
- Map Generation
- Test for Randomness

DAISY PROFESSIONAL STATISTICS SYSTEM
Stone House Systems
515 Cumnor Rd.
Kenilworth, IL 60043
(312) 256 - 5813
Contact Person: Deborah Stonehouse

CONFIGURATIONS SUPPORTED

Computer	Language	Operating System	RAM	Number Drives	Cost
APPLE II		DOS	48K	1	$199

NUMBER OF CURRENT USERS 2000
DATE OF FIRST RELEASE 1981
VERSION 2.4 RELEASED Jan 86

PROGRAM DESCRIPTION

Daisy Professional is a system of powerful analytical tools in use by over 1600 researchers, educators, business planners, scientists, marketers, government analysis, and students.

The Daisy Professional statistics system includes; descriptive statistics, moments, medians, correlations, partial correlations, covariances, autocorrelation, hypothesis tests and nonparametric correlation. Daisy offers six types of regression analysis, with detailed summaries, residual analysis, ANOVA, model validation and predictions. Crosstabs include a variety of cell statistics, plus chi-square (with Yates correction), phi, Cramer's V and Pearson's coefficient. Graphic displays include histogram, sequence and scatter plots, with linear or log scaling. Data is entered through a spreadsheet-style window, or can be read directly from a standard DIF file. Data sets can be appended or overlayed. Daisy offers 21 math transforms, 4 time-series transforms, sorts, ranks and 6 types of random number generation. "Hide" commands allow analysis of subsets of the data. Missing values are fully supported. Daisy is accompanied by a 300 page indexed manual and tutorial, and an additional disk of examples.

PRODUCT REVIEWS

Brand, Stewart (Editor), Liswood, Woody (Reviewer). Whole Earth Software Catalog for 1986, pp. 74, (1986).

TYPE OF PROGRAM
Statistical Package

PROGRAM DESIGNED FOR
Data Analysis

PROGRAM STYLE
Command Driven
Integrated System

MISCELLANEOUS PROGRAM FEATURES
Source Code Available
Copyable Disk

DOCUMENTATION
User's Manual - 300 pages, 20 technical references
Table of Contents
Index
Tutorial or Example Lessons
Sample Runs
Formulas Provided
Tutorials and Examples on Disk

DATA MANAGEMENT
Keyboard Data Entry
Data Manipulations and Transformations
Missing Values Allowed in Data

DATA EDITING
Change
Add
Delete

FOREIGN DATA ACCESS
DIF Files

GRAPHICS FEATURES
Graphics Appear in Color on the Monitor
Graphics can be Output to a Printer
Graphics can be Saved to a File
Titles and/or Labels Available
Uses Pixel Graphics

GRAPHICS
Histograms
Scatter (x-y) Plots

PRODUCT SUPPORT
User may call at own Expense
No Classes or Instruction Available

STATISTICAL FEATURES SUPPORTED

DESCRIPTIVE STATISTICS
- Mean
- Standard Deviation or Variance
- Standard Error of the Mean
- Minimum, Maximum
- Median
- Skewness
- Kurtosis

t-TESTS
- One Sample t-Test
- Independent Group t-Test/Equal Variance
- Independent Group t-Test/Unequal Var
- Paired t-Test

CORRELATION AND REGRESSION
- Pearson Correlation Coefficient
- Simple Linear Regression
- Multiple Linear Regression
- Stepwise Multiple Linear Regression
- Residuals Calculated
- **REGRESSION PLOTS**
  - Residuals

CATEGORICAL DATA ANALYSIS
- Chi-Square Contingency Table Analysis
- Goodness-of-Fit Tests

ANALYSIS OF VARIANCE
- One-Way ANOVA
- Two-Way ANOVA

NONPARAMETRIC TESTS
- Sign Test (Signed Rank)
- Wilcoxon One Sample Test
- Mann-Whitney U
- Kruskal-Wallis Test
- Friedman Chi-Square Test
- Spearman or Kendall Correlation

TIME SERIES ANALYSIS
- Autocorrelations

MISCELLANEOUS
- Random Number Generation

DATA DESK

Data Description, Inc.
Box 4555
Ithaca, NY 14852
(607) 257 - 1000
Contact Person: Paul Velleman

CONFIGURATIONS SUPPORTED

Computer	Language	Operating System	RAM	Number Drives	Cost
MACINTOSH		DOS	512K	1	$175

NUMBER OF CURRENT USERS 1200
DATE OF FIRST RELEASE Sept 85
VERSION 1.0 RELEASED Sept 86

PROGRAM DESCRIPTION

The Data Desk is a full-function statistics package for the Macintosh family of computers designed to faciliate high-interaction data analysis. It is widely used for teaching (in a low-priced Student version) and research. The Data Desk provides a graphic desktop interface in which variables and the results of statistical analyses appear as icons in windows on the screen and are manipulated with a mouse pointing device. This provides an environment that encourages users to think about relationships among variables rather than about calculations on columns of numbers. The environment is easy for a novice to learn yet efficient and powerful for the experienced user. The package includes a 220-page tutorial handbook complete with examples and descriptions of when and why to use various statistics. Because of its unique user interface and design concept, the Data Desk does not fit comfortably into the standard descriptions of statistics software.

The Data Desk takes full advantage of the high quality of Macintosh graphics. All displays are interactive to help the user communicate with the program (as well as letting the program display data). With a click of the mouse, histograms can be rescaled, scatterplots can be focused on one region of the plot, and either kind of display can be reshaped. Three-dimensional rotating plots animate the movement of point clouds to let you see high-dimensional structure. Rotating plots are fully integrated with the rest of the program so that, for example, a subset selected in a rotating plot can define an I/0 dummy variable, which can then be used to restrict any other analysis to that subset. The Data Desk is also fully integrated with the Macintosh environment, providing transparant porting of data and graphics to and from other Macintosh applications.

TYPE OF PROGRAM
Statistical Package

PROGRAM DESIGNED FOR
Data Analysis
Educational use

PROGRAM STYLE
Integrated System

MISCELLANEOUS PROGRAM FEATURES
Copyable Disk

DOCUMENTATION
User's Manual - 220 pages, 15 technical references
- Table of Contents
- Index
- Tutorial or Example Lessons
- Sample Runs
- Formulas Provided

Tutorials and Examples on Disk

DATA MANAGEMENT
Keyboard Data Entry
Data Manipulations and Transformations
Missing Values Allowed in Data

DATA EDITING
Change
Add
Delete

FOREIGN DATA ACCESS
Standard Rectangular ASCII Files
Can Pass Variable Names
Most Macintosh Programs

GRAPHICS FEATURES
Graphics can be Output to a Printer
Graphics can be Saved to a File
Titles and/or Labels Available
Uses Pixel Graphics

GRAPHICS
- Histograms
- Scatter (x-y) Plots
- 3-D Plotting
- Box Plots
- 3-D Rotating Plots

PRODUCT SUPPORT
- User may call at own Expense
- No Classes or Instruction Available

STATISTICAL FEATURES SUPPORTED

DESCRIPTIVE STATISTICS
- Mean
- Standard Deviation or Variance
- Minimum, Maximum
- Median
- Percentiles
- Skewness
- Kurtosis
- Number of Numeric Values
- K% Difference
- Mid K%
- K-th Smallest
- K-th Largest
- Range
- Interquartile Range
- Count
- Midrange
- Biweight

t-TESTS
- One Sample t-Test
- Independent Group t-Test/Equal Variance
- Independent Group t-Test/Unequal Var
- Paired t-Test
- Bonferroni Adjustment for Multiple Tests

CORRELATION AND REGRESSION

- Pearson Correlation Coefficient
- Simple Linear Regression
- Multiple Linear Regression
- Non-Linear Regression
- Residuals Calculated
- Cook's Distance
- DFFits
- Externally Studentized Rediduals
- Interally Studentized Residuals
- Leverage
- Regression Through the Origin
- **REGRESSION PLOTS**
  - Residuals

CONFIDENCE INTERVALS

- Means
- Difference Between Two Means
- Variances
- Ratio of Variances
- Bonferroni Adjustment for Intervals

CATEGORICAL DATA ANALYSIS

- Chi-Square Contingency Table Analysis

ANALYSIS OF VARIANCE

- One-Way ANOVA
- Two-Way ANOVA
- Analysis of Covariance

MISCELLANEOUS

- Random Number Generation
- Snapshot Transformed Variable
- Set Selector Variable
- Split into Seperate Variables
- Append Variables
- Generate Patterned Data
- Sort/Unsort
- Ranking
- Data Transformations

DATAMYTE FAN II SOFTWARE

DataMyte Corporation
14960 Industrial Road
Minnetonka, MN 55345
(612) 935 - 7704
Contact Person: Technical Marketing Support Department

CONFIGURATIONS SUPPORTED

Computer	Language	Operating System	RAM	Number Drives	Cost
IBM PC	C	DOS 2.1	256K	2	$ 995

NUMBER OF CURRENT USERS 500
DATE OF FIRST RELEASE Jun 86
VERSION 1.5 RELEASED Oct 86

PROGRAM DESCRIPTION

The FAN II Software program is a statistical process control (SPC) data base that stores and analyzes SPC data collected by the DataMyte DataTruck, and DataMyte 750, 760, 860, 1500/1700 and 2000 series data collectors in the Factory Area Network (FAN). Analysis of the data transforms it into X-bar and R, X-bar and sigma, moving X-bar and R, moving X-bar and sigma, CuSum, histogram, capability and data reports. The program will print and display attribute charts for files coming from the DataMyte 2000 that contain attribute data. Data contained in charts may be selected by date or subgroup and the graphs may be viewed on a color/graphics system before printing. The charts and reports contain various statistics such as skewness, kurtosis, critical and calculated chi square values, CP, CR and CPK. Extensive editing and review capabilities allow data files to be saved, copied, deleted, edited and converted to formats for use by popular spreadsheet and data base programs.

The FAN II Software program is also used to set up the DataTruck and DataMyte data collectors with information used for data collection. Setup files are created and edited in the FAN II Software program and contain such information as the number of characteristics to be measured, engineering and control limits, and the number of samples per subgroup, and so on.

TYPE OF PROGRAM
Quality Control or Reliability

PROGRAM DESIGNED FOR
Data Analysis

PROGRAM STYLE
Menu Driven
Integrated System

MISCELLANEOUS PROGRAM FEATURES
Copyable Disk

DOCUMENTATION
User's Manual - 80 pages, ? technical references
Table of Contents
Tutorial or Example Lessons

DATA MANAGEMENT
Keyboard Data Entry
Missing Values Allowed in Data

DATA EDITING
Change
Add
Delete

GRAPHICS FEATURES
Graphics Appear in Color on the Monitor
Graphics can be Output to a Printer
Titles and/or Labels Available
Uses Pixel Graphics

GRAPHICS
Histograms
Scatter (x-y) Plots
SEE QC Plots

PRODUCT SUPPORT
User may call at own Expense
Classes or Instruction Available

STATISTICAL FEATURES SUPPORTED

DESCRIPTIVE STATISTICS

- Mean
- Standard Deviation or Variance
- Skewness
- Kurtosis

DISTRIBUTION FUNCTION EVALUATION

- Chi Square

CONTROL CHARTS

- X-Bar
- s

MISCELLANEOUS

- Test for Normality of Data

DATAMYTEtm ATTRIBUTE SOFTWARE

DataMyte Corporation
14960 Industrial Road
Minnetonka, MN 55345
(612) 985 - 7704
Contact Person: Chris Kruell

CONFIGURATIONS SUPPORTED

Computer	Language	Operating System	RAM	Number Drives	Cost
IBM PC	C	DOS	256K	2	$995

NUMBER OF CURRENT USERS 100
DATE OF FIRST RELEASE Aug 85
VERSION 3.2 RELEASED Oct 86

PROGRAM DESCRIPTION

The DataMyte Attribute Software program stores and analyzes attribute data collected by DataMyte 1000 series data collectors. The data is analyzed and turned into Pareto, p-, np-, c-, u-charts and summary reports. The charts contain the prompts and attributes selected for the chart. The summary report lists the attributes and counts for each prompt level. Graphs may be viewed on a color or graphics system before printing. Editing and review capabilities allow data files to be saved, copied, deleted, edited and converted to formats for use by popular spreadsheet and data base programs. The DataMyte Attribute Software program can set up the data collector with prompt loops for data collection and the program can also print bar code labels for bar code collection.

Computer configuration: IBM PC, PC/XT, PC-AT, or compatible, with 256K memory, at least two disk drives and RS-232 communications. Requires a dot-matrix printer for printing charts. Color or graphics card optional.

TYPE OF PROGRAM

Quality Control or Reliability

PROGRAM DESIGNED FOR

Data Analysis

PROGRAM STYLE
- Menu Driven
- Integrated System

MISCELLANEOUS PROGRAM FEATURES
- Copyable Disk

DOCUMENTATION
- User's Manual - 90 pages, ? technical references
  - Table of Contents
  - Index
  - Tutorial or Example Lessons
  - Sample Runs

DATA MANAGEMENT
- Keyboard Data Entry
- Missing Values Allowed in Data

DATA EDITING
- Change
- Add
- Delete

FOREIGN DATA ACCESS
- DIF Files

GRAPHICS FEATURES
- Graphics Appear in Color on the Monitor
- Graphics can be Output to a Printer
- Titles and/or Labels Available
- Uses Pixel Graphics

GRAPHICS
- Histograms
- Scatter (x-y) Plots
- Control Charts

PRODUCT SUPPORT
- User may call at own Expense
- Classes or Instruction Available

STATISTICAL FEATURES SUPPORTED

CONTROL CHARTS

Number of Defects
Number of Defectives
p-Chart
np-Chart
c-Chart
u-Chart
C/1000
C/100
Pareto

DATASTAT

ZiaSoft, Inc.
522 Kansas Avenue
Grand Junction, Co. 81503
(303) 241 - 0308
Contact Person: Dr. Robert K. Alexander

CONFIGURATIONS SUPPORTED

Computer	Language	Operating System	RAM	Number Drives	Cost
IBM PC	BASICA	DOS	64K	2	$275

NUMBER OF CURRENT USERS 10
DATE OF FIRST RELEASE May 85
VERSION 1.1 RELEASED May 85

PROGRAM DESCRIPTION

DataStat is a general statistics package combining some broadly used techniques and data file management in a convenient, modestly priced unit. It is designed to be used quickly without requiring memorization of (or repeated reference to) complex command structures. Its menu oriented design allows user interaction and facilitates exploratory research on a set of data.

DataStat is capable of handling both numeric and text data, and is quite useful for market research or other research utilizing nmemonically oriented coded data sets. Both numeric and non-numeric data files may be conveniently edited, automatically recoded or transformed, filtered, etc. by the extensive data base managers included in the package. Likewise, reports of raw or transformed data and statistics (including graphs) may be output to disk files for incorporation into word processed reports.

TYPE OF PROGRAM

Statistical Package

PROGRAM DESIGNED FOR

Data Analysis

PROGRAM STYLE
Menu Driven
Integrated System

MISCELLANEOUS PROGRAM FEATURES
Copyable Disk

DOCUMENTATION
User's Manual - 150 pages, 0 technical references
Table of Contents
Index
Tutorial or Example Lessons
Formulas Provided

DATA MANAGEMENT
Keyboard Data Entry
Data Manipulations and Transformations

DATA EDITING
Change
Add
Delete

FOREIGN DATA ACCESS
Standard Rectangular ASCII Files
DIF Files
dBase II Files
Writing a File Transform Algorithm

GRAPHICS FEATURES
Graphics can be Output to a Printer
Graphics can be Saved to a File
Titles and/or Labels Available
Uses Pixel Graphics
Uses Character Graphics

GRAPHICS
Histograms
Scatter (x-y) Plots
Rectilinear with Two Variables

PRODUCT SUPPORT
User may call at own Expense
No Classes or Instruction Available

STATISTICAL FEATURES SUPPORTED

DESCRIPTIVE STATISTICS

- Mean
- Standard Deviation or Variance
- Standard Error of the Mean
- Coefficient of Variation
- Minimum, Maximum
- Median
- Skewness
- Kurtosis
- Mode
- Range
- Sum X
- N-Size
- SE of CV, Skewness, Kurtosis

t-TESTS

- Independent Group t-Test/Equal Variance
- Independent Group t-Test/Unequal Var
- Paired t-Test

CORRELATION AND REGRESSION

- Pearson Correlation Coefficient
- Simple Linear Regression
- Multiple Linear Regression
- Non-Linear Regression
- Residuals Calculated
- Generation of Y Estimates for X(s)
- ANOVA
- **REGRESSION PLOTS**
  - Residuals

CATEGORICAL DATA ANALYSIS

- Chi-Square Contingency Table Analysis
- Cross-Tabulations from Coded Files

ANALYSIS OF VARIANCE

- One-Way ANOVA
- One-Way with Repeated Measures
- Two-Way ANOVA
- Two-Way Unequal Cell Sizes Allowed
- Nested One-Way

MISCELLANEOUS

Random Number Generation
Test for Normality of Data
Test for Equality of Variances
Coded Data Tallied

DCS MULTISTAT
Davell Custom Software
PO Box 4162
Cleveland, TN 37311
(615) 336 - 3055
Contact Person: David W. Cawlfield

CONFIGURATIONS SUPPORTED

Computer	Language	Operating System	RAM	Number Drives	Cost
IBM PC		DOS	192K	1	$ 290

NUMBER OF CURRENT USERS ?
DATE OF FIRST RELEASE Mar 83
VERSION 2.5 RELEASED Apr 85

PROGRAM DESCRIPTION

DCS Multistat is a statistical tool for non-statisticians; specifically engineers, managers, scientists, and investors. This program is interactively used to create models to analyze and optimize factory production, product demand, or spending budgets; experimental data, process variables, or complex data tables; and time dependent behavior of economic data, stock prices, and other investment vehicles.

DCS Multistat is a unique program for data analysis on an IBM PC. This tool combines database, spreadsheet, statistics, graphics, and report writing in a single tool. A friendly, interactive approach to multiple regression helps you to explore the meaning of your data. However, the powerful statistical tools and their use are thoroughly explained from the viewpoint of a non-statistician. The information you need to build a model is clearly displayed. All commands are single keystrokes that make sense, such as H-help screens or L-load new data set.

PRODUCT REVIEWS

Siegal, Jay. Econometric Reports, (1985).

TYPE OF PROGRAM

Statistical Package

PROGRAM DESIGNED FOR
Data Analysis

PROGRAM STYLE
Command Driven
Integrated System

MISCELLANEOUS PROGRAM FEATURES
Copyable Disk
On Screen Help Function

DOCUMENTATION
User's Manual - 116 pages, 7 technical references
Table of Contents
Index
Tutorial or Example Lessons
Sample Runs
Formulas Provided
Tutorials and Examples on Disk

DATA MANAGEMENT
Keyboard Data Entry
Data Manipulations and Transformations
Missing Values Allowed in Data

DATA EDITING
Change
Add
Delete

FOREIGN DATA ACCESS
Standard Rectangular ASCII Files

GRAPHICS FEATURES
Graphics Appear in Color on the Monitor
Graphics can be Output to a Printer
Graphics can be Saved to a File
Uses Pixel Graphics

GRAPHICS
Scatter (x-y) Plots
User Defined Functions

PRODUCT SUPPORT
User may call at own Expense
No Classes or Instruction Available

STATISTICAL FEATURES SUPPORTED

DESCRIPTIVE STATISTICS
- Mean
- Standard Deviation or Variance
- Standard Error of the Mean
- Coefficient of Variation
- Minimum, Maximum
- Percentiles
- Best Correlation Analysis

t-TESTS
- One Sample t-Test
- Independent Group t-Test/Unequal Var
- Paired t-Test

CORRELATION AND REGRESSION
- Pearson Correlation Coefficient
- Simple Linear Regression
- Multiple Linear Regression
- Stepwise Multiple Linear Regression
- Residuals Calculated
- Estimate Asymptotic Standard Errors
- Prediction
- Standard Error of the Estimate
- Correlation Matrices
- Standard Deviation of Coefficients
- Standard Deviation of Residuals
- Covariance Matrices

CONFIDENCE INTERVALS
- Means
- Difference Between Two Means

DISTRIBUTION FUNCTION EVALUATION
- Normal

TIME SERIES ANALYSIS
- Moving Average Smoothing
- **TIME SERIES ANALYSIS - FORECASTING**
  - Seasonal Decomposition
  - Leading/Lagging Indicators
  - Regression on Differences
- **TIME SERIES ANALYSIS - PLOTS**
  - Nth order Differences
- **TIME SERIES ANALYSIS - SPECTRAL ESTIMATE**
  - Regression to Fourier Series

MISCELLANEOUS

Select If
Data Sorting
Report Writing

DESCRIPTIVE STATISTICS

COMPress
P.O. Box 102
Wentworth, NH 03282
(603) 764 - 5831
Contact Person: John P. Spancake

CONFIGURATIONS SUPPORTED

Computer	Language	Operating System	RAM	Number Drives	Cost
APPLE	BASIC	DOS	48K	1	$ 70

NUMBER OF CURRENT USERS ?
DATE OF FIRST RELEASE 1981
CURRENT VERSION RELEASED ?

PROGRAM DESCRIPTION

Descriptive Statistics is designed to be a brief supplement to standard textbooks on elementary statistics and probability. The programs allow students to experiment with principles explained in the text.

Several methods of describing and summarizing raw data are illustrated. These can prepare students for understanding of probability and the methods of statistical inference. The BASIC programs are modifiable and some optional programming exercises are provided for interested students, but programming skills are not presumed or taught in the package.

TYPE OF PROGRAM
Statistical Package

PROGRAM DESIGNED FOR
Educational use

PROGRAM STYLE
Menu Driven
Integrated System

DOCUMENTATION

User's Manual - 58 pages, 0 technical references
- Table of Contents
- Index
- Tutorial or Example Lessons
- Sample Runs
- Formulas Provided

Tutorials and Examples on Disk

DATA MANAGEMENT

Keyboard Data Entry

DATA EDITING

Change
Add
Delete

PRODUCT SUPPORT

Free Phone Support Available
No Classes or Instruction Available

STATISTICAL FEATURES SUPPORTED

DESCRIPTIVE STATISTICS

Mean
Standard Deviation or Variance
Median

DESIGN-EASEtm
Stat-Ease, Inc.
4108 Aldrich Ave. So.
Minneapolis, MN 55409
(612) 822 - 5574
Contact Person: Pat Whitcomb

CONFIGURATIONS SUPPORTED

Computer	Language	Operating System	RAM	Number Drives	Cost
IBM PC		DOS	256K	1	$300

NUMBER OF CURRENT USERS 150
DATE OF FIRST RELEASE JUN 85
VERSION 1.10 RELEASED OCT 86

PROGRAM DESCRIPTION

DESIGN-EASE makes it possible for non-statisticians to design and analyze experiments. Designs are selected from easy to understand menus for two-level full factorial, fractional factorial and Plackett & Burman designs. The program produces data sheets with the actual levels of each variable for each experiment. Normal and half normal probability plots are used to analyze the responses. Residual analysis is done using normal probability, residuals versus predicted values, residuals versus run order and residuals versus single factor plots. If a transformation of the response data is required, many are available. Interaction plots are used to interpret two-factor interactions.

DESIGN-EASE is an incredibly easy to use, yet powerful, program for design and analysis of two-level factorial and fractional factorial designs. It has a full-screen editor for data entry and editing and very good use of graphics for data analysis. The documentation is good, though almost unnecessary, because of the excellent user interface. Included with DESIGN-EASE is a complete tutorial using data from the book Statistics for Experimenters by Box, Hunter, and Hunter.

TYPE OF PROGRAM

Design of Experiments

PROGRAM DESIGNED FOR
Data Analysis

PROGRAM STYLE
Menu Driven
Integrated System

MISCELLANEOUS PROGRAM FEATURES
Copyable Disk

DOCUMENTATION
User's Manual - 26 pages, ? technical references
Table of Contents
Tutorial or Example Lessons
Formulas Provided
Tutorials and Examples on Disk

DATA MANAGEMENT
Keyboard Data Entry
Data Manipulations and Transformations

DATA EDITING
Change
Add
Delete

FOREIGN DATA ACCESS
Standard Rectangular ASCII Files

GRAPHICS FEATURES
Graphics Appear in Color on the Monitor
Graphics can be Output to a Printer

PRODUCT SUPPORT
User may call at own Expense
Classes or Instruction Available

DISTRIB/ACCEPT

Center for Statistics, QC and Design
SUNY -Binghamton
Binghamton, NY 13901
(607) 777 - 2619
Contact Person: Ellen Tattenbaum

CONFIGURATIONS SUPPORTED

Computer	Language	Operating System	RAM	Number Drives	Cost
IBM PC	TURBO PASCAL	DOS	256K	1	$ 50

NUMBER OF CURRENT USERS 300
DATE OF FIRST RELEASE Jan 84
CURRENT VERSION RELEASED Aug 86

PROGRAM DESCRIPTION

DISTRIB/ACCEPT is a set of two menu-driven programs, designed primarily for the quality control practitioner. DISTRIB computes tables of the PDF and CDF for the binomial, hypergeometric, and Poisson distributions, as well as computing probabilities associated with the exponential and normal distributions. It performs plots of these five distributions. ACCEPT performs a variety of computations associated with single, double, and sequential sampling plans by attributes. In particular, it will design single-stage plans to any desired specifications, for any lot size. It will also compute and plot OC curves for specified plans.

These programs provide the user with the means to custom-design sampling plans, as well as to evaluate the characteristics of existing plans. Efficient algorithms are used to provide exact computations wherever possible, and approximations are identified wherever used.

TYPE OF PROGRAM

Statistical Package

PROGRAM DESIGNED FOR
Data Analysis

PROGRAM STYLE
Menu Driven
Integrated System

MISCELLANEOUS PROGRAM FEATURES
Copyable Disk

DOCUMENTATION
User's Manual - 0 pages, 0 technical references
Table of Contents
Index
Tutorial or Example Lessons
Sample Runs
Formulas Provided

GRAPHICS FEATURES
Graphics can be Output to a Printer
Uses Character Graphics

GRAPHICS
PDF
CDF
OC Curves

PRODUCT SUPPORT
User may call at own Expense
No Classes or Instruction Available

STATISTICAL FEATURES SUPPORTED

DISTRIBUTION FUNCTION EVALUATION
Normal
Binomial
Hypergeometric
Poisson
Exponential

CONTROL CHARTS
OTHER QUALITY CONTROL PROCEDURES
Acceptance Sampling by Attributes
Sequential Sampling Plans

DYNACOMP STATISTICAL PROGRAMS

DYNACOMP
P.O. Box 18129
Rochchester, NY 14618
(800) 828-6772
Contact Person: B. Rivers

CONFIGURATIONS SUPPORTED

Computer	Language	Operating System	RAM	Number Drives	Cost
See Paragraph					

NUMBER OF CURRENT USERS Thousands
DATE OF FIRST RELEASE ?
CURRENT VERSION RELEASED ?

ADDITIONAL SOFTWARE REQUIRED
Applesoft for Apple etc.
(Microsoft) Basic

PROGRAM DESCRIPTION

DYNACOMP offers a large selection of microcomputer programs covering a variety of topics. Among the DYNACOMP listings are over 20 statistics programs. Several general statistical packages are available along with special purpose programs for multivariate analysis, regression analysis, factor analysis, analysis of variance, quality control and forecasting.

DYNACOMP publishes a catalog listing the programs offered. A wide variety of computers are supported by DYNACOMP programs. The catalog listing indicates which computers are supported for a particular program.

TYPE OF PROGRAM
Several Different Programs

PROGRAM DESIGNED FOR
UNKNOWN

PROGRAM STYLE
Separate Programs for each Procedure

PRODUCT SUPPORT
No Classes or Instruction Available

ECONOMIST WORKSTATION
Data Resourses
24 Hartwell Avenue
Lexington, Mass 02173
(617) 863 - 5100
Contact Person: Nem Jain

CONFIGURATIONS SUPPORTED

Computer	Language	Operating System	RAM	Number Drives	Cost
IBM PC	FORTRAN	DOS	640K	2	

NUMBER OF CURRENT USERS 88
DATE OF FIRST RELEASE Apr 86
VERSION 2.0 RELEASED Sept 86

ADDITIONAL SOFTWARE REQUIRED
Nobler

PROGRAM DESCRIPTION
The ECONOMIST WORKSTATION is designed for analysts who want to focus their efforts on problem solving without having to learn a language, remember command syntax, or be a computer expert. The ECONOMIST WORKSTATION lets users store and manipulate data; perform econometric, statistical, or financial analysis; and display results in tabular or graphic form.

Applications include the following: Banking--Loan Analysis, cost analysis, and forecasting interest and foreign exchange rates. Marketing--sales and lead tracking, product-line forecasting, and promotional analysis. Manufacturing--Demand forecasting, inventory control, and order analysis. Government--Revenue forecasting and policy formulation. Utilities--Load forecasting and rate studies. Key features include: A command mode as well as a menu-and-form mode. Automatic downloading of data from Data Resources' mainframe computer offering access to the world's largest private collection of economic and financial information. Automatic downloading from in-house computers. Complete data base management capabilities. A full range of diagnostic and basic summary statistics as well as a complete library of mathematical functions including Census Bureau's X-11 Method. A wide range of analytic techniques including ordinary and two-stage least square; polynomial distributed lags; Almon lags; Hildreth-Lu and Cochrane-Orcutt autoregressive corrections. Sophisticated model-building and simulation capabilities such as normalization and renormalization of equations; transferring equations between models; simulating linear, nonlinear, simultaneous, recursive, dynamic, and static equations. Solution methods include Gauss-Seidel, Jacobi and Newton. Advanced report-writing capabilities. A full range of quality graphical display options.

TYPE OF PROGRAM
Regression Analysis

PROGRAM DESIGNED FOR
Data Analysis

PROGRAM STYLE
Menu Driven
Command Driven
Integrated System

MISCELLANEOUS PROGRAM FEATURES
Copyable Disk
On Screen Help Function
Optional Support for 8087 or 80287 Mathematical Chip

DOCUMENTATION
User's Manual - 100 pages, ? technical references
Table of Contents
Tutorial or Example Lessons
Sample Runs
Formulas Provided
Tutorials and Examples on Disk

DATA MANAGEMENT
Keyboard Data Entry
Data Manipulations and Transformations
Missing Values Allowed in Data

DATA EDITING
Change
Add
Delete

FOREIGN DATA ACCESS
Standard Rectangular ASCII Files
DIF Files
dBase II Files
WKS Files
PRN Files

GRAPHICS FEATURES
- Graphics Appear in Color on the Monitor
- Graphics can be Output to a Printer
- Graphics can be Saved to a File
- Titles and/or Labels Available
- Uses Pixel Graphics
- Uses Character Graphics

GRAPHICS
- Histograms
- Scatter (x-y) Plots
- Full Screen Editing of Plots
- Logarithmic
- Mixed Line & Bar Charts

PRODUCT SUPPORT
- Free Phone Support Available
- Classes or Instruction Available

STATISTICAL FEATURES SUPPORTED

DESCRIPTIVE STATISTICS
- Mean
- Standard Deviation or Variance
- Standard Error of the Mean
- Coefficient of Variation
- Minimum, Maximum
- Median
- Crowth Triangle

t-TESTS
- One Sample t-Test

CORRELATION AND REGRESSION
- Pearson Correlation Coefficient
- Simple Linear Regression
- Multiple Linear Regression
- Non-Linear Regression
- Residuals Calculated
- Seemingly Unrelated Squares
- Restricted Least Squares
- Weighted Least Squares
- 3-Stage Least Squares
- 2-Stage Least Squares
- Ridge Regression
- Polynomial Distributed Lags
- **REGRESSION PLOTS**
  - Residuals

CONFIDENCE INTERVALS
Means

ANALYSIS OF VARIANCE
One-Way ANOVA

TIME SERIES ANALYSIS
Moving Average Smoothing
TIME SERIES ANALYSIS - FORECASTING
Newton
Jacob
Gauss-Seidel
TIME SERIES ANALYSIS - PLOTS
Bar, Scatter, and Line Plots

MISCELLANEOUS
Random Number Generation

ELF - THE STATISTICAL PACKAGE
The Winchendon Group, Inc.
3907 Lakota Road
Alexandria, VA 22310
(703) 960 - 2587
Contact Person: Sheila Weiss

CONFIGURATIONS SUPPORTED

Computer	Language	Operating System	RAM	Number Drives	Cost
APPLE	BASIC	DOS	48K	1	$ 250
IBM PC	PASCAL	DOS	192K	2	$ 350

NUMBER OF CURRENT USERS 1500
DATE OF FIRST RELEASE 1980
CURRENT VERSION RELEASED 1984

PROGRAM DESCRIPTION

ELF is a general purpose statistical package designed for anyone who wishes to do statistical analysis. It is generally used by persons wishing to break away from mainframe usage.

ELF has the following capabilities:factor analysis; stepwise discriminant analysis; stepwise regression with residuals and forecasting; crosstabs; frequencies; histograms; scattergrams; means; standard deviations; correlation coefficients; 1 and 2 way ANOVA; report writer; t-test on means; interfaces with standard files and card-image files; full database entry, updating and correction facilities; and much more.

PRODUCT REVIEWS

Carpenter, James et al. "Statistical Software Available for Microcomputers", BYTE, pp. 234-264, (April 19, 1984).

Siegel, Jay. "Quantitative Software Reports", Econometric Report, (1984, 1985).

"ELF Arrives", Your Computer Magazine, pp. 36-37, (Feb 1982).

Stanton, Jeffrey (edited by). The Book of Apple Software, pp. 117-118.

TYPE OF PROGRAM
Statistical Package

PROGRAM DESIGNED FOR
Data Analysis

PROGRAM STYLE
Menu Driven
Integrated System

MISCELLANEOUS PROGRAM FEATURES
Optional Support for 8087 Mathematical Chip

DOCUMENTATION
User's Manual - 100 pages, 6 technical references
Table of Contents
Index
Tutorial or Example Lessons
Sample Runs
Formulas Provided
Tutorials and Examples on Disk

DATA MANAGEMENT
Data Manipulations and Transformations
Missing Values Allowed in Data

DATA EDITING
Change
Add
Delete

FOREIGN DATA ACCESS
Standard Rectangular ASCII Files
DIF Files
dBase II Files
1-2-3 PRN Format

GRAPHICS FEATURES
Graphics Appear in Color on the Monitor
Graphics can be Output to a Printer
Graphics can be Saved to a File
Uses Pixel Graphics

GRAPHICS
Histograms
Scatter (x-y) Plots

PRODUCT SUPPORT
User may call at own Expense
No Classes or Instruction Available

STATISTICAL FEATURES SUPPORTED

DESCRIPTIVE STATISTICS
Mean
Standard Deviation or Variance
Standard Error of the Mean
Minimum, Maximum
Skewness
Kurtosis
Range

t-TESTS
One Sample t-Test
Independent Group t-Test/Equal Variance
Independent Group t-Test/Unequal Var
Paired t-Test

CORRELATION AND REGRESSION
Pearson Correlation Coefficient
Simple Linear Regression
Multiple Linear Regression
Stepwise Multiple Linear Regression
Durbin-Watson

CATEGORICAL DATA ANALYSIS
Chi-Square Contingency Table Analysis
Multi-Dimensional Tables
Frequencies Can be Entered Directly

ANALYSIS OF VARIANCE
One-Way ANOVA
Two-Way ANOVA

DISTRIBUTION FUNCTION EVALUATION
Normal
t
Chi Square
F

MISCELLANEOUS

Test for Equality of Variances
Linear Discriminant Function Calculation

ENGINEERING TOOL KIT

Sof-ware Tools
P.O. Box 8751
Boise, Idaho 83707
(208) 343 - 1437
Contact Person: Joan Heitzeberg

CONFIGURATIONS SUPPORTED

Computer	Language	Operating System	RAM	Number Drives	Cost
MACINTOSH	BASIC	DOS	512K	1	$99
APPLE II	BASIC	DOS	48K	2	$59
IBM PC	BASIC	DOS	240K	2	$129

NUMBER OF CURRENT USERS 150
DATE OF FIRST RELEASE Mar 85
CURRENT VERSION RELEASED May 86

PROGRAM DESCRIPTION

ENGINEERING TOOL KIT is an extremely easy to use statistical and graphics package used for recording numeric engineering and scientific data, translating this data into meaningful graphics forms and generating statistical analysis reports. It has been on the market for over a year and is being used by many major scientific, educational and engineering institutions across the country and overseas.

ETK features: trend charts, scatter plots, histograms, polynomial regression analysis and graphs, multiple linear regression, one-way anova, random number generation, base conversion. Statistics include: standard deviation, mean, range, minimum-maximum values, kurtosis, skewness, standard error of the mean, correlation coefficient, regression equations, moments and others. Graphs and statistics can be viewed on screen, as well as in hardcopy format. ETK offers optional curve-fitting and statistics for each graph type, features not obtainable in other general graphics packages.

TYPE OF PROGRAM

Statistical Package

PROGRAM DESIGNED FOR
Data Analysis

PROGRAM STYLE
Menu Driven
Integrated System

DOCUMENTATION
User's Manual - 60 pages, ? technical references
Table of Contents
Index
Sample Runs

DATA MANAGEMENT
Keyboard Data Entry
Data Manipulations and Transformations
Missing Values Allowed in Data

DATA EDITING
Change
Add
Delete

FOREIGN DATA ACCESS
Standard Rectangular ASCII Files
DIF Files
Cutting and Pasting From Spreadsheets

GRAPHICS FEATURES
Graphics can be Output to a Printer
Titles and/or Labels Available
Uses Pixel Graphics

GRAPHICS
Histograms
Scatter (x-y) Plots

PRODUCT SUPPORT
User may call at own Expense
No Classes or Instruction Available

STATISTICAL FEATURES SUPPORTED

DESCRIPTIVE STATISTICS
- Mean
- Standard Deviation or Variance
- Standard Error of the Mean
- Coefficient of Variation
- Minimum, Maximum
- Skewness
- Kurtosis

CORRELATION AND REGRESSION
- Pearson Correlation Coefficient
- Simple Linear Regression
- Multiple Linear Regression
- Residuals Calculated

CONFIDENCE INTERVALS
- Means
- Variances
- Ratio of Variances

CATEGORICAL DATA ANALYSIS
- Chi-Square Contingency Table Analysis
- Frequencies Can be Entered Directly

ANALYSIS OF VARIANCE
- One-Way ANOVA

DISTRIBUTION FUNCTION EVALUATION
- Normal

MISCELLANEOUS
- Random Number Generation

EPILOG

Epicenter Software
PO BOX 90073
Pasadena, CA 91109
(818) 304 - 9487
Contact Person: Jonathan Buckley

CONFIGURATIONS SUPPORTED

Computer	Language	Operating System	RAM	Number Drives	Cost
IBM PC	FORTRAN	DOS	448K	2	$ 945

NUMBER OF CURRENT USERS 150
DATE OF FIRST RELEASE Oct 84
VERSION 3.0 RELEASED Aug 86

PROGRAM DESCRIPTION

EPILOG is an integrated statistical package for epidemiological and clinical trials applications. Procedures are available to carry out all the common epidemiological analyses, including simple descriptive statistics, calculation of rates either directly or indirectly standardized, relative risk estimation for matched or unmatched analyses. Survival analyses include curve estimation and plotting, logrank and other tests of homogeneity, relative survival, Cox regression, and multiple linear regression for censored data. Common to all procedures is a set of commands that control input/output, flag missing values, transform and recode the raw data and create new variables, label variables, tables and values, and select cases for analyses. Utility procedures are available to check, correct, full-screen edit, and sort the raw data set.

The unique feature of EPILOG is its orientation towards epidemiological applications. The procedures are integrated so that tables created at one step may be passed to a second procedure. Commands may be stored on disk, or entered interactively. Although only a monochrome screen is required, high-resolution printer plots may be requested.

TYPE OF PROGRAM
Epidemiology and Clinical Trials

PROGRAM DESIGNED FOR
Data Analysis

PROGRAM STYLE
Command Driven
Integrated System

MISCELLANEOUS PROGRAM FEATURES
Supports 8087 Mathematical Chip

DOCUMENTATION
User's Manual - 165 pages, 30 technical references
Table of Contents
Tutorial or Example Lessons
Sample Runs
Tutorials and Examples on Disk

DATA MANAGEMENT
Keyboard Data Entry
Data Manipulations and Transformations
Missing Values Allowed in Data

DATA EDITING
Change
Add
Delete

FOREIGN DATA ACCESS
Standard Rectangular ASCII Files

GRAPHICS FEATURES
Graphics can be Output to a Printer
Uses Pixel Graphics
Uses Character Graphics

GRAPHICS
Survival Curves

PRODUCT SUPPORT
User may call at own Expense
No Classes or Instruction Available

STATISTICAL FEATURES SUPPORTED

DESCRIPTIVE STATISTICS
- Mean
- Standard Deviation or Variance
- Standard Error of the Mean
- Minimum, Maximum
- Median
- Percentiles
- Skewness
- Kurtosis

t-TESTS
- Independent Group t-Test/Equal Variance
- Paired t-Test

CORRELATION AND REGRESSION
- Pearson Correlation Coefficient
- Simple Linear Regression
- Multiple Linear Regression
- Stepwise Multiple Linear Regression
- Logistic Regression
- Cox Regression
- Censored Linear Regression

CATEGORICAL DATA ANALYSIS
- Chi-Square Contingency Table Analysis
- Multi-Dimensional Tables
- Fisher's Exact Test
- Frequencies Can be Entered Directly

ANALYSIS OF VARIANCE
- One-Way ANOVA

NONPARAMETRIC TESTS
- Wilcoxon One Sample Test
- Mann-Whitney U
- Kruskal-Wallis Test

MISCELLANEOUS

- Life Table Analysis
- Random Number Generation
- p-Values Given With Tests
- Relative Risk Estimation
- Relative Survival Rate Estimation
- Cohort Analysis
- Rate Standardization
- Tests of Seasonality
- Space-Time Cluster Analysis

EPISTAT STATISTICAL PACKAGE VER 3.2

Epistat Services
2011 Cap Rock Circle
Richardson, TX 75080
(512) 255 - 3847
Contact Person: Tracy Gustafson

CONFIGURATIONS SUPPORTED

Computer	Language	Operating System	RAM	Number Drives	Cost
IBM PC	BASICA	DOS	96K	1	$ 25

NUMBER OF CURRENT USERS 10,000
DATE OF FIRST RELEASE Jun 83
VERSION 3.2 RELEASED July 85

PROGRAM DESCRIPTION

EPISTAT is a statistical package written in BASICA for the IBM-PC or other compatible microcomputers. It is designed to allow rapid analysis of smaller data sets (under 2000 data items). The package is ideal for the analysis of case-control studies performed for the medical or social sciences.

EPISTAT provides versatility and user-friendliness at an affordable price. All functions are accurate to at least 3 decimal places. Few if any statistical packages provide ALL of the functions in EPISTAT, and any one function is worth the purchase price.

PRODUCT REVIEWS

Toy, Larry G. "Statistics for the PC: EPISTAT: A Program with Medical App", Medical Times, pp. 75-76, (1984).

Lee, RS., Cohen, J. "Good with Stats: SYSTAT AND EPISTAT", PC Magazine, pp. 179-186, (March 5, 1985).

Editorial - Business Computing, pp. 15-16, (April 1984).

McKeough, W.J. "EPISTAT Review", Mathematics and Computer Education, pp. 135-137, (1986).

TYPE OF PROGRAM
Statistical Package

PROGRAM DESIGNED FOR
Data Analysis

PROGRAM STYLE
Menu Driven
Separate Programs for each Procedure

MISCELLANEOUS PROGRAM FEATURES
Source Code Available
Copyable Disk

DOCUMENTATION
User's Manual - 10 pages, 4 technical references
Table of Contents
Index
Tutorial or Example Lessons
Sample Runs
Formulas Provided
Tutorials and Examples on Disk

DATA MANAGEMENT
Keyboard Data Entry
Data Manipulations and Transformations
Missing Values Allowed in Data

DATA EDITING
Change
Add
Delete

FOREIGN DATA ACCESS
Standard Rectangular ASCII Files
dBase II Files

GRAPHICS FEATURES
Graphics Appear in Color on the Monitor
Graphics can be Output to a Printer
Titles and/or Labels Available
Uses Pixel Graphics

GRAPHICS
Histograms
Scatter (x-y) Plots

PRODUCT SUPPORT

User may call at own Expense
No Classes or Instruction Available

STATISTICAL FEATURES SUPPORTED

DESCRIPTIVE STATISTICS

Mean
Standard Deviation or Variance
Median

t-TESTS

Independent Group t-Test/Equal Variance
Paired t-Test

CORRELATION AND REGRESSION

Pearson Correlation Coefficient
Simple Linear Regression

CONFIDENCE INTERVALS

Means
Difference Between Two Means
Odds Ratios

CATEGORICAL DATA ANALYSIS

Chi-Square Contingency Table Analysis
Fisher's Exact Test
Goodness-of-Fit Tests
Mantel-Haenszel Chi-Square
McNemar's Test
MH Chi-square for Multiple Controls

ANALYSIS OF VARIANCE

One-Way ANOVA
Two-Way ANOVA

NONPARAMETRIC TESTS

Sign Test (Signed Rank)
Mann-Whitney U
Spearman or Kendall Correlation

DISTRIBUTION FUNCTION EVALUATION

Normal
t
Chi Square
F
Binomial
Poisson

MISCELLANEOUS

- Random Number Generation
- Test for Equality of Variances
- Sample Size Estimation
- p-Values Given With Tests
- Bayes' Theorem
- Crosstabs
- Select If
- Data Sorting

EXEC*U*STAT

Exec*U*Stat, Inc.
Research Park, 2 Wall Street
Princeton, NJ 08540
(609) 924 - 9357
Contact Person: Mr Robert Erickson

CONFIGURATIONS SUPPORTED

Computer	Language	Operating System	RAM	Number Drives	Cost
IBM PC	APL	DOS	320K	2	$ 495

NUMBER OF CURRENT USERS 1500
DATE OF FIRST RELEASE Nov 84
VERSION 1.4 RELEASED Aug 86

PROGRAM DESCRIPTION

EXEC*U*STAT is an integrated system of statistical and graphics procedures designed to enable today's executives to make use of modern statistical and data analysis techniques. EXEC*U*STAT includes routines for basic plotting, descriptive methods, estimation, forecasting, regression, financial calculations, and several advanced procedures. Also included is an executive desk containing a pull-down calculator, scratch pad, appointment calendar and other features. Re: data management, EXEC*U*STAT will now directly import 1-2-3 files (Versions 1 or 2), Symphony files, dBASE II or III files or Multiplan SYLK files.

PRODUCT REVIEWS

PC Magazine, pp. 218, (Aug 1986).

TYPE OF PROGRAM

Statistical Package

PROGRAM DESIGNED FOR

Data Analysis
Educational use

PROGRAM STYLE
- Menu Driven
- Integrated System

MISCELLANEOUS PROGRAM FEATURES
- On Screen Help Function
- Optional Support for 8087 Mathematical Chip

DOCUMENTATION
- User's Manual - 400 pages, 10 technical references
  - Table of Contents
  - Index
  - Tutorial or Example Lessons

DATA MANAGEMENT
- Keyboard Data Entry
- Data Manipulations and Transformations
- Missing Values Allowed in Data

DATA EDITING
- Change
- Add
- Delete

FOREIGN DATA ACCESS
- Standard Rectangular ASCII Files
- DIF Files
- Multiplan SYLK Files
- dBASE II or III
- Symphony
- Lotus 1-2-3

GRAPHICS FEATURES
- Graphics Appear in Color on the Monitor
- Graphics can be Output to a Printer
- Graphics can be Saved to a File
- Titles and/or Labels Available
- Uses Pixel Graphics

GRAPHICS
- Histograms
- Pie Charts
- Scatter (x-y) Plots
- Box Plots
- SEE Time Series Plots
- Bar Charts
- Line Graphs

PRODUCT SUPPORT
User may call at own Expense
Classes or Instruction Available

STATISTICAL FEATURES SUPPORTED

DESCRIPTIVE STATISTICS
Mean
Standard Deviation or Variance
Standard Error of the Mean
Coefficient of Variation
Minimum, Maximum
Median
Percentiles
Skewness
Kurtosis

t-TESTS
One Sample t-Test
Independent Group t-Test/Equal Variance
Independent Group t-Test/Unequal Var
Paired t-Test

CORRELATION AND REGRESSION
Pearson Correlation Coefficient
Simple Linear Regression
Multiple Linear Regression
Non-Linear Regression
Residuals Calculated
Estimate Asymptotic Standard Errors
Polynomial Regression

CONFIDENCE INTERVALS
Means
Difference Between Two Means
Variances
Ratio of Variances

CATEGORICAL DATA ANALYSIS
Chi-Square Contingency Table Analysis
Frequencies Can be Entered Directly

ANALYSIS OF VARIANCE
One-Way ANOVA
One-Way with Repeated Measures

NONPARAMETRIC TESTS
- Sign Test (Signed Rank)
- Wilcoxon One Sample Test
- Mann-Whitney U
- Kruskal-Wallis Test
- Friedman Chi-Square Test
- Spearman or Kendall Correlation

EXPLORATORY DATA ANALYSIS
- Box Plots
- Notched Box Plots

TIME SERIES ANALYSIS
- Moving Average Smoothing
- **TIME SERIES ANALYSIS - FORECASTING**
    - Exponential Smoothing
    - Trend
- **TIME SERIES ANALYSIS - PLOTS**
    - Seasonal Subseries

MISCELLANEOUS
- Random Number Generation
- p-Values Given With Tests

EXPERIMENTAL STAT BOOK AND 2 DISKS

Lionheart Press, Inc.
P. O. Box 379
Alburg, VT 05440
(514) 933 - 4918

CONFIGURATIONS SUPPORTED

Computer	Language	Operating System	RAM	Number Drives	Cost
MS-DOS	COMPILED	DOS	64K	1	
CP/M 5 1/4"	COMPILED	CP/M	64K	1	
APPLE	COMPILED	DOS	64K	1	

NUMBER OF CURRENT USERS 300+
DATE OF FIRST RELEASE ?
CURRENT VERSION RELEASED 1986

PROGRAM DESCRIPTION

A clear text which will allow you to develop a useful understanding of statistics. The mathematics is left to the computer programs so that you can concentrate on the understanding of the principles. Topics covered include uncertainties, sampling distributions, the applications of the normal distribution, hypothesis tests, significance levels and the calculations, Type II errors, the analysis of variance and the design of experiments, linear and multilinear regression, orthogonal polynomials, covariance, response surface experiments. Many practical examples are given. An extensive Glossary of statistical terms is provided. An easy to read book with practical user-friendly programs.

TYPE OF PROGRAM

Statistical Package

PROGRAM DESIGNED FOR

Data Analysis

PROGRAM STYLE
Command Driven
Separate Programs for each Procedure

DOCUMENTATION
User's Manual - 0 pages, 0 technical references
Table of Contents
Index
Tutorial or Example Lessons
Sample Runs
Formulas Provided
Tutorials and Examples on Disk

DATA MANAGEMENT
Keyboard Data Entry
Data Manipulations and Transformations

DATA EDITING
Change
Add
Delete

FOREIGN DATA ACCESS
Standard Rectangular ASCII Files

PRODUCT SUPPORT
User may call at own Expense
No Classes or Instruction Available

EXPERTIMENTAL DESIGN

Statistical Programs
9941 Rowlett, Suite 6
Houston, TX 77075
(713) 947 - 1551
Contact Person: Bonnie Deming

CONFIGURATIONS SUPPORTED

Computer	Language	Operating System	RAM	Number Drives	Cost
IBM PC	PASCAL	DOS	256K	1	$295

NUMBER OF CURRENT USERS ?
DATE OF FIRST RELEASE Oct 86
VERSION 2.1 RELEASED Oct 86

PROGRAM DESCRIPTION

EXPERtIMENTAL DESIGN tm is an expert system program that helps researchers determine the statistical requirements of their research projects, thereby guiding them toward the most appropriate of thirteen experimental design methods: Comparison of means, Calibration, factorial, paired comparisons, fractional factorial, Latin squares, saturated fractional factorial, Plackett-Burman, simplex mixture designs, central composite, fixed-size sequential simplex, Box-Behnken, variable-size sequential simplex. It is intended for the use of scientists, engineers and statisticians involved in R & D.

Through a series of questions posed to the user, EXPERtIMENTAL DESIGN tm ranks the possible designs in order of suitability. Because of inherent unknown in much research, the answers to questions placed by the program need not be "yes" or "no". EXPERtIMENTAL DESIGN tm has been programmed to deal with "fuzziness" in the user's answers by assigning desirabilities based on answers by the user. Thus, the final ranking by EXPERtIMENTAL DESIGN tm is unique to each researcher's different set of requirements.

TYPE OF PROGRAM

Expert System

PROGRAM DESIGNED FOR
Data Analysis
Educational use

PROGRAM STYLE
Menu Driven
Integrated System

MISCELLANEOUS PROGRAM FEATURES
Copyable Disk
On Screen Help Function

DOCUMENTATION
User's Manual - 230 pages, 20 technical references
Table of Contents
Tutorial or Example Lessons

DATA MANAGEMENT
Keyboard Data Entry

PRODUCT SUPPORT
User may call at own Expense
No Classes or Instruction Available

STATISTICAL FEATURES SUPPORTED

MISCELLANEOUS
Aids in Design Selection

EXPLORATORY DATA ANALYSIS

CONDUIT
Univ of Iowa - Oakdale Campus
Iowa City, IA 52242
(319) 353 - 5789
Contact Person: Jim Leaven

CONFIGURATIONS SUPPORTED

Computer	Language	Operating System	RAM	Number Drives	Cost
APPLE II	BASIC		48K	2	$ 165

NUMBER OF CURRENT USERS ?
DATE OF FIRST RELEASE 1981
CURRENT VERSION RELEASED 1981

PROGRAM DESCRIPTION

These programs accompany the author's book, Applications, Basics, and Computing of Exploratory Data Analysis. The programs analyze data according to EDA techniques and would be useful in any course in which EDA is taught. Methods included in the package are stem-and-leaf displays, letter-value displays, boxplots, x-y plots, resistant lines, data smoothing, coded table displays, median polish, and rootograms. The book presents selected basic techniques of exploratory data analysis, illustrates their application to real data and explains the accompanying program from this software package.

The student learning EDA soon becomes familiar with many pencil-and-paper techniques for data display and analysis. In addition, the computer programs permit students and teachers alike to concentrate on the results rather than the arithmetic, explore large amounts of data, eliminate tedious arithmetic and the errors that inevitably creep in, and combine exploratory methods with other data analytic techniques already programmed. Listings of FORTRAN programs are also given in the book.

PRODUCT REVIEWS

BYTE, (April 1984).

TYPE OF PROGRAM
Statistical Package

PROGRAM DESIGNED FOR
Data Analysis

PROGRAM STYLE
Command Driven
Integrated System

MISCELLANEOUS PROGRAM FEATURES
Source Code Available
Copyable Disk
On Screen Help Function

DOCUMENTATION
User's Manual - 0 pages, 0 technical references
Table of Contents
Index
Tutorial or Example Lessons
Sample Runs
Formulas Provided
Tutorials and Examples on Disk

DATA MANAGEMENT
Keyboard Data Entry
Data Manipulations and Transformations

DATA EDITING
Change
Add
Delete

GRAPHICS FEATURES
Uses Pixel Graphics

GRAPHICS
SEE EDA Plots

PRODUCT SUPPORT
Free Phone Support Available
No Classes or Instruction Available

STATISTICAL FEATURES SUPPORTED

EXPLORATORY DATA ANALYSIS

- Stem-and-Leaf Displays
- Letter-Value Displays
- Resistant Line
- Smoothing Techniques
- Median Polish
- Rootograms
- Box Plots
- Coded Tables
- Condensed x-y Plots

EXPLORING STATISTICS WITH THE IBM PC

Addison-Wesley Publishing Co. Inc.
Jacob Way
Reading, MA 01867
(617) 944 - 3700
Contact Person: Cindy Johnson

CONFIGURATIONS SUPPORTED

Computer	Language	Operating System	RAM	Number Drives	Cost
IBM PC	BASIC	DOS	64K	1	$ 40

NUMBER OF CURRENT USERS 7000
DATE OF FIRST RELEASE Jan 85
CURRENT VERSION RELEASED Mar 87

PROGRAM DESCRIPTION

Exploring Statistics is a set of 20 statistical programs and combination casebook and user's manual designed for the IBM PC microcomputer. While accessible to the beginning student of statistics, the programs are equally well-suited for analysis of small data sets in any setting.

The package contains a program diskette, with programs for analysis from boxplots to multiple regression, and a data diskette with two databases. The databases, one with interesting facts about fifty states and one with time series data, allow users to explore statistics even before they enter their own data for analysis

TYPE OF PROGRAM
Statistical Package

PROGRAM DESIGNED FOR
Educational use

PROGRAM STYLE
Menu Driven
Separate Programs for each Procedure

MISCELLANEOUS PROGRAM FEATURES
Source Code Available
On Screen Help Function

DOCUMENTATION
User's Manual - 320 pages, 12 technical references
Table of Contents
Index
Tutorial or Example Lessons
Sample Runs
Formulas Provided
Tutorials and Examples on Disk

DATA MANAGEMENT
Keyboard Data Entry
Data Manipulations and Transformations

DATA EDITING
Change
Add
Delete

FOREIGN DATA ACCESS
Standard Rectangular ASCII Files

GRAPHICS FEATURES
Graphics can be Output to a Printer

GRAPHICS
Histograms
Scatter (x-y) Plots
Box Plots
SEE Time Series Plots

PRODUCT SUPPORT
Free Phone Support Available
No Classes or Instruction Available

STATISTICAL FEATURES SUPPORTED

DESCRIPTIVE STATISTICS

- Mean
- Standard Deviation or Variance
- Standard Error of the Mean
- Coefficient of Variation
- Minimum, Maximum
- Median
- Skewness
- Kurtosis
- Outlier Detection

t-TESTS

- Independent Group t-Test/Equal Variance
- Independent Group t-Test/Unequal Var

CORRELATION AND REGRESSION

- Pearson Correlation Coefficient
- Simple Linear Regression
- Multiple Linear Regression
- Residuals Calculated
- Estimate Asymptotic Standard Errors

CATEGORICAL DATA ANALYSIS

- Chi-Square Contingency Table Analysis
- Goodness-of-Fit Tests
- Frequencies Can be Entered Directly

ANALYSIS OF VARIANCE

- One-Way ANOVA
- One-Way with Repeated Measures
- Two-Way ANOVA

DISTRIBUTION FUNCTION EVALUATION

- Normal
- t
- Chi Square
- F
- Binomial
- Poisson

EXPLORATORY DATA ANALYSIS

- Box Plots

TIME SERIES ANALYSIS

- **TIME SERIES ANALYSIS - FORECASTING**
  - Trend
- **TIME SERIES ANALYSIS - PLOTS**
  - Time Series

MISCELLANEOUS

Random Number Generation
Test for Normality of Data
Test for Equality of Variances

FILESTAT
COMPress
P. O. Box 102
Wentworth, NH 03282
(603) 764 - 5831
Contact Person: Ellen Young

CONFIGURATIONS SUPPORTED

Computer	Language	Operating System	RAM	Number Drives	Cost
APPLE II	BASIC	DOS	48K	1	$ 154

NUMBER OF CURRENT USERS ?
DATE OF FIRST RELEASE Sep 85
VERSION 1.0 RELEASED Sep 85

PROGRAM DESCRIPTION

FILESTAT is a 3-disk statistical package with each disk addressing a particular data type (interval/ratio, ordinal, or nominal). Data entry and management are accomplished through the use of the Data Management menu. Permanent data files are stored on a separate disk. In addition to standard tabular output, graphic display options include histogram, frequency polygon, scatterplot (with line-of-best-fit) and pie chart. Output may be directed to a viewscreen or a printer. A comprehensive user's manual provides illustrated step-by-step instructions for efficient use of this package.

FILESTAT's user friendliness makes this product particularly attractive. For example, most menu selections require only a single keypress, and auditory plus visual feedback immediately cue inappropriate menu selections. The menu architecture is designed to allow the user to move efficiently across entry, management, stat selection and output display modes without getting 'lost' along the way. The Data Management menu, for example, offers central guidance for managing a data set prior to submitting it to statistical analysis. Menu options include data add, delete, edit, find, reformat, print and disk store. The Stat Selector menu offers guidance as to appropriate statistical choices. Finally, a special help feature called System Aids offers continual visual symbols which inform the user how to end a current operation and return (or move to) an appropriate major FILESTAT menu.

TYPE OF PROGRAM
Statistical Package

PROGRAM DESIGNED FOR
Data Analysis

PROGRAM STYLE
Menu Driven
Integrated System

DOCUMENTATION
User's Manual - 160 pages, 0 technical references
Table of Contents
Index
Tutorial or Example Lessons
Sample Runs
Formulas Provided
Tutorials and Examples on Disk

DATA MANAGEMENT
Keyboard Data Entry
Data Manipulations and Transformations

DATA EDITING
Change
Add
Delete

FOREIGN DATA ACCESS
DIF Files

GRAPHICS FEATURES
Graphics can be Output to a Printer
Uses Pixel Graphics

GRAPHICS
Histograms
Pie Charts
Scatter (x-y) Plots
Frequency Polygon

PRODUCT SUPPORT
User may call at own Expense
No Classes or Instruction Available

STATISTICAL FEATURES SUPPORTED

DESCRIPTIVE STATISTICS

- Mean
- Standard Deviation or Variance
- Minimum, Maximum
- Median
- Percentiles
- Skewness
- Kurtosis
- Range
- Mode

t-TESTS

- Independent Group t-Test/Unequal Var
- Paired t-Test

CORRELATION AND REGRESSION

- Pearson Correlation Coefficient
- Simple Linear Regression
- Prediction

CATEGORICAL DATA ANALYSIS

- Chi-Square Contingency Table Analysis
- Goodness-of-Fit Tests
- Frequencies Can be Entered Directly
- McNemar's Test

ANALYSIS OF VARIANCE

- One-Way ANOVA
- One-Way with Repeated Measures

NONPARAMETRIC TESTS

- Kruskal-Wallis Test
- Friedman Chi-Square Test
- Spearman or Kendall Correlation
- Median Test
- Wilcoxon Matched Pairs Test

MISCELLANEOUS

- Z and T score Calculation
- Display of Ranked Scores

FORECAST MASTER
Scientific Systems Inc.
One Alewife Place
Cambridge, MA 02140
(617) 661 - 6364
Contact Person: Robert Goodrich

CONFIGURATIONS SUPPORTED

Computer	Language	Operating System	RAM	Number Drives	Cost
IBM PC	MICROSOFT C	DOS	512K	2	$795

NUMBER OF CURRENT USERS 500
DATE OF FIRST RELEASE July 85
VERSION 2.0 RELEASED June 86

PROGRAM DESCRIPTION

FORECAST MASTER is a statistical forecasting program offering seven major forecasting techniques: curve fitting, X11, exponential smoothing, Box-Jenkins, state space, Bayesian vector autoregression, and dynamic regression. It also includes time series graphics both to the screen and to a variety of output devices (plotters, laser printers, printers), as well as a DOS interface and data management utilities. The purpose of the package is to make sophisicated and powerful forecasting methodologies available to the non specialist, through the use of an intelligent, menu-driven user interface. FORECAST MASTER was written for the intelligent layman in business, government, utilities, financial institutions and telecommunications, as well as for academics and business schools. It is used by numerous institutions in all of these categories.

FORECAST MASTER is distinctive for its easy-to-use interface and for several methodologies not available elsewhere for microcomputers. These include state space, variable parameter regression, and autoregression conditional heteroscedastic regression models. It includes a context sensitive on-screen help facility to assist the user in using these complex methodologies.

PRODUCT REVIEWS

Bryan, Marvin. "Business Forecasting", PC Magazine, Vol 5, No. 14, pp. 211-234, (Aug 1986).

Sandberg-Diment, Erik. "Statistical Forecasting Made Simple, Almost", New York Times, (June 24, 1986).

TYPE OF PROGRAM
Time Series Analysis

PROGRAM DESIGNED FOR
Data Analysis

PROGRAM STYLE
Menu Driven
Integrated System

MISCELLANEOUS PROGRAM FEATURES
Copyable Disk
On Screen Help Function
Optional Support for 8087, 80287 Mathematical Chip

DOCUMENTATION
User's Manual - 120 pages, 30 technical references
Table of Contents
Index
Tutorial or Example Lessons
Sample Runs
Formulas Provided

DATA MANAGEMENT
Keyboard Data Entry
Data Manipulations and Transformations

FOREIGN DATA ACCESS
Standard Rectangular ASCII Files

GRAPHICS FEATURES
Graphics Appear in Color on the Monitor
Graphics can be Output to a Printer
Graphics can be Saved to a File
Uses Pixel Graphics
Uses Character Graphics

GRAPHICS
Histograms
Time Series Line Plots

PRODUCT SUPPORT
User may call at own Expense
Classes or Instruction Available

STATISTICAL FEATURES SUPPORTED

DESCRIPTIVE STATISTICS
- Mean
- Standard Deviation or Variance
- Standard Error of the Mean

t-TESTS
- One Sample t-Test

CORRELATION AND REGRESSION
- Simple Linear Regression
- Multiple Linear Regression
- Non-Linear Regression
- Residuals Calculated
- **REGRESSION PLOTS**
  - Residuals

DISTRIBUTION FUNCTION EVALUATION
- Normal
- t
- Chi Square
- F

TIME SERIES ANALYSIS
- Autocorrelations
- Cross Correlations
- AUTOREGRESSIVE MOVING AVERAGE
  - Model Identification
  - Parameter Estimation
- **TIME SERIES ANALYSIS - FORECASTING**
  - Exponential Smoothing
  - Dynamic Regression
  - Curvefitting
  - Vector AR
  - State Space
  - ARMA
  - X11
- **TIME SERIES ANALYSIS - PLOTS**
  - Correlation Functions
  - Original Data

FORECAST PLUS (TM)
Walonick Associates, Inc
6500 Nicollet, Avenue S
Minneapolis, MN 55423
(800) 328 - 4907
(612) 866 - 9022
Contact Person: David Walonick

CONFIGURATIONS SUPPORTED

Computer	Language	Operating System	RAM	Number Drives	Cost
IBM PC	COMPILED	DOS	192K	2	$ 595

NUMBER OF CURRENT USERS 1000+
DATE OF FIRST RELEASE Oct 84
VERSION 2.1 RELEASED Aug 86

PROGRAM DESCRIPTION

FORECAST PLUS is a comprehensive exploratory graphics and forecasting package with an easy to use data manager built in. By analyzing historical data to provide estimates of the future, Forecast Plus becomes a powerful management tool targeted for managers, economists, scientists, engineers, anyone involved in business planning. Forecast Plus uses sophisticated statistical techniques to predict future values of important variables, thereby reducing risk in decision making and eliminating some losses resulting from uncertainty with those decisions. Forecasting can be profitably utilized in all aspects of business: marketing/sales for reliable demand forecasts in finance for predictions to cash flow/interest rates in personnel for employee scheduling in production for inventory control, process control, scheduling...

FORECAST PLUS data management includes data files creation and editing, algebraic transformations, lags and differencing. Exploratory graphic features include time plots, 4253HT smoothing, autocorrelation function and others. Forecasting procedures include simple moving averages, single exponential smoothing, double exponential smoothing, Holt's 2 paramater smoothing, Harrison's harmonic smoothing, Brown's quadratic exponential smoothing, Winter's multiplicative and additive seasonal smoothing, robust decomposition, Census X-11 decomposition, regression trend analysis, multiple regression analysis, generalized adaptive filtering, and Box-Jenkins analysis.

PRODUCT REVIEWS

Computerized Investing, Vol. 4, No. 3, (May 1985).

PC Magazine, (Aug 1986).

The Journal of Business Forecasting, Vol. 4, No. 3, (Fall 1985).

Business Software Magazine, (May 1985).

TYPE OF PROGRAM

Statistical Package

PROGRAM DESIGNED FOR

Data Analysis

PROGRAM STYLE

Menu Driven
Integrated System

MISCELLANEOUS PROGRAM FEATURES

Copyable Disk
On Screen Help Function

DOCUMENTATION

User's Manual - 210 pages, 80 technical references
- Table of Contents
- Index
- Tutorial or Example Lessons
- Sample Runs
- Formulas Provided

Tutorials and Examples on Disk

DATA MANAGEMENT

Keyboard Data Entry
Data Manipulations and Transformations
Missing Values Allowed in Data

DATA EDITING

Change
Add
Delete

FOREIGN DATA ACCESS
- Standard Rectangular ASCII Files
- DIF Files
- dBase II Files
- StatPac or StatPac Gold Files

GRAPHICS FEATURES
- Graphics can be Output to a Printer
- Graphics can be Saved to a File
- Uses Pixel Graphics
- Uses Character Graphics
- Titles and/or Labels Available

GRAPHICS
- Scatter (x-y) Plots
- Box Plots
- SEE Time Series Plots
- SEE EDA Plots
- ACF Plots
- Spread vs Level Plots
- Decomposition Plots

PRODUCT SUPPORT
- User may call at own Expense
- No Classes or Instruction Available

STATISTICAL FEATURES SUPPORTED

CORRELATION AND REGRESSION
- Pearson Correlation Coefficient
- Simple Linear Regression
- Multiple Linear Regression
- Residuals Calculated
- Estimate Asymptotic Standard Errors
- Durbin-Watson

EXPLORATORY DATA ANALYSIS
- Smoothing Techniques
- Box Plots
- Aggregate Box Plots
- Time Plots
- Spread vs Level Plots
- ACF Plots

TIME SERIES ANALYSIS
- Autocorrelations
- Moving Average Smoothing
- AUTOREGRESSIVE MOVING AVERAGE
  - Model Identification
  - Parameter Estimation
- **TIME SERIES ANALYSIS - FORECASTING**
  - Exponential Smoothing
  - Harrison's Harmonics Smoothing
  - Adaptive Filtering
  - Robust SABL Decomposition
  - Census X-11 Decomposition
  - Winter's Seasonal Smoothing
  - Moving Average
  - Box-Jenkins
  - Regression
  - Holts two-parameter Smoothing
- **TIME SERIES ANALYSIS - PLOTS**
  - Autocorrelations
  - Original Data
  - Spread vs Level Plots
  - Box Plots
  - Decomposition Plots
  - Observed and Expected Error Plots
  - Smoothed Data Plots
  - Seasonal Component by Month Plots

FORECASTING AND TIME SERIES BOOK & DISK
Lionheart Press, Inc.
P. O. Box 379
Alburg, VT 05440
(514) 933 - 4918

CONFIGURATIONS SUPPORTED

Computer	Language	Operating System	RAM	Number Drives	Cost
MS-DOS	COMPILED	DOS	64K	1	
CP/M 5 1/4"	COMPILED	CP/M	64K	1	
APPLE	COMPILED	DOS	64K	1	

NUMBER OF CURRENT USERS 300
DATE OF FIRST RELEASE ?
CURRENT VERSION RELEASED 1986

PROGRAM DESCRIPTION

The statistical analysis of time-series is a subject which has been the turf of the experts until now. The expertise is on Lionhart disks and you can employ it at home or in your office without hiring a consultant. Topics covered include the nature of time-series, time-series analysis (correlation, autocorrelation and spectrum analysis by Fast Fourier Transforms), forecasting techniques (moving averages, exponential smoothing, regression model, and Box-Jenkins ARIMA-type models). A set of time-series and examples is provided so that you can test your knowledge and understanding of the programs. Examples of time series include stock and bond prices, utilities index, and multiple time-series. If you have heard of circadian rhythms or of periodicity you need this book.

TYPE OF PROGRAM

Statistical Package

PROGRAM DESIGNED FOR
Data Analysis

PROGRAM STYLE
Command Driven
Separate Programs for each Procedure

DOCUMENTATION
User's Manual - 0 pages, 0 technical references
Table of Contents
Index
Tutorial or Example Lessons
Sample Runs
Formulas Provided
Tutorials and Examples on Disk

DATA MANAGEMENT
Keyboard Data Entry
Data Manipulations and Transformations

DATA EDITING
Change
Add
Delete

FOREIGN DATA ACCESS
Standard Rectangular ASCII Files

PRODUCT SUPPORT
User may call at own Expense
No Classes or Instruction Available

FORECASTING EDGE
Human Edge
1875 S. Grant #480
San Mateo, CA 94402
(415) 573 - 1593

CONFIGURATIONS SUPPORTED

Computer	Language	Operating System	RAM	Number Drives	Cost
IBM PC		DOS	256K	2	$100

NUMBER OF CURRENT USERS 1000
DATE OF FIRST RELEASE Feb 86
VERSION 1.1 RELEASED ?

PROGRAM DESCRIPTION

The most sophisticated statisticians, analysts, educational institutions and research groups have adopted the Box-Jenkins method of forecasting. It has been found to be extremely accurate for modeling everything from industrial processes, business forecasts and inventory control, to environmental data.

Software that combines expert systems intelligence with this complex forecasting formula; Easy and Accurate; expert statistician on a disk; interfaces directly with Lotus 1-2-3 and most other popular spreadsheet and word processing programs.

PRODUCT REVIEWS

Wujcik, Erick. "Program Provides Edge on Forecasting", Detroit News, (May 15, 1986).

TYPE OF PROGRAM

Time Series Analysis

PROGRAM DESIGNED FOR

Data Analysis

PROGRAM STYLE

Menu Driven
Integrated System

MISCELLANEOUS PROGRAM FEATURES
- Copyable Disk
- On Screen Help Function
- Optional Support for 8087 Mathematical Chip

DOCUMENTATION
- User's Manual - 150 pages, 5 technical references
  - Table of Contents
  - Index
  - Tutorial or Example Lessons
  - Sample Runs
  - Formulas Provided
- Tutorials and Examples on Disk

DATA MANAGEMENT
- Keyboard Data Entry
- Data Manipulations and Transformations
- Missing Values Allowed in Data

DATA EDITING
- Change
- Add
- Delete

FOREIGN DATA ACCESS
- Standard Rectangular ASCII Files
- DIF Files
- dBase II Files

GRAPHICS FEATURES
- Graphics Appear in Color on the Monitor
- Graphics can be Output to a Printer
- Graphics can be Saved to a File
- Titles and/or Labels Available
- Uses Character Graphics

GRAPHICS
- Histograms
- Pie Charts
- Scatter (x-y) Plots
- Box Plots

PRODUCT SUPPORT
- Free Phone Support Available
- No Classes or Instruction Available

STATISTICAL FEATURES SUPPORTED

TIME SERIES ANALYSIS

TIME SERIES ANALYSIS - FORECASTING

Box-Jenkins

GAGETROL SOFTWARE

Paul Hertzler & Co., Inc.
P.O. Box 578
Gochen, IN 46526
(219) 533 - 0571
Contact Person: Evan J. Miller

CONFIGURATIONS SUPPORTED

Computer	Language	Operating System	RAM	Number Drives	Cost
IBM PC	PASCAL/ ASSEMBLY	DOS	640K	1	$495
HP 150 TOUCHSCRN.	PASCAL/ ASSEMBLY	DOS	640K	1	$495

NUMBER OF CURRENT USERS 28
DATE OF FIRST RELEASE July 85
VERSION 2.30 RELEASED July 86

PROGRAM DESCRIPTION

GageTrol software is a complete system for scheduling and controlling gage calibration and capability studies.

Features:
-control an unlimited number of gages;
-data entry via keyboard or digital gages;
-eight sort fields for gage identification;
-automatic date increment for schedulting tests or calibrations;
-reports of all gages past due for GR&R test or calibration, gages due for testing in a particular week, all gages that failed the last test, and many more;
-Gage Performance Curves.
-Standard (GM based) long and short-form analysis including repeatability, reproducibility, accuracy, linearity and stability. GageTrol also maintains gage calibration procedures, measurement records and pass/fail flags.

TYPE OF PROGRAM
Quality Control or Reliability

PROGRAM DESIGNED FOR
Data Analysis

PROGRAM STYLE
Menu Driven
Integrated System

DOCUMENTATION
User's Manual - 150 pages, ? technical references
Table of Contents
Formulas Provided

DATA MANAGEMENT
Keyboard Data Entry
Data Manipulations and Transformations
Missing Values Allowed in Data

DATA EDITING
Change
Add
Delete

FOREIGN DATA ACCESS
Digital Gages

GRAPHICS FEATURES
Graphics can be Output to a Printer
Titles and/or Labels Available
Uses Pixel Graphics

GRAPHICS
GP. Curve with Normal Curve Superimposed
Gage Performance Curve

PRODUCT SUPPORT
User may call at own Expense
Classes or Instruction Available

STATISTICAL FEATURES SUPPORTED

DESCRIPTIVE STATISTICS
- Mean
- Minimum, Maximum
- R-Bar
- Linearity
- Stability
- Accuracy
- GR&R
- Reproducibility
- Repeatability

RELIABILITY
- % Gage Rejection
- % Gage Acceptance
- In-Spec Data Rejected
- Out-Of-Spec Data Accepted
- In-Spec Data Affected by Gage Error
- Out-Of-Spec Data Affected by Gage Error

GAUSS
Aptech Systems, Inc
P.O. Box 6487
Kent, WA 98064
631 - 6679
Contact Person: Cheryl Jones

CONFIGURATIONS SUPPORTED

Computer	Language	Operating System	RAM	Number Drives	Cost
IBM PC		DOS	320K	2	$300

NUMBER OF CURRENT USERS 1500+
DATE OF FIRST RELEASE July 84
VERSION 1.49B RELEASED Sep 86

PROGRAM DESCRIPTION

The GAUSS Mathematical and Statistical System is an extremely high performance software package for IBM PC/XT/AT's and compatibles. It provides statistical, graphical, data base, and mathematical capabilities. It combines speed, power, flexibility, and ease of use. The system consists of the GAUSS Programming Language, plus a set of applications modules written in this language. GAUSS is used by: statisticians; data base managers; financial analysts; business managers; engineers; physical, biological, medical, and social scientists; actuaries; and others. GAUSS is used to do tasks that have previously been done by: conventional statistics packages (descriptive statistics, crosstabs, regression, non-parametric statistics, and so on); graphics packages (2 and 3D); spreadsheet programs; data base programs; and specialized FORTRAN programs (maximum likelihood estimation, general optimization, linear algebra, eigen analysis, signal processing).

GAUSS has by far the fastest computational speed, and the fastest I/O, of any program available for PC'S. It allows serious number crunching to be done on a desktop. It provides the convenience of "canned" statistical, graphics, data base, and mathematical programs, but also allows programs easily to be tailored to specific needs. For considerably less than the cost of many conventional off-the-shelf statistics programs, Aptech Systems can customize a package to a users' exact needs, or users can, if they want, modify the applications programs provided.

PRODUCT REVIEWS

Platt, Gerald W. "GAUSS", The American Statistician, VOL. 40, No. 2, pp. 167-169, (May 1986).

Bryan, Marvin. "Business Forecasting: 16 Ways to Predict the Future", PC MAGAZINE, Vol. 5, No. 14, pp. 211-234, (August 1986).

TYPE OF PROGRAM

Statistical Package

PROGRAM DESIGNED FOR

Data Analysis

PROGRAM STYLE

Command Driven
Integrated System

MISCELLANEOUS PROGRAM FEATURES

Source Code Available
Copyable Disk
On Screen Help Function
Supports 8087 Mathematical Chip

DOCUMENTATION

User's Manual - 550 pages, many technical references
- Table of Contents
- Index
- Tutorial or Example Lessons
- Sample Runs
- Formulas Provided

Quick Reference Card
Tutorials and Examples on Disk

DATA MANAGEMENT

Keyboard Data Entry
Data Manipulations and Transformations
Missing Values Allowed in Data

DATA EDITING

Change
Add
Delete

FOREIGN DATA ACCESS

Standard Rectangular ASCII Files
DIF Files
dBase II Files
STATA
SYSTAT
SPSS
Lotus
dBASE II and III Files

GRAPHICS FEATURES

Graphics Appear in Color on the Monitor
Graphics can be Output to a Printer
Graphics can be Saved to a File
Titles and/or Labels Available
Uses Pixel Graphics
Uses Character Graphics

GRAPHICS

Histograms
Pie Charts
Scatter (x-y) Plots
3-D Plotting
Box Plots
Likelihood Surfaces
Graphs of Functions

PRODUCT SUPPORT

User may call at own Expense
No Classes or Instruction Available

STATISTICAL FEATURES SUPPORTED

DESCRIPTIVE STATISTICS

Mean
Standard Deviation or Variance
Standard Error of the Mean
Coefficient of Variation
Minimum, Maximum
Median
Percentiles
Skewness
Kurtosis

t-TESTS

One Sample t-Test
Independent Group t-Test/Equal Variance
Independent Group t-Test/Unequal Var
Paired t-Test

CORRELATION AND REGRESSION

- Pearson Correlation Coefficient
- Simple Linear Regression
- Multiple Linear Regression
- Non-Linear Regression
- Residuals Calculated
- 2 and 3 Stage Least Squares
- **REGRESSION PLOTS**
  - Residuals

CONFIDENCE INTERVALS

- Means
- Difference Between Two Means
- Proportions
- Difference Between Two Proportions
- Variances
- Ratio of Variances

CATEGORICAL DATA ANALYSIS

- Chi-Square Contingency Table Analysis
- Multi-Dimensional Tables
- Fisher's Exact Test
- Goodness-of-Fit Tests
- Frequencies Can be Entered Directly

ANALYSIS OF VARIANCE

- One-Way ANOVA
- One-Way with Repeated Measures
- Analysis of Covariance

NONPARAMETRIC TESTS

- Get Rank-Ties for any Data Set
- Bootstrap any Statistical Algorithm

DISTRIBUTION FUNCTION EVALUATION

- Normal
- t
- Chi Square
- F
- Binomial
- Hypergeometric
- Poisson
- Gamma
- Beta
- Non-Central F
- Non-Central t

TIME SERIES ANALYSIS

- Autocorrelations
- Cross Correlations
- Moving Average Smoothing
- AUTOREGRESSIVE MOVING AVERAGE
  - Model Identification
  - Parameter Estimation
- **TIME SERIES ANALYSIS - FORECASTING**
  - Several Methods
- **TIME SERIES ANALYSIS - SPECTRAL ESTIMATE**
  - FFT

MISCELLANEOUS

- Random Number Generation
- p-Values Given With Tests
- Eigen Analysis
- General Covariance-Structure Models
- Multinomial Logit
- Multinomial Probit
- Log-Linear Models
- Ordinal Logit
- Ordinal Probit
- Logit (Logistic Regression)
- Probit
- General Non-Linear Least Squares
- General Maximum Likelihood

GAUSSIAN PROBABILITY PLOTTING

Team
Box 25
Tamworth, NH 03886
(603) 323 - 8843
Contact Person: JR King

CONFIGURATIONS SUPPORTED

Computer	Language	Operating System	RAM	Number Drives	Cost
OSBORNE I	MBASIC	CP/M	64K	2	$ 240
APPLE	APPLESOFT	DOS	64K	2	$ 240
IBM PC	MBASIC	DOS	64K	2	$ 240

NUMBER OF CURRENT USERS 12
DATE OF FIRST RELEASE Dec 83
CURRENT VERSION RELEASED Aug 84

ADDITIONAL SOFTWARE REQUIRED
MICROSOFT BASIC

PROGRAM DESCRIPTION

This is a dedicated software package for converting raw data sets into normal probability plots for performing calculations to obtain plotting positions and a linear regression line for validating data and, after validation, for estimating conventional statistical parameters and confidence limits for both the data set and the regression line. It is for statistical data analysts and is used for exploratory and confirmatory analysis in process control and product assurance studies.

This program validates data by testing for randomness and normality before obtaining conventional parameter estimates and is the only probability plotting program which generates confidence limits for the entire plot.

TYPE OF PROGRAM
Statistical Package

PROGRAM DESIGNED FOR
Data Analysis

PROGRAM STYLE
Menu Driven
Integrated System

MISCELLANEOUS PROGRAM FEATURES
Copyable Disk
On Screen Help Function

DOCUMENTATION
User's Manual - 6 pages, 52 technical references
Table of Contents
Index
Tutorial or Example Lessons
Sample Runs
Formulas Provided
Tutorials and Examples on Disk

DATA MANAGEMENT
Keyboard Data Entry

DATA EDITING
Change
Add
Delete

FOREIGN DATA ACCESS
Standard Rectangular ASCII Files
dBase II Files

GRAPHICS FEATURES
Graphics can be Output to a Printer

GRAPHICS
Probability Plots

PRODUCT SUPPORT
Free Phone Support Available
No Classes or Instruction Available

STATISTICAL FEATURES SUPPORTED

DESCRIPTIVE STATISTICS
- Mean
- Standard Deviation or Variance
- Minimum, Maximum
- Median
- Percentiles

CORRELATION AND REGRESSION
- Simple Linear Regression
- Residuals Calculated
- Estimate Asymptotic Standard Errors

CONFIDENCE INTERVALS
- Regression Line

DISTRIBUTION FUNCTION EVALUATION
- Normal
- Log Normal

MISCELLANEOUS
- Test for Normality of Data
- Test for Randomness
- Test for Homogeneity

GPSS/PC

MINUTEMAN Software
P.O.Box 171
Stow, MA 01775
(617) 897 - 5662
Contact Person: Alice Cox

CONFIGURATIONS SUPPORTED

Computer	Language	Operating System	RAM	Number Drives	Cost
IBM PC	GPSS	DOS	320K	1	$995

NUMBER OF CURRENT USERS 500+
DATE OF FIRST RELEASE July 84
VERSION 2.0 RELEASED July 86

PROGRAM DESCRIPTION

GPSS/PC is a full powered version of GPSS, the General Purpose Simulation System, the most popular discrete event mainframe simulation language which now includes graphics and animation capabilities. More than just a language, GPSS/PC is a simulation environment specifically designed for today's high speed microprocessors. If the user is responsible for a business, warehousing, manufacturing, distribution or traffic system, a computer network, LAN or any complex discrete system he/she will need to be able to predict results of decisions. GPSS/PC was designed to deliver predictions.

Highlights: (3-10 items of less than 15 words each) * Interactive- Named values, and even the block structure of models, may be changed on the fly. Block statements may be used as keyboard commands. * Integrated - GPSS/PC is a simulation environment making all edit, compile, link run, debug functions available in a single phase. Errors can be corrected immediately without requiring recompilation.* Powerful - GPSS/PC implements over 70 GPSS blocks and commends and 50 System Numerical Attributes. * Advanced - GPSS/PC features unlimited precision integers (superior to even double precision floating point format), random number generators, and a sophisticated math library. * Easy - GPSS/PC presents the user with a variety of usability features including syntax error prevention, online help, command recognition, cursor prompting, and automatic spacing.

PRODUCT REVIEWS
Karian, Zaven. BYTE, pp. 265.

TYPE OF PROGRAM
Simulation Programming Language

PROGRAM DESIGNED FOR
Data Analysis

PROGRAM STYLE
Command Driven
Integrated System

MISCELLANEOUS PROGRAM FEATURES
Copyable Disk
On Screen Help Function
Supports 8087, 80287 Mathematical Chip

DOCUMENTATION
User's Manual - 500 pages, 6 technical references
- Table of Contents
- Index
- Tutorial or Example Lessons

Quick Reference Card
Tutorials and Examples on Disk
Tutorial Manual

DATA MANAGEMENT
Keyboard Data Entry
Data Manipulations and Transformations
Missing Values Allowed in Data

DATA EDITING
Change
Add
Delete

FOREIGN DATA ACCESS
DIF Files
ASCII

GRAPHICS FEATURES
Graphics Appear in Color on the Monitor
Graphics can be Output to a Printer
Uses Character Graphics

GRAPHICS
- Histograms
- Symbolic Block Diagram
- Animation

PRODUCT SUPPORT
- Free Phone Support Available
- User may call at own Expense
- No Classes or Instruction Available

STATISTICAL FEATURES SUPPORTED

DESCRIPTIVE STATISTICS
- Mean
- Standard Deviation or Variance
- Minimum, Maximum
- Percentiles

CONFIDENCE INTERVALS
- Means

MISCELLANEOUS
- Animation Plus Five Graphics Windows

HP STATISTICS LIBRARY/200/300

Hewlett Packard
3404 E Harmony Road
Fort Collins, CO 80525
(303) 226 - 3800
Contact Person: Dan Sherwood

CONFIGURATIONS SUPPORTED

Computer	Language	Operating System	RAM	Number Drives	Cost
HP 9000/ 200, 300	BASIC	BASIC	260K	1	$1500

NUMBER OF CURRENT USERS 2500+
DATE OF FIRST RELEASE ?
CURRENT VERSION RELEASED Jul 86

PROGRAM DESCRIPTION

The HP Statistical Library/200/300 consists of ten professionally prepared programs servicing a wide spectrum of users ranging from managers to scientists, engineers, and researchers. The integrated routines allow for broad data manipulation capabilities. The data may be subjected to comprehensive basic statistics routines through advanced statistical techniques such as analysis of variance, regression analysis, and principal component and factor analysis. Created in conjuction with a major university, the programs are easy to use, with CRT prompts guiding the user through the programs. In order to satisfy the individual user's needs, the Stat Pack may be purchased as a whole or in two separate parts.

The HP Statistical Library/200/300 supports an impressive 32,000 data elements which may be saved on mass storage indefinitely and never have to be reentered. To assist the user even further, the original ten discs of the HP Statistical Library/200/300 may be copied onto a single hard disk. The HP Statistical Library/200/300 generates presentation quality charts and graphs in minutes to the specification of the user. The HP Statistical Library's ability to plot-to-file may be used with the HP TechWriter (document editor) to combine text and graphics for sophisticated report generation. The HP Statistical Library has existed for over a decade and been improved through the years by the inclusion of user requested enhancements.

TYPE OF PROGRAM
Statistical Package

PROGRAM DESIGNED FOR
Data Analysis

PROGRAM STYLE
Menu Driven
Integrated System

MISCELLANEOUS PROGRAM FEATURES
Source Code Available
Copyable Disk

DOCUMENTATION
User's Manual - 425 pages, 119 technical references
Table of Contents
Index
Tutorial or Example Lessons
Sample Runs
Formulas Provided
Tutorials and Examples on Disk

DATA MANAGEMENT
Keyboard Data Entry
Data Manipulations and Transformations
Missing Values Allowed in Data

DATA EDITING
Change
Add
Delete

FOREIGN DATA ACCESS
Standard Rectangular ASCII Files
HP9111A Graphics Tablet
User Supplied Data Program

GRAPHICS FEATURES
Graphics Appear in Color on the Monitor
Graphics can be Output to a Printer
Graphics can be Saved to a File
Titles and/or Labels Available
Uses Pixel Graphics

GRAPHICS

- Histograms
- Scatter (x-y) Plots
- 3-D Plotting
- Probability Plots
- Andrew's Fourier Plots
- SEE Time Series Plots
- ANOVA Interaction Plots
- Semi-log Plots
- Log-log Plots

PRODUCT SUPPORT

- Free Phone Support Available
- No Classes or Instruction Available

STATISTICAL FEATURES SUPPORTED

DESCRIPTIVE STATISTICS

- Mean
- Standard Deviation or Variance
- Standard Error of the Mean
- Coefficient of Variation
- Minimum, Maximum
- Median
- Percentiles
- Skewness
- Kurtosis
- Midrange
- Tukey's Middle Means

t-TESTS

- One Sample t-Test
- Independent Group t-Test/Equal Variance
- Independent Group t-Test/Unequal Var
- Paired t-Test

CORRELATION AND REGRESSION

- Pearson Correlation Coefficient
- Simple Linear Regression
- Multiple Linear Regression
- Stepwise Multiple Linear Regression
- Non-Linear Regression
- Residuals Calculated
- Estimate Asymptotic Standard Errors
- Test for Innocuous Components
- Logarithmic Regression
- Residual Sum of Squares
- Polynomial Regression
- Correlation Matrix

CONFIDENCE INTERVALS
- Means
- Regression Coefficients

CATEGORICAL DATA ANALYSIS
- Chi-Square Contingency Table Analysis
- Goodness-of-Fit Tests

ANALYSIS OF VARIANCE
- One-Way ANOVA
- Two-Way ANOVA
- Two-Way Unequal Cell Sizes Allowed
- Analysis of Covariance
- Nested Factors
- Split Plot
- Multiway Factorials
- **MULTIPLE COMPARISONS**
  - Fisher's LSD
  - Duncan's Multiple Range
  - Scheffe
  - Newman-Keuls
  - Tukey
  - Orthogonal Polynomials
  - Treatment Contrasts

NONPARAMETRIC TESTS
- Sign Test (Signed Rank)
- Mann-Whitney U
- Kruskal-Wallis Test
- Spearman or Kendall Correlation
- Runs Tests
- Kolmogorov-Smirnov Test
- Median Test
- Taha Squared Rank Test
- Wilcoxon Signed Rank Test

DISTRIBUTION FUNCTION EVALUATION
- Normal
- t
- Chi Square
- F
- Binomial
- Hypergeometric
- Poisson
- Beta
- Negative Binomial
- Gamma
- LaPlace
- Logistic
- Weibull

TIME SERIES ANALYSIS

- Autocorrelations
- Cross Correlations
- **TIME SERIES ANALYSIS - PLOTS**
  - Time Series

MISCELLANEOUS

- Random Number Generation
- Test for Normality of Data
- p-Values Given With Tests
- Factor Analysis
- Principal Components Analysis
- Random Deviate Generators (22 distrib.)
- Tests for Randomness (7 kinds)
- Random Sampling Without Replacement
- Shuffling

HSD STATS
Human Systems Dynamics
9010 Reseda Blvd, Suite 222
Northridge, CA 91324
(818) 993 - 8536
Contact Person: Merideth Wiberg

CONFIGURATIONS SUPPORTED

Computer	Language	Operating System	RAM	Number Drives	Cost
APPLE II	BASIC	DOS	48K	1	$ 50

NUMBER OF CURRENT USERS 700
DATE OF FIRST RELEASE Aug 81
VERSION 1 RELEASED Aug 81

PROGRAM DESCRIPTION

HSD STATS is designed for quick analysis of small data sets. Students can sit down with HSD STATS for the first time and finish their statistics homework in minutes. With HSD STATS, you can enter up to 8 samples of 250 cases each from the keyboard or disk. After entering the samples, the user can choose an analysis option from the program menu. HSD STATS then runs the analysis on specified samples.

HSD STATS is menu driven. There is no need to learn any commands. Enter data by keyboard, edit and save to disk. Get a printer copy of all numeric results, disk copies of data files, and hi-resolution screen graphs of scatterplots and bar graphs.

TYPE OF PROGRAM

Statistical Package

PROGRAM DESIGNED FOR

Data Analysis
Educational use

PROGRAM STYLE

Menu Driven
Integrated System

DOCUMENTATION
User's Manual - 48 pages, 0 technical references
Index
Sample Runs

DATA MANAGEMENT
Keyboard Data Entry
Data Manipulations and Transformations

DATA EDITING
Change
Add
Delete

GRAPHICS FEATURES
Graphics can be Saved to a File
Titles and/or Labels Available
Uses Pixel Graphics

GRAPHICS
Histograms
Scatter (x-y) Plots

PRODUCT SUPPORT
Free Phone Support Available
No Classes or Instruction Available

STATISTICAL FEATURES SUPPORTED

DESCRIPTIVE STATISTICS
Mean
Standard Deviation or Variance

t-TESTS
One Sample t-Test
Independent Group t-Test/Equal Variance
Independent Group t-Test/Unequal Var
Paired t-Test

CORRELATION AND REGRESSION
Pearson Correlation Coefficient
Correlation Matrices

CATEGORICAL DATA ANALYSIS
Chi-Square Contingency Table Analysis

MISCELLANEOUS
Frequency Distribution

INSTAT

Statistical Consulting Services
517 East Lodge Dr.
Tempe, AZ 85283
(602) 838 - 7784
Contact Person: Mikel Aickin

CONFIGURATIONS SUPPORTED

Computer	Language	Operating System	RAM	Number Drives	Cost
IBM PC	none	DOS	64K	2	$ 30
TANDY 2000	none	DOS	64K	2	$ 30

NUMBER OF CURRENT USERS ?
DATE OF FIRST RELEASE Spr 83
CURRENT VERSION RELEASED Spr 83

PROGRAM DESCRIPTION

INSTAT provides some of the most frequently used statistical computations and displays. It is designed for the novice, but experienced statisticians will find it useful for screening data.

All variables are referenced by name in a very simple command structure. The unique DESCRIBE command only requires the user to provide the names of the variables to be displayed or related to each other: the program chooses the most appropriate form of display and the relevant computations. Repeated analyses are easily requested for subgroups of data by specifying control variables. Length of data files is limited only by online disk storage. Output can be viewed on screen, stored in a file or sent to any printer.

PRODUCT REVIEWS

Wang, Deane. "Statistics with the IBM Personal Computer", Science Software Quarterly, pp. 37-41, (Spring 1984).

TYPE OF PROGRAM

Statistical Package

PROGRAM DESIGNED FOR
Data Analysis

PROGRAM STYLE
Command Driven
Integrated System

MISCELLANEOUS PROGRAM FEATURES
Copyable Disk
On Screen Help Function

DOCUMENTATION
User's Manual - 92 pages, 0 technical references
Table of Contents
Index
Tutorial or Example Lessons
Sample Runs
Formulas Provided
Tutorials and Examples on Disk

DATA MANAGEMENT
Keyboard Data Entry
Missing Values Allowed in Data

FOREIGN DATA ACCESS
Standard Rectangular ASCII Files

GRAPHICS FEATURES
Graphics can be Output to a Printer
Graphics can be Saved to a File
Titles and/or Labels Available

GRAPHICS
Histograms
Scatter (x-y) Plots

PRODUCT SUPPORT
User may call at own Expense
No Classes or Instruction Available

STATISTICAL FEATURES SUPPORTED

DESCRIPTIVE STATISTICS
- Mean
- Standard Deviation or Variance
- Minimum, Maximum

t-TESTS
- One Sample t-Test
- Independent Group t-Test/Equal Variance
- Paired t-Test

CORRELATION AND REGRESSION
- Simple Linear Regression

CONFIDENCE INTERVALS
- Means
- Proportions
- Difference Between Two Proportions

CATEGORICAL DATA ANALYSIS
- Chi-Square Contingency Table Analysis
- Frequencies Can be Entered Directly

DISTRIBUTION FUNCTION EVALUATION
- t
- Chi Square

MISCELLANEOUS
- p-Values Given With Tests

INSTAT-D:Discrete Data Analysis

Statistical Consulting Services
517 East Lodge Dr.
Tempe, AZ 85283
(602) 838 - 7784
Contact Person: Mikel Aickin

CONFIGURATIONS SUPPORTED

Computer	Language	Operating System	RAM	Number Drives	Cost
IBM PC	none	DOS	128K	1	$ 150
TANDY 2000	none	DOS	128K	1	$ 150

NUMBER OF CURRENT USERS ?
DATE OF FIRST RELEASE 1983
CURRENT VERSION RELEASED 1983

PROGRAM DESCRIPTION

INSTAT-D is a program for fitting linear and log-linear models to contingency table data. It will be of most use to professional statisticians.

The methodology on which INSTAT-D is based is described in its theoretical and applied aspects in Linear Statistical Analysis of Discrete Data by Mikel Aickin (Wiley 1983). The program provides parameter estimates, their variances and covariances, and residual statistics for models specified by the user. Because of its flexibility INSTAT-D can also fit non-standard versions of standard contingency table models. The wide variety of data manipulation options (including packing a large file into a contingency table, and ordering the data with regard to a group of variables simultaneously) make this a spreadsheet for discrete data analysis.

TYPE OF PROGRAM

Statistical Package

PROGRAM DESIGNED FOR
Data Analysis

PROGRAM STYLE
Command Driven
Integrated System

MISCELLANEOUS PROGRAM FEATURES
Copyable Disk

DOCUMENTATION
User's Manual - 41 pages, 0 technical references
Table of Contents
Index
Tutorial or Example Lessons
Sample Runs
Formulas Provided
Tutorials and Examples on Disk

DATA MANAGEMENT
Keyboard Data Entry
Data Manipulations and Transformations
Missing Values Allowed in Data

DATA EDITING
Change
Add
Delete

FOREIGN DATA ACCESS
Standard Rectangular ASCII Files

GRAPHICS FEATURES
Graphics can be Output to a Printer
Graphics can be Saved to a File

GRAPHICS
Scatter (x-y) Plots

PRODUCT SUPPORT
User may call at own Expense
No Classes or Instruction Available

STATISTICAL FEATURES SUPPORTED

DESCRIPTIVE STATISTICS
- Mean
- Standard Deviation or Variance

CORRELATION AND REGRESSION
- Simple Linear Regression
- Multiple Linear Regression
- Residuals Calculated
- Estimate Asymptotic Standard Errors
- Standardization
- Orthogonalization
- Correlation Matrices
- Inverse Correlation Matrices

CATEGORICAL DATA ANALYSIS
- Chi-Square Contingency Table Analysis
- Multi-Dimensional Tables
- Goodness-of-Fit Tests
- Frequencies Can be Entered Directly
- Linear Parameter Estimation
- Log-linear Parameter Estimation
- Covariance Matrices

INSTAT-P:Poisson Regression

Statistical Consulting Services
517 East Lodge Dr
Tempe, AZ 85283
(602) 838 - 7784
Contact Person: Mikel Aickin

CONFIGURATIONS SUPPORTED

Computer	Language	Operating System	RAM	Number Drives	Cost
IBM PC	none	DOS	128K	1	$ 50
TANDY 2000	none	DOS	128K	1	$ 50

NUMBER OF CURRENT USERS ?
DATE OF FIRST RELEASE Spr 84
CURRENT VERSION RELEASED Spr 84

PROGRAM DESCRIPTION

INSTAT-P carries out multiple regression analysis in the special case where the dependent variable is a Poisson distributed count. This technique is widely used in biomedical statistics and census analysis. The manual explains the method in detail, so no additional reading is necessary.

The program uses the same interactive menu as INSTAT-R. The logarithm of the expected Poisson count is expressed as a regression function, so that log-linear analysis of contingency table data can be performed. Residual and multicollinearity analyses are provided, along with a backward stepwise routine. Length of data files is limited only be online disk storage. Output can be viewed on screen, stored in a file or sent to any printer.

TYPE OF PROGRAM
Statistical Package

PROGRAM DESIGNED FOR
Data Analysis

PROGRAM STYLE
Menu Driven
Integrated System

MISCELLANEOUS PROGRAM FEATURES
Copyable Disk

DOCUMENTATION
User's Manual - 48 pages, 11 technical references
Table of Contents
Index
Tutorial or Example Lessons
Sample Runs
Formulas Provided
Tutorials and Examples on Disk

DATA MANAGEMENT
Keyboard Data Entry
Missing Values Allowed in Data

FOREIGN DATA ACCESS
Standard Rectangular ASCII Files

GRAPHICS FEATURES
Graphics can be Output to a Printer
Graphics can be Saved to a File

GRAPHICS
Scatter (x-y) Plots

PRODUCT SUPPORT
User may call at own Expense
No Classes or Instruction Available

STATISTICAL FEATURES SUPPORTED

DESCRIPTIVE STATISTICS
- Mean
- Standard Deviation or Variance
- Minimum, Maximum

CATEGORICAL DATA ANALYSIS
- Chi-Square Contingency Table Analysis
- Multi-Dimensional Tables
- Goodness-of-Fit Tests
- Frequencies Can be Entered Directly
- Log-linear Poisson Regression Function

DISTRIBUTION FUNCTION EVALUATION
- Chi Square

MISCELLANEOUS
- p-Values Given With Tests

INSTAT-QC: QUALITY CONTROL CHARTS

Statistical Consulting Services
517 E. Lodge Dr.
Tempe, AZ 85283
(602) 838 - 7784
Contact Person: Mikel Aickin

CONFIGURATIONS SUPPORTED

Computer	Language	Operating System	RAM	Number Drives	Cost
IBM PC		DOS	64K	1	$125

NUMBER OF CURRENT USERS ?
DATE OF FIRST RELEASE 1984
VERSION 1.0 RELEASED Jan. 85

PROGRAM DESCRIPTION

INSTAT-QC is designed for quality assurance personnel who need to set up an on-going control chart system.

The program permits independent definition of data and chart files. Target values, control limits and specification limits can be set for means, standard deviations, defective fraction and counts of defects. Charts can be produced in either interactive or batch (unattended) mode. The user can customize the program for any printer.

TYPE OF PROGRAM
Quality Control or Reliability

PROGRAM DESIGNED FOR
Data Analysis

PROGRAM STYLE
Command Driven
Integrated System

MISCELLANEOUS PROGRAM FEATURES
Copyable Disk
On Screen Help Function

DOCUMENTATION
User's Manual - 40 pages, 1 technical references
Table of Contents
Tutorial or Example Lessons
Sample Runs
Formulas Provided

DATA MANAGEMENT
Keyboard Data Entry
Missing Values Allowed in Data

DATA EDITING
Change
Add
Delete

FOREIGN DATA ACCESS
Standard Rectangular ASCII Files

GRAPHICS FEATURES
Graphics can be Output to a Printer
Graphics can be Saved to a File
Titles and/or Labels Available
Uses Character Graphics

GRAPHICS
QC Charts

PRODUCT SUPPORT
No Classes or Instruction Available

STATISTICAL FEATURES SUPPORTED

DESCRIPTIVE STATISTICS
Mean
Standard Deviation or Variance
Standard Error of the Mean
Minimum, Maximum

CONTROL CHARTS
X-Bar
s
Proportions
Number of Defects
Number of Defectives

INSTAT-QF:Quick Forecaster

Statistical Consulting Services
517 East Lodge Dr.
Tempe, AZ 85283
(602) 838 - 7784
Contact Person: Mikel Aickin

CONFIGURATIONS SUPPORTED

Computer	Language	Operating System	RAM	Number Drives	Cost
IBM PC	none	DOS	64K	1	$ 20

NUMBER OF CURRENT USERS ?
DATE OF FIRST RELEASE Sum 84
CURRENT VERSION RELEASED Sum 84

PROGRAM DESCRIPTION

INSTAT-QF is designed to provide quick forecasts for a univariate time series. Among its users are investment analysts and stock traders.

Without requiring any technical knowledge, the program permits the user to specify an ARIMA forecasting method, and within seconds provides forecasts based on the best fitting model. Data files are easily updated, so that near-term forecasts can be revised on a daily basis.

PRODUCT REVIEWS

Financial and Invesment Software Review, (May/June 1984).

TYPE OF PROGRAM

Statistical Package

PROGRAM DESIGNED FOR

Data Analysis

PROGRAM STYLE

Menu Driven
Integrated System

MISCELLANEOUS PROGRAM FEATURES
Copyable Disk

DOCUMENTATION
User's Manual - 7 pages, 0 technical references
Table of Contents
Index
Tutorial or Example Lessons
Sample Runs
Formulas Provided
Tutorials and Examples on Disk

DATA MANAGEMENT
Keyboard Data Entry

DATA EDITING
Change
Add
Delete

FOREIGN DATA ACCESS
Standard Rectangular ASCII Files

GRAPHICS
SEE Time Series Plots

PRODUCT SUPPORT
User may call at own Expense
No Classes or Instruction Available

STATISTICAL FEATURES SUPPORTED

TIME SERIES ANALYSIS
AUTOREGRESSIVE MOVING AVERAGE
Parameter Estimation
TIME SERIES ANALYSIS - FORECASTING
ARIMA
TIME SERIES ANALYSIS - PLOTS
Residuals
Forecasts
Time Series
Detrended Series

INSTAT-R:Multiple Regression
Statistical Consulting Services
517 East Lodge Dr
Tempe, AZ 85283
(602) 838 - 7784
Contact Person: Mikel Aickin

CONFIGURATIONS SUPPORTED

Computer	Language	Operating System	RAM	Number Drives	Cost
IBM PC	none	DOS	64K	1	$ 50
TANDY 2000	none	DOS	96K	1	$ 50

NUMBER OF CURRENT USERS ?
DATE OF FIRST RELEASE Fall 83
CURRENT VERSION RELEASED Spr 84

PROGRAM DESCRIPTION

INSTAT-R is a full-featured multiple regression program with capabilities formerly available only on mainframe statistical packages. The manual constitutes a mini-course on regression explaining not only the program operation but also interpretation of output and the strategy of regression analysis.

Dual on-screen interactive menus permit the user to quickly specify and analyze different models. Five aspects of residual analysis (including correct P-values) are immediately available as additional variables, and can be used in subsequent regressions or plots. The ingeneous multicollinearity diagnostics of Belsley, Kuh and Welch are provided, as well as casewise deletion statistics. Length of data files is limited only by on-line disk storage. Output can be viewed on the screen, stored to a file or sent to any printer.

PRODUCT REVIEWS

Wang, Deane. "Statistics with the IBM Personal Computer", Science Software Quarterly, pp. 37-41, (Spring 1984).

TYPE OF PROGRAM
Statistical Package

PROGRAM DESIGNED FOR
Data Analysis

PROGRAM STYLE
Menu Driven
Integrated System

MISCELLANEOUS PROGRAM FEATURES
Copyable Disk

DOCUMENTATION
User's Manual - 76 pages, 19 technical references
Table of Contents
Index
Tutorial or Example Lessons
Sample Runs
Formulas Provided
Tutorials and Examples on Disk

DATA MANAGEMENT
Keyboard Data Entry
Missing Values Allowed in Data

FOREIGN DATA ACCESS
Standard Rectangular ASCII Files

GRAPHICS FEATURES
Graphics can be Output to a Printer
Graphics can be Saved to a File

GRAPHICS
Scatter (x-y) Plots

PRODUCT SUPPORT
User may call at own Expense
No Classes or Instruction Available

STATISTICAL FEATURES SUPPORTED

DESCRIPTIVE STATISTICS
- Mean
- Standard Deviation or Variance
- Minimum, Maximum

t-TESTS
- One Sample t-Test
- Independent Group t-Test/Equal Variance
- Paired t-Test

CORRELATION AND REGRESSION
- Pearson Correlation Coefficient
- Simple Linear Regression
- Multiple Linear Regression
- Stepwise Multiple Linear Regression
- Residuals Calculated
- Estimate Asymptotic Standard Errors
- Weighted Regression
- Ridge Regression
- Multicollinearity Diagnostic
- Sensitivity Analysis

DISTRIBUTION FUNCTION EVALUATION
- t

TIME SERIES ANALYSIS
- Autocorrelations

MISCELLANEOUS
- p-Values Given With Tests

INSTAT-SC:THE STATISTICAL CALCULATOR

Statistical Consulting Services
517 E. Lodge Dr.
Tempe, AZ 85283
(602) 838 - 7784
Contact Person: Mikel Aickin

CONFIGURATIONS SUPPORTED

Computer	Language	Operating System	RAM	Number Drives	Cost
IBM PC		DOS	64K	1	$ 30

NUMBER OF CURRENT USERS ?
DATE OF FIRST RELEASE 1984
CURRENT VERSION RELEASED 1984

PROGRAM DESCRIPTION

INSTAT-SC is an on-screen statistical calculator. With single keystroke commands, data can be entered into four stacks, and then a parametric statistical procedure can be chosen for analysis. The program performs the procedures most commonly taught in introductory statistics courses, and so it is ideal for students, teachers, researchers, and business decision-makers.

The attractive screen layout, simple command keys, and on-screen help feature, make INSTAT-SC fun to use and far more efficient for small data sets than larger, more cumbersome programs.

PRODUCT REVIEWS

Sparks, Leslie E.. "INSTAT-SC", Access, Vol. 3, No. 5, pp. 6, (Sept/Oct 1984).

Gabaldon, Diana J.. "Statistics Fast and Easy", Science Software Quarterly, Vol. 1, No.4, pp. 70-72, (1984).

TYPE OF PROGRAM

Statistical Package

PROGRAM DESIGNED FOR
Educational use

PROGRAM STYLE
Command Driven
Integrated System

MISCELLANEOUS PROGRAM FEATURES
Copyable Disk
On Screen Help Function

DOCUMENTATION
User's Manual - 0 pages, 0 technical references
Table of Contents
Index
Tutorial or Example Lessons
Sample Runs
Formulas Provided
Tutorials and Examples on Disk

DATA MANAGEMENT
Keyboard Data Entry
Data Manipulations and Transformations

DATA EDITING
Change
Add
Delete

PRODUCT SUPPORT
User may call at own Expense
No Classes or Instruction Available

STATISTICAL FEATURES SUPPORTED

DESCRIPTIVE STATISTICS
- Mean
- Standard Deviation or Variance
- Standard Error of the Mean

t-TESTS
- One Sample t-Test
- Independent Group t-Test/Equal Variance
- Independent Group t-Test/Unequal Var
- Paired t-Test

CORRELATION AND REGRESSION
- Pearson Correlation Coefficient
- Simple Linear Regression

CONFIDENCE INTERVALS
- Means
- Difference Between Two Means
- Proportions
- Difference Between Two Proportions
- Correlation Coefficients

CATEGORICAL DATA ANALYSIS
- Chi-Square Contingency Table Analysis
- Frequencies Can be Entered Directly

ANALYSIS OF VARIANCE
- One-Way ANOVA

DISTRIBUTION FUNCTION EVALUATION
- Normal
- t
- Chi Square
- F
- Binomial

MISCELLANEOUS
- Random Number Generation
- p-Values Given With Tests

INSTAT-U:UTILITIES

Statistical Consulting Services
517 East Lodge Dr
Tempe, AZ 85283
(602) 838 - 7748
Contact Person: Mikel Aickin

CONFIGURATIONS SUPPORTED

Computer	Language	Operating System	RAM	Number Drives	Cost
IBM PC	none	DOS	64K	2	$ 20
TANDY 2000	none	DOS	64K	2	$ 20

NUMBER OF CURRENT USERS ?
DATE OF FIRST RELEASE Spr 83
CURRENT VERSION RELEASED Win 83

PROGRAM DESCRIPTION

INSTAT-U is a collection of programs for data file creation and manipulation. The files created are in SCS.DAT format (a version of standard ASCII files), which is required for most INSTAT series programs.

Each program solicits information from the user, and then performs its operations. Data can be viewed, edited, recoded and transformed; variables can be selected, deleted and renamed; files can be merged, subfiles selected, and translation to and from DIF format can be carried out. dBaseII files can also be converted to SCS.DAT format.

PRODUCT REVIEWS

Wang, Deane. "Statistics with the IBM Personal Computer", Science Software Quarterly, pp. 37-41, (Spring 1984).

TYPE OF PROGRAM

Statistical Package

PROGRAM DESIGNED FOR

Data Analysis

PROGRAM STYLE
Menu Driven
Separate Programs for each Procedure

MISCELLANEOUS PROGRAM FEATURES
Copyable Disk

DOCUMENTATION
User's Manual - 41 pages, 0 technical references
Table of Contents
Index
Tutorial or Example Lessons
Sample Runs
Formulas Provided
Tutorials and Examples on Disk

DATA MANAGEMENT
Keyboard Data Entry
Data Manipulations and Transformations
Missing Values Allowed in Data

DATA EDITING
Change
Add
Delete

FOREIGN DATA ACCESS
Standard Rectangular ASCII Files
DIF Files
dBase II Files

PRODUCT SUPPORT
User may call at own Expense
No Classes or Instruction Available

STATISTICAL FEATURES SUPPORTED

MISCELLANEOUS

- Select If
- Merge Files

INTRODUCTORY STATISTICS

Brooks/Cole Publishing Company
555 Abrego
Monterey, CA 93940
(408) 373 - 0728
Contact Person: Robert Evans

CONFIGURATIONS SUPPORTED

Computer	Language	Operating System	RAM	Number Drives	Cost
APPLE II	BASIC	DOS	48K	1	$26
IBM PC	BASIC	DOS	64K	1	$26

NUMBER OF CURRENT USERS 600
DATE OF FIRST RELEASE 1984
VERSION 2.0 RELEASED Oct 86

PROGRAM DESCRIPTION

The book and accompanying microcomputer diskette give an integrated approach to teaching statistics, allowing the student to gain a conceptual understanding of the processes without becoming immersed in the tedium of the actual calculations. It is designed as an instruction program for a first course in statistics at the undergraduate or graduate level. It covers the commonly used parametric and non-parametric techniques and is appropriate for students in many disciplines.

The combination of text and microcomputer diskette is unique in that it provides a comprehensive instructional approach to statistics that combines presentation of fundamental statistical concepts and techniques with computer capability for applying these techniques to data. The diskette contains a series of statistical programs that will perform the calculations for all of the statistical techniques introduced in the text. The appropriate computer program for each technique is referenced and the formulas it employs specified. Part II of the text supplies summary descriptions of each computer program and detailed instructions on the use of the programs.

TYPE OF PROGRAM
Statistical Package

PROGRAM DESIGNED FOR
Educational use

PROGRAM STYLE
Menu Driven
Separate Programs for each Procedure

MISCELLANEOUS PROGRAM FEATURES
Source Code Available
Copyable Disk
On Screen Help Function

DOCUMENTATION
User's Manual - 298 pages, 0 technical references
Table of Contents
Index
Tutorial or Example Lessons
Sample Runs
Formulas Provided
Really a Statistics Text

DATA MANAGEMENT
Keyboard Data Entry
Data Manipulations and Transformations
Missing Values Allowed in Data

DATA EDITING
Change
Add
Delete

GRAPHICS FEATURES
Titles and/or Labels Available
Uses Pixel Graphics

GRAPHICS
Histograms
Pie Charts
Scatter (x-y) Plots

PRODUCT SUPPORT
No Classes or Instruction Available

STATISTICAL FEATURES SUPPORTED

DESCRIPTIVE STATISTICS
- Mean
- Standard Deviation or Variance
- Standard Error of the Mean
- Minimum, Maximum
- Median

t-TESTS
- Independent Group t-Test/Equal Variance
- Independent Group t-Test/Unequal Var
- Paired t-Test

CORRELATION AND REGRESSION
- Pearson Correlation Coefficient
- Simple Linear Regression

CONFIDENCE INTERVALS
- Means

CATEGORICAL DATA ANALYSIS
- Chi-Square Contingency Table Analysis
- Goodness-of-Fit Tests
- Frequencies Can be Entered Directly

ANALYSIS OF VARIANCE
- One-Way ANOVA
- One-Way with Repeated Measures
- Two-Way ANOVA
- Analysis of Covariance

NONPARAMETRIC TESTS
- Wilcoxon One Sample Test
- Mann-Whitney U
- Kruskal-Wallis Test
- Friedman Chi-Square Test
- Spearman or Kendall Correlation

DISTRIBUTION FUNCTION EVALUATION
- Normal
- t
- Chi Square
- F

MISCELLANEOUS
- p-Values Given With Tests

INTROSTAT 2.2
Ideal Systems
P.O. Box 681
Fairfield, Iowa 52556
(515) 472 - 4507
Contact Person: Christopher Dennen

CONFIGURATIONS SUPPORTED

Computer	Language	Operating System	RAM	Number Drives	Cost
APPLE II	BASIC	DOS	48K	2	$ 125
IBM PC	BASIC	DOS	64K	2	$ 125
ATARI	ATARI BASIC	DOS	48K	2	$ 125

NUMBER OF CURRENT USERS
DATE OF FIRST RELEASE 81
VERSION 2.2 RELEASED 84

PROGRAM DESCRIPTION

INTROSTAT is the original statistical package for the AppleII computer. Since its introduction in 1981 it has undergone significant evolution and today stands as a well refined, well tested product. Originally designed for students and researchers in the behavioral sciences, INTROSTAT quickly gained a reputation for ease of use, flexibility, and power. Today INTROSTAT is used widely by independent researchers, universities, public schools, and business.

The statistical procedures contained in INTROSTAT include those which are commonly encountered in introductory and intermediate statistics courses. Some non-parametric tests which are rarely available in introductory statistics packages are also included. INTROSTAT has no equal for ease of use and value. The INTROSTAT package includes a full 55 page manual that takes the user through each of the tests in a friendly, informative way. The disk contains a sample data set adapted from Statlab: An Empirical Introduction to Statistics by Hodges et al (McGraw-Hill, 1975).

TYPE OF PROGRAM
Statistical Package

PROGRAM DESIGNED FOR
Data Analysis
Educational use

PROGRAM STYLE
Menu Driven
Integrated System

MISCELLANEOUS PROGRAM FEATURES
Source Code Available
Copyable Disk

DOCUMENTATION
User's Manual - 55 pages, ? technical references
Table of Contents
Index
Tutorial or Example Lessons
Sample Runs

DATA MANAGEMENT
Keyboard Data Entry
Data Manipulations and Transformations
Missing Values Allowed in Data

DATA EDITING
Change
Add
Delete

GRAPHICS FEATURES
Uses Pixel Graphics

GRAPHICS
Scatter (x-y) Plots
SEE Regression Plots

PRODUCT SUPPORT
User may call at own Expense
No Classes or Instruction Available

STATISTICAL FEATURES SUPPORTED

DESCRIPTIVE STATISTICS
- Mean
- Standard Deviation or Variance
- Standard Error of the Mean
- Minimum, Maximum
- Median
- Frequency Table

t-TESTS
- One Sample t-Test
- Independent Group t-Test/Equal Variance
- Paired t-Test

CORRELATION AND REGRESSION
- Pearson Correlation Coefficient
- Simple Linear Regression
- **REGRESSION PLOTS**
  - Regression Line

ANALYSIS OF VARIANCE
- One-Way ANOVA
- Two-Way ANOVA

NONPARAMETRIC TESTS
- Wilcoxon One Sample Test
- Mann-Whitney U

MISCELLANEOUS
- Crosstabs

JASS(TM)

Joiner Associates Inc.
P.O. Box 5445, 3800 Regent Street
Madison, WI 53705
(608) 238 - 6417
Contact Person: Jessie Gwynne

CONFIGURATIONS SUPPORTED

Computer	Language	Operating System	RAM	Number Drives	Cost
IBM PC		DOS	512K	HD	$895

NUMBER OF CURRENT USERS ?
DATE OF FIRST RELEASE Feb 85
VERSION 2.0 RELEASED Aug 86

PROGRAM DESCRIPTION

Jass software includes the tools needed for the design and analysis of two-level factorial experiments. Engineers, technicians, scientists, statisticians and others can use Jass to increase the efficiency of experimentation and the operation of industrial processes. Jass emphasizes graphical display of results; tailors input and output for two-level factorial designs; and has convenient and readily understood documentation. Full, fractional, blocked, and replicated factorials are supported as well as designs with center points, missing data or fuzzy factor levels.

Jass prompts the user for the information needed to design an experiment. Jass will select the appropriate design for experiments with up to 15 factors (10 IBM PC) and up to 256 runs. For each experiment Jass prints a report form that is useful for data collection. Full, fractional, blocked and replicated factorials are supported as well as designs with center points, missing data or fuzzy factor levels. Jass output includes tables of effects, residuals, fitted values; cell statistics, cubeplots, normal plots, dotplots, scatterplots, interaction plots, and complete alias structure. Model reduction as well as the saving and documenting of your worksheet, commands and output is simple. Data may be entered from the keyboard or from a file. All output may be sent to files. Sophisticated data transformations and data editing capabilities are included. Documentation includes complete on-line HELP, a users guide with index, and a testdrive for new users.

PRODUCT REVIEWS

Karlin, Ernest W.and Procopio, A. John. "Personal Computers Make Statistical Analysis Easy", ASQC 40th Anniversary Quality Congress Transactions, pp. 740, (1986).

TYPE OF PROGRAM

Statistical Package

PROGRAM DESIGNED FOR

Data Analysis

PROGRAM STYLE

Menu Driven
Command Driven
Integrated System

MISCELLANEOUS PROGRAM FEATURES

On Screen Help Function
Optional Support for 8087 Mathematical Chip

DOCUMENTATION

User's Manual - 200 pages, ? technical references
- Table of Contents
- Index
- Tutorial or Example Lessons
- Sample Runs
- Formulas Provided

Quick Reference Card
Tutorials and Examples on Disk

DATA MANAGEMENT

Keyboard Data Entry
Data Manipulations and Transformations
Missing Values Allowed in Data

DATA EDITING

Change
Add
Delete

FOREIGN DATA ACCESS

Standard Rectangular ASCII Files

GRAPHICS FEATURES

Graphics can be Output to a Printer
Graphics can be Saved to a File
Titles and/or Labels Available
Uses Character Graphics

GRAPHICS

- Histograms
- Scatter (x-y) Plots
- Interaction Plots
- Reference Distribution Plots
- Normal Probability Plots
- Cube Plots

PRODUCT SUPPORT

- User may call at own Expense
- Classes or Instruction Available

STATISTICAL FEATURES SUPPORTED

DESCRIPTIVE STATISTICS

- Mean
- Standard Deviation or Variance
- Minimum, Maximum
- Median
- Percentiles

CORRELATION AND REGRESSION

- Pearson Correlation Coefficient
- Simple Linear Regression
- Multiple Linear Regression

ANALYSIS OF VARIANCE

- 2-level Factorial
- Multiway Factorials
- Alias structure printed
- Unbalanced Designs
- Test for curvature

MISCELLANEOUS

- Random Number Generation

KWIKSTAT
Mission Technologies
P.O. Box 1169 Dept: MD
Cedar Hill, TX 75104
(214) 291 - 2115
Contact Person: A. Elliott

CONFIGURATIONS SUPPORTED

Computer	Language	Operating System	RAM	Number Drives	Cost
IBM PC	COMPILED	DOS	196K	2	$25

NUMBER OF CURRENT USERS New
DATE OF FIRST RELEASE Oct 86
VERSION 1.0 RELEASED Oct 86

PROGRAM DESCRIPTION

KWIKSTAT is a general purpose statistical analysis program which can be used to quickly perform the most common statistical techniques. Data can be entered from the keyboard, from a standard ASCII file, or read directly from a dBASE III file. Data can also be transferred from other popular programs such as LOTUS 1-2-3, Framework, Supercalc, etc. In addition, KWIKSTAT can produce some very nice graphics plots, including scatterplots, bar charts, histograms, and a 3-dimensional bar chart. Also, KWIKSTAT has a quick report facility that produces a formatted listing of the data similar to SAS's PROC PRINT.

Since KWIKSTAT shares the dBase III file structure, dBase users can take advantage of the powerful data manuipulation tools in dBase to prepare data for analysis. Data created in KWIKSTAT can be output easily in an ASCII format that is shareable with many other programs such as SAS, SPSS, LOTUS 1-2-3, and others. This low-cost program may be shared freely with other users by copying the diskettes. Unregistered users are encouraged to send in a modest registration fee.

TYPE OF PROGRAM

Statistical Package

PROGRAM DESIGNED FOR
Data Analysis

PROGRAM STYLE
Menu Driven
Integrated System

MISCELLANEOUS PROGRAM FEATURES
Copyable Disk
On Screen Help Function

DOCUMENTATION
User's Manual - 25 pages, 5 technical references
Table of Contents
Index
Tutorial or Example Lessons
Tutorials and Examples on Disk

DATA MANAGEMENT
Keyboard Data Entry
Missing Values Allowed in Data

DATA EDITING
Change
Add
Delete

FOREIGN DATA ACCESS
Standard Rectangular ASCII Files
dBASE III Files

GRAPHICS FEATURES
Graphics can be Output to a Printer
Titles and/or Labels Available
Uses Pixel Graphics
Uses Character Graphics

GRAPHICS
Histograms
Scatter (x-y) Plots
3-D Plotting
Box Plots
Multiple Comparison
Survival Analysis
SEE Regression Plots

PRODUCT SUPPORT
User may call at own Expense
No Classes or Instruction Available

STATISTICAL FEATURES SUPPORTED

DESCRIPTIVE STATISTICS
- Mean
- Standard Deviation or Variance
- Standard Error of the Mean
- Minimum, Maximum
- Median
- Percentiles
- Sum
- Tukey's 5 Number Summary

t-TESTS
- Independent Group t-Test/Equal Variance
- Paired t-Test

CORRELATION AND REGRESSION
- Pearson Correlation Coefficient
- Simple Linear Regression
- Multiple Linear Regression
- Residuals Calculated
- **REGRESSION PLOTS**
  - Residuals

CATEGORICAL DATA ANALYSIS
- Chi-Square Contingency Table Analysis
- Fisher's Exact Test
- Frequencies Can be Entered Directly

ANALYSIS OF VARIANCE
- One-Way ANOVA
- One-Way with Repeated Measures
- **MULTIPLE COMPARISONS**
  - Newman-Keuls

DISTRIBUTION FUNCTION EVALUATION
- Normal
- t
- Chi Square
- F

EXPLORATORY DATA ANALYSIS
- Box Plots

MISCELLANEOUS
- Life Table Analysis
- p-Values Given With Tests

KYPPAD

Professional Applications Development
12 Sandy Way
Weymouth, MA 02191
(617) 331 - 4062
Contact Person: John A. Clements

CONFIGURATIONS SUPPORTED

Computer	Language	Operating System	RAM	Number Drives	Cost
IBM PC		DOS	256	2	$65

NUMBER OF CURRENT USERS 50+
DATE OF FIRST RELEASE June 86
VERSION A1.1 RELEASED Jun 86

ADDITIONAL SOFTWARE REQUIRED
Symphony
Lotus 1-2-3

PROGRAM DESCRIPTION

Integrated process capability and control templates. For use with 1-2-3 (Release 2, and 2.01) and symphony. Analysis and charting of Quality Assurance Variables Data. Separate templates are provided for both specification limits (U & L) given, one limit (U or L) given, no limits given, no standards given. The following parameters are calculated: Subgroup sum, mean, size, standard deviation, max, min, range. All data mean (M), All data SD (S), Pooled Subgroup Standard Deviation, All data count (N), Max subgroup count (n), All data max, All data min, {M+3S}, {M-3S}, {M+3S/sqrt(n)}, {M-3S/sqrt(n)}, {m+3S/sqrt(N)}, {M-3S/sqrt(N)}, {U-M)/S}, {M-L/S}, Estimated % above U, Estimated % below L, {(U-L)/S}, Estimated % out of spec, {(U-M/3S}, CpU, {(M-L)/3S}, CpL, {(U-L)/6S}, Cp, MIN(CpL,CpU), Cpk. Analysis of variance with F-test and p. All data distribution.

The advantages are process control and capability analysis included in one program so that process may be continuously monitored for conformance to specification. Analysis and charts may be customized by user.

TYPE OF PROGRAM
Quality Control or Reliability

PROGRAM DESIGNED FOR
Data Analysis

PROGRAM STYLE
Menu Driven
Separate Programs for each Procedure

MISCELLANEOUS PROGRAM FEATURES
Source Code Available
Copyable Disk

DOCUMENTATION
User's Manual - 50 pages, ? technical references
Table of Contents
Tutorial or Example Lessons
Sample Runs

DATA MANAGEMENT
Keyboard Data Entry
Data Manipulations and Transformations
Missing Values Allowed in Data

DATA EDITING
Change
Add
Delete

FOREIGN DATA ACCESS
Standard Rectangular ASCII Files
DIF Files
dBase II Files
Symphony
1-2-3

GRAPHICS FEATURES
Graphics Appear in Color on the Monitor
Graphics can be Output to a Printer
Graphics can be Saved to a File
Titles and/or Labels Available
Uses Pixel Graphics

GRAPHICS
Histograms
Normal Probability Chart
Control Charts
Histogram with Superimposed Normal
Cumulative Percentile Chart

PRODUCT SUPPORT
User may call at own Expense
Classes or Instruction Available

STATISTICAL FEATURES SUPPORTED

DESCRIPTIVE STATISTICS
Mean
Standard Deviation or Variance
Minimum, Maximum
Percentiles

CONFIDENCE INTERVALS
Means

DISTRIBUTION FUNCTION EVALUATION
Normal

CONTROL CHARTS
X-Bar
s
R
Max-Min-Spec
Adjusted X-Bar
OTHER QUALITY CONTROL PROCEDURES
Process Capability

LAB STATISTICS PACKAGE

High Technology Software Products Inc
PO Box 60406
Oklahoma City, OK 73146
(405) 848 - 0480

CONFIGURATIONS SUPPORTED

Computer	Language	Operating System	RAM	Number Drives	Cost
APPLE	APPLESOFT		48K	1	$ 50

NUMBER OF CURRENT USERS 200
DATE OF FIRST RELEASE Apr 82
VERSION 1.03 RELEASED Apr 82

PROGRAM DESCRIPTION

The Lab Statistics Package(tm), developed by a college Physics professor, provides an easy method of introducing laboratory students to statistical procedures used for the analysis of raw data. The students can actually have fun while they learn. The concepts presented are applicable to Physics, Chemistry, Biology, Engineering, and the behavioral sciences. Lab Statistics consists of two main programs, Least Squares Demo and Statistical Calculations.

TYPE OF PROGRAM

Statistical Package

PROGRAM DESIGNED FOR

Educational use

PROGRAM STYLE

Menu Driven
Integrated System

DOCUMENTATION

User's Manual - 20 pages, 0 technical references

Index

Tutorial or Example Lessons

Sample Runs

Formulas Provided

Tutorials and Examples on Disk

PRODUCT SUPPORT

User may call at own Expense

No Classes or Instruction Available

STATISTICAL FEATURES SUPPORTED

DESCRIPTIVE STATISTICS

Mean

Standard Deviation or Variance

Standard Error of the Mean

CORRELATION AND REGRESSION

Simple Linear Regression

Quadratic, Cubic Regression

Exponential Regression

Cochrane-Orcutt and Hildreth-Lu

Box-Jenkins

Residuals Can be Fitted and Saved

LIMDEP

Dr. William H. Greene
517 12th Street
Brooklyn, NY 11215
(718) 499 - 2674
Contact Person: William Greene

CONFIGURATIONS SUPPORTED

Computer	Language	Operating System	RAM	Number Drives	Cost
IBM PC	FORTRAN	DOS	256K	2	$250

NUMBER OF CURRENT USERS 500
DATE OF FIRST RELEASE 1980
VERSION IV RELEASED Mar 86

PROGRAM DESCRIPTION

LIMDEP is a general purpose econometric modelling program. It is useable for estimating the linear regression model by ordinary and many types of generalized least squares as well as numerous types of survival and qualitative and limited dependent variable models. Nearly all of the standard cross section and time series econometric techniques are included. The program is written primarily for professional researchers and graduate students in the social sciences, but is now widely used in graduate econometrics and statistics courses as well.

LIMDEP's menu of regression models and statistical features range from simple descriptive statistics and linear regression to intricate and highly nonlinear models such as the nested logit model. All models are specified with the same simple, English-like command structure. Data entry is from a keyboard, ASCII files, or binary or DIF files written by other programs and a data editor is provided. There is no internal limit on the size of a data set. Transformed variables are created algebraically and can involve dozens of functions such as log, exp, gamma, and functions of the normal distribution. A powerful matrix algebra package is fully integrated into the estimation routines, so any estimation results are useable in later matrix calculations. All program features may be used in sequentially executed commands or in user written procedures which are then accessed like subroutines. About twenty classes of models are included in the program, but many others can be estimated by using the matrix algebra language and other program features. What distinguishes this program from others is the availability of its power and versatility at a fraction of the cost of other packages.

PRODUCT REVIEWS
ESRC (London School of Economics) Software Directory.

TYPE OF PROGRAM
Statistical Package

PROGRAM DESIGNED FOR
Data Analysis

PROGRAM STYLE
Command Driven
Integrated System

MISCELLANEOUS PROGRAM FEATURES
Copyable Disk
Optional Support for 8087 Mathematical Chip

DOCUMENTATION
User's Manual - 315 pages, 20+ technical references
Table of Contents
Index
Tutorial or Example Lessons
Sample Runs
Formulas Provided
Tutorials and Examples on Disk

DATA MANAGEMENT
Keyboard Data Entry
Data Manipulations and Transformations
Missing Values Allowed in Data

DATA EDITING
Change
Add
Delete

FOREIGN DATA ACCESS
Standard Rectangular ASCII Files
DIF Files
Binary

GRAPHICS FEATURES
- Graphics can be Output to a Printer
- Graphics can be Saved to a File
- Uses Character Graphics

GRAPHICS
- Histograms
- Scatter (x-y) Plots

PRODUCT SUPPORT
- User may call at own Expense
- No Classes or Instruction Available

STATISTICAL FEATURES SUPPORTED

DESCRIPTIVE STATISTICS
- Mean
- Standard Deviation or Variance
- Standard Error of the Mean
- Coefficient of Variation
- Minimum, Maximum
- Median
- Percentiles
- Skewness
- Kurtosis
- Cross Tabulations
- Correlation Matrices
- Covariance

t-TESTS
- t-Tests using Matrix Capabilities

CORRELATION AND REGRESSION
- Pearson Correlation Coefficient
- Simple Linear Regression
- Multiple Linear Regression
- Non-Linear Regression
- Residuals Calculated
- **REGRESSION PLOTS**
  - Residuals

CONFIDENCE INTERVALS
- Using Program Commands

CATEGORICAL DATA ANALYSIS
- Chi-Square Contingency Table Analysis

ANALYSIS OF VARIANCE
- One-Way ANOVA
- Analysis of Covariance

DISTRIBUTION FUNCTION EVALUATION
- Normal
- t
- Chi Square
- F
- Binomial
- Poisson
- Exponential
- Inverse Normal
- Beta

TIME SERIES ANALYSIS
- Autocorrelations
- Cross Correlations
  - Model Identification
- **TIME SERIES ANALYSIS - PLOTS**
  - PACF
  - ACF

RELIABILITY
- Exponential
- Weibull
- Logistic
- Log-normal

MISCELLANEOUS
- Life Table Analysis
- Random Number Generation
- Test for Normality of Data
- Test for Equality of Variances
- Linear Discriminant Function Calculation
- p-Values Given With Tests
- Matrix Programming Language
- Matrix Algebra

LINEAR AND NON-LINEAR PROGRAMMING

Lionheart Press, Inc.
P. O. Box 379
Alburg, VT 05440
(514) 933 - 4918

CONFIGURATIONS SUPPORTED

Computer	Language	Operating System	RAM	Number Drives	Cost
MS-DOS	COMPILED	DOS	64K	1	
CP/M 5 1/4"	COMPILED	CP/M	64K	1	
APPLE	COMPILED	DOS	64K	1	

NUMBER OF CURRENT USERS 200
DATE OF FIRST RELEASE Mar 84
CURRENT VERSION RELEASED 1986

PROGRAM DESCRIPTION

The availablity of powerful computing techniques allows easy application of "hard" topics such as linear programming, quadratic programming, and non-linear programming in general. In this book the mathematics is left to the computer programs and the emphasis is on how to formulate problems which can be solved usefully by linear and non-linear programming techniques.

TYPE OF PROGRAM
Statistical Package

PROGRAM DESIGNED FOR
Data Analysis

PROGRAM STYLE
Command Driven
Separate Programs for each Procedure

DOCUMENTATION

User's Manual - 0 pages, 0 technical references

Table of Contents

Index

Tutorial or Example Lessons

Sample Runs

Formulas Provided

Tutorials and Examples on Disk

DATA MANAGEMENT

Keyboard Data Entry

Data Manipulations and Transformations

DATA EDITING

Change

Add

Delete

FOREIGN DATA ACCESS

Standard Rectangular ASCII Files

PRODUCT SUPPORT

User may call at own Expense

No Classes or Instruction Available

LOLITA

Dept. Management
University of West. Australia, AUSTRALIA

Contact Person: B.P. Murphy

CONFIGURATIONS SUPPORTED

Computer	Language	Operating System	RAM	Number Drives	Cost
Z-80	PASCAL	CP/M	256K	1	$ 200
8086-87	PASCAL	DOS CP/M-86	256K	1	$ 200

NUMBER OF CURRENT USERS 40
DATE OF FIRST RELEASE 1982
VERSION 3.5 RELEASED 1985

PROGRAM DESCRIPTION

Lolita fits log-linear models to pure contingency tables of less than 8 dimensions. Iterative proportional scaling is used for computation of expected values; approximate estimates and their s.e. are obtained by matrix operation on expected values and inverses.

The program allows considerable searching via branch and bound techniques, suitable to explatory analyses. 'Graphical' model and complete hierarchical model searches are available. The program can be built upon in modular fashion by users - some knowledge of the Pascal language is necessary.

TYPE OF PROGRAM
Statistical Package

PROGRAM DESIGNED FOR
Data Analysis

PROGRAM STYLE
Menu Driven
Integrated System

MISCELLANEOUS PROGRAM FEATURES
Copyable Disk
On Screen Help Function
Supports 8087, Mathematical Chip

DOCUMENTATION
User's Manual - 70 pages, 30 technical references
Table of Contents
Index
Tutorial or Example Lessons
Sample Runs
Formulas Provided
Tutorials and Examples on Disk

DATA MANAGEMENT
Keyboard Data Entry
Data Manipulations and Transformations
Missing Values Allowed in Data

DATA EDITING
Change
Add
Delete

FOREIGN DATA ACCESS
Standard Rectangular ASCII Files

PRODUCT SUPPORT
User may call at own Expense
No Classes or Instruction Available

LOTUS STAT
Rapid Data
1237 Clark Way
San Jose, CA 95125
(408) 266 - 5174
Contact Person: John Flaig

CONFIGURATIONS SUPPORTED

Computer	Language	Operating System	RAM	Number Drives	Cost
IBM PC	NA		256K	2	$ 50

NUMBER OF CURRENT USERS 50
DATE OF FIRST RELEASE MAR 85
VERSION 1.1 RELEASED Sept 86

ADDITIONAL SOFTWARE REQUIRED
LOTUS 1-2-3

PROGRAM DESCRIPTION
The menu-driven program has the following modules: Descriptive statistics, (no. of entries, sum, mean, median, max, min, std dev (n & n-1), variance, skewness, kurtosis, quartiles, normality test); histograms by quantity, percentage and cum percentages with superimposed normal distribution; control charts (X, Xbar, R, S, P, NP, C and U); linear regression and correlation; OC curves with AOQL, AOQ, AQL, ATI; Process capability (Cp, Cpk, Cpu, Cpl); t-Tests for means and proportions; F-test for variances; paired and unpaired t-Test; sample size for experiments, measurement error study; reliability computation using sum of components method; X-Y scatter plots; distributions (normal, poisson, t and F); outline for defining and controlling a process.

TYPE OF PROGRAM
Statistical Package

PROGRAM DESIGNED FOR
Data Analysis

PROGRAM STYLE
Menu Driven
Separate Programs for each Procedure

MISCELLANEOUS PROGRAM FEATURES
Source Code Available
Copyable Disk

DOCUMENTATION
User's Manual - ? pages, ? technical references
Quick Reference Card
Tutorials and Examples on Disk

DATA MANAGEMENT
Keyboard Data Entry

DATA EDITING
Change
Add
Delete

FOREIGN DATA ACCESS
Standard Rectangular ASCII Files
DIF Files
dBase II Files

GRAPHICS FEATURES
Graphics Appear in Color on the Monitor
Graphics can be Output to a Printer
Graphics can be Saved to a File
Titles and/or Labels Available
Uses Pixel Graphics

GRAPHICS
Histograms
Pie Charts
Scatter (x-y) Plots
Histograms with Normal Curve

PRODUCT SUPPORT
User may call at own Expense
No Classes or Instruction Available

STATISTICAL FEATURES SUPPORTED

DESCRIPTIVE STATISTICS

- Mean
- Standard Deviation or Variance
- Minimum, Maximum
- Median
- First and Third Quartiles
- Range

t-TESTS

- Independent Group t-Test/Equal Variance
- Independent Group t-Test/Unequal Var
- Paired t-Test

CONTROL CHARTS

- X-Bar
- s
- R
- p-Chart
- np-Chart
- c-Chart
- u-Chart
- Sum of Components Reliability Template
- X-Chart

MAC REGRESSION

Cuide Systems
Nard Singel 142
3032 Bk Rotterdam, NETHERLANDS
010-4659965
Contact Person: C. Bongers

CONFIGURATIONS SUPPORTED

Computer	Language	Operating System	RAM	Number Drives	Cost
MACINTOSH			512K		$49

NUMBER OF CURRENT USERS 25
DATE OF FIRST RELEASE Sep 86
VERSION 1.0 RELEASED Sep 86

PROGRAM DESCRIPTION

The program is written for use at educational institutions. Its major use concerns explaining regression analysis and its pitfalls.

In order to teach regression to students, you need a program that provides immediate feedback on the behavior of the model in response to changes in the observations. MAC REGRESSION is designed with this purpose in mind. It is graphically oriented; when an observation is moved (with the mouse) the regression line is recomputed and redrawn immediately. For more details see Wheels of the Mind.

TYPE OF PROGRAM
Regression Analysis

PROGRAM DESIGNED FOR
Educational use

PROGRAM STYLE
Integrated System

MISCELLANEOUS PROGRAM FEATURES
Copyable Disk

DOCUMENTATION
User's Manual - 30 pages, 0 technical references
Table of Contents
Tutorial or Example Lessons
Formulas Provided
Tutorials and Examples on Disk

DATA MANAGEMENT
Keyboard Data Entry
Data Manipulations and Transformations
Missing Values Allowed in Data

DATA EDITING
Change
Add
Delete

FOREIGN DATA ACCESS
Clipboard Access

GRAPHICS FEATURES
Graphics Appear in Color on the Monitor
Graphics can be Output to a Printer
Uses Pixel Graphics

GRAPHICS
Scatter (x-y) Plots

PRODUCT SUPPORT
User may call at own Expense
No Classes or Instruction Available

STATISTICAL FEATURES SUPPORTED

DESCRIPTIVE STATISTICS
Mean
Standard Deviation or Variance
Standard Error of the Mean

CORRELATION AND REGRESSION
Pearson Correlation Coefficient
Simple Linear Regression
Residuals Calculated
Confidence Interval
REGRESSION PLOTS
Residuals

MACSPIN

D2 Software, Inc.
3001 N. Lamar Blvd., Suite 110
Austin, TX 78705
(512) 482 - 8933
Contact Person: Amy Ledbetter

CONFIGURATIONS SUPPORTED

Computer	Language	Operating System	RAM	Number Drives	Cost
MACINTOSH			512K		$200

NUMBER OF CURRENT USERS 1600
DATE OF FIRST RELEASE Jan 86
VERSION 1.1 RELEASED Sept 86

PROGRAM DESCRIPTION

MacSpin is a revolutionary tool for graphical data analysis. It can help anyone who needs to analyze and understand complex numerical data. MacSpin allows you to visualize your data and easily discover pattems, trends, associations and outliers. MacSpin will make looking at data more stimulating and productive than you have ever imagined. Data analysis will become an engaging, interesting process-visual and intuitive. In a few minutes of visual exploration you can gain insights that you might never find from numerical summaries or lengthy printouts.

MacSpin does this providing many new ways for you to look at and interact with your data: three-dimensional display via rotation, a fourth dimension via animation, highlighting for categorical data and instant "Pop-Up" of background information. MacSpin is the first tool to bring these research techniques out of the laboratory and make them available to the working data analyst. MacSpin can transform and manipulate data, giving you the flexibility to get real leverage out of its graphical capabilities. It is easy to get your data into MacSpin, either from outside computers or from other Macintosh software.

PRODUCT REVIEWS

Holloway, Greg. "Preview: MacSpin", MACazine, pp. 82-89, (Feb 86).

Shapiro, Neil L.. "The Editor's Desktop", MacUser, pp.

9-10, (May 86).

Hirame, Ellen. "Look at it This Way", MacUser, pp. 40-44, (June 86).

Schmerken, Ivy. "Man and Machine", Wall Street Computer Review, pp. 46-47, (July 86).

Steen, Lynn A.. American Mathematical Monthly, (Aug-Sept 86).

Foster, David L., McManus, Reed. "3-d Data", MacWorld, pp. 96-99, (Aug 86).

Pournelle, Jerry. "The Show Goes On?", Byte, pp. 279-281, (Oct 86).

TYPE OF PROGRAM
Graphics

PROGRAM DESIGNED FOR
Data Analysis

PROGRAM STYLE
Integrated System

MISCELLANEOUS PROGRAM FEATURES
Optional Support for 68881 Mathematical Chip

DOCUMENTATION
User's Manual - 186 pages, 8 technical references
- Table of Contents
- Index
- Tutorial or Example Lessons
- Sample Runs
- Formulas Provided

Tutorials and Examples on Disk

DATA MANAGEMENT
Keyboard Data Entry
Data Manipulations and Transformations
Missing Values Allowed in Data

DATA EDITING
Change
Add
Delete

FOREIGN DATA ACCESS
Standard Rectangular ASCII Files

GRAPHICS FEATURES
Graphics can be Output to a Printer
Graphics can be Saved to a File
Titles and/or Labels Available
Uses Pixel Graphics
Uses Character Graphics

GRAPHICS
3-D Plotting
3-D Rotating Plots

PRODUCT SUPPORT
User may call at own Expense
No Classes or Instruction Available

STATISTICAL FEATURES SUPPORTED

DESCRIPTIVE STATISTICS
Mean
Standard Deviation or Variance

MISCELLANEOUS
Random Number Generation

MACSS (MACINTOSH STATISTICAL SYSTEM)

Statsoft, Inc.
2832 East 10th Street, Suite 4
Tulsa, OK 74104
(918) 583 - 4149
Contact Person: Sales Office

CONFIGURATIONS SUPPORTED

Computer	Language	Operating System	RAM	Number Drives	Cost
MACINTOSH	FORTRAN	HFS	512K	1	$245
MACINTOSH SE	FORTRAN	HFS	1M	1	$245
MACINTOSH II	FORTRAN	HFS	1M	1	$245

NUMBER OF CURRENT USERS ?
DATE OF FIRST RELEASE Dec 86
VERSION 1A RELEASED Dec 86

PROGRAM DESCRIPTION

General Purpose, advanced statistical package (basic, nonparametric, multivariate statistics), with graphics, and complete statistical database management functions. Unlimited size of files, double precision calculation and mini computer speed.

Macintosh statistical packages are either advanced (i.e., comprehensive and powerful) or "true-macintosh" (i.e., follow the mac user interface). MacSS is both advanced and "true-macintosh". It features a comprehensive selection of advanced statistics (e.g., general MANOVA/ANOVA with up to 128 dependent variables, not available in any other program), and complete statistical database management functions (including a spreadsheet editor). Cases can be selected for every statistical analysis following user specified selection conditions of unlimited complexity. Unlimited size of data files, double precision calculations and mini computer speed.

TYPE OF PROGRAM

Statistical Package

PROGRAM DESIGNED FOR
- Data Analysis
- Educational use

PROGRAM STYLE
- Menu Driven
- Integrated System

MISCELLANEOUS PROGRAM FEATURES
- Copyable Disk

DOCUMENTATION
- User's Manual - 300 pages, 85 technical references
  - Table of Contents
  - Index
  - Tutorial or Example Lessons
  - Sample Runs
  - Formulas Provided
- Tutorials and Examples on Disk

DATA MANAGEMENT
- Keyboard Data Entry
- Data Manipulations and Transformations
- Missing Values Allowed in Data

DATA EDITING
- Change
- Add
- Delete

FOREIGN DATA ACCESS
- Standard Rectangular ASCII Files
- Scratchbook
- Clipboard
- Any Text Files

GRAPHICS FEATURES
- Graphics can be Output to a Printer
- Graphics can be Saved to a File
- Titles and/or Labels Available
- Uses Pixel Graphics

GRAPHICS
- Histograms
- Scatter (x-y) Plots
- Trend Plots
- Graph of Means

PRODUCT SUPPORT
User may call at own Expense
No Classes or Instruction Available

STATISTICAL FEATURES SUPPORTED

DESCRIPTIVE STATISTICS
Mean
Standard Deviation or Variance
Standard Error of the Mean
Coefficient of Variation
Minimum, Maximum
Median
Percentiles
Skewness
Kurtosis

t-TESTS
Independent Group t-Test/Equal Variance
Independent Group t-Test/Unequal Var
Paired t-Test

CORRELATION AND REGRESSION
Pearson Correlation Coefficient
Simple Linear Regression
Multiple Linear Regression
Residuals Calculated
Durbin Watson Statistic
Regression Based Forecasting
REGRESSION PLOTS
Residuals

CATEGORICAL DATA ANALYSIS
Chi-Square Contingency Table Analysis
Frequencies Can be Entered Directly

ANALYSIS OF VARIANCE

- Analysis of Covariance
- Complete Contrast Analysis
- Fixed or Random
- Incomplete
- Unbalanced
- Nested
- 128 Dependent Variables in MANOVA
- Up to 10 Independent Variables (between/within factors)
- General ANOVA/ANCOVA/MANOVA

NONPARAMETRIC TESTS

- Wilcoxon One Sample Test
- Mann-Whitney U
- Wald-Wolfowitz Test
- Kruskal-Wallis Test
- Spearman or Kendall Correlation
- Phi-Square
- V-Square
- Chi-Square

DISTRIBUTION FUNCTION EVALUATION

- Normal
- t
- Chi Square
- F

TIME SERIES ANALYSIS

- Autocorrelations
- **TIME SERIES ANALYSIS - FORECASTING**
  - Regression

MISCELLANEOUS

- Linear Discriminant Function Calculation
- p-Values Given With Tests

MASS VERSION 4

Westat Associates Pty.Ltd.
60 Bruce Street
Nedlands, Western Australia, 6009
(09) 386 4647
Contact Person: B. P. Murphy

CONFIGURATIONS SUPPORTED

Computer	Language	Operating System	RAM	Number Drives	Cost
IBM PC	PASCAL	DOS	256K	2	$ 295
MACINTOSH	PASCAL	MAC	512K	1	$ 225

NUMBER OF CURRENT USERS 300
DATE OF FIRST RELEASE JUN 84
VERSION 4 RELEASED JAN 87

PROGRAM DESCRIPTION

MASS is an interactive statistics package for general data analysis in research, business, and education. It provides a wide range of standard analyses, and a number of quite sophisticated techniques, with accent on numerical power and reliability, and ease of use.

MASS allows the user to create, edit, transform data, and proceed through statistical procedures, saving output if required, all within the one program. It also allows the user to load other programs from within it, subject to RAM store. Data can be read from and written to external files. The user can choose to be prompted at various levels from verbose to terse, and is also able to use batch files for independent or routine processing. Use of the standard techniques is thus made very quick and easy. Sophisticated facilities include extensive data transformations, a very powerful tabulation module, general factorial ANOVA, subset searching in linear and log-linear models, general non-linear estimation by Levenberg-Marquardt methods, high resolution graphics and an expanding multivariate section.

PRODUCT REVIEWS

Micro World (Australian), (Sept/Oct 1984).

TYPE OF PROGRAM
Statistical Package

PROGRAM DESIGNED FOR
Data Analysis
Educational use

PROGRAM STYLE
Menu Driven
Integrated System

MISCELLANEOUS PROGRAM FEATURES
Copyable Disk
On Screen Help Function
Optional Support for 8087 Mathematical Chip

DOCUMENTATION
User's Manual - 150 pages, 10 technical references
Table of Contents
Index
Tutorial or Example Lessons
Sample Runs
Formulas Provided
Tutorials and Examples on Disk

DATA MANAGEMENT
Keyboard Data Entry
Data Manipulations and Transformations
Missing Values Allowed in Data

DATA EDITING
Change
Add
Delete

FOREIGN DATA ACCESS
Standard Rectangular ASCII Files
DIF Files

GRAPHICS FEATURES
Graphics Appear in Color on the Monitor
Graphics can be Output to a Printer
Titles and/or Labels Available
Uses Pixel Graphics
Uses Character Graphics

GRAPHICS
- Histograms
- Pie Charts
- Scatter (x-y) Plots
- 3-D Plotting
- Box Plots
- See Regression Plots

PRODUCT SUPPORT
- User may call at own Expense
- No Classes or Instruction Available

STATISTICAL FEATURES SUPPORTED

DESCRIPTIVE STATISTICS
- Mean
- Standard Deviation or Variance
- Standard Error of the Mean
- Minimum, Maximum
- Median
- Percentiles
- Skewness
- Kurtosis

t-TESTS
- One Sample t-Test
- Independent Group t-Test/Equal Variance
- Independent Group t-Test/Unequal Var
- Paired t-Test

CORRELATION AND REGRESSION
- Pearson Correlation Coefficient
- Simple Linear Regression
- Multiple Linear Regression
- Stepwise Multiple Linear Regression
- Non-Linear Regression
- Residuals Calculated
- **REGRESSION PLOTS**
  - Residuals

CATEGORICAL DATA ANALYSIS
- Chi-Square Contingency Table Analysis
- Multi-Dimensional Tables
- Fisher's Exact Test
- Goodness-of-Fit Tests
- Frequencies Can be Entered Directly
- Searching Graphical & Hierachical Models

ANALYSIS OF VARIANCE

- One-Way ANOVA
- One-Way with Repeated Measures
- Two-Way ANOVA
- General Factorial < 8 Factors
- Multiple Comparisons

NONPARAMETRIC TESTS

- Sign Test (Signed Rank)
- Wilcoxon One Sample Test
- Mann-Whitney U
- Kruskal-Wallis Test
- Friedman Chi-Square Test
- Spearman or Kendall Correlation

DISTRIBUTION FUNCTION EVALUATION

- Normal

TIME SERIES ANALYSIS

- Autocorrelations

MISCELLANEOUS

- Random Number Generation
- Test for Equality of Variances
- Linear Discriminant Function Calculation
- p-Values Given With Tests

MEDLOG

Information Analysis Corporation
201 San Antonio Circle, Suite 125
Mountain View, CA 94040
(415) 948 - 1640
Contact Person: Sarah Strauss

CONFIGURATIONS SUPPORTED

Computer	Language	Operating System	RAM	Number Drives	Cost
IBM PC	PL/I, C	DOS	256K	2	$7500

NUMBER OF CURRENT USERS 75
DATE OF FIRST RELEASE Nov 83
VERSION 86.8 RELEASED Aug 86

PROGRAM DESCRIPTION

MEDLOG is a microcomputer-based data management and statistical analysis system designed for medical research applications such as clinical trials. No programming skills are required to use MEDLOG - it is intended for use by medical personnel as well as statisticians. MEDLOG can efficiently handle large amounts of clinical data, and provides very fast access to data listings and analytical results.

MEDLOG is a completely interactive system designed to maximize retrieval speed so that statistical analysis of large amounts of data can be performed on-line. This objective is achieved partly by such technical features as file inversion, and partly by eliminating the need to write programs to extract data for analysis. A key element in making MEDLOG a programmerless system is its facility for forming data subsets on the basis of time and measurement differentials. For example, the user can easily identify for each patient the blood pressure measurement recorded closest to 6 months after an event such as surgery. Another example of program-free subsetting is identifying encounters where body weight increased by 10% within two months - this involves searching within a time window as it ranges over each patient's entire observation period.

TYPE OF PROGRAM
Statistical Package

PROGRAM DESIGNED FOR
Data Analysis

PROGRAM STYLE
Menu Driven
Integrated System

MISCELLANEOUS PROGRAM FEATURES
Copyable Disk
On Screen Help Function

DOCUMENTATION
User's Manual - 350 pages, 0 technical references
Table of Contents
Index
Tutorial or Example Lessons
Sample Runs
Formulas Provided
Tutorials and Examples on Disk

DATA MANAGEMENT
Keyboard Data Entry
Data Manipulations and Transformations
Missing Values Allowed in Data

DATA EDITING
Change
Add
Delete

FOREIGN DATA ACCESS
DIF Files
Formatted ASCII Files

GRAPHICS FEATURES
Graphics can be Output to a Printer
Graphics can be Saved to a File

GRAPHICS
Histograms
Scatter (x-y) Plots
Bar Charts
Survival Curves
Patient Time Plots

PRODUCT SUPPORT
User may call at own Expense
Classes or Instruction Available

STATISTICAL FEATURES SUPPORTED

DESCRIPTIVE STATISTICS
Mean
Standard Deviation or Variance
Standard Error of the Mean
Minimum, Maximum
Median
Percentiles
Skewness
Kurtosis

t-TESTS
One Sample t-Test
Independent Group t-Test/Equal Variance
Paired t-Test

CORRELATION AND REGRESSION
Pearson Correlation Coefficient
Simple Linear Regression
Multiple Linear Regression
Residuals Calculated
Estimate Asymptotic Standard Errors
Logistic Regression

CONFIDENCE INTERVALS
Confidence Limits on Predicted Values
Confidence Limits on Predicted Means

CATEGORICAL DATA ANALYSIS
Chi-Square Contingency Table Analysis
Fisher's Exact Test

ANALYSIS OF VARIANCE
One-Way ANOVA

NONPARAMETRIC TESTS
Sign Test (Signed Rank)
Mann-Whitney U
Kruskal-Wallis Test
Spearman or Kendall Correlation

MISCELLANEOUS

Life Table Analysis
p-Values Given With Tests
Cox Regression of Survival Data
Network Version Available - Novell

MICRANAL-BJ

Gwilym Jenkins & Partners Ltd
Parkfield, Greaves Rd
Lancaster, U.K. LA1 4TZ
(405) 364 - 4708
Contact Person: J.F. Horrel, 1700 Echo Tr, Norman OK USA

CONFIGURATIONS SUPPORTED

Computer	Language	Operating System	RAM	Number Drives	Cost
IBM PC	FORTRAN	DOS	256K	2	$ 350

NUMBER OF CURRENT USERS 52
DATE OF FIRST RELEASE Jun 84
CURRENT VERSION RELEASED Dec 86

PROGRAM DESCRIPTION

"MICRANAL" is an integrated Box-Jenkins forecasting system. The product has been developed from the mini/mainframe products offered since 1974 and developed under the supervision of one of the originators of the Box-Jenkins Approach.

MICRANAL provides the user with the capability to perform univariate stochastic (past history only) and transfer function/intervention (leading indicator) forecasting plus associated seasonal adjustment and decomposition. The system offers the user the option of four interactive command driven modules which are embraced with a data and model handling framework.

TYPE OF PROGRAM
Statistical Package

PROGRAM DESIGNED FOR
Data Analysis

PROGRAM STYLE
Command Driven
Integrated System

MISCELLANEOUS PROGRAM FEATURES
Copyable Disk
On Screen Help Function
Optional Support for 8087 Mathematical Chip

DOCUMENTATION
User's Manual - 200 pages, 5 technical references
Table of Contents
Index
Tutorial or Example Lessons
Sample Runs
Formulas Provided
Tutorials and Examples on Disk

DATA MANAGEMENT
Keyboard Data Entry
Data Manipulations and Transformations

DATA EDITING
Change
Add
Delete

FOREIGN DATA ACCESS
ASCII Files
Lotus 1-2-3

GRAPHICS FEATURES
Graphics can be Output to a Printer
Graphics can be Saved to a File
Titles and/or Labels Available
Uses Pixel Graphics
Uses Character Graphics

GRAPHICS
Histograms
Box Plots
SEE Time Series Plots

PRODUCT SUPPORT
User may call at own Expense
Classes or Instruction Available

STATISTICAL FEATURES SUPPORTED

TIME SERIES ANALYSIS
- Autocorrelations
- Cross Correlations
- AUTOREGRESSIVE MOVING AVERAGE
  - Model Identification
  - Parameter Estimation
- Transfer Function Models
- Intervention Models
- **TIME SERIES ANALYSIS - FORECASTING**
  - ARIMA
- **TIME SERIES ANALYSIS - PLOTS**
  - Autocorrelations
  - Partial Autocorrelations
  - Original Data
  - Residuals

MICRO DATA ANALYZER (MDA)

Compumetrix Corp.
174 Willowdale Ave., Suite 201
Willowdale, Ontario, CANADA M2N 4Y8
(416) 222 - 4099
Contact Person: Robert Wolfe

CONFIGURATIONS SUPPORTED

Computer	Language	Operating System	RAM	Number Drives	Cost
IBM PC	FORTRAN	DOS	128K	2	$ 349

NUMBER OF CURRENT USERS 250
DATE OF FIRST RELEASE Jun 83
CURRENT VERSION RELEASED Jun 85

PROGRAM DESCRIPTION

MICRO DATA ANALYZER (MDA) is a versatile statistical package found to be useful by a wide range of people. Current users include transportation consultants, medical researchers, economists, and quality control engineers. MDA is currently used in a number of universities around the United States. MDA has two major advantages. The size of the data set MDA can analyze is limited only by the available disk storage capacity. MDA is written in FORTRAN so it executes quickly. However, the user need not know any computer languages or memorize any command instructions.

MDA can perform a number of statistical functions. MDA does statistical summaries, histograms, plots, crosstabulation tables, breakdowns by category group, correlation and covariance analysis, least squares regression, and multinomial logit analysis (something no other statistical program on micros offers). The user can create new variables or modify existing variables by using a wide variety of logical and algebraic operations. MDA can read and write ASCII and DIF files. There is a missing data feature and Boolean variables can be used to analyze subsets. Data can be directed to printer or displayed on the terminal and selected variables can be written to external disk files in character form for use with other software.

PRODUCT REVIEWS

"Popular Reviews:Software, review of Version 1.1", Popular Computing, (March 1984).

TYPE OF PROGRAM
Statistical Package

PROGRAM DESIGNED FOR
Data Analysis

PROGRAM STYLE
Menu Driven
Separate Programs for each Procedure

MISCELLANEOUS PROGRAM FEATURES
Copyable Disk
On Screen Help Function
Optional Support for 8087 Mathematical Chip

DOCUMENTATION
User's Manual - 205 pages, 10 technical references
Table of Contents
Index
Tutorial or Example Lessons
Sample Runs
Formulas Provided
Tutorials and Examples on Disk

DATA MANAGEMENT
Keyboard Data Entry
Data Manipulations and Transformations
Missing Values Allowed in Data

DATA EDITING
Change
Add
Delete

FOREIGN DATA ACCESS
Standard Rectangular ASCII Files
Binary Files

GRAPHICS FEATURES
Graphics can be Output to a Printer
Titles and/or Labels Available
Uses Character Graphics

GRAPHICS
Histograms
Scatter (x-y) Plots
SEE Regression Plots

PRODUCT SUPPORT

User may call at own Expense
No Classes or Instruction Available

STATISTICAL FEATURES SUPPORTED

DESCRIPTIVE STATISTICS

Mean
Standard Deviation or Variance
Standard Error of the Mean
Coefficient of Variation
Minimum, Maximum

CORRELATION AND REGRESSION

Simple Linear Regression
Multiple Linear Regression
Residuals Calculated
Weighted Least Squares

REGRESSION PLOTS

Residuals

CATEGORICAL DATA ANALYSIS

Chi-Square Contingency Table Analysis
Multi-Dimensional Tables
Frequencies Can be Entered Directly

MISCELLANEOUS

Multinomial Logit Analysis

MICROSTAT

Ecosoft, Inc
6413 N. College
Indianapolis, IN 46220
(317) 255 - 6476
Contact Person: Emma Alkire

CONFIGURATIONS SUPPORTED

Computer	Language	Operating System	RAM	Number Drives	Cost
IBM PC	APC BASIC	DOS	64K	1	$ 375
KAYPRO II IV 10	APC BASIC	CP/M	64K	2	
8" Z80	APC BASIC	CP/M	64K	1	$ 375

NUMBER OF CURRENT USERS 3000
DATE OF FIRST RELEASE 1978
VERSION 4.1 RELEASED

PROGRAM DESCRIPTION

MICROSTAT is a general purpose interactive statistics package. Its menu driven approach allows use by students and occasional users, yet it has many powerful features for professional use, including a batch option for large or repetitive operations.

MICROSTAT is file oriented. Data can be entered, edited, and transformed by the Data Management Subsystem or it can also read ASCII, DIF and dBASEII files. All output can be redirected to a text file for further editing or merging into other reports via a word processor. Microstat has been on the market for over four years and there are versions that run on a wide variety of systems.

PRODUCT REVIEWS

PC Magazine, pp. 214, (Aug 1986).

TYPE OF PROGRAM
Statistical Package

PROGRAM DESIGNED FOR
Data Analysis

PROGRAM STYLE
Menu Driven
Integrated System

MISCELLANEOUS PROGRAM FEATURES
Copyable Disk

DOCUMENTATION
User's Manual - 100 pages, 8 technical references
Table of Contents
Index
Tutorial or Example Lessons
Sample Runs
Formulas Provided
Tutorials and Examples on Disk

DATA MANAGEMENT
Keyboard Data Entry
Data Manipulations and Transformations
Missing Values Allowed in Data

DATA EDITING
Change
Add
Delete

FOREIGN DATA ACCESS
Standard Rectangular ASCII Files
DIF Files
dBase II Files
Comma Delimited ASCII Files

GRAPHICS FEATURES
Titles and/or Labels Available

GRAPHICS
Histograms
Scatter (x-y) Plots

PRODUCT SUPPORT
User may call at own Expense
No Classes or Instruction Available

STATISTICAL FEATURES SUPPORTED

DESCRIPTIVE STATISTICS

- Mean
- Standard Deviation or Variance
- Standard Error of the Mean
- Coefficient of Variation
- Minimum, Maximum
- Skewness
- Kurtosis

t-TESTS

- One Sample t-Test
- Independent Group t-Test/Equal Variance
- Independent Group t-Test/Unequal Var
- Paired t-Test

CORRELATION AND REGRESSION

- Pearson Correlation Coefficient
- Simple Linear Regression
- Multiple Linear Regression
- Stepwise Multiple Linear Regression
- Residuals Calculated

CATEGORICAL DATA ANALYSIS

- Chi-Square Contingency Table Analysis
- Fisher's Exact Test
- Goodness-of-Fit Tests
- Frequencies Can be Entered Directly

ANALYSIS OF VARIANCE

- One-Way ANOVA
- One-Way with Repeated Measures
- Two-Way ANOVA

NONPARAMETRIC TESTS

- Sign Test (Signed Rank)
- Wilcoxon One Sample Test
- Mann-Whitney U
- Kruskal-Wallis Test
- Friedman Chi-Square Test
- Spearman or Kendall Correlation
- Wald-Wolfowitz Runs Test
- Absolute Normal Scores Test

DISTRIBUTION FUNCTION EVALUATION

- Normal
- t
- Chi Square
- F
- Binomial
- Hypergeometric
- Poisson

TIME SERIES ANALYSIS

- Moving Average Smoothing

MISCELLANEOUS

- Random Number Generation
- Test for Normality of Data
- p-Values Given With Tests

MICROSURVEY

MVA Systematica
MVA House, Victoria Way
Woking, Surrey, Guzi IDD, ENGLAND
04862 28051
Contact Person: Hugn Neffendorf

CONFIGURATIONS SUPPORTED

Computer	Language	Operating System	RAM	Number Drives	Cost
Almost Any	FORTRAN	Most	128K	2	1500

NUMBER OF CURRENT USERS 75
DATE OF FIRST RELEASE 1980
CURRENT VERSION RELEASED 1986

PROGRAM DESCRIPTION

MICROSURVEY is an integrated package of programs for data validation, data correction, data manipulation or transformation, cross tabulation, multiple regression and descriptive statistics. It is intended for users involved in survey research and current users cover a broad spectrum of central and local government, universities and consulting firms. It is designed for experienced survey analysts, but not only computer specialists.

Principal characteristics of MICROSURVEY are: availability from micros to mainframes, interactive or batch modes, handling of hierarchic data files in a single pass, and no limit on file sizes.

PRODUCT REVIEWS

Gentleman, H.. "Internal User Note", Scottish Office, (1983).

TYPE OF PROGRAM

Statistical Package - Survey Analysis

PROGRAM DESIGNED FOR

Data Analysis

PROGRAM STYLE
Menu Driven
Integrated System

MISCELLANEOUS PROGRAM FEATURES
Supports 8087 Mathematical Chip

DOCUMENTATION
User's Manual - 200 pages, 0 technical references
Table of Contents
Index
Tutorial or Example Lessons
Sample Runs
Formulas Provided
Tutorials and Examples on Disk

DATA MANAGEMENT
Data Manipulations and Transformations
Missing Values Allowed in Data

DATA EDITING
Change
Add
Delete

FOREIGN DATA ACCESS
Standard Rectangular ASCII Files
Hierarchical Files

PRODUCT SUPPORT
User may call at own Expense
No Classes or Instruction Available

STATISTICAL FEATURES SUPPORTED

DESCRIPTIVE STATISTICS

Mean
Standard Deviation or Variance
Minimum, Maximum

CORRELATION AND REGRESSION

Multiple Linear Regression

MISCELLANEOUS

Crosstabs

MICROTSP 5.0

Quantitative Micro Software
4521 Campus Dr. # 336
Irvine, CA 92715
(714) 856 - 3368
Contact Person: Carolyn Stone

CONFIGURATIONS SUPPORTED

Computer	Language	Operating System	RAM	Number Drives	Cost
IBM PC		DOS		1	$ 595

NUMBER OF CURRENT USERS ?
DATE OF FIRST RELEASE 81
VERSION 5.0 RELEASED Mar 86

PROGRAM DESCRIPTION

MicroTSP is a software package for forecasting and regression analysis. With MicroTSP, users can find the best statistical relationships among data and prepare forecasts using those relationships. MicroTSP provides all the power necessary to analyze time series data and work moderate sized cross-section problems. Invaluable for financial analysis, sales forecasting, interest rate forecasting, and scientific data analysis and evaluation, MicroTSP supplies all statistical techniques commonly used in econometrics and forecasting.

Features: Fast processing; complete regression with 5 variables and 100 observations in 5 seconds; even faster with the 8087 co-processor. Autoregressive and moving average models using Box-Jenkins method. Completely flexible polynomial distributed lags. Seasonal adjustment capabilities.

PRODUCT REVIEWS

Forrest, N. B.. "Reviews", PC Magazine, (July 1985).

TYPE OF PROGRAM

Statistical Package

PROGRAM DESIGNED FOR

Data Analysis
Educational use

PROGRAM STYLE
- Menu Driven
- Command Driven
- Integrated System

MISCELLANEOUS PROGRAM FEATURES
- On Screen Help Function
- Optional Support for 8087 Mathematical Chip

DOCUMENTATION
- User's Manual - 350 pages, many technical references
  - Table of Contents
  - Index
  - Tutorial or Example Lessons
  - Sample Runs
- Tutorials and Examples on Disk

DATA MANAGEMENT
- Keyboard Data Entry
- Data Manipulations and Transformations
- Missing Values Allowed in Data

DATA EDITING
- Change
- Add
- Delete

FOREIGN DATA ACCESS
- Standard Rectangular ASCII Files
- DIF Files
- Lotus

GRAPHICS FEATURES
- Graphics can be Output to a Printer
- Graphics can be Saved to a File
- Titles and/or Labels Available
- Uses Pixel Graphics
- Uses Character Graphics

GRAPHICS
- Scatter (x-y) Plots
- Line Graphs

PRODUCT SUPPORT
- User may call at own Expense
- No Classes or Instruction Available

STATISTICAL FEATURES SUPPORTED

DESCRIPTIVE STATISTICS
- Mean
- Standard Deviation or Variance
- Minimum, Maximum

CORRELATION AND REGRESSION
- Multiple Linear Regression
- Non-Linear Regression
- Residuals Calculated
- **REGRESSION PLOTS**
  - Residuals

EXPLORATORY DATA ANALYSIS
- Smoothing Techniques

TIME SERIES ANALYSIS
- Autocorrelations
- Cross Correlations
- Moving Average Smoothing
- AUTOREGRESSIVE MOVING AVERAGE
  - Model Identification
  - Parameter Estimation
- Forecasting
- **TIME SERIES ANALYSIS - PLOTS**
  - Autocorrelations

MISCELLANEOUS
- Random Number Generation

MINITAB DATA ANALYSIS SOFTWARE

Minitab, Inc.
3081 Enterprise Drive
State College, PA 16801
(814) 238 - 3280
Contact Person: Vicki L. Jodon

CONFIGURATIONS SUPPORTED

Computer	Language	Operating System	RAM	Number Drives	Cost
IBM PC	Fortran	DOS	320K	HD	$500
VICTOR	FORTRAN	DOS	384K	HD	$500
FORTUNE	FORTRAN	FOR:PRO	512K	HD	$750
DEC PRO	FORTRAN	P/OS	256K	HD	$500

NUMBER OF CURRENT USERS 600
DATE OF FIRST RELEASE Jan 84
VERSION 5.1 RELEASED Aug 86

PROGRAM DESCRIPTION

Minitab is a general purpose analysis system, designed for anyone with data to organize and analyze. Emphasis is on ease of use for engineers, social and physical scientists, managers, educators, students, statisticians, and others who need to learn from data. It has 100% compatible interactive and batch modes. Minitab is also completely compatible among all supported processors . Data analysis features include: descriptive statistics; flexible plotting including histograms and other displays; multiway tables in a wide variety of layouts; regression with residual analysis; diagnostics and stepwise procedures; analysis of variance; nonparametric methods; exploratory data analysis including Box-Jenkins procedures. General features include: easy transformations and coding; automatic handling of missing values; data editing and manipulation; and input/output from terminals or files. Complete documentation is available in the Minitab Reference Manual, the Minitab Primer, the Minitab Handbook, the Quick Reference Card and through on-line HELP facility. Most Minitab sessions require just a few straight forward commands; new users need less than one hour of instruction to get started.

PRODUCT REVIEWS

Bryan, Marvin. "Business Forecasting", PC Magazine, pp. 218, (Aug 1986).

TYPE OF PROGRAM

Statistical Package

PROGRAM DESIGNED FOR

Data Analysis

PROGRAM STYLE

Command Driven
Integrated System

MISCELLANEOUS PROGRAM FEATURES

On Screen Help Function

DOCUMENTATION

User's Manual - 375 pages, 0 technical references
- Table of Contents
- Index
- Tutorial or Example Lessons
- Sample Runs
- Formulas Provided

Quick Reference Card
Primer
Handbook

DATA MANAGEMENT

Keyboard Data Entry
Data Manipulations and Transformations
Missing Values Allowed in Data

DATA EDITING

Change
Add
Delete

FOREIGN DATA ACCESS

Standard Rectangular ASCII Files
1-2-3 PRN Format

GRAPHICS FEATURES

Graphics can be Output to a Printer

GRAPHICS
- Histograms
- Scatter (x-y) Plots
- SEE EDA Plots
- Contour Plots

PRODUCT SUPPORT
- User may call at own Expense
- Classes or Instruction Available

STATISTICAL FEATURES SUPPORTED

DESCRIPTIVE STATISTICS
- Mean
- Standard Deviation or Variance
- Standard Error of the Mean
- Minimum, Maximum
- Median
- Quartiles

t-TESTS
- One Sample t-Test
- Independent Group t-Test/Equal Variance
- Independent Group t-Test/Unequal Var
- Paired t-Test

CORRELATION AND REGRESSION
- Pearson Correlation Coefficient
- Simple Linear Regression
- Multiple Linear Regression
- Stepwise Multiple Linear Regression
- Residuals Calculated
- Variance Inflation Factors
- Lack-of-Fit
- Leverage
- **REGRESSION PLOTS**
  - Residuals

CONFIDENCE INTERVALS
- Means
- Difference Between Two Means

CATEGORICAL DATA ANALYSIS
- Chi-Square Contingency Table Analysis
- Multi-Dimensional Tables
- Goodness-of-Fit Tests
- Frequencies Can be Entered Directly

ANALYSIS OF VARIANCE

- One-Way ANOVA
- Two-Way ANOVA
- Two-Way Unequal Cell Sizes Allowed
- Three-Way ANOVA

NONPARAMETRIC TESTS

- Sign Test (Signed Rank)
- Wilcoxon One Sample Test
- Mann-Whitney U
- Kruskal-Wallis Test
- Spearman or Kendall Correlation

DISTRIBUTION FUNCTION EVALUATION

- Normal
- t
- Chi Square
- F
- Binomial
- Poisson
- Exponential
- Beta
- Gamma
- Log Normal
- LaPlace
- Logistic
- Weibull
- Uniform
- Integer
- Bernoulli

EXPLORATORY DATA ANALYSIS

- Stem-and-Leaf Displays
- Letter-Value Displays
- Resistant Line
- Smoothing Techniques
- Median Polish
- Rootograms

TIME SERIES ANALYSIS

- Autocorrelations
- Cross Correlations
- AUTOREGRESSIVE MOVING AVERAGE
  - Model Identification
  - Parameter Estimation
- **TIME SERIES ANALYSIS - FORECASTING**
  - ARIMA

MISCELLANEOUS

Random Number Generation
Test for Normality of Data
p-Values Given With Tests
Macro Capabilities

MINITAB/1-2-3 & MULTIPLAN INTERFACE

Minitab, Inc.
3081 Enterprise Drive
State College, PA 16801
(814) 238 - 3280
Contact Person: Cheryl Ferrin

CONFIGURATIONS SUPPORTED

Computer	Language	Operating System	RAM	Number Drives	Cost
IBM PC		DOS	320K	HD	
VICTOR		DOS	384K	HD	
FORTUNE		FOR:PRO	512K	HD	
DEC PRO		P/OS	256K	HD	

NUMBER OF CURRENT USERS 100
DATE OF FIRST RELEASE May 85
VERSION 2.1 RELEASED Fall 86

ADDITIONAL SOFTWARE REQUIRED

Symphony
Lotus 1-2-3
Minitab Data Analysis Software

PROGRAM DESCRIPTION

The Minitab/1-2-3 Interface is a stand-alone product allowing the user to directly translate Lotus 1-2-3 or Symphony worksheets into Minitab saved format or Minitab worksheets into 1-2-3 or Symphony worksheet format. All data is translated regardless of format. In addition, formula cells, ERR, missing values, and Minitab column names and constants are supported. This easy conversion allows users to combine the statistical and graphing capabilities of the Minitab packages with the entering, editing, reporting, and graphing capabilities of 1-2-3 and Symphony. The Minitab/Multiplan Interface is used with Minitab on the Fortune 32:16 microcomputer, enabling Minitab to read and write data files in the 'symbolic' format used by Multiplan. Price is $30 for the Minitab/1-2-3 Interface and $100 for the Minitab/Multiplan Interface.

For information regarding program features, capabilities, statistical procedures, please refer to Minitab Data Analysis Software description. The Interface packages are used in conjunction with the Data Analysis Software.

TYPE OF PROGRAM
UNKNOWN

PROGRAM DESIGNED FOR
UNKNOWN

PROGRAM STYLE
Separate Programs for each Procedure

PRODUCT SUPPORT
User may call at own Expense
Classes or Instruction Available

MIPSAQ

Center for Statistics, QC and Design
SUNY - Binghamton
Binghamton, NY 13901
(607) 777 - 2619
Contact Person: Ellen Tattenbaum

CONFIGURATIONS SUPPORTED

Computer	Language	Operating System	RAM	Number Drives	Cost
IBM PC	TURBO PASCAL	DOS	256K	1	$ 100

NUMBER OF CURRENT USERS 350
DATE OF FIRST RELEASE Jan 84
VERSION 5.01 RELEASED Sept 86

PROGRAM DESCRIPTION

MIPSAQ is an interactive statistical package for the microcomputer similar to the mainframe package MINITAB. It is capable of data manipulation and editing, simple statistical and graphical analysis of moderate-sized datasets, simulation of data from various distributions, and control charting. Originally developed as a teaching tool for an industrial statistical quality control workshop, MIPSAQ is extremely well suited for educational uses.

With its free-format command structure, column-based manipulations and extensive help facilities, MIPSAQ is an extremely flexible, easy to use package. It has undergone thousands of hours of user testing.

TYPE OF PROGRAM
Statistical Package

PROGRAM DESIGNED FOR
Educational use

PROGRAM STYLE
Command Driven
Integrated System

MISCELLANEOUS PROGRAM FEATURES
Copyable Disk
On Screen Help Function

DOCUMENTATION
User's Manual - 0 pages, 0 technical references
Table of Contents
Index
Tutorial or Example Lessons
Sample Runs
Formulas Provided
Tutorials and Examples on Disk

DATA MANAGEMENT
Keyboard Data Entry
Data Manipulations and Transformations
Missing Values Allowed in Data

DATA EDITING
Change
Add
Delete

GRAPHICS FEATURES
Graphics Appear in Color on the Monitor
Graphics can be Output to a Printer
Titles and/or Labels Available
Uses Pixel Graphics
Uses Character Graphics

GRAPHICS
Histograms
Scatter (x-y) Plots
Multiple Plots
Control Charts

PRODUCT SUPPORT
User may call at own Expense
No Classes or Instruction Available

STATISTICAL FEATURES SUPPORTED

DESCRIPTIVE STATISTICS
- Mean
- Standard Deviation or Variance
- Minimum, Maximum
- Median

t-TESTS
- One Sample t-Test

CORRELATION AND REGRESSION
- Pearson Correlation Coefficient
- Simple Linear Regression
- Residuals Calculated
- Prediction

CONFIDENCE INTERVALS
- Means

CATEGORICAL DATA ANALYSIS
- Goodness-of-Fit Tests

ANALYSIS OF VARIANCE
- One-Way ANOVA

NONPARAMETRIC TESTS
- Runs Tests

DISTRIBUTION FUNCTION EVALUATION
- Normal

EXPLORATORY DATA ANALYSIS
- Stem-and-Leaf Displays
- Letter-Value Displays

CONTROL CHARTS
- X-Bar
- s

MISCELLANEOUS
- Random Number Generation
- Test for Normality of Data
- p-Values Given With Tests
- One-Sample Z-Test
- Can Use Computer as Calculator
- Frequency Distribution

MLR

Morgan Computing Company, Inc.
2520 Tarpley Road- Suite 500
Carrollton, TX 75006
(214) 245 - 4763
Contact Person: Charles Kroboth

CONFIGURATIONS SUPPORTED

Computer	Language	Operating System	RAM	Number Drives	Cost
IBM PC	COMPILED	DOS	128K	1	$ 100

NUMBER OF CURRENT USERS 100
DATE OF FIRST RELEASE Aug 83
CURRENT VERSION RELEASED ?

PROGRAM DESCRIPTION

MLR(tm) is a program written for the IBM PC which solves the classical multiple linear regression problem. It incorporates several features which allow for quick, easy entry and editing of problem observation sets. It is a menu driven program written in compiled BASIC and requires a computer with a minimum of 128K of RAM memory.

MLR allows the user to enter up to 999 observations for 9 independent variables. Each variable can be named and that name is used in output reports. A subset of the observations set can be selected and the regression statistics calculated based just on that designated subset. Data from any source can be used in MLR. Output includes the estimates for each independent variable coefficient, t statistic for each coefficient, rsquare, variances of the dependent variable and F ratio.

TYPE OF PROGRAM

Statistical Package

PROGRAM DESIGNED FOR

Data Analysis

PROGRAM STYLE
Menu Driven
Integrated System

DOCUMENTATION
User's Manual - 20 pages, 10 technical references
Table of Contents
Index
Tutorial or Example Lessons
Sample Runs
Formulas Provided
Tutorials and Examples on Disk

DATA MANAGEMENT
Keyboard Data Entry

DATA EDITING
Change
Add
Delete

FOREIGN DATA ACCESS
Standard Rectangular ASCII Files

PRODUCT SUPPORT
No Classes or Instruction Available

STATISTICAL FEATURES SUPPORTED

CORRELATION AND REGRESSION
Multiple Linear Regression

MODISTAT

Modicom Ltd.
241 Victoria Rd., Alexandra Palace
London, ENGLAND N22 4XH
01 (888) - 4946
Contact Person: Michael Smith

CONFIGURATIONS SUPPORTED

Computer	Language	Operating System	RAM	Number Drives	Cost
IBM PC	BASIC	DOS	256K	2	$275
DEC	BASIC	DOS	256K	2	$275
APRICOT	BASIC	DOS	256K	2	$275
VICTOR 9000	BASIC	DOS	256K	2	$275

NUMBER OF CURRENT USERS 2000+
DATE OF FIRST RELEASE Jan 84
CURRENT VERSION RELEASED Jan 84

PROGRAM DESCRIPTION

MODISTAT is a comprehensive and multi-purpose interactive statistics package, designed for anyone wishing to do data analysis who requires access to a wide range of fundamental statistical analyses. This program is suitable for the teaching or study of statistics in any discipline at university or college. It is likewise equally suitable for statistical applications in business, government, industry and research.

Using the most efficient algorithms and containing its own data base management system, MODISTAT offers flexibility, numerical stability and pixel graphics to the screen or a wide range of printers and plotters. MODISTAT can also pick up data from databases, spreadsheets, and data loggers for laboratory work.

TYPE OF PROGRAM

Statistical Package

PROGRAM DESIGNED FOR
Data Analysis
Educational use

PROGRAM STYLE
Menu Driven
Integrated System

MISCELLANEOUS PROGRAM FEATURES
Copyable Disk
On Screen Help Function

DOCUMENTATION
User's Manual - 150 pages, 3 technical references
Table of Contents
Index
Tutorial or Example Lessons
Sample Runs
Formulas Provided
Tutorials and Examples on Disk

DATA MANAGEMENT
Keyboard Data Entry
Data Manipulations and Transformations
Missing Values Allowed in Data

DATA EDITING
Change
Add
Delete

FOREIGN DATA ACCESS
Standard Rectangular ASCII Files
DIF Files
dBase II Files

GRAPHICS FEATURES
Graphics Appear in Color on the Monitor
Graphics can be Output to a Printer
Titles and/or Labels Available
Uses Pixel Graphics

GRAPHICS
- Histograms
- Pie Charts
- Scatter (x-y) Plots
- Box Plots
- User Defined Functions
- SEE Time Series Plots
- SEE EDA Plots

PRODUCT SUPPORT
- User may call at own Expense
- No Classes or Instruction Available

STATISTICAL FEATURES SUPPORTED

DESCRIPTIVE STATISTICS
- Mean
- Standard Deviation or Variance
- Minimum, Maximum
- Median
- Range

t-TESTS
- One Sample t-Test
- Independent Group t-Test/Equal Variance
- Independent Group t-Test/Unequal Var
- Paired t-Test

CORRELATION AND REGRESSION
- Pearson Correlation Coefficient
- Simple Linear Regression
- Multiple Linear Regression
- Residuals Calculated
- Estimate Asymptotic Standard Errors
- Weighted Regression
- Through Origin

CATEGORICAL DATA ANALYSIS
- Chi-Square Contingency Table Analysis

ANALYSIS OF VARIANCE
- One-Way ANOVA
- One-Way with Repeated Measures
- Two-Way ANOVA
- Analysis of Covariance
- Crossed Designs - Balanced
- Crossed Designs - Unbalanced

NONPARAMETRIC TESTS

- Wilcoxon One Sample Test
- Mann-Whitney U
- Kruskal-Wallis Test
- Friedman Chi-Square Test
- Spearman or Kendall Correlation

DISTRIBUTION FUNCTION EVALUATION

- Normal
- t
- Chi Square
- F
- Binomial
- Poisson

EXPLORATORY DATA ANALYSIS

- Stem-and-Leaf Displays
- Box Plots

TIME SERIES ANALYSIS

- Autocorrelations
- **TIME SERIES ANALYSIS - PLOTS**
    - Correlogram
    - Exponential Smoothing

CONTROL CHARTS

- X-Bar
- s
- CuSum Chart

MODULAR STATISTICAL SYSTEM

Persimmon Software
910 Memory Lane
Mobile, AL 36608
(205) 342 - 0341
Contact Person: Charles F. Cicciarella

CONFIGURATIONS SUPPORTED

Computer	Language	Operating System	RAM	Number Drives	Cost
IBM PC	BASIC	DOS	256K	2	$500

NUMBER OF CURRENT USERS ?
DATE OF FIRST RELEASE July 87
CURRENT VERSION RELEASED ?

PROGRAM DESCRIPTION

This is a system of statistical analysis modules which can be selected by the purchaser to construct a statistical analysis package tailored to specific needs of the user.

The most unique feature of this product is its modularity which permits the user to buy only those forms of analysis that are needed and then add modules as needs change. These modules can be purchased for $19.95 each.

TYPE OF PROGRAM
Statistical Package

PROGRAM DESIGNED FOR
Data Analysis

PROGRAM STYLE
Menu Driven
Command Driven
Integrated System

MISCELLANEOUS PROGRAM FEATURES
Copyable Disk
On Screen Help Function

DOCUMENTATION
User's Manual - ? pages, ? technical references

DATA MANAGEMENT
Keyboard Data Entry
Data Manipulations and Transformations
Missing Values Allowed in Data

DATA EDITING
Change
Add
Delete

FOREIGN DATA ACCESS
Standard Rectangular ASCII Files

PRODUCT SUPPORT
User may call at own Expense
No Classes or Instruction Available

MPSS

Functional Solutions, Inc
235 Bleecker St.
Utica, NY 13501
(315) 735 - 6421
Contact Person: Deby LaGrand

CONFIGURATIONS SUPPORTED

Computer	Language	Operating System	RAM	Number Drives	Cost
IBM PC	PASCAL	P-SYSTEM	256K	2	$495
APPLE II	PASCAL	P-SYSTEM	128K	2	$495
ALPHA	PASCAL	AMOS .	64K	HD	$995

NUMBER OF CURRENT USERS 30
DATE OF FIRST RELEASE Jan 85
VERSION 1.02 RELEASED July 86

PROGRAM DESCRIPTION

Munger Pascal Statistical System (MPSS) is a comprehensive system of computer programs created for the analysis of data. The system is menu-driven to promote easy access to the data analysis programs. MPSS is a robust statistical tool kit that contains flexible routines for data and file manipulation, and offers the researcher a wide variety of parametric and nonparametric statistical routines. The program is primarily for researchers, professionals in the medical fields, and large institutions which need a 'number-crunching' statistical package.

MPSS has been designed to be as easy to use as possible, and thus is easily accessible to users with little or no computer experience; yet its routines are varied and sophisticated enough to appeal to any professional.

TYPE OF PROGRAM

Statistical Package

PROGRAM DESIGNED FOR

Data Analysis

PROGRAM STYLE
- Menu Driven
- Integrated System

MISCELLANEOUS PROGRAM FEATURES
- Copyable Disk

DOCUMENTATION
- User's Manual - 250 pages, 17 technical references
  - Table of Contents
  - Index
  - Tutorial or Example Lessons

DATA MANAGEMENT
- Keyboard Data Entry
- Data Manipulations and Transformations
- Missing Values Allowed in Data

DATA EDITING
- Change
- Add
- Delete

FOREIGN DATA ACCESS
- Standard Rectangular ASCII Files
- Lotus 1-2-3 Files

GRAPHICS FEATURES
- Graphics can be Output to a Printer
- Graphics can be Saved to a File
- Titles and/or Labels Available
- Uses Character Graphics

GRAPHICS
- Histograms
- Scatter (x-y) Plots
- Dendrograms
- Factor Plots

PRODUCT SUPPORT
- User may call at own Expense
- No Classes or Instruction Available

STATISTICAL FEATURES SUPPORTED

DESCRIPTIVE STATISTICS
- Mean
- Standard Deviation or Variance
- Standard Error of the Mean
- Coefficient of Variation
- Minimum, Maximum
- Median
- Skewness
- Kurtosis

t-TESTS
- One Sample t-Test
- Independent Group t-Test/Equal Variance
- Paired t-Test

CORRELATION AND REGRESSION
- Pearson Correlation Coefficient
- Simple Linear Regression
- Multiple Linear Regression
- Stepwise Multiple Linear Regression
- Residuals Calculated
- **REGRESSION PLOTS**
  - Residuals

CONFIDENCE INTERVALS
- Means
- Difference Between Two Means

CATEGORICAL DATA ANALYSIS
- Chi-Square Contingency Table Analysis
- Multi-Dimensional Tables
- Fisher's Exact Test
- Goodness-of-Fit Tests

ANALYSIS OF VARIANCE
- One-Way ANOVA
- Two-Way ANOVA
- Two-Way Unequal Cell Sizes Allowed
- Analysis of Covariance
- Repeated Measures for Split Plot/Nested
- MANOVA
- **MULTIPLE COMPARISONS**
  - Scheffe
  - LSD
  - Modified LSD

NONPARAMETRIC TESTS

Mann-Whitney U
Kruskal-Wallis Test
Friedman Chi-Square Test
Spearman or Kendall Correlation
Wald-Wolfowitz Runs
Kolmogorov-Smirnov

DISTRIBUTION FUNCTION EVALUATION

Normal
t
Chi Square
F
Binomial
Poisson

EXPLORATORY DATA ANALYSIS

Dendrograms

TIME SERIES ANALYSIS

Autocorrelations
Moving Average Smoothing
AUTOREGRESSIVE MOVING AVERAGE
Parameter Estimation

MISCELLANEOUS

Cluster Analysis
Linear Discriminant Function Calculation
p-Values Given With Tests

MSUSTAT

Research and Development Institute Inc
Montana State University:Attn RE Lund
Boseman, MT 59717-0002
(406) 994 - 3271
Contact Person: Richard E Lund

CONFIGURATIONS SUPPORTED

Computer	Language	Operating System	RAM	Number Drives	Cost
IBM PC	FORTRAN	DOS	256K	2	$ 193

NUMBER OF CURRENT USERS 700
DATE OF FIRST RELEASE Jan 84
VERSION 3.2 RELEASED Sept 86

PROGRAM DESCRIPTION

MSUSTAT offers 40 general purpose statistical procedures used frequently by scientists and appearing in most intermediate level statistical methods texts. The computational code has been user tested through 8 years of mainframe use (micro version 4 years) in both the classroom and for research data analysis at Montana State University. Program design emphasizes the simplicity of control demanded by the beginner, but includes many features demanded by the advanced data analyst. Programs are fast compiled Fortran giving main-frame accuracy. Only ready-to-run units are distributed; no compiler is needed.

Control simplicity is achieved by use of a question-answer format. Prompt lines include potential responses and parameter limits. A user can always respond HELP to obtain additional explanation. Incorrect responses lead to display of assistance messages, followed by re-display of the prompt. No-entry defaults frequently control the program correctly for the simpler more standard problems. Consequently the new user can operate MSUSTAT successfully with almost no reference to the user's manual by stepping through slowly, reading all messages and prompt lines and requesting additional help as needed. The defaults and brevity of needed control-input also fulfills the needs of the experienced user for a quick "few-frills" analysis.

PRODUCT REVIEWS

Foxwell, Harry. "MSUSTAT", Capital PC Monitor, (June 1984).

Marasinghi, Mervyn G.. "MSUSTAT, MS/PC-DOS and CP/M-80 Version 2.20", American Statistician, Vol 39, pp. 72-74, (Feb 1985).

Isitt, John. "MSUSTAT - An Interactive Package", Computational Statistics and Data Analysis, Vol 2, pp. 331-336, (Feb 1985).

Mauriello, David. "MSUSTAT", Science Software Quarterly, Vol 1, pp. 51-56, (Fall 1984).

TYPE OF PROGRAM

Statistical Package

PROGRAM DESIGNED FOR

Data Analysis
Educational use

PROGRAM STYLE

Menu Driven
Integrated System

MISCELLANEOUS PROGRAM FEATURES

Copyable Disk
On Screen Help Function
Supports 8087 Mathematical Chip

DOCUMENTATION

User's Manual - 200 pages, 36 technical references
- Table of Contents
- Index
- Tutorial or Example Lessons
- Sample Runs
- Formulas Provided

Tutorials and Examples on Disk

DATA MANAGEMENT

Keyboard Data Entry
Data Manipulations and Transformations
Missing Values Allowed in Data

FOREIGN DATA ACCESS

Standard Rectangular ASCII Files

GRAPHICS FEATURES

Graphics can be Output to a Printer
Graphics can be Saved to a File
Titles and/or Labels Available

GRAPHICS

Histograms
Scatter (x-y) Plots
Normal Distribution Plot

PRODUCT SUPPORT

No Classes or Instruction Available

STATISTICAL FEATURES SUPPORTED

DESCRIPTIVE STATISTICS

Mean
Standard Deviation or Variance
Standard Error of the Mean
Minimum, Maximum
Median
Skewness
Kurtosis

t-TESTS

One Sample t-Test
Independent Group t-Test/Equal Variance
Paired t-Test
Multivariate T-square (Hotelling's)

CORRELATION AND REGRESSION

Pearson Correlation Coefficient
Simple Linear Regression
Multiple Linear Regression
Stepwise Multiple Linear Regression
Residuals Calculated
Estimate Asymptotic Standard Errors

CONFIDENCE INTERVALS

Means
Difference Between Two Means

CATEGORICAL DATA ANALYSIS

Chi-Square Contingency Table Analysis
Multi-Dimensional Tables
Fisher's Exact Test
Frequencies Can be Entered Directly

ANALYSIS OF VARIANCE
- One-Way ANOVA
- One-Way with Repeated Measures
- Two-Way ANOVA
- Two-Way Unequal Cell Sizes Allowed
- Analysis of Covariance
- Three-Way ANOVA
- Four-Way ANOVA
- MANOVA
- Lattice Designs
- Multiple Comparisons and Contrasts

NONPARAMETRIC TESTS
- Sign Test (Signed Rank)
- Wilcoxon One Sample Test
- Mann-Whitney U
- Kruskal-Wallis Test
- Friedman Chi-Square Test
- Spearman or Kendall Correlation
- Nonparametric Confidence Intervals

DISTRIBUTION FUNCTION EVALUATION
- Normal
- t
- Chi Square
- F
- Binomial
- Hypergeometric
- Beta
- Non-central F
- Studentized Range

MISCELLANEOUS
- Random Number Generation
- Linear Discriminant Function Calculation
- p-Values Given With Tests

MTS

Automatic Forecasting Systems Inc.
P. O. Box 563
Hatboro, PA 19040
(215) 675 - 0652
Contact Person: David P. Reilly

CONFIGURATIONS SUPPORTED

Computer	Language	Operating System	RAM	Number Drives	Cost
IBM PC	FORTRAN	DOS	320K	2	$995

NUMBER OF CURRENT USERS 10
DATE OF FIRST RELEASE Jan 86
CURRENT VERSION RELEASED Mar 86

PROGRAM DESCRIPTION

AFS'S products for time series analysis were designed to meet all of your software needs pertaining to Box-Jenkins or ARIMA model building. MTS is a valuable, time-efficient forecasting tool when you don't have time to build structural models or when you have to produce forecasts of many items. If you are new to Vector ARIMA modeling, you can use MTS not only in generating forecasts quickly, but also as a computer-assisted learning device to further your understanding of the modeling process. MTS is a program that can be used for building models either automatically or not.

* Complete vector ARIMA modeling.
* Includes both automatic and non-automatic modeling.
* Some of the advanced modeling features included are: (all are optional)
  1) Exogenous Time Series Variables may be Included
  2) Automatic Model Stepdown
  3) Extended Matrix Method of Estimation

TYPE OF PROGRAM

Statistical Package

PROGRAM DESIGNED FOR
Data Analysis
Educational use

PROGRAM STYLE
Menu Driven
Integrated System

MISCELLANEOUS PROGRAM FEATURES
On Screen Help Function
Supports 8087 Mathematical Chip

DOCUMENTATION
User's Manual - 80 pages, 3 technical references
Table of Contents
Index
Tutorial or Example Lessons
Sample Runs
Formulas Provided
Tutorials and Examples on Disk

DATA MANAGEMENT
Keyboard Data Entry
Data Manipulations and Transformations

DATA EDITING
Change
Add
Delete

FOREIGN DATA ACCESS
Standard Rectangular ASCII Files
DIF Files
Multiple Records Per ASCII File

GRAPHICS FEATURES
Graphics can be Output to a Printer
Graphics can be Saved to a File
Titles and/or Labels Available

GRAPHICS
Scatter (x-y) Plots
SEE Time Series Plots

PRODUCT SUPPORT
User may call at own Expense
Classes or Instruction Available

STATISTICAL FEATURES SUPPORTED

TIME SERIES ANALYSIS
- Autocorrelations
- Cross Correlations
- AUTOREGRESSIVE MOVING AVERAGE
  - Model Identification
  - Parameter Estimation
- Transfer Function Models
- Intervention Models
- Vector ARIMA
- **TIME SERIES ANALYSIS - FORECASTING**
  - Non-linear Least Squares
- **TIME SERIES ANALYSIS - PLOTS**
  - Autocorrelations
  - Partial Autocorrelations
  - Original Data
  - Residuals
  - Forecasts
  - Cross Correlation

MISCELLANEOUS
- Test for Normality of Data

MULTIPLE FACTOR ANALYSIS
Mathematical Software Co.
P.O. Box 12349
El Cajon, CA 92022
(619) 940 - 0343
Contact Person: Dr. Allan Easton

CONFIGURATIONS SUPPORTED

Computer	Language	Operating System	RAM	Number Drives	Cost
APPLE II	COMPILED BASIC		48K	2	$50
IBM PC	COMPILED BASIC		64K	2	$50

NUMBER OF CURRENT USERS ?
DATE OF FIRST RELEASE 1982
VERSION 2.0 RELEASED ?

PROGRAM DESCRIPTION

MULTIPLE FACTOR ANALYSIS accepts three types of data: (1) primary data, (2) intercorrelation matrices, and (3) matrices of factor loadings. Thus, the user can factor analyze new primary data generated from multiple-variable measurements on many subjects. The user can factor analyse intercorrelation matrices reported in journal articles. Alternatively, the user can try different rotational schemes on his/her own data or on those created by other researchers. In general, MFA can help make sense of multiple measurements made on a multiplicity of subjects (objects). Primary data can be entered either by variable (column order) or by case (row order).

Also available is SON OF MULTIPLE FACTOR ANALYSIS. As its name implies, SOMFA is a companion program that extends the capabilities of the MULTIPLE FACTOR ANALYSIS software. SOMFA picks up where the typical multiple factor analytic study stops. The input to a typical factor analysis is a battery of measurements on M variables for N test subjects. The output is a matrix of properly rotated factor-loadings plus M communalities that reveal the variances of the M variables in the common-factor space.

TYPE OF PROGRAM
Statistical Package

PROGRAM DESIGNED FOR
Data Analysis

PROGRAM STYLE
Menu Driven
Integrated System

MISCELLANEOUS PROGRAM FEATURES
Source Code Available
Copyable Disk
On Screen Help Function
Optional Support for 8087 on IBM PC Mathematical Chip

DOCUMENTATION
User's Manual - 50+ pages, ? technical references
Table of Contents
Tutorial or Example Lessons
Tutorials and Examples on Disk

DATA MANAGEMENT
Keyboard Data Entry
Data Manipulations and Transformations

DATA EDITING
Change
Add
Delete

FOREIGN DATA ACCESS
Standard Rectangular ASCII Files

GRAPHICS FEATURES
Graphics can be Output to a Printer
Uses Pixel Graphics

GRAPHICS
Scatter (x-y) Plots
Factor Loading Patterns Pair-by-Pair

PRODUCT SUPPORT
User may call at own Expense
No Classes or Instruction Available

STATISTICAL FEATURES SUPPORTED

DESCRIPTIVE STATISTICS

Mean
Standard Deviation or Variance
Standard Error of the Mean

CORRELATION AND REGRESSION

Pearson Correlation Coefficient

MISCELLANEOUS

Factor Analysis

N

IDV Datenanalyse und Versuchsplanung
Wessobrunner Str. 6
8035 Gauting, W. GERMANY
(089) 850 - 8001
Contact Person: Dr. V. W. Rahlfs

CONFIGURATIONS SUPPORTED

Computer	Language	Operating System	RAM	Number Drives	Cost
IBM PC	FORTRAN/ C	DOS	320K	1	$450

NUMBER OF CURRENT USERS 140
DATE OF FIRST RELEASE Nov 86
VERSION 1.3 RELEASED April 87

PROGRAM DESCRIPTION

Since February 1987 the version No. 1.3 of the program "N" for microcomputers is available from the software house IDV, Institut fur Datenanalyse und Versuchsplanung. "N" is a management and research tool for the planning and intrepretation of scientific studies involving sample size calculations. With this software package the following questions may be answered, provided that all other input has been defined: Number of cases required for a study, smallest difference, alpha error and beta error. Three study situations have been implemented: Comparison of a sample with a fixed constant, comparison of two correlated samples (e.g. pre-post design) and the comparison of two uncorrelated samples (parallel group design). The program handles the two well-known data types: Event data (binomial test situation) and quantitative data (t-test situation). In addition to tests for differences, all procedures include tests for equivalence (bioequivalence) according to E.L. Lehmann or Patel and Gupta. Admitted are, of course, one-sided and two-sided alternative hypotheses as well as unbalanced group sizes in parallel group designs.

If desired, the user can obtain values of the operation characteristics (OC) wherever this makes sense. A special file can be generated which allows instant plotting of the OC curve by means of the program Graph-in-the-Box (or any other program). It should be pointed out that the program is based largely on exact algorithms which e.g. involve the use of the non-central t-distribution and its inverse in the case of the t-test situation. Of course, the program is user friendly in the following sense: The menus for asking questions have been designed according to the principles of gestalt-psychology, for each input or output field there are two possibilities of help: "help" for program use, and "info" for program content. There is ample use of function/special keys and modern window technique. Both the program and the documentation are available in German and English language.

TYPE OF PROGRAM
Sample Size Calculation

PROGRAM DESIGNED FOR
Data Analysis

PROGRAM STYLE
Menu Driven
Integrated System

MISCELLANEOUS PROGRAM FEATURES
Copyable Disk
On Screen Help Function

DOCUMENTATION
User's Manual - 200 pages, ? technical references
Table of Contents
Tutorial or Example Lessons
Formulas Provided
Program Validation

DATA MANAGEMENT
Keyboard Data Entry

PRODUCT SUPPORT
User may call at own Expense
Classes or Instruction Available

STATISTICAL FEATURES SUPPORTED

MISCELLANEOUS

Sample Size Estimation

NORMAL PROBABILITY PLOTTING

Technical and Engineering for Management
Box 25
Tamworth, NH 03886
(603) 323 - 8843
Contact Person: James R. King

CONFIGURATIONS SUPPORTED

Computer	Language	Operating System	RAM	Number Drives	Cost
APPLE II	APPLESOFT	PROPRIETAR	64k	2	$ 240
OSBORNE	MS-BASIC	CP/M	64K	2	$ 240
IBM	BASIC	DOS	64K	2	$ 240

NUMBER OF CURRENT USERS 12
DATE OF FIRST RELEASE July 83
VERSION 1.5 RELEASED July 85

ADDITIONAL SOFTWARE REQUIRED
MBASIC

PROGRAM DESCRIPTION

Normal Probability Plotting is a dedicated mini-expert system program for all data analysts. It converts data sets up to n-100 into normal probability plots, fits a regression line and confidence limits, tests for data randomness, calculates standard statistical parameters, and calculates and tests residuals.

This program offers the following features and options: 1. Choice of normal or log-normal distribution. 2. Choice of generalized least squares or Ferrell's median regression. 3. Six different confidence levels. 4. Allows simple visual test of the normality assumption. 5. Automatic test for randomness of the data set. 6. Choice of computing residuals for regression diagnostics.

TYPE OF PROGRAM
Regression Analysis

PROGRAM DESIGNED FOR
Data Analysis

PROGRAM STYLE
Menu Driven
Integrated System

MISCELLANEOUS PROGRAM FEATURES
Source Code Available
Copyable Disk

DOCUMENTATION
User's Manual - 96 pages, 52 technical references
Table of Contents
Index
Tutorial or Example Lessons
Sample Runs

DATA MANAGEMENT
Keyboard Data Entry

DATA EDITING
Change
Add
Delete

FOREIGN DATA ACCESS
Standard Rectangular ASCII Files

GRAPHICS FEATURES
Graphics can be Output to a Printer
Graphics can be Saved to a File
Uses Character Graphics

GRAPHICS
Scatter (x-y) Plots
SEE Regression Plots

PRODUCT SUPPORT
User may call at own Expense
Classes or Instruction Available

STATISTICAL FEATURES SUPPORTED

DESCRIPTIVE STATISTICS
- Mean
- Standard Deviation or Variance
- Standard Error of the Mean

CORRELATION AND REGRESSION
- Simple Linear Regression
- Residuals Calculated
- **REGRESSION PLOTS**
  - Residuals

CONFIDENCE INTERVALS
- Means
- Regression Line

DISTRIBUTION FUNCTION EVALUATION
- Normal

MISCELLANEOUS
- Test for Normality of Data
- Test for Randomness

NTSYS-PC
Applied Biostatistics
3 Heritage Lane
Setauket, NY 11733
(516) 751 - 1203
Contact Person: F. James Rohlf

CONFIGURATIONS SUPPORTED

Computer	Language	Operating System	RAM	Number Drives	Cost
IBM PC	PASCAL	DOS	256K	1	$90

NUMBER OF CURRENT USERS New
DATE OF FIRST RELEASE Oct 86
VERSION 1 RELEASED Oct 86

PROGRAM DESCRIPTION
None Given

TYPE OF PROGRAM
Multivariate Analysis

PROGRAM DESIGNED FOR
Data Analysis
Educational use

PROGRAM STYLE
Menu Driven
Integrated System

MISCELLANEOUS PROGRAM FEATURES
Copyable Disk
On Screen Help Function
Optional Support for 8087, 80287 Mathematical Chip

DOCUMENTATION
User's Manual - ? pages, ? technical references
Table of Contents
Tutorial or Example Lessons
Sample Runs
Tutorials and Examples on Disk

DATA MANAGEMENT
Keyboard Data Entry
Missing Values Allowed in Data

FOREIGN DATA ACCESS
Standard Rectangular ASCII Files

GRAPHICS FEATURES
Graphics Appear in Color on the Monitor
Graphics can be Output to a Printer
Graphics can be Saved to a File
Uses Pixel Graphics
Uses Character Graphics

GRAPHICS
Scatter (x-y) Plots
3-D Plotting
Cladograms
Phenograms

PRODUCT SUPPORT
User may call at own Expense
No Classes or Instruction Available

STATISTICAL FEATURES SUPPORTED

DESCRIPTIVE STATISTICS
Mean
Standard Deviation or Variance
Minimum, Maximum

MISCELLANEOUS
Cluster Analysis
Minimum Spanning Tree
Principal Coordinates Analysis
Principal Components Analysis

NUMBER CRUNCHER STATISTICAL SYSTEM

NCSS
865 East 400 North
Kaysville, UT 84037
(801) 546 - 0445
Contact Person: Dr Jerry L Hintze

CONFIGURATIONS SUPPORTED

Computer	Language	Operating System	RAM	Number Drives	Cost
IBM PC	OBJECT	DOS	256K	2	$79
MACINTOSH	BASIC	MAC	512K	2	$79

NUMBER OF CURRENT USERS 3000+
DATE OF FIRST RELEASE 1980
VERSION 4.21 RELEASED Aug 86

PROGRAM DESCRIPTION

NCSS is an integrated statistical analysis system designed for students, teachers and professionals who desire a menu-driven system to complete various statistical and data analyses on microcomputers. The system is easy to use and accurate.

The NCSS system includes a wide variety of statistical and data analytic tools. This means that data may be entered, transformed, and analyzed in several ways. It has its own spread sheet for easy data handling. Data may be imported from other programs.

PRODUCT REVIEWS

BYTE, (April 1984).

American Statistician, (Nov 1985).

TYPE OF PROGRAM

Statistical Package

PROGRAM DESIGNED FOR
Data Analysis

PROGRAM STYLE
Menu Driven
Integrated System

MISCELLANEOUS PROGRAM FEATURES
Source Code Available
Copyable Disk

DOCUMENTATION
User's Manual - 250 pages, 50 technical references
Index
Tutorial or Example Lessons
Sample Runs
Formulas Provided
Tutorials and Examples on Disk

DATA MANAGEMENT
Keyboard Data Entry
Data Manipulations and Transformations
Missing Values Allowed in Data

DATA EDITING
Change
Add
Delete

FOREIGN DATA ACCESS
Standard ASCII Files

GRAPHICS FEATURES
Graphics Appear in Color on the Monitor
Graphics can be Output to a Printer
Graphics can be Saved to a File
Titles and/or Labels Available
Uses Pixel Graphics

GRAPHICS
Histograms
Scatter (x-y) Plots
Box Plots
Control Charts
Stem-Leaf

PRODUCT SUPPORT
User may call at own Expense
No Classes or Instruction Available

STATISTICAL FEATURES SUPPORTED

DESCRIPTIVE STATISTICS

Mean
Standard Deviation or Variance
Standard Error of the Mean
Coefficient of Variation
Minimum, Maximum
Median
Percentiles
Skewness
Kurtosis

t-TESTS

One Sample t-Test
Independent Group t-Test/Equal Variance
Independent Group t-Test/Unequal Var
Paired t-Test

CORRELATION AND REGRESSION

Pearson Correlation Coefficient
Simple Linear Regression
Multiple Linear Regression
Stepwise Multiple Linear Regression
Residuals Calculated
Estimate Asymptotic Standard Errors
Durbin-Watson
Robust Regression
Partial Correlation
Adjusted R-squared
Press

CONFIDENCE INTERVALS

Means
Regression Coefficients

CATEGORICAL DATA ANALYSIS

Chi-Square Contingency Table Analysis
Frequencies Can be Entered Directly

ANALYSIS OF VARIANCE
- One-Way ANOVA
- One-Way with Repeated Measures
- Two-Way ANOVA
- Two-Way Unequal Cell Sizes Allowed
- Analysis of Covariance
- Four-Way ANOVA
- **MULTIPLE COMPARISONS**
  - Fisher's LSD
  - User Defined Comparisons
  - Duncan's Multiple Range
  - Newman-Keuls

NONPARAMETRIC TESTS
- Sign Test (Signed Rank)
- Wilcoxon One Sample Test
- Mann-Whitney U
- Kruskal-Wallis Test
- Friedman Chi-Square Test
- Spearman or Kendall Correlation
- Wald-Wolfowitz Runs Test
- Fisher's 2X2 Test

DISTRIBUTION FUNCTION EVALUATION
- Normal
- t
- Chi Square
- F
- Binomial
- Poisson
- Gamma
- Beta

EXPLORATORY DATA ANALYSIS
- Stem-and-Leaf Displays
- Smoothing Techniques

TIME SERIES ANALYSIS
- Autocorrelations
- Moving Average Smoothing
- **TIME SERIES ANALYSIS - FORECASTING**
  - Exponential Smoothing
  - Double Exponential Smoothing
  - Seasonal Decomposition

MISCELLANEOUS

- Cluster Analysis
- Linear Discriminant Function Calculation
- Principal Components Analysis
- Factor Analysis
- Spreadsheet Editing
- Copy/Paste Editing

NWA QUALITY ANALYST
Northwest Analytical, Inc.
520 NW Davis St.
Portland, OR 97209
(503) 224 - 7727
Contact Person: J. L. Cawley

CONFIGURATIONS SUPPORTED

Computer	Language	Operating System	RAM	Number Drives	Cost
IBM PC	BASIC	DOS	384K	2	$495
NCR Burroughs	BASIC	CTOS/BTOS	512K	2	$ 495
HP 150	BASIC	DOS	256K	2	$ 495

NUMBER OF CURRENT USERS 500
DATE OF FIRST RELEASE May 85
VERSION 2.1 RELEASED Jun 86

PROGRAM DESCRIPTION

NWA QUALITY ANALYST is a complete personal computer based system for statistical quality control. QUALITY ANALYST provides control charting, process capability analysis, general statistics, and data management. QUALITY ANALYST interfaces with other manufacturing software such as CAMM (CENTEC), Instrument systems (e.g. DATaMYTE), and data interface cards and software such as LABTEC NOTEBOOK (Laboratory Technologies).

QUALITY ANALYST is a modular program and can be configured to serve the needs of staff ranging from the process engineer to the machine operator. There are no upper limits on the number of points or subgroups that can be plotted on charts. QUALITY ANALYST offers a full complement of procedures for continuous process in addition to discrete manufacturing.

TYPE OF PROGRAM

Quality Control or Reliability

PROGRAM DESIGNED FOR
Data Analysis

PROGRAM STYLE
Menu Driven
Integrated System

MISCELLANEOUS PROGRAM FEATURES
Source Code Available
Copyable Disk

DOCUMENTATION
User's Manual - 350 pages, 15 technical references
Table of Contents
Index
Tutorial or Example Lessons
Sample Runs
Formulas Provided
Tutorials and Examples on Disk

DATA MANAGEMENT
Keyboard Data Entry
Data Manipulations and Transformations
Missing Values Allowed in Data

DATA EDITING
Change
Add
Delete

FOREIGN DATA ACCESS
Standard Rectangular ASCII Files
DIF Files
SYLK
Specialty Measuring Devices -DataMYTE

GRAPHICS FEATURES
Graphics Appear in Color on the Monitor
Graphics can be Output to a Printer
Graphics can be Saved to a File
Titles and/or Labels Available
Uses Pixel Graphics
Uses Character Graphics

GRAPHICS
- Histograms
- Scatter (x-y) Plots
- Process Capability
- Probability Plots
- Pareto Diagram
- Control Charts

PRODUCT SUPPORT
- User may call at own Expense
- No Classes or Instruction Available

STATISTICAL FEATURES SUPPORTED

DESCRIPTIVE STATISTICS
- Mean
- Standard Deviation or Variance
- Standard Error of the Mean
- Coefficient of Variation
- Minimum, Maximum
- Median
- Percentiles
- Skewness
- Kurtosis

t-TESTS
- One Sample t-Test
- Independent Group t-Test/Equal Variance
- Independent Group t-Test/Unequal Var
- Paired t-Test

CORRELATION AND REGRESSION
- Pearson Correlation Coefficient
- Simple Linear Regression
- Multiple Linear Regression
- Non-Linear Regression
- Residuals Calculated
- **REGRESSION PLOTS**
  - Residuals

CATEGORICAL DATA ANALYSIS
- Fisher's Exact Test
- Goodness-of-Fit Tests

ANALYSIS OF VARIANCE
- One-Way ANOVA

NONPARAMETRIC TESTS
- Wald-Wolfowitz

DISTRIBUTION FUNCTION EVALUATION

Binomial
Hypergeometric
Poisson
Negative Binomial

CONTROL CHARTS

X-Bar
s
Proportions
Number of Defects
Number of Defectives
R
CuSum Chart
p-Chart
Pareto Analysis
Process Capability
Moving Range
Moving Average
Individual Measures

MISCELLANEOUS

Random Number Generation

NWA STATPAK
Northwest Analytical Inc.
520 NW Davis St.
Portland, OR 97209
(503) 224 - 7727
Contact Person: J. L. Cawley

CONFIGURATIONS SUPPORTED

Computer	Language	Operating System	RAM	Number Drives	Cost
IBM PC	BASIC	DOS	384K	2	$495
NCR Burroughs	BASIC	CTOS/BTOS	512K	2	$495
HP 150	BASIC	DOS	256K	2	$495

NUMBER OF CURRENT USERS 13,500
DATE OF FIRST RELEASE Mar 80
VERSION 4.1 RELEASED Aug 86

PROGRAM DESCRIPTION

NWA STATPAK is a multifunction statistical analysis and graphics package. STATPAK is targeted to the professional user of statistics (i.e. chemist, biologist, financial modeler, etc.) and is designed so that the user can become proficient rapidly and yet have the power and resources for major projects.

NWA STATPAK is a modular library which works under a common dispatch manager. The system is flexible, configurable, and interfaces well with other software and instrumentation. STATPAK provides excellent graphics capability.

PRODUCT REVIEWS

Science Software Quarterly, pp. 67-70, (Summer 1984).

Butler and Camon. Behavior Research Methods, Instruments and Computers, pp. 352-358, (1985).

TYPE OF PROGRAM

Statistical Package

PROGRAM DESIGNED FOR
Data Analysis

PROGRAM STYLE
Menu Driven
Integrated System

MISCELLANEOUS PROGRAM FEATURES
Source Code Available
Copyable Disk

DOCUMENTATION
User's Manual - 400 pages, 20 technical references
Table of Contents
Index
Tutorial or Example Lessons
Sample Runs
Formulas Provided
Tutorials and Examples on Disk

DATA MANAGEMENT
Keyboard Data Entry
Data Manipulations and Transformations
Missing Values Allowed in Data

DATA EDITING
Change
Add
Delete

FOREIGN DATA ACCESS
Standard Rectangular ASCII Files
DIF Files
SYLK

GRAPHICS FEATURES
Graphics Appear in Color on the Monitor
Graphics can be Output to a Printer
Graphics can be Saved to a File
Titles and/or Labels Available
Uses Pixel Graphics
Uses Character Graphics

GRAPHICS
- Histograms
- Scatter (x-y) Plots
- Box Plots
- Seasonal Index
- Residual Plots
- Normality Plots

PRODUCT SUPPORT
- User may call at own Expense
- No Classes or Instruction Available

STATISTICAL FEATURES SUPPORTED

DESCRIPTIVE STATISTICS
- Mean
- Standard Deviation or Variance
- Standard Error of the Mean
- Coefficient of Variation
- Minimum, Maximum
- Median
- Percentiles
- Skewness
- Kurtosis

t-TESTS
- One Sample t-Test
- Independent Group t-Test/Equal Variance
- Independent Group t-Test/Unequal Var
- Paired t-Test

CORRELATION AND REGRESSION
- Pearson Correlation Coefficient
- Simple Linear Regression
- Multiple Linear Regression
- Stepwise Multiple Linear Regression
- Non-Linear Regression
- Residuals Calculated
- **REGRESSION PLOTS**
    - Residuals

CONFIDENCE INTERVALS
- Means
- Difference Between Two Means
- Proportions
- Difference Between Two Proportions
- Computed for All Regression Functions

CATEGORICAL DATA ANALYSIS
- Chi-Square Contingency Table Analysis
- Multi-Dimensional Tables
- Fisher's Exact Test
- Goodness-of-Fit Tests
- Frequencies Can be Entered Directly

ANALYSIS OF VARIANCE
- One-Way ANOVA
- One-Way with Repeated Measures
- Two-Way ANOVA
- Two-Way Unequal Cell Sizes Allowed
- 3-Way
- **MULTIPLE COMPARISONS**
    - Duncan's Multiple Range
    - Newman-Keuls
    - Least Significant Difference
    - Dunnett's
    - Tukey's

NONPARAMETRIC TESTS
- Sign Test (Signed Rank)
- Wilcoxon One Sample Test
- Mann-Whitney U
- Kruskal-Wallis Test
- Friedman Chi-Square Test
- Spearman or Kendall Correlation
- Wald-Wolfowitz
- Kolmogorov-Smirnov

DISTRIBUTION FUNCTION EVALUATION
- Normal
- t
- Chi Square
- F
- Binomial
- Hypergeometric
- Poisson
- Exponential
- Negative Binomial
- Gamma
- Inverse Normal
- Log Normal
- Incomplete Gamma
- Khrgian-Mazin
- Bivariate Normal

EXPLORATORY DATA ANALYSIS
- Stem-and-Leaf Displays
- Letter-Value Displays
- Resistant Line
- Smoothing Techniques
- Box Plots

TIME SERIES ANALYSIS
- Autocorrelations
- Cross Correlations
- Moving Average Smoothing
- **TIME SERIES ANALYSIS - PLOTS**
  - Residuals
  - Y/Y-Hat

MISCELLANEOUS
- Random Number Generation
- Test for Normality of Data
- Test for Equality of Variances
- p-Values Given With Tests

OPTIMIZATION BOOK AND DISK

Lionheart Press, Inc.
P. O. Box 379
Alburg, VT 05440
(514) 933 - 4918

CONFIGURATIONS SUPPORTED

Computer	Language	Operating System	RAM	Number Drives	Cost
MS-DOS	COMPILED	DOS	64K	1	
APPLE	COMPILED	DOS	64K	1	
CP/M 5 1/4"	COMPILED	CP/M	64K	1	
				1	

NUMBER OF CURRENT USERS 200
DATE OF FIRST RELEASE Mar 84
CURRENT VERSION RELEASED 1986

PROGRAM DESCRIPTION

In business and technology there ia s wide variety of problems - usually non-linear - which require optimization. These range from the optimization of return on an investment portfolio to finding the minimum costs associated with inventory and production schedules. The programs associated with this book allow you to enter the paramaters of a situation that you have formulated and obtain an optimum solution - a minimum or maximum, (or maybe a "saddle point"). "Real Life" examples are given of the application of the programs, and both the sensitivity and the limitation of the typical solutions are examined.

TYPE OF PROGRAM

Statistical Package

PROGRAM DESIGNED FOR
Data Analysis

PROGRAM STYLE
Command Driven
Separate Programs for each Procedure

DOCUMENTATION
User's Manual - 0 pages, 0 technical references
Table of Contents
Index
Tutorial or Example Lessons
Sample Runs
Formulas Provided
Tutorials and Examples on Disk

DATA MANAGEMENT
Keyboard Data Entry
Data Manipulations and Transformations

DATA EDITING
Change
Add
Delete

FOREIGN DATA ACCESS
Standard Rectangular ASCII Files

PRODUCT SUPPORT
User may call at own Expense
No Classes or Instruction Available

P-STAT (R)
P-Stat, Inc
P.O. Box AH
Princeton, NJ 08542
(609) 924 - 9100
Contact Person: Ms Sebbie Buhler

CONFIGURATIONS SUPPORTED

Computer	Language	Operating System	RAM	Number Drives	Cost
IBM PC	FORTRAN	DOS	640	?	$695

NUMBER OF CURRENT USERS N/A
DATE OF FIRST RELEASE 1963
CURRENT VERSION RELEASED Aug 86

PROGRAM DESCRIPTION

P-STAT offers a unique combination of data management and display, crosstabulation, and statistics all within a single, easy to use program. It features a non-procedural, conversational command language that allows the user to perform complex data analyses easily. P-STAT can be run in either conversational or batch mode from the same module. The package was begun at Princeton University in the early 1960's and since 1979 has been supported by P-STAT, Inc.

P-STAT contains about 280,000 Fortran statements and is supported on a variety of different computers. All conversions and implementations are developed and updated from a single master source file. P-STAT is used internationally by educational, commerical, and government installations. Typical applications include market research, personnel research, clinical trials, quality assurance, systems performance analysis and teaching of statistical methods. P-STAT is extremely versatile and can be used by different departments within an organization for a variety of purposes.

TYPE OF PROGRAM

Statistical Package

PROGRAM DESIGNED FOR
Data Analysis

PROGRAM STYLE
Command Driven
Integrated System

MISCELLANEOUS PROGRAM FEATURES
On Screen Help Function
Supports 8087 Mathematical Chip

DOCUMENTATION
User's Manual - 850 pages, ? technical references
Table of Contents
Index
Tutorial or Example Lessons
Sample Runs
Formulas Provided
Tutorials and Examples on Disk

DATA MANAGEMENT
Keyboard Data Entry
Data Manipulations and Transformations
Missing Values Allowed in Data

DATA EDITING
Change
Add
Delete

FOREIGN DATA ACCESS
Standard Rectangular ASCII Files
DIF Files
Column-Binary Data
Multipunch Data

GRAPHICS FEATURES
Graphics can be Output to a Printer
Graphics can be Saved to a File
Titles and/or Labels Available

GRAPHICS
Histograms
Scatter (x-y) Plots
Box Plots

PRODUCT SUPPORT
User may call at own Expense
Classes or Instruction Available

STATISTICAL FEATURES SUPPORTED

DESCRIPTIVE STATISTICS
- Mean
- Standard Deviation or Variance
- Standard Error of the Mean
- Minimum, Maximum
- Median
- Percentiles
- Skewness
- Kurtosis

t-TESTS
- Independent Group t-Test/Equal Variance
- Independent Group t-Test/Unequal Var
- Paired t-Test

CORRELATION AND REGRESSION
- Pearson Correlation Coefficient
- Simple Linear Regression
- Multiple Linear Regression
- Stepwise Multiple Linear Regression
- Residuals Calculated
- Estimate Asymptotic Standard Errors
- Durbin-Watson

CATEGORICAL DATA ANALYSIS
- Chi-Square Contingency Table Analysis
- Fisher's Exact Test
- Goodness-of-Fit Tests
- Lambda
- McNemar's Test

ANALYSIS OF VARIANCE
- One-Way ANOVA
- One-Way with Repeated Measures
- Two-Way ANOVA
- Two-Way Unequal Cell Sizes Allowed
- Analysis of Covariance
- Nested Factors
- Latin Square
- Multiple Repeated Measures
- Multiway Factorials

NONPARAMETRIC TESTS
- Spearman or Kendall Correlation
- Rank Command
- Others

EXPLORATORY DATA ANALYSIS

- Stem-and-Leaf Displays
- Letter-Value Displays
- Resistant Line
- Smoothing Techniques
- Median Polish
- Rootograms
- Box Plots
- Coded Tables
- Condensed x-y Plots
- Notched Box Plots

MISCELLANEOUS

- Random Number Generation
- Test for Equality of Variances
- p-Values Given With Tests
- Factor Analysis
- Stepwise Discriminant Analysis
- Matrix Operations

P-STATISTICS

Information Systems Corporation
6033 W. Century Blvd., Suite 400
Los Angeles, CA 90045
(213) 412 - 8435
Contact Person: Jim Hicks

CONFIGURATIONS SUPPORTED

Computer	Language	Operating System	RAM	Number Drives	Cost
IBM PC	PASCAL	UCSD-P	64K	2	$ 340

NUMBER OF CURRENT USERS 217
DATE OF FIRST RELEASE Jul 84
CURRENT VERSION RELEASED Jul 84

PROGRAM DESCRIPTION

P-statistics is a modular set of statistical analysis routines designed for both the experienced and novice user of statistical techniques. Each analysis routine is called by an executive program in response to the user selecting an appropriate single letter command. Each analysis routine reads input data from a standard work file and generates analysis results in a standard output work file as well as on the user's display. The output work file (for some analysis routines) can be used directly as the input work file for other analysis routines. These same input/output work files can be used as input to LOTUS and VisiCalc. p-Statistics is ideal in an educational teaching environment, research environment, and for anyone with a need to analyze data statistically. The documentation is tutorial and has many examples.

Data preparation is easy and straightforward. Data is entered in a free-form style. There are no format restrictions placed on the data. In most cases the size of the data array (sample size) is limited only by the size of available disk storage. Command prompt lines are always displayed to instruct the user in what analysis routines can be called at any given level in the analysis routine command hierarchy. The name p-Statistics reflects the fact that the system was developed in PASCAL which compiles into p-Code which runs under the USCD p-Systems.

TYPE OF PROGRAM
Statistical Package

PROGRAM DESIGNED FOR
Data Analysis

PROGRAM STYLE
Menu Driven
Separate Programs for each Procedure

MISCELLANEOUS PROGRAM FEATURES
On Screen Help Function

DOCUMENTATION
User's Manual - 100 pages, 17 technical references
Table of Contents
Index
Tutorial or Example Lessons
Sample Runs
Formulas Provided
Tutorials and Examples on Disk

DATA MANAGEMENT
Keyboard Data Entry
Data Manipulations and Transformations

DATA EDITING
Change
Add
Delete

FOREIGN DATA ACCESS
Standard Rectangular ASCII Files
dBase II Files
VisiCalc

PRODUCT SUPPORT
Free Phone Support Available
No Classes or Instruction Available

STATISTICAL FEATURES SUPPORTED

DESCRIPTIVE STATISTICS

- Mean
- Standard Deviation or Variance
- Standard Error of the Mean
- Coefficient of Variation
- Minimum, Maximum
- Median
- Percentiles
- Skewness
- Kurtosis
- Moments (2nd,3rd,4th)
- Ratios
- Quartiles
- Deciles
- Mean deviation
- Percentage

t-TESTS

- One Sample t-Test
- Independent Group t-Test/Equal Variance
- Independent Group t-Test/Unequal Var
- Paired t-Test

CORRELATION AND REGRESSION

- Pearson Correlation Coefficient
- Simple Linear Regression
- Multiple Linear Regression
- Stepwise Multiple Linear Regression
- Non-Linear Regression
- Residuals Calculated

CONFIDENCE INTERVALS

- Means
- Difference Between Two Means
- Proportions
- Difference Between Two Proportions
- Variances
- Ratio of Variances

CATEGORICAL DATA ANALYSIS

- Chi-Square Contingency Table Analysis
- Multi-Dimensional Tables
- Fisher's Exact Test
- Goodness-of-Fit Tests
- Frequencies Can be Entered Directly
- Frequencies Can Also be Calculated

ANALYSIS OF VARIANCE

One-Way ANOVA
One-Way with Repeated Measures
Two-Way ANOVA
Two-Way Unequal Cell Sizes Allowed
Analysis of Covariance

NONPARAMETRIC TESTS

Wilcoxon One Sample Test
Mann-Whitney U
Kruskal-Wallis Test
Friedman Chi-Square Test
Spearman or Kendall Correlation

DISTRIBUTION FUNCTION EVALUATION

Normal
t
Chi Square
F
Binomial
Hypergeometric
Poisson
Beta
Gamma

MISCELLANEOUS

Random Number Generation
Test for Normality of Data
Test for Equality of Variances
p-Values Given With Tests
Frequency Distribution
Probability Calculations
Combinatorial Analysis

PASE

Ideal Systems
P.O. Box 681
Fairfield, Iowa 52556
(515) 472 - 4507
Contact Person: Christopher Dennen

CONFIGURATIONS SUPPORTED

Computer	Language	Operating System	RAM	Number Drives	Cost
APPLE II	BASIC	DOS	48K	1	$ 125

NUMBER OF CURRENT USERS ?
DATE OF FIRST RELEASE ?
VERSION ? RELEASED ?

PROGRAM DESCRIPTION

PASE is a program for the advanced user. It starts where multiple regression in ADVANCESTAT leaves off. First of all PASE provides the coefficients obtained in linear multiple regression. This allows for the building of models with one dependent variable caused by one or more independent variables. For more complicated causal models, which may include multiple dependent variables often arranged in a hierarchical causal structure, PASE also provides all total causal effects, direct effects, and total indirect effects.

PASE is easy to operate. It is self-documenting and menu driven. Data files can be read from STUDENTSTAT, INTROSTAT, and ADVANCESTAT or it can act as a stand alone package with data entered directly into the program. For speed parts of the program have been compiled although the BASIC source code is also included. The accuracy of PASE has been found to be at least as accurate as regression results produced by SPSS on an IBM mainframe. The PASE package includes a complete 63 page manual containing a clear introduction to causal modeling, numerous references, a bibliography, and several detailed examples of causal modeling using the PASE package. The author of the program and manual, Dr. Lee M. Wolfe, is thoroughly familiar with the strengths and weaknesses of this statistical procedure and conveys his understanding in a clear precise manner.

TYPE OF PROGRAM
UNKNOWN

PROGRAM DESIGNED FOR
Data Analysis
Educational use

PROGRAM STYLE
Menu Driven
Separate Programs for each Procedure

MISCELLANEOUS PROGRAM FEATURES
Source Code Available
Copyable Disk

DOCUMENTATION
User's Manual - 63 pages, many technical references
Table of Contents
Index
Tutorial or Example Lessons
Sample Runs

DATA MANAGEMENT
Keyboard Data Entry
Missing Values Allowed in Data

DATA EDITING
Change
Add
Delete

FOREIGN DATA ACCESS
Files from INTROSTAT/ADVANCESTAT
STUDENTSTAT

PRODUCT SUPPORT
User may call at own Expense
No Classes or Instruction Available

STATISTICAL FEATURES SUPPORTED

CORRELATION AND REGRESSION

- Simple Linear Regression
- Multiple Linear Regression
- Multicollinearity Diagnostic
- Standard Deviation of Coefficients

PC - MATRIX

Qtec Services Ltd.
1601 - 925 West Georgia Street
Vancouver B.C., CANADA V6C 1R5
(604) 683 - 5757
Contact Person: Piet de Jong

CONFIGURATIONS SUPPORTED

Computer	Language	Operating System	RAM	Number Drives	Cost
IBM PC	ASSEMBLER/ PASCAL	DOS	128K	1	$95

NUMBER OF CURRENT USERS 200
DATE OF FIRST RELEASE 1981
VERSION 4 RELEASED July 86

PROGRAM DESCRIPTION

PC-Matrix makes an IBM microcomputer or compatible into an interactive matrix calculator. A good way to envision PC-Matrix is to picture an ordinary calculator. Now add matrix capabilities to it. For example the command + adds two matrices, ' transposes a matrix. Complicated matrix expressions can be evaluated in the same way as ordinary calculators are used to deal with arithmetical expressions. Over 60 commands are implemented, including inversion, eigenvalues and eigenvectors, the singular value decomposition and generalized inverses. No programming skills are required. Using PC-Matrix is as simple as using an ordinary calculator. Of course one has to appreciate matrix concepts. Any statistical or other problem that can be stated in terms of matrix calculations can be easily dealt with. Matrices of up to 4000 elements can be accommodated. The calculator has a memory of arbitrary size. Files permit the transfer of information from session to session or to and from other programs.

PC-Matrix is ideal for smaller research type situations where "once-off" matrix type calculations are needed. For example, what is the inverse of this matrix? There is no straight-jacket as with the conventional packages. It is also extremely effective for teaching. Students are forced to do the actual calculations step by step and without the arithmetical tedium, instead of submitting them to a "black-box" type of program.

PRODUCT REVIEWS
"Gauss - A Matrix Calculator Program", The American Statistician, Vol 38, No. 2, (May 1984).

TYPE OF PROGRAM
Matrix Calculator

PROGRAM DESIGNED FOR
Data Analysis
Educational use

PROGRAM STYLE
Command Driven
Integrated System

MISCELLANEOUS PROGRAM FEATURES
Copyable Disk
Optional Support for 8087 Mathematical Chip

DOCUMENTATION
User's Manual - 35 pages, ? technical references
Table of Contents
Index
Tutorial or Example Lessons
Sample Runs
Quick Reference Card

DATA MANAGEMENT
Keyboard Data Entry
Data Manipulations and Transformations

DATA EDITING
Change
Add
Delete

FOREIGN DATA ACCESS
Standard Rectangular ASCII Files

PRODUCT SUPPORT
User may call at own Expense
No Classes or Instruction Available

STATISTICAL FEATURES SUPPORTED

DESCRIPTIVE STATISTICS

- Mean
- Standard Deviation or Variance
- Standard Error of the Mean
- Coefficient of Variation
- Minimum, Maximum
- Skewness
- Kurtosis

t-TESTS

- One Sample t-Test
- Independent Group t-Test/Equal Variance
- Independent Group t-Test/Unequal Var
- Paired t-Test

CORRELATION AND REGRESSION

- Pearson Correlation Coefficient
- Simple Linear Regression
- Multiple Linear Regression
- Stepwise Multiple Linear Regression
- Residuals Calculated

CONFIDENCE INTERVALS

- Means
- Difference Between Two Means
- Proportions
- Difference Between Two Proportions
- Variances
- Ratio of Variances

CATEGORICAL DATA ANALYSIS

- Chi-Square Contingency Table Analysis
- Multi-Dimensional Tables
- Frequencies Can be Entered Directly

ANALYSIS OF VARIANCE

- One-Way ANOVA
- One-Way with Repeated Measures
- Analysis of Covariance

DISTRIBUTION FUNCTION EVALUATION

Normal
t
Chi Square
F
Binomial
Poisson

TIME SERIES ANALYSIS

Autocorrelations
Cross Correlations
Moving Average Smoothing

MISCELLANEOUS

Random Number Generation
Test for Equality of Variances
Linear Discriminant Function Calculation
p-Values Given With Tests
Procedures Formulated in Matrix Terms

PC ANOVA

Human Systems Dynamics
9010 Reseda Blvd, Suite 222
Northridge, CA 91324
(818) 993 - 8536
Contact Person: Merideth Wiberg

CONFIGURATIONS SUPPORTED

Computer	Language	Operating System	RAM	Number Drives	Cost
IBM PC	BASIC COMPILED	DOS	256K	2	$ 200

NUMBER OF CURRENT USERS 600
DATE OF FIRST RELEASE Jan 85
CURRENT VERSION RELEASED Jun 86

PROGRAM DESCRIPTION

PC ANOVA is a comprehensive analysis of variance package for the IBM-PC. PC ANOVA produces a complete analysis of variance summary table as well as descriptive statistics for each cell of an experimental design. The package also includes separate programs for file creation and review/edit, data transformations, and high-resolution plots and bar graphs of treatment means.

PC ANOVA requires no previous computer experience. By following documentation examples the user can start analyzing experimental data immediately. The program is menu driven, so no commands are necessary. Detailed descriptions of each program and procedure are given in the manual.

TYPE OF PROGRAM
Statistical Package

PROGRAM DESIGNED FOR
Data Analysis

PROGRAM STYLE
Menu Driven
Integrated System

DOCUMENTATION
User's Manual - 129 pages, 11 technical references
Index
Tutorial or Example Lessons
Sample Runs
Practice Files on Disk

DATA MANAGEMENT
Keyboard Data Entry
Data Manipulations and Transformations

DATA EDITING
Change
Add
Delete

FOREIGN DATA ACCESS
Standard Rectangular ASCII Files
DIF Files

GRAPHICS FEATURES
Graphics can be Output to a Printer
Graphics can be Saved to a File
Titles and/or Labels Available
Uses Pixel Graphics

GRAPHICS
Histograms
Graph of Treatment Means

PRODUCT SUPPORT
Free Phone Support Available
No Classes or Instruction Available

STATISTICAL FEATURES SUPPORTED

ANALYSIS OF VARIANCE

One-Way ANOVA
One-Way with Repeated Measures
Two-Way ANOVA
Two-Way Unequal Cell Sizes Allowed
Latin Square
Multiway Factorials
One to five way ANOVA
Between-within Design

PC STATISTICIAN

Human Systems Dynamics
9010 Reseda Blvd, Suite 222
Northridge, CA 91324
(818) 993 - 8536
Contact Person: Merideth Wiberg

CONFIGURATIONS SUPPORTED

Computer	Language	Operating System	RAM	Number Drives	Cost
IBM PC	COMPILED	DOS	256K	2	$ 300

NUMBER OF CURRENT USERS 1500
DATE OF FIRST RELEASE Dec 83
VERSION 1 RELEASED Aug 86

PROGRAM DESCRIPTION

PC STATISTICIAN is a comprehensive statistics package for persons in diverse fields who need to deal accurately and rapidly with statistics. The user needs no previous computer experience. By following documentation examples, the user can start analyzing experimental or survey data immediately. The program is menu-driven, so no commands are necessary.

PC STATISTICIAN has a research database for data files up to 48 fields or variables. The program can review/edit, merge files, create subfiles, search and select records on up to 4 variables, delete records, delete files, rename files or select a random sample of records. Missing data is handled automatically. To produce reports, specify the analysis, then the variables and variable levels. If all the data is in a single file, PC STATISTICIAN can choose the records and variables for analysis automatically.

PRODUCT REVIEWS

"Focus on Statistical Software", PC Week, (June 12, 1984).

TYPE OF PROGRAM

Statistical Package

PROGRAM DESIGNED FOR
Data Analysis

PROGRAM STYLE
Menu Driven
Integrated System

DOCUMENTATION
User's Manual - 120 pages, 14 technical references
Index
Tutorial or Example Lessons
Sample Runs
Sample Data Files on Disk

DATA MANAGEMENT
Keyboard Data Entry
Data Manipulations and Transformations
Missing Values Allowed in Data

DATA EDITING
Change
Add
Delete

FOREIGN DATA ACCESS
Standard Rectangular ASCII Files
DIF Files

GRAPHICS FEATURES
Graphics can be Output to a Printer
Graphics can be Saved to a File
Titles and/or Labels Available
Uses Pixel Graphics

GRAPHICS
Histograms
Scatter (x-y) Plots

PRODUCT SUPPORT
Free Phone Support Available
No Classes or Instruction Available

STATISTICAL FEATURES SUPPORTED

DESCRIPTIVE STATISTICS

- Mean
- Standard Deviation or Variance
- Standard Error of the Mean
- Minimum, Maximum
- Median
- Percentiles

t-TESTS

- One Sample t-Test
- Independent Group t-Test/Equal Variance
- Independent Group t-Test/Unequal Var
- Paired t-Test

CORRELATION AND REGRESSION

- Pearson Correlation Coefficient
- Simple Linear Regression
- Multiple Linear Regression
- Residuals Calculated
- Estimate Asymptotic Standard Errors
- Partial Correlation
- Multiple Correlation

CONFIDENCE INTERVALS

- Means

CATEGORICAL DATA ANALYSIS

- Chi-Square Contingency Table Analysis
- Multi-Dimensional Tables
- Fisher's Exact Test

ANALYSIS OF VARIANCE

- One-Way ANOVA
- One-Way with Repeated Measures
- **MULTIPLE COMPARISONS**
  - Newman-Keuls

NONPARAMETRIC TESTS

- Sign Test (Signed Rank)
- Wilcoxon One Sample Test
- Mann-Whitney U
- Kruskal-Wallis Test
- Spearman or Kendall Correlation
- Friedman 2-way ANOVA

MISCELLANEOUS

- Test for Equality of Variances
- p-Values Given With Tests
- Crosstabs
- Frequency Distribution
- Tabulation

PCNONLIN
Statistical Consultants,Inc.
462 East High St.
Lexington, KY 40508
(606) 252 3890
Contact Person: Susan Williams

CONFIGURATIONS SUPPORTED

Computer	Language	Operating System	RAM	Number Drives	Cost
IBM PC	MS-FORTRAN 77	DOS	320K	2	$575
HP 150	FORTRAN	DOS	320K		$575

NUMBER OF CURRENT USERS 150
DATE OF FIRST RELEASE Dec 84
VERSION Vol-B RELEASED Jan 86

PROGRAM DESCRIPTION

PCNONLIN is a software package for the statistical analysis of general nonlinear models, including pharmacokinetic models. Analysis of virtually any nonlinear model requires little to no programming on the part of the user.

PCNONLIN can execute commands started in a text file or run interactively. A large library of commonly used pharmacokinetic models is available to the user. These models can be referenced by number only. User-defined models not in the pharmacokinetic library can be easily specified. Models may be specified as systems of integrated or differential equations. Functions of parameters in the model, such as peak effect and area under the curve can be estimated along with their asymptotic standard errors. Residual analysis, including diagnostic plots, are performed. Three minimization methods are available to the user; the Nelder Mead simplex and two variations of the Gauss-Newton method.

TYPE OF PROGRAM

Statistical Package

PROGRAM DESIGNED FOR
Data Analysis

PROGRAM STYLE
Command Driven
Integrated System

MISCELLANEOUS PROGRAM FEATURES
On Screen Help Function
Supports 8087, Mathematical Chip

DOCUMENTATION
User's Manual - 157 pages, 16 technical references
Table of Contents
Index
Sample Runs
Examples on Disk

DATA MANAGEMENT
Keyboard Data Entry
Data Manipulations and Transformations

FOREIGN DATA ACCESS
Standard Rectangular ASCII Files

GRAPHICS FEATURES
Graphics can be Output to a Printer
Graphics can be Saved to a File
Titles and/or Labels Available
Uses Character Graphics

GRAPHICS
Scatter (x-y) Plots

PRODUCT SUPPORT
User may call at own Expense
Classes or Instruction Available

STATISTICAL FEATURES SUPPORTED

CORRELATION AND REGRESSION
- Simple Linear Regression
- Multiple Linear Regression
- Non-Linear Regression
- Residuals Calculated
- **REGRESSION PLOTS**
  - Residuals

PERT & CRITICAL PATH TECHNIQUES

Lionheart Press, Inc
PO Box 379
Alburg, VT 05440
(514) 933 - 4918

CONFIGURATIONS SUPPORTED

Computer	Language	Operating System	RAM	Number Drives	Cost
MS-DOS	COMPILED	DOS	64K	1	
CP/M 5 1/4"	COMPILED	CP/M	64k	1	
APPLE II	COMPILED	DOS	64K	1	

NUMBER OF CURRENT USERS 200
DATE OF FIRST RELEASE Mar 84
CURRENT VERSION RELEASED Mar 86

PROGRAM DESCRIPTION

Project scheduling methods have been among those "good ideas" that are not used all that much, mainly because it has just been too much trouble for the average manager to get all the information into and out of the mainframe computer. Now Lionhart has changed all that if you have a microcomputer of standard capacity. The book gives a review of the ideas behind the techniques - and of network theory, in general. As usual with Lionhart publications we concentrate on the ideas and the applications and leave the mathematics to the computer programs. The programs allow the user to supervise a project on his own, with instant answers changing specialized techniques into an immediate management tool.

TYPE OF PROGRAM

Statistical Package

PROGRAM DESIGNED FOR

Data Analysis

PROGRAM STYLE
Command Driven
Separate Programs for each Procedure

DOCUMENTATION
User's Manual - 0 pages, 0 technical references
Table of Contents
Index
Tutorial or Example Lessons
Sample Runs
Formulas Provided
Tutorials and Examples on Disk

DATA MANAGEMENT
Keyboard Data Entry
Data Manipulations and Transformations

DATA EDITING
Change
Add
Delete

FOREIGN DATA ACCESS
Standard Rectangular ASCII Files

PRODUCT SUPPORT
User may call at own Expense
No Classes or Instruction Available

POINT FIVE tm

Pacific Crest Software, Inc.
887 N.W. Grant Avenue
Corvallis, OR 97330
(503) 754 - 1067
Contact Person: Dan Apple

CONFIGURATIONS SUPPORTED

Computer	Language	Operating System	RAM	Number Drives	Cost
IBM PC	PASCAL	DOS	256K	2	$295
HERCULES	PASCAL	DOS	256K	2	$295

NUMBER OF CURRENT USERS 750
DATE OF FIRST RELEASE Nov 1985
VERSION 1 RELEASED Nov 1985

PROGRAM DESCRIPTION

POINT FIVE is a flexible, multi-purpose problem-solving tool. It is for statistical, financial, and mathematical analysis and works with matrices, vectors, and scalars. It can be used for both numerical and graphical modeling and analysis across a wide range of disciplines and functional areas. Anyone who works with numbers or solves numerical problems can use POINT FIVE. POINT FIVE has a simple user interface that is consistent through all 5 aspects of the program (Calculator, analysis system, modeling tool, graphics, and application development).

POINT FIVE is distinctive from other programs because it incorporates the power of a programmable calculator with 150 built-in functions and the ability to perform data: entry, editing, management, and analysis all very simply. Logic and data are stored separately. Other unique features are: a random number generator, statistical distributions, one command draws a graph and one keystroke recreates it with new data (scatter and regression plots; line and multiple line graphs; regular, hidden, hanging, stacked, and area bar graphs), scaling, generating reports, and automatic labeling. Lastly, POINT FIVE is an understandable 4th generation programming language for developing, modifying and testing users own applications.

PRODUCT REVIEWS

Aarons, Richard. "Point Five: A New Way of Looking at Numbers", PC Magazine, pp. 38, (August 1986).

Gillin, Paul. "Company Announces Quantitative-Analysis Tool", PC Week, pp. 32, (June 24, 1986).

Burke, Steven. "Flexible Modeling Program Announced", Infoworld, pp. 60, (May 12, 1986).

Gibson, Stanley. "Statistical Analysis Package Debuts", Computerworld, pp. 40, (May 19, 1986).

TYPE OF PROGRAM

Statistical Package

PROGRAM DESIGNED FOR

Educational use

PROGRAM STYLE

Command Driven
Separate Programs for each Procedure

MISCELLANEOUS PROGRAM FEATURES

Copyable Disk
On Screen Help Function
Optional Support for 8087, 80286, 80287 Mathematical Chip

DOCUMENTATION

User's Manual - 174 pages, 0 technical references
- Table of Contents
- Index
- Tutorial or Example Lessons
- Sample Runs
- Formulas Provided

Quick Reference Card
Tutorials and Examples on Disk

DATA MANAGEMENT

Keyboard Data Entry
Data Manipulations and Transformations
Missing Values Allowed in Data

DATA EDITING

Change
Add
Delete

FOREIGN DATA ACCESS
- Standard Rectangular ASCII Files
- DIF Files

GRAPHICS FEATURES
- Graphics Appear in Color on the Monitor
- Graphics can be Output to a Printer
- Titles and/or Labels Available
- Uses Pixel Graphics

GRAPHICS
- Histograms
- Scatter (x-y) Plots
- Line Bargraphs
- Regression Plots
- Hidden-Bar Graphs
- Hanging-Bar Graphs
- Line Plots

PRODUCT SUPPORT
- User may call at own Expense
- Classes or Instruction Available

STATISTICAL FEATURES SUPPORTED

DESCRIPTIVE STATISTICS
- Mean
- Standard Deviation or Variance
- Standard Error of the Mean
- Coefficient of Variation
- Minimum, Maximum
- Median
- Percentiles
- Skewness
- Kurtosis
- Range
- Number of Valid Entries

t-TESTS
- One Sample t-Test
- Independent Group t-Test/Equal Variance
- Independent Group t-Test/Unequal Var
- Paired t-Test

NONPARAMETRIC TESTS
- Sign Test (Signed Rank)
- Wilcoxon One Sample Test
- Spearman or Kendall Correlation

DISTRIBUTION FUNCTION EVALUATION
- Normal
- Chi Square
- Binomial
- Poisson

TIME SERIES ANALYSIS
- **TIME SERIES ANALYSIS - FORECASTING**
  - GLM
- **TIME SERIES ANALYSIS - PLOTS**
  - Regression Plot
  - Scatterplot

CONTROL CHARTS
- X-Bar
- Number of Defects
- Number of Defectives
- **OTHER QUALITY CONTROL PROCEDURES**
  - Acceptance Sampling by Attributes
  - Acceptance Sampling by Variables

MISCELLANEOUS
- Random Number Generation

POWER
Epicenter Software
P.O. Box 90073
Pasadena, CA 91109
(818) 304 - 9487
Contact Person: Jonathan Buckley

CONFIGURATIONS SUPPORTED

Computer	Language	Operating System	RAM	Number Drives	Cost
IBM PC	FORTRAN	DOS	192K	1	$ 155

NUMBER OF CURRENT USERS 15
DATE OF FIRST RELEASE AUG 85
VERSION 1.0 RELEASED AUG 85

PROGRAM DESCRIPTION

POWER is a program for calculation of power, sample size, study duration, follow-up period, relative risk, exposure period, survival rate, or statistical significance (as appropriate) for the following study designs: comparison of proportions, comparison of means, case-control study - proportions, case-control study - continuous exposure variable cohort study - internal controls, cohort study - external controls, comparison of survival rates, comparison of survival rate with cure, phase II/Toxicity study.

Tables of estimates may be produced for a range of possible study characteristics. The user determines which characteristics or parameter is to be estimated for a given study design, and which parameters should be given a range of alternative values.

TYPE OF PROGRAM
Sample Size Estimation

PROGRAM DESIGNED FOR
Data Analysis

PROGRAM STYLE
Menu Driven
Integrated System

MISCELLANEOUS PROGRAM FEATURES
On Screen Help Function
Optional Support for 8087 Mathematical Chip

DOCUMENTATION
User's Manual - 17 pages, 5 technical references
Formulas Provided

DATA MANAGEMENT
Keyboard Data Entry

PRODUCT SUPPORT
User may call at own Expense
No Classes or Instruction Available

STATISTICAL FEATURES SUPPORTED

MISCELLANEOUS
Sample Size Estimation

PROCESS CONTROL CHART TOOL KIT

Sof-Ware Tools
P.O. Box 8751
Boise, Idaho 83707
(208) 343 - 1437
Contact Person: Joan Heitzeberg

CONFIGURATIONS SUPPORTED

Computer	Language	Operating System	RAM	Number Drives	Cost
MACINTOSH	BASIC	DOS	512K	1	$99
APPLE II	BASIC	DOS	48K	2	$99
IBM PC	BASIC	DOS	240K	2	$129

NUMBER OF CURRENT USERS 100
DATE OF FIRST RELEASE May 1985
VERSION 1.94 RELEASED May 86

PROGRAM DESCRIPTION

PROCESS CONTROL CHART TOOL KIT is a graphics and statistical package that provides a variety of control charts and graphs based on Deming's philosophy of statistical quality control systems. Many major firms have found this package to be extremely user-friendly and characteristic of their statistical quality control needs and are implementing it as a part of their overall control quality.

PCCTK provides: trend charts, scatter plots, histograms, pareto charts, x-bar-r charts, moving pairs x-bar-r charts, and control charts for attributes (P, NP, U, C-Charts) in one single package. PCCTK is menu-driven and provides not only the graphs and charts, but also the statistics asociated with each graph type. It offers a variety of options such as: graph symbols, grids, auto or manual scaling capability, statistics, curve-fitting, user-supplied control lines or computer generated control limits, titles, axis labels and other numerous features.

TYPE OF PROGRAM

Statistical Package

PROGRAM DESIGNED FOR
Data Analysis
Educational use

PROGRAM STYLE
Menu Driven
Integrated System

DOCUMENTATION
User's Manual - 60 pages, 6 technical references
Table of Contents
Index
Sample Runs
Formulas Provided

DATA MANAGEMENT
Keyboard Data Entry
Data Manipulations and Transformations
Missing Values Allowed in Data

DATA EDITING
Change
Add
Delete

FOREIGN DATA ACCESS
Standard Rectangular ASCII Files
Read Clipboard Data - Multiplan, Excel

GRAPHICS FEATURES
Graphics can be Output to a Printer
Titles and/or Labels Available
Uses Pixel Graphics

GRAPHICS
Histograms
Scatter (x-y) Plots
Trend
Control Charts

PRODUCT SUPPORT
User may call at own Expense
No Classes or Instruction Available

STATISTICAL FEATURES SUPPORTED

DESCRIPTIVE STATISTICS
- Mean
- Standard Deviation or Variance
- Standard Error of the Mean
- Minimum, Maximum
- Skewness
- Kurtosis

CORRELATION AND REGRESSION
- Pearson Correlation Coefficient
- Simple Linear Regression

DISTRIBUTION FUNCTION EVALUATION
- Normal

CONTROL CHARTS
- X-Bar
- Number of Defects
- Number of Defectives
- R
- p-Chart
- np-Chart
- c-Chart
- u-Chart
- Pareto

OTHER QUALITY CONTROL PROCEDURES
- Acceptance Sampling by Attributes
- Acceptance Sampling by Variables

MISCELLANEOUS
- Random Number Generation

PRODAS

Conceptual Software
P.O. Box 56627
Houston, TX 77256
(713) 667- 4222
Contact Person: Henry Feldman

CONFIGURATIONS SUPPORTED

Computer	Language	Operating System	RAM	Number Drives	Cost
IBM PC	C	DOS	320	HD	$1790

NUMBER OF CURRENT USERS 200
DATE OF FIRST RELEASE July 84
VERSION 3.2 RELEASED Aug. 86

PROGRAM DESCRIPTION

PRODAS is the only system that combines advanced database management, statistics, graphics, and matrix programming into an integrated system. Among major statistics packages, only PRODAS has database management capabilities that rival the leading database packages. PRODAS is a command drive system with syntax similar to SAS. Our users choose PRODAS because it solves both database management and statistics requirements. Full screen data entry and online error check make an excellent data entry system. The PRODAS programming language has the ability to process up to 100 databases simulataneously The statistics covers the range from cross tables and regression to generalized linear models and logistic regression.

PRODAS is both fast and powerful. PRODAS is 2 to 8 times faster than other packages and it processes databases with hundreds of variables and tens of thousands of records. Only PRODAS provides both sequential and random-access databases. Random access is the state-of-the-art method for storing and retrieving data. PRODAS offers equivalents to 30 of mainframe SAS/STAT procedures. The PRODAS Matrix programming language is very similar to the SAS Matrix procedure. The graphics are bit-mapped, not character plots. PRODAS consists of 4 modules: Database, Statistics, Graphics, and Matrix. These can be purchased separately.

PRODUCT REVIEWS

Teitel, Robert. "Statistical Database Management on Microcomputers", Computer Science and Statistics:Proceedings of the Symposium, pp. 195-197, (March 1986).

Rizzo, Tony. "Project Database II", PC Magazine, pp. 221-222, (June 24, 1986).

Jeffries, Ron. "PC-SAS: A Big Sigh!", The Jeffries Report, pp. 6, (Jan 1986).

TYPE OF PROGRAM

Statistical Package

PROGRAM DESIGNED FOR

Data Analysis

PROGRAM STYLE

Command Driven
Integrated System

MISCELLANEOUS PROGRAM FEATURES

Copyable Disk
Optional Support for 8078, 80287 Mathematical Chip

DOCUMENTATION

User's Manual - 600+ pages, ? technical references
- Table of Contents
- Tutorial or Example Lessons
- Sample Runs

Tutorials and Examples on Disk

DATA MANAGEMENT

Keyboard Data Entry
Data Manipulations and Transformations
Missing Values Allowed in Data

DATA EDITING

Change
Add
Delete

FOREIGN DATA ACCESS

Standard Rectangular ASCII Files
DIF Files
dBase II Files
dBase III
Lotus

GRAPHICS FEATURES
- Graphics Appear in Color on the Monitor
- Graphics can be Output to a Printer
- Graphics can be Saved to a File
- Titles and/or Labels Available
- Uses Pixel Graphics

GRAPHICS
- Histograms
- Pie Charts
- Scatter (x-y) Plots

PRODUCT SUPPORT
- User may call at own Expense
- Classes or Instruction Available

STATISTICAL FEATURES SUPPORTED

DESCRIPTIVE STATISTICS
- Mean
- Standard Deviation or Variance
- Standard Error of the Mean
- Coefficient of Variation
- Minimum, Maximum
- Median
- Percentiles
- Skewness
- Kurtosis
- Prob-T
- T
- Mode

t-TESTS
- One Sample t-Test
- Independent Group t-Test/Equal Variance
- Independent Group t-Test/Unequal Var
- Paired t-Test

CORRELATION AND REGRESSION
- Pearson Correlation Coefficient
- Simple Linear Regression
- Multiple Linear Regression
- Stepwise Multiple Linear Regression
- Residuals Calculated
- All Possible Regressions
- Partial Correlations
- Spearman and Kendall Correlations
- **REGRESSION PLOTS**
    - Residuals

CONFIDENCE INTERVALS

- Means
- Difference Between Two Means

CATEGORICAL DATA ANALYSIS

- Chi-Square Contingency Table Analysis
- Multi-Dimensional Tables
- Fisher's Exact Test
- Goodness-of-Fit Tests
- Frequencies Can be Entered Directly

ANALYSIS OF VARIANCE

- One-Way ANOVA
- Two-Way ANOVA
- Two-Way Unequal Cell Sizes Allowed
- Analysis of Covariance
- Generalized Linear Models
- Nested, Mixed Effects, Interactions
- **MULTIPLE COMPARISONS**
  - Fisher's LSD
  - Duncan's Multiple Range
  - Scheffe
  - Bonferroni
  - Newman-Keuls
  - Studentized Range
  - Studentized Maximum Modulus

NONPARAMETRIC TESTS

- Sign Test (Signed Rank)
- Wilcoxon One Sample Test
- Mann-Whitney U
- Kruskal-Wallis Test
- Friedman Chi-Square Test
- Spearman or Kendall Correlation
- Median Scores
- Von Der Waerden
- Savage Scores

DISTRIBUTION FUNCTION EVALUATION
- Normal
- t
- Chi Square
- F
- Binomial
- Hypergeometric
- Poisson
- Beta
- Negative Binomial
- Inverse t
- Inverse N
- Inverse F
- Inverse Chi Square
- Inverse Binomial
- Gamma
- Inverse Beta

EXPLORATORY DATA ANALYSIS
- Stem-and-Leaf Displays
- Letter-Value Displays

TIME SERIES ANALYSIS
- Moving Average Smoothing
- **TIME SERIES ANALYSIS - FORECASTING**
  - Exponential Smoothing
  - Winters
- **TIME SERIES ANALYSIS - PLOTS**
  - Date Scaled

CONTROL CHARTS
- X-Bar
- s

MISCELLANEOUS

- Cluster Analysis
- Life Table Analysis
- Random Number Generation
- Linear Discriminant Function Calculation
- p-Values Given With Tests
- Hierarchical Cross Table Generator
- Probit and Logit
- Logistic Regression
- Cox Regression
- Multiresponse and Dichotomy Cross Tables
- Least Absolute Value
- Rank Variables
- Standardized Variables
- Stepwise Discriminant
- Principal Components
- Canonical Correlation
- Factor Analysis

PSYCHOSTAT-3

Statsoft, Inc.
2832 East 10th Street, Suite 4
Tulsa, OK 74104
(918) 583 - 4149
Contact Person: Sales Office

CONFIGURATIONS SUPPORTED

Computer	Language	Operating System	RAM	Number Drives	Cost
CP/M	BASIC	CP/M	64	1	$99

NUMBER OF CURRENT USERS 5000
DATE OF FIRST RELEASE 1984
VERSION 1.1 RELEASED 1985

PROGRAM DESCRIPTION

A general purpose statistical package (basic statistics, nonparametrics, multivariate statistics) with graphics and statistical database management functions.

Extremely easy to use, even for novices (menu driven), advanced statistics.

TYPE OF PROGRAM
Statistical Package

PROGRAM DESIGNED FOR
Data Analysis
Educational use

PROGRAM STYLE
Menu Driven
Integrated System

MISCELLANEOUS PROGRAM FEATURES
Source Code Available
Copyable Disk

DOCUMENTATION

User's Manual - ? pages, 10 technical references
- Table of Contents
- Tutorial or Example Lessons
- Sample Runs

DATA MANAGEMENT
- Keyboard Data Entry
- Data Manipulations and Transformations
- Missing Values Allowed in Data

DATA EDITING
- Change
- Add
- Delete

FOREIGN DATA ACCESS
- Standard Rectangular ASCII Files
- Any ASCII Data File

GRAPHICS FEATURES
- Graphics can be Output to a Printer
- Titles and/or Labels Available
- Uses Character Graphics

GRAPHICS
- Histograms
- Scatter (x-y) Plots

PRODUCT SUPPORT
- User may call at own Expense
- No Classes or Instruction Available

STATISTICAL FEATURES SUPPORTED

DESCRIPTIVE STATISTICS
- Mean
- Standard Deviation or Variance
- Standard Error of the Mean

t-TESTS
- One Sample t-Test
- Independent Group t-Test/Equal Variance
- Independent Group t-Test/Unequal Var
- Paired t-Test

CORRELATION AND REGRESSION
- Pearson Correlation Coefficient
- Simple Linear Regression
- Multiple Linear Regression
- Residuals Calculated

CATEGORICAL DATA ANALYSIS
- Chi-Square Contingency Table Analysis
- Frequencies Can be Entered Directly

ANALYSIS OF VARIANCE
- One-Way ANOVA
- One-Way with Repeated Measures
- Two-Way ANOVA
- Two-Way Unequal Cell Sizes Allowed
- Analysis of Covariance
- Up to 5-Way ANCOVA Incl. A Covariate
- Repeated Measures
- Incomplete Designs
- **MULTIPLE COMPARISONS**
  - Planned Comparisons

NONPARAMETRIC TESTS
- Phi-Square
- Nu-Square

DISTRIBUTION FUNCTION EVALUATION
- Normal
- t
- Chi Square
- F

MISCELLANEOUS
- p-Values Given With Tests

QA/S SYSTEM

Paul Hertzlert & Co., Inc.
P.O. Box 578
Goshen, IN 46526
(219) 533 - 0571
Contact Person: Evan J. Miller

CONFIGURATIONS SUPPORTED

Computer	Language	Operating System	RAM	Number Drives	Cost
IBM PC	PASCAL/ ASSEMBLY	DOS	640K	HD	$995
HP 150 TOUCH SCREEN	PASCAL/ ASSEMBLY	DOS	640	HD	$995

NUMBER OF CURRENT USERS 45
DATE OF FIRST RELEASE Mar 83
VERSION 2.31 RELEASED July 86

PROGRAM DESCRIPTION

QA/S software is a complete data base SPC system for manufacturers. Variable and attribute data may be entered into the data base manually, or automatically via digital gages. Industry-standard SPC techniques are available. These include control charts, scatter diagrams, process capability studies, capability analysis, and Pareto analysis.

QA/S software features a sophisticated data base. All data is stored in one indexed file on a hard disc. This eliminates the need to keep track of numerous part files on multiple floppy discs. Data may be retrieved from the data base by part number, characteristic and data window, and sorted by lot, machine tool, etc.

TYPE OF PROGRAM

Quality Control or Reliability

PROGRAM DESIGNED FOR

Data Analysis

PROGRAM STYLE
Menu Driven
Integrated System

MISCELLANEOUS PROGRAM FEATURES
Copyable Disk

DOCUMENTATION
User's Manual - 300 pages, ? technical references
Table of Contents
Formulas Provided

DATA MANAGEMENT
Keyboard Data Entry
Data Manipulations and Transformations
Missing Values Allowed in Data

DATA EDITING
Change
Add
Delete

FOREIGN DATA ACCESS
Standard Rectangular ASCII Files
dBase II Files
Digital Gages
1-2-3 Files

GRAPHICS FEATURES
Graphics can be Output to a Printer
Titles and/or Labels Available
Uses Pixel Graphics

GRAPHICS
Histograms
Pie Charts
Scatter (x-y) Plots
Capability Analysis
Pareto Diagram
Control Charts

PRODUCT SUPPORT
User may call at own Expense
Classes or Instruction Available

STATISTICAL FEATURES SUPPORTED

DESCRIPTIVE STATISTICS
- Mean
- Standard Deviation or Variance
- Minimum, Maximum
- Percentiles
- Skewness
- Kurtosis

t-TESTS
- Independent Group t-Test/Equal Variance
- Independent Group t-Test/Unequal Var
- Paired t-Test

CORRELATION AND REGRESSION
- Pearson Correlation Coefficient
- Simple Linear Regression

CATEGORICAL DATA ANALYSIS
- Chi-Square Contingency Table Analysis

CONTROL CHARTS
- X-Bar
- Number of Defects
- Number of Defectives
- R
- Control Limits Based on A2 Factor
- Cpk
- Cp
- Actual and Predicted Out of Spec.
- NP
- P
- U
- C
- X
- **RELIABILITY**
  - For both Variables and Attributes
  - Run Sum or Cumulative Sum Analysis
- **OTHER QUALITY CONTROL PROCEDURES**
  - Acceptance Sampling by Attributes
  - Acceptance Sampling by Variables

QC PLOT
Human Systems Dynamics
9010 Reseda Blvd, Suite 222
Northridge, CA 91324
(818) 993 - 8536
Contact Person: Merideth Wiberg

CONFIGURATIONS SUPPORTED

Computer	Language	Operating System	RAM	Number Drives	Cost
APPLE II	BASIC	DOS 3.3	48K	1	$ 400

NUMBER OF CURRENT USERS 150
DATE OF FIRST RELEASE Jan 85
CURRENT VERSION RELEASED Jul 85

PROGRAM DESCRIPTION

QC PLOT takes quality control data and automatically creates statistical quality control charts. You can choose from six variable control charts: mean, range, standard deviation, individual values, subgroup sums, or trend. You can also choose from five attribute control charts:p, %p, np, c or u. The program also provides six distribution charts: hypergeometric, binomial, Poisson, normal, exponential and Weibull.

QC PLOT provides a data base, a powerful data editor, and data transformations.

TYPE OF PROGRAM
Quality Control or Reliability

PROGRAM DESIGNED FOR
Data Analysis

PROGRAM STYLE
Menu Driven
Integrated System

DOCUMENTATION
User's Manual - 110 pages, 3 technical references
Index
Sample Runs
Tutorials and Examples on Disk

DATA MANAGEMENT
Keyboard Data Entry
Data Manipulations and Transformations

DATA EDITING
Change
Add
Delete

GRAPHICS FEATURES
Graphics can be Output to a Printer
Graphics can be Saved to a File
Titles and/or Labels Available
Uses Pixel Graphics

GRAPHICS
Histograms

PRODUCT SUPPORT
Free Phone Support Available
No Classes or Instruction Available

STATISTICAL FEATURES SUPPORTED

CONTROL CHARTS
X-Bar
s
R
p-Chart
np-Chart
c-Chart
u-Chart
Individual Values
Subgroup Sums
Trend
%p

OTHER QUALITY CONTROL PROCEDURES
Acceptance Sampling by Attributes
Acceptance Sampling by Variables

QC-PRO ATTRIBUTE DATA ANALYSIS

G.R. Technologies Inc.
26911 Northwestern Highway, Suite 300
Southfield, MI 48034
(313) 262 - 1423
Contact Person: G. Pister

CONFIGURATIONS SUPPORTED

Computer	Language	Operating System	RAM	Number Drives	Cost
APPLE II	BASIC	DOS	48K	2	$ 300
IBM PC	BASIC	DOS	128K	2	$ 300

NUMBER OF CURRENT USERS 75+
DATE OF FIRST RELEASE Jun 84
VERSION 2.0 RELEASED Sept 84

PROGRAM DESCRIPTION

QC-PRO Attribute Data Analysis is used to monitor descriptive type part data. The program is written for people in quality control.

The software includes Pareto analysis on defect types with both graphic and numeric indications of worst defect categories. Charts available are P (percent defect), C(defects per sample) and U(defects per unit).

PRODUCT REVIEWS

Quality Progress, (March 85, 86).

Quality Magazine, (Aug 85, June 86).

TYPE OF PROGRAM

Statistical Package

PROGRAM DESIGNED FOR

Data Analysis

PROGRAM STYLE
Menu Driven
Integrated System

MISCELLANEOUS PROGRAM FEATURES
Copyable Disk
On Screen Help Function

DOCUMENTATION
User's Manual - 11 pages, 5 technical references
Table of Contents
Index
Tutorial or Example Lessons
Sample Runs
Formulas Provided
Tutorials and Examples on Disk

DATA MANAGEMENT
Keyboard Data Entry
Data Manipulations and Transformations

DATA EDITING
Change
Add
Delete

FOREIGN DATA ACCESS
Standard Rectangular ASCII Files
DIF Files

GRAPHICS FEATURES
Graphics Appear in Color on the Monitor
Graphics can be Output to a Printer
Graphics can be Saved to a File
Titles and/or Labels Available
Uses Pixel Graphics

GRAPHICS
Histograms
SEE QC Plots

PRODUCT SUPPORT
User may call at own Expense
Classes or Instruction Available

STATISTICAL FEATURES SUPPORTED

DESCRIPTIVE STATISTICS

- Mean
- Standard Deviation or Variance
- Minimum, Maximum

CONTROL CHARTS

- Proportions
- Number of Defects
- Number of Defectives
- p-Chart
- c-Chart
- u-Chart
- Pareto Diagrams

QC-PRO DESIGNED EXPERIMENTS

G.R. Technologies Inc.
26911 Northwestern Highway Suite 300
Southfield, MI 48034
(313) 262 - 1423
Contact Person: G. Pister

CONFIGURATIONS SUPPORTED

Computer	Language	Operating System	RAM	Number Drives	Cost
IBM PC	BASIC	DOS	256K	1	CALL

NUMBER OF CURRENT USERS ?
DATE OF FIRST RELEASE Aug 86
VERSION 1.0 RELEASED Aug 86

PROGRAM DESCRIPTION

The program is written for people in design, process and quality engineering. Major uses are to optimize component parameters and tolerances in the design phase, problem solving and optimizing the various parameters and tolerances in a given process before and during final manufacture of a product.

The Following Functions are Available: A. Tests of Significance 1. t - Test 2. F - Test 3. Chi Square Test B. Analysis of Variance C. Designed Experiments 1. Full Factorial 2. Latin Square 3. Taguchi Orthogonal Arrays 4. Blocked

PRODUCT REVIEWS

Quality Progress, (March 1986).

Quality Magazine, (June 1986).

TYPE OF PROGRAM

Statistical Package

PROGRAM DESIGNED FOR

Data Analysis

PROGRAM STYLE
Command Driven
Integrated System

MISCELLANEOUS PROGRAM FEATURES
Source Code Available
Copyable Disk
On Screen Help Function

DOCUMENTATION
User's Manual - 45 pages, 7 technical references
Table of Contents
Index
Tutorial or Example Lessons
Sample Runs
Formulas Provided
Tutorials and Examples on Disk

DATA MANAGEMENT
Keyboard Data Entry
Data Manipulations and Transformations
Missing Values Allowed in Data

DATA EDITING
Change
Add
Delete

FOREIGN DATA ACCESS
Standard Rectangular ASCII Files
DIF Files
dBase II Files

GRAPHICS FEATURES
Graphics Appear in Color on the Monitor
Graphics can be Output to a Printer
Titles and/or Labels Available
Uses Character Graphics

GRAPHICS
Scatter (x-y) Plots

PRODUCT SUPPORT
User may call at own Expense
Classes or Instruction Available

STATISTICAL FEATURES SUPPORTED

DESCRIPTIVE STATISTICS

- Mean
- Standard Deviation or Variance
- Standard Error of the Mean
- Minimum, Maximum

t-TESTS

- One Sample t-Test
- Independent Group t-Test/Equal Variance
- Independent Group t-Test/Unequal Var
- Paired t-Test

CORRELATION AND REGRESSION

- Pearson Correlation Coefficient
- Simple Linear Regression
- Multiple Linear Regression
- Stepwise Multiple Linear Regression

CONFIDENCE INTERVALS

- Means
- Difference Between Two Means
- Variances
- Ratio of Variances

CATEGORICAL DATA ANALYSIS

- Chi-Square Contingency Table Analysis
- Fisher's Exact Test

ANALYSIS OF VARIANCE

- One-Way ANOVA
- One-Way with Repeated Measures
- Two-Way ANOVA
- Two-Way Unequal Cell Sizes Allowed
- Multiple Comparisons

DISTRIBUTION FUNCTION EVALUATION

- t
- Chi Square
- F

QC-PRO GAGE CONTROL/CAPABILITY

G. R. Technologies Inc.
26911 Northwestern Highway, Suite 300
Southfield, MI 48034
(313) 262 - 1423
Contact Person: G. Pister

CONFIGURATIONS SUPPORTED

Computer	Language	Operating System	RAM	Number Drives	Cost
APPLE II	BASIC	DOS	48K	2	$ 395
IBM PC	BASIC	PC-DOS	128K	2	$ 395

NUMBER OF CURRENT USERS 50+
DATE OF FIRST RELEASE Aug 84
VERSION 3.0 RELEASED Aug 86

PROGRAM DESCRIPTION

OC-PRO Gage Capability Analysis is designed to evaluate measurement systems. The program is for the Quality Control sector.

The program looks at five areas. These include gage accuracy, repeatability, reproducibility, stability and linearity. Both variable and attribute type gage studies may be performed. Gage control gives a listing of calibration scheduling. The list contains all overdue gages as well as gages due for calibration today, within seven days and this month.

PRODUCT REVIEWS

Quality Progress, (March 85, 86).

Quality Magazine, (Aug 85, June 86).

TYPE OF PROGRAM

Statistical Package

PROGRAM DESIGNED FOR

Data Analysis

PROGRAM STYLE
Menu Driven
Integrated System

MISCELLANEOUS PROGRAM FEATURES
Copyable Disk
On Screen Help Function

DOCUMENTATION
User's Manual - 15 pages, 3 technical references
Index
Tutorial or Example Lessons
Sample Runs
Formulas Provided
Tutorials and Examples on Disk

DATA MANAGEMENT
Keyboard Data Entry
Data Manipulations and Transformations

DATA EDITING
Change
Add
Delete

FOREIGN DATA ACCESS
Standard Rectangular ASCII Files
DIF Files

GRAPHICS FEATURES
Graphics Appear in Color on the Monitor
Graphics can be Output to a Printer
Graphics can be Saved to a File
Titles and/or Labels Available
Uses Pixel Graphics

GRAPHICS
Scatter (x-y) Plots

PRODUCT SUPPORT
User may call at own Expense
Classes or Instruction Available

STATISTICAL FEATURES SUPPORTED

DESCRIPTIVE STATISTICS
- Standard Deviation or Variance

CONTROL CHARTS
- **OTHER QUALITY CONTROL PROCEDURES**
  - Gage Capability Analysis

QC-PRO STATISTICAL PROCESS CONTROL

G. R. Technologies Inc.
26911 Northwestern Highway, Suite 300
Southfield, MI 48034
(313) 262 - 1423
Contact Person: G. Pister

CONFIGURATIONS SUPPORTED

Computer	Language	Operating System	RAM	Number Drives	Cost
APPLE	BASIC	DOS	48K	2	$ 535
IBM PC	BASIC	DOS	128K	2	$ 535

NUMBER OF CURRENT USERS 300+
DATE OF FIRST RELEASE Feb 83
VERSION 3.2 RELEASED May 86

PROGRAM DESCRIPTION

QC-PRO Statistical Process Control assists in evaluating and monitoring measurements related to discrete or continuous process data . The program is written for people involved in quality control and manufacturing engineering.

The program provides in depth statistics as well as graphic charting, Included are Shewhart Control Charts (XBar, Range, Individuals) with control limits computer calculated or user set. Machine-Process capability shows the process in proportion to specification and estimates percent outside tolerance. Histogram shows the sample distribution with tests for normality, +/- sigma limits, average and tolerance drawn in. Statistics include process average, standard deviation, capability index/ratio, Cpk, skewness, kurtosis, probability of occurrence.

PRODUCT REVIEWS

Quality Progress, ASQC, (March 84, 85, & 86).

Quality, Hitchcock Publications, (May 1984, July 1985).

CIME, A.S.M.E., (March 1984).

TYPE OF PROGRAM
Statistical Package

PROGRAM DESIGNED FOR
Data Analysis

PROGRAM STYLE
Menu Driven
Integrated System

MISCELLANEOUS PROGRAM FEATURES
Copyable Disk
On Screen Help Function

DOCUMENTATION
User's Manual - 80+ pages, 5 technical references
Index
Tutorial or Example Lessons
Sample Runs
Formulas Provided
Tutorials and Examples on Disk

DATA MANAGEMENT
Keyboard Data Entry
Data Manipulations and Transformations
Missing Values Allowed in Data

DATA EDITING
Change
Add
Delete

FOREIGN DATA ACCESS
Standard Rectangular ASCII Files
DIF Files
dBASE III Files
Lotus 1-2-3

GRAPHICS FEATURES
Graphics Appear in Color on the Monitor
Graphics can be Output to a Printer
Graphics can be Saved to a File
Titles and/or Labels Available
Uses Pixel Graphics

GRAPHICS
- Histograms
- Scatter (x-y) Plots
- Normal Distribution Plot
- SEE QC Plots
- Normal Probability Paper

PRODUCT SUPPORT
- User may call at own Expense
- Classes or Instruction Available

STATISTICAL FEATURES SUPPORTED

DESCRIPTIVE STATISTICS
- Mean
- Standard Deviation or Variance
- Minimum, Maximum
- Skewness
- Kurtosis

DISTRIBUTION FUNCTION EVALUATION
- Normal
- Non-Normal

CONTROL CHARTS
- X-Bar
- s
- R
- Moving Range

MISCELLANEOUS
- Test for Normality of Data
- Chart Pattern Analysis
- Comments with each Sample
- Multi-Characteristic Data Entry

QC-PRO WEIBULL RELIABILITY ANALYSIS

G. R. Technologies
26911 Northwestern Highway, Suite 300
Southfield, MI 48034
(313) 262 - 1423
Contact Person: G. Pister

CONFIGURATIONS SUPPORTED

Computer	Language	Operating System	RAM	Number Drives	Cost
APPLE II	BASIC	DOS	48K	1	$ 450
IBM PC	BASIC	DOS	128K	2	$ 450

NUMBER OF CURRENT USERS 75+
DATE OF FIRST RELEASE Jul 83
VERSION 2.0 RELEASED Dec 84

PROGRAM DESCRIPTION

QC-PRO Weibull Reliability Analysis is designed to assist in evaluating Product Reliability. The program is geared towards people involved in product assurance/reliability.

The program plots the reliability function and performs reliability modelling. Data is plotted on Weibull probability paper using linear regression techniques to derive the best fit line. Target testing is a feature which permits sample size reduction while maintaining the same level of confidence. Statistics include Weibull parameters, reliability based on specifications and correlation coefficient. Options include minimum life estimation and confidence bands.

PRODUCT REVIEWS

Quality Progress, ASQC, (March 84, 85, 86).

Quality Magazine, (Aug 85, June 86).

TYPE OF PROGRAM

Statistical Package

PROGRAM DESIGNED FOR
Data Analysis

PROGRAM STYLE
Menu Driven
Integrated System

MISCELLANEOUS PROGRAM FEATURES
Copyable Disk
On Screen Help Function

DOCUMENTATION
User's Manual - 15 pages, 8 technical references
Table of Contents
Index
Tutorial or Example Lessons
Sample Runs
Formulas Provided
Tutorials and Examples on Disk

DATA MANAGEMENT
Keyboard Data Entry
Data Manipulations and Transformations

DATA EDITING
Change
Add
Delete

FOREIGN DATA ACCESS
Standard Rectangular ASCII Files
DIF Files

GRAPHICS FEATURES
Graphics Appear in Color on the Monitor
Graphics can be Output to a Printer
Graphics can be Saved to a File
Titles and/or Labels Available
Uses Pixel Graphics

GRAPHICS
Weibull Plot

PRODUCT SUPPORT
User may call at own Expense
Classes or Instruction Available

STATISTICAL FEATURES SUPPORTED

DESCRIPTIVE STATISTICS
Percentiles

CORRELATION AND REGRESSION
Pearson Correlation Coefficient
Simple Linear Regression

RELIABILITY
Weibull

QCPAC

Marcel Dekker
270 Madison Ave.
New York, NY 10016
(212) 696 - 9000
Contact Person: SM Zimmerman / 205-460-6411

CONFIGURATIONS SUPPORTED

Computer	Language	Operating System	RAM	Number Drives	Cost
IBM PC	BASIC	DOS	?	1	$165

NUMBER OF CURRENT USERS ?
DATE OF FIRST RELEASE SEPT 85
CURRENT VERSION RELEASED ?

PROGRAM DESCRIPTION

QCPAC is a system of quality control programs for both acceptance sampling and incoming inspection of variables and attributes. It plots x-bar, sigma, range, p (variable sample size), and c control charts. The package is designed for the quality control professional, manager, engineer, and technician to perform fast and accurate statistical analyses. The package allows data entry and storage, analysis, and presentation.

The package will plot most of the control charts needed by the quality control professional and will perform a process capability analysis including a goodness of fit test for the normal distribution.

TYPE OF PROGRAM
Quality Control or Reliability

PROGRAM DESIGNED FOR
Data Analysis

PROGRAM STYLE
Menu Driven
Separate Programs for each Procedure

MISCELLANEOUS PROGRAM FEATURES
Source Code Available
Copyable Disk
On Screen Help Function

DOCUMENTATION
User's Manual - 168 pages, 0 technical references
Table of Contents
Tutorial or Example Lessons
Sample Runs
Formulas Provided

DATA MANAGEMENT
Keyboard Data Entry

DATA EDITING
Change
Add
Delete

FOREIGN DATA ACCESS
Standard Rectangular ASCII Files

GRAPHICS FEATURES
Graphics can be Output to a Printer
Titles and/or Labels Available
Uses Pixel Graphics
Uses Character Graphics

GRAPHICS
Histograms
Control Charts
OC Curves

PRODUCT SUPPORT
User may call at own Expense
No Classes or Instruction Available

STATISTICAL FEATURES SUPPORTED

DESCRIPTIVE STATISTICS

- Mean
- Standard Deviation or Variance
- Standard Error of the Mean
- Coefficient of Variation
- Minimum, Maximum
- Percentiles

CATEGORICAL DATA ANALYSIS

- Goodness-of-Fit Tests

DISTRIBUTION FUNCTION EVALUATION

- Normal
- Binomial
- Hypergeometric
- Poisson

CONTROL CHARTS

- X-Bar
- s
- Proportions
- Number of Defects
- Number of Defectives
- R
- **OTHER QUALITY CONTROL PROCEDURES**
  - Acceptance Sampling by Attributes
  - Acceptance Sampling by Variables

QCPACK

Micropack, Inc
5633 S. Woodlawn
Chicago, IL 60637
(312) 752 - 3112

CONFIGURATIONS SUPPORTED

Computer	Language	Operating System	RAM	Number Drives	Cost
IBM PC	BASIC	DOS	128K	1	$ 100

NUMBER OF CURRENT USERS 100
DATE OF FIRST RELEASE Aug 83
CURRENT VERSION RELEASED Mar 84

PROGRAM DESCRIPTION

QCPACK is a set of five computer programs that let you perform Statistical Process Control, and custom-design and analyze your Attribute Sampling Plans and Variable Sampling Plans.

XBARR-xbar and R statistical control charts with process capability. PUC-P-chart, U-chart, C-chart. This program handles both cases of known and unknown standard values for three control charts. LBLAOQL-Design optimum lot-by-lot single-sampling plans based on average outgoing quality limit (AOQL). AQLLTFD-sampling plans based on Average Quality Limit (AQL) and Lot Tolerance Fraction Defective (LTFD). LBLSDV-Design of lot-by-lot single sampling plans for variables for single and double specification limits.

TYPE OF PROGRAM

Quality Control

PROGRAM DESIGNED FOR

Data Analysis
Educational use

PROGRAM STYLE

Menu Driven
Separate Programs for each Procedure

MISCELLANEOUS PROGRAM FEATURES
Copyable Disk
On Screen Help Function

DOCUMENTATION
User's Manual - 4 pages, 1 technical references
Table of Contents
Index
Tutorial or Example Lessons
Sample Runs
Formulas Provided
Tutorials and Examples on Disk

DATA MANAGEMENT
Keyboard Data Entry

DATA EDITING
Change
Add
Delete

GRAPHICS FEATURES
Graphics can be Output to a Printer

PRODUCT SUPPORT
No Classes or Instruction Available

STATISTICAL FEATURES SUPPORTED

CONTROL CHARTS
X-Bar
Proportions

OTHER QUALITY CONTROL PROCEDURES
Acceptance Sampling by Attributes
Acceptance Sampling by Variables

QUALITY ASSURANCE/STAT PROCESS CONTROL

Logical Design Corporation
23933 Research Drive
Farmington Hills, MI 48024
(313) 474 - 2300
Contact Person: Michael Bass

CONFIGURATIONS SUPPORTED

Computer	Language	Operating System	RAM	Number Drives	Cost
IBM PC	COBOL	DOS	256K	HD	$2500
BURROUGHS B20	COBOL	BTOS	384K	HD	$2500
HP VECTRA	COBOL	DOS	512K	HD	$2500

NUMBER OF CURRENT USERS 35
DATE OF FIRST RELEASE ?
CURRENT VERSION RELEASED ?

PROGRAM DESCRIPTION

Quality Assurance--Statistical Analysis allows manufacturers to utilize the power of a computer to calculate sophisticated statistics. Designed to be useable by all members of the organization. QA provides control charts that monitor continuous process control. QA consists of 5 basic elements: 1. Definition of a part's critical dimensions and attributes off the blueprint. 2. Capability analysis to determine the process capability before going into full production. 3. Ongoing testing of critical dimensions and attributes to ensure process capability throughout the production run. 4 Reports and charts for data analysis (X Bar, R, s, histograms, n, np, u, c). 5. Maintaining history for future reference by part, machine and operator.

TYPE OF PROGRAM

Quality Control or Reliability

About the Authors

WAYNE WOODWARD is Associate Professor of Statistics at Southern Methodist University, Dallas, Texas. Dr. Woodward's research interests include time series analysis, robust estimation, and statistical computing, particularly on microcomputers, and he is author of over 30 articles on these topics; he also serves as an Associate Editor for *Computational Statistics and Data Analysis*. A member of the American Statistical Association, Dr. Woodward received the M.S. and Ph.D. degrees (1971 and 1974) in mathematics from Texas Tech University, Lubbock, Texas.

ALAN C. ELLIOTT is a faculty member at the University of Texas Health Science Center, Dallas, Texas, where he manages a User Support Group, which provides campus-wide training, technical support, and consultations for personal computer users. The author of a book on IBM PC programming techniques, he is also a member of the American Statistical Association. Mr. Elliott received the B.A. degree (1974) from Dallas Baptist University, and M.A.S. degree (1976) from Southern Methodist University.

HENRY L. GRAY is Charles F. Frensley Professor of Mathematics and Statistics, and Associate Dean of Academic Affairs, at Southern Methodist University, Dallas, Texas. Dr. Gray is the coauthor with William R. Schucany of *The Generalized Jackknife Statistics* (Marcel Dekker, Inc.) and author of over 50 papers in the fields of statistics, numerical analysis, and differential equations.

DOUGLAS C. MATLOCK is a graduate student in statistics at Southern Methodist University, Dallas, Texas, as well as a Consulting Associate with SMU's Center for Statistical Consulting and Research, which serves both academic and business clients. He received two B.S. degrees, one in mathematical science (1982) and the other in computer science (1983), from Lamar University, Beaumont, Texas, and M.S. degree (1985) in statistics from Southern Methodist University.

THE STATISTICIAN

Quant Systems
Box 628
Charleston, SC 29402
(803) 571 - 2825
Contact Person: Dr James Hawkes

CONFIGURATIONS SUPPORTED

Computer	Language	Operating System	RAM	Number Drives	Cost
IBM PC	C	DOS	128K	2	$350
CP/M BASED	BASIC	CP/M	64K	2	$150
UNIX BASED	C	XENIX UNIX	1MEG	HD	$750
TRS-80	BASIC	TRS-DOS	64K	2	$150

NUMBER OF CURRENT USERS 2000
DATE OF FIRST RELEASE 1978
VERSION 3.1 RELEASED Aug 86

PROGRAM DESCRIPTION

THE STATISTICIAN is a powerful menu driven program designed to aid in statistician analysis and forecasting. It contains a data editor with search and sort functions, five multiple regression procedures, non-parametric tests, descriptive statistics, plotting, ten forecasting models, random variate generation, random sampling, twenty-four data transformations, hypothesis testing including one and two way ANOVA, correlation analysis, and many other features. The package is designed to accommodate missing values.

The principal strengths of the program are in the multiple regression and forecasting components. We are aware of no other program available for microcomputers that performs all of the regression procedures available in THE STATISTICIAN. Also, the program produces extremely accurate estimates --using the Longley data provided in the Journal of the American Statistical Association.

TYPE OF PROGRAM
Statistical Package

PROGRAM DESIGNED FOR
Data Analysis

PROGRAM STYLE
Menu Driven
Integrated System

MISCELLANEOUS PROGRAM FEATURES
Source Code Available
Copyable Disk
On Screen Help Function

DOCUMENTATION
User's Manual - 200+ pages, 0 technical references
- Table of Contents
- Index
- Tutorial or Example Lessons
- Sample Runs
- Formulas Provided

Tutorials and Examples on Disk

DATA MANAGEMENT
Keyboard Data Entry
Data Manipulations and Transformations
Missing Values Allowed in Data

DATA EDITING
Change
Add
Delete

FOREIGN DATA ACCESS
Standard Rectangular ASCII Files
DIF Files
dBase II Files
1-2-3 PRN Format

GRAPHICS FEATURES
Graphics can be Output to a Printer
Graphics can be Saved to a File
Titles and/or Labels Available

GRAPHICS

Histograms
Scatter (x-y) Plots
Line Graphs
SEE Time Series Plots

PRODUCT SUPPORT

User may call at own Expense
No Classes or Instruction Available

STATISTICAL FEATURES SUPPORTED

DESCRIPTIVE STATISTICS

Mean
Standard Deviation or Variance
Minimum, Maximum
Median
Skewness
Kurtosis

t-TESTS

One Sample t-Test
Independent Group t-Test/Equal Variance
Paired t-Test

CORRELATION AND REGRESSION

Pearson Correlation Coefficient
Simple Linear Regression
Multiple Linear Regression
Stepwise Multiple Linear Regression
Non-Linear Regression
Residuals Calculated
Estimate Asymptotic Standard Errors
Prediction
Ridge Regression
Multi-stage Least Squares
Estimates

CONFIDENCE INTERVALS

Confidence Limits on Predicted Values

CATEGORICAL DATA ANALYSIS

Chi-Square Contingency Table Analysis

ANALYSIS OF VARIANCE

One-Way ANOVA
Two-Way ANOVA with Repeated Measures

NONPARAMETRIC TESTS
- Sign Test (Signed Rank)
- Wilcoxon One Sample Test
- Mann-Whitney U
- Kruskal-Wallis Test
- Spearman or Kendall Correlation

EXPLORATORY DATA ANALYSIS
- Stem-and-Leaf Displays

TIME SERIES ANALYSIS
- Moving Average Smoothing
- Classical Decomposition
- Holt's 4 and 6 term Sinusoidal
- Adaptive Filtering
- **TIME SERIES ANALYSIS - FORECASTING**
  - Exponential Smoothing
  - Double Exponential Smoothing
  - Winters
- **TIME SERIES ANALYSIS - PLOTS**
  - Time Series

MISCELLANEOUS
- Random Number Generation
- Test for Equality of Variances
- Predicted Values Written to Database

THE SURVEY SYSTEM

Creative Research Systems
1649 Del Oro
Petaluma, CA 94952
(707) 765 - 1001

CONFIGURATIONS SUPPORTED

Computer	Language	Operating System	RAM	Number Drives	Cost
IBM PC	COMPILED	PC-DOS	256K	1	$ 500
TI PROF	COMPILED	MS-DOS	192K	1	$ 500
WANG PC	COMPILED	MS-DOS	192K	1	$ 500

NUMBER OF CURRENT USERS 600
DATE OF FIRST RELEASE May 83
VERSION 3.0 RELEASED July 86

PROGRAM DESCRIPTION

The Survey System is an integrated series of programs for the entry, editing, processing and presentation of questionnaire data. It is designed primarily for marketing and opinion research. The system can produce crosstabs and scores in "banner" format (several column variables on one page). Summary and probability statistics can be included. The system can also produce bar charts. Analysis of variance, correlation and regression are available through an optional module. All tables and charts are camera ready for professional presentations.

The survey system is distinguished by a variety of features professional researchers require. It has full data entry, editing and manipulation abilities, including variable transformations, questionnaire weighting and sub-sample selection. The system can handle up to 3000 variables per questionnaire and up to 32,000 questionnaires. An open ended question analysis option adds the ability to use categories and sub-categories of answers. With another option the system can also code and report the actual text of responses to open-ended questions. The system is easily used by people who have no prior computer experience.

TYPE OF PROGRAM
Statistical Package

PROGRAM DESIGNED FOR
Data Analysis

PROGRAM STYLE
Menu Driven
Integrated System

MISCELLANEOUS PROGRAM FEATURES
Copyable Disk
Optional Support for 8087 Mathematical Chip

DOCUMENTATION
User's Manual - 200 pages, 0 technical references
Table of Contents
Index
Tutorial or Example Lessons
Sample Runs
Tutorials and Examples on Disk

DATA MANAGEMENT
Keyboard Data Entry
Data Manipulations and Transformations
Missing Values Allowed in Data

DATA EDITING
Change
Add
Delete

FOREIGN DATA ACCESS
Standard Rectangular ASCII Files
DIF Files

GRAPHICS FEATURES
Graphics can be Output to a Printer
Titles and/or Labels Available
Uses Pixel Graphics

GRAPHICS
Histograms

PRODUCT SUPPORT
User may call at own Expense
No Classes or Instruction Available

STATISTICAL FEATURES SUPPORTED

DESCRIPTIVE STATISTICS

- Mean
- Standard Deviation or Variance
- Standard Error of the Mean
- Minimum, Maximum
- Median
- Percentiles

t-TESTS

- Independent Group t-Test/Equal Variance
- Paired t-Test

CORRELATION AND REGRESSION

- Pearson Correlation Coefficient
- Simple Linear Regression
- Multiple Linear Regression
- Stepwise Multiple Linear Regression
- Residuals Calculated
- Partial Correlation

CATEGORICAL DATA ANALYSIS

- Chi-Square Contingency Table Analysis

ANALYSIS OF VARIANCE

- One-Way ANOVA
- One-Way with Repeated Measures
- Two-Way ANOVA
- Two-Way Unequal Cell Sizes Allowed

TRAJECTORIES TS

DBi Software Products
One Energy Place, 5805 E.Pickard Road
Mt. Pleasant, MI 48858
(517) 772 - 5055
Contact Person: Kris Kirby

CONFIGURATIONS SUPPORTED

Computer	Language	Operating System	RAM	Number Drives	Cost
IBM PC	BASIC	DOS	128K	1	$ 495
DEC RAINBOW	BASIC	DOS CP/M	128K	1	$ 495
HP-150	BASIC	DOS	128K	1	$ 495
WANG PC	BASIC	DOS	128K	1	$ 495

NUMBER OF CURRENT USERS 1300
DATE OF FIRST RELEASE Sept 83
VERSION 5.0 RELEASED Jan 85

ADDITIONAL SOFTWARE REQUIRED
Microsoft BASIC

PROGRAM DESCRIPTION

TRAJECTORIES TS is a superbly programmed analytical research tool that provides professionals with over 48 separate programs. TRAJECTORIES TS is without an equal when it comes to regression analysis. TRAJECTORIES TS is the most resourceful, most powerful research-oriented software system available. TRAJECTORIES TS user level acceptance includes Corporate, Government and Educational environments.

TRAJECTORIES TS is menu and prompt driven, and is provided with BASIC source code. TRAJECTORIES TS can be implemented on a wide variety of micro-computers with CP/M, MS DOS, operating systems with a minimum of 128K memory, one disk drive (although two are preferred) an 80-column printer. Down loading from main-frames is possible along with interfacing capabilities with popular data base managers. TRAJECTORIES TS includes 48 separate statistical programs providing over 120 of the most desired statistical applications. These programs are designed by statisticians for the experienced or novice user. TRAJECTORIES TS will

please the best statistician: - available on a wide variety of micro computers - supplied with BASIC source code - modeled after popular mainframe statistical packages - will read any comma or space delimited ASC-II format - data entry similar to popular spread sheets - mainframe interface capabilities - toll free technical support.

TYPE OF PROGRAM
Statistical Package

PROGRAM DESIGNED FOR
Data Analysis

PROGRAM STYLE
Menu Driven
Separate Programs for each Procedure

MISCELLANEOUS PROGRAM FEATURES
Source Code Available
Copyable Disk
On Screen Help Function

DOCUMENTATION
User's Manual - 95 pages, 6 technical references
- Table of Contents
- Index
- Sample Runs
- Formulas Provided

Tutorials and Examples on Disk

DATA MANAGEMENT
Keyboard Data Entry
Data Manipulations and Transformations
Missing Values Allowed in Data

DATA EDITING
Change
Add
Delete

FOREIGN DATA ACCESS
Standard Rectangular ASCII Files
dBase II Files
Mainframe Interface Capabilities

GRAPHICS FEATURES

- Graphics can be Output to a Printer
- Graphics can be Saved to a File
- Titles and/or Labels Available
- Uses Character Graphics

GRAPHICS

- Histograms
- Scatter (x-y) Plots
- Box Plots
- Frequency Distribution

PRODUCT SUPPORT

- Free Phone Support Available
- No Classes or Instruction Available

STATISTICAL FEATURES SUPPORTED

DESCRIPTIVE STATISTICS

- Mean
- Standard Deviation or Variance
- Standard Error of the Mean
- Minimum, Maximum
- Median
- Percentiles
- Skewness
- Kurtosis

t-TESTS

- One Sample t-Test
- Independent Group t-Test/Equal Variance
- Independent Group t-Test/Unequal Var
- Paired t-Test

CORRELATION AND REGRESSION

- Pearson Correlation Coefficient
- Simple Linear Regression
- Multiple Linear Regression
- Non-Linear Regression
- Residuals Calculated
- Barlett's Chi Square Test
- Test for Pooling Models
- **REGRESSION PLOTS**
  - Residuals

CONFIDENCE INTERVALS

- Means
- Difference Between Two Means

CATEGORICAL DATA ANALYSIS

- Chi-Square Contingency Table Analysis
- Fisher's Exact Test

ANALYSIS OF VARIANCE

- One-Way ANOVA
- Two-Way ANOVA
- **MULTIPLE COMPARISONS**
  - Fisher's LSD
  - Duncan's Multiple Range
  - Tukey
  - Dunnetts

NONPARAMETRIC TESTS

- Wilcoxon One Sample Test
- Kruskal-Wallis Test
- Spearman or Kendall Correlation

DISTRIBUTION FUNCTION EVALUATION

- Normal
- t
- Chi Square
- F

TIME SERIES ANALYSIS

- Moving Average Smoothing
- **TIME SERIES ANALYSIS - FORECASTING**
  - Exponential Smoothing
  - Regression
  - Moving Averages
  - Advance or Lag a Variable
  - Create Time Period Vector
  - Time Series Seasonal Indices
  - Polynomial Regression

TRUESTAT

True Basic, Inc.
39 S. Main St.
Hanover, NH 03755
(603) 643 - 3882
Contact Person: Ruth Tucker Bogart

CONFIGURATIONS SUPPORTED

Computer	Language	Operating System	RAM	Number Drives	Cost
IBM PC	BASIC	DOS	256K	1	$80
MACINTOSH	BASIC		512K	1	$80
COMMODORE AMIGA	BASIC		512K	1	$80

NUMBER OF CURRENT USERS ?
DATE OF FIRST RELEASE May 86
VERSION 1.0 RELEASED May 86

PROGRAM DESCRIPTION

TrueSTAT is a simple, interactive statistical simulation and analysis system. It is designed primarily for teaching, including self study, although it may also be used for quick statistical analyses of small datasets.

TrueSTAT is easy to learn and use. It emphasizes graphical output, can produce several types of plots, and can overlay several plots on a single picture. TrueSTAT is rich in simulation capabilities -- it includes the ability to generate a variety of random test data following normal, binomial, and other distributions. TrueSTAT's most important feature is that you can construct statistical programs much like ordinary True BASIC programs. You can do this with a simple built-in screen editor, or you can create and save these programs as text files in the underlying system.

TYPE OF PROGRAM

Statistical Package

PROGRAM DESIGNED FOR

Educational use

PROGRAM STYLE
- Menu Driven
- Integrated System

MISCELLANEOUS PROGRAM FEATURES
- Copyable Disk
- On Screen Help Function

DOCUMENTATION
- User's Manual - 53 pages, ? technical references
  - Table of Contents
  - Tutorial or Example Lessons
  - Sample Runs

DATA MANAGEMENT
- Keyboard Data Entry
- Data Manipulations and Transformations
- Missing Values Allowed in Data

DATA EDITING
- Change
- Add
- Delete

FOREIGN DATA ACCESS
- Standard Rectangular ASCII Files

GRAPHICS FEATURES
- Graphics Appear in Color on the Monitor
- Graphics can be Output to a Printer
- Graphics can be Saved to a File
- Titles and/or Labels Available
- Uses Pixel Graphics

GRAPHICS
- Histograms
- Scatter (x-y) Plots
- Box Plots
- Confidence Interval Plots
- Normal Curve
- SEE Regression Plots

PRODUCT SUPPORT
- User may call at own Expense
- No Classes or Instruction Available

STATISTICAL FEATURES SUPPORTED

DESCRIPTIVE STATISTICS
- Mean
- Standard Deviation or Variance
- Minimum, Maximum
- Median
- Letter Values

t-TESTS
- One Sample t-Test
- Independent Group t-Test/Equal Variance
- Paired t-Test

CORRELATION AND REGRESSION
- Pearson Correlation Coefficient
- Simple Linear Regression
- Residuals Calculated
- **REGRESSION PLOTS**
  - Residuals
  - Fitted Line

CONFIDENCE INTERVALS
- Means
- Difference Between Two Means

DISTRIBUTION FUNCTION EVALUATION
- Normal
- t

EXPLORATORY DATA ANALYSIS
- Letter-Value Displays

MISCELLANEOUS
- Random Number Generation
- p-Values Given With Tests
- Statistical Programming Language

UNIX/STAT

Gary Perlman
Wang Institute, Tyng Road
Tyngsboro, MA 01879

CONFIGURATIONS SUPPORTED

Computer	Language	Operating System	RAM	Number Drives	Cost
IBM PC	C	DOS	96K	1	$15
MINI'S	C	UNIX	64K	NA	$20

NUMBER OF CURRENT USERS 1000+
DATE OF FIRST RELEASE 1980
VERSION 5.2 RELEASED Sept 86

PROGRAM DESCRIPTION

UNIX/STAT is a set of over 25 programs for data manipulation and analysis on MSDOS and UNIX (where the package was developed). The programs are written for analysts familar with running commands in the MSDOS or UNIX command interpreter. Analyses consists of pipelines of commands in which copies of data are extracted, transformed, formatted, and analyzed.

UNIX/STAT data manipulation programs work with each other and with standard utilities like sort or any file manipulation programs. MSDOS batch files and UNIX shell scripts provide a flexible and portable programming capability. The liberal copyright on the programs and documentation make the package ideal for sites with many users.

TYPE OF PROGRAM
Statistical Package

PROGRAM DESIGNED FOR
Data Analysis

PROGRAM STYLE
Command Driven
Separate Programs for each Procedure

MISCELLANEOUS PROGRAM FEATURES
- Source Code Available
- Copyable Disk
- On Screen Help Function
- Optional Support for 8087 Mathematical Chip

DOCUMENTATION
- User's Manual - 100 pages, 15 technical references
  - Table of Contents
  - Tutorial or Example Lessons
  - Sample Runs
  - Formulas Provided
- Quick Reference Card
- Example Disk

DATA MANAGEMENT
- Keyboard Data Entry
- Data Manipulations and Transformations
- Missing Values Allowed in Data

DATA EDITING
- Change
- Add
- Delete

FOREIGN DATA ACCESS
- Standard Rectangular ASCII Files

GRAPHICS FEATURES
- Graphics can be Output to a Printer
- Graphics can be Saved to a File
- Titles and/or Labels Available
- Uses Character Graphics

GRAPHICS
- Histograms
- Scatter (x-y) Plots
- Error-Bar Plots

PRODUCT SUPPORT
- No Classes or Instruction Available

STATISTICAL FEATURES SUPPORTED

DESCRIPTIVE STATISTICS
- Mean
- Standard Deviation or Variance
- Standard Error of the Mean
- Minimum, Maximum
- Median
- Percentiles
- Skewness
- Kurtosis
- Harmonic Mean
- Geometric Mean

t-TESTS
- One Sample t-Test
- Independent Group t-Test/Equal Variance
- Paired t-Test

CORRELATION AND REGRESSION
- Pearson Correlation Coefficient
- Simple Linear Regression
- Multiple Linear Regression
- Non-Linear Regression
- Residuals Calculated
- Partial Correlation Analysis
- **REGRESSION PLOTS**
    - Residuals

CATEGORICAL DATA ANALYSIS
- Chi-Square Contingency Table Analysis
- Multi-Dimensional Tables
- Fisher's Exact Test
- Frequencies Can be Entered Directly

ANALYSIS OF VARIANCE
- One-Way ANOVA
- One-Way with Repeated Measures
- Two-Way ANOVA
- Two-Way Unequal Cell Sizes Allowed
- N-Way ANOVA-To Ten Factors

NONPARAMETRIC TESTS
- Sign Test (Signed Rank)
- Spearman or Kendall Correlation
- Rank Order Transformations

DISTRIBUTION FUNCTION EVALUATION
- Normal
- t
- Chi Square
- F
- Uniform

TIME SERIES ANALYSIS
- Autocorrelations
- **TIME SERIES ANALYSIS - PLOTS**
  - Bar Plots

MISCELLANEOUS
- Random Number Generation
- p-Values Given With Tests
- Signal Detection Theory

WORMSTAT

Small Business Computers of New England
Box 397 4 Limbo Lane
Amherst, NH 03031
(603) 673 - 0228
Contact Person: Gene Calvano

CONFIGURATIONS SUPPORTED

Computer	Language	Operating System	RAM	Number Drives	Cost
MACINTOSH	PASCAL		128K	1	$79

NUMBER OF CURRENT USERS Over 300
DATE OF FIRST RELEASE Aug 85
VERSION 1.1 RELEASED Jan 86

PROGRAM DESCRIPTION

WormStat was designed both as a general purpose statistical package for the Macintosh and as a tool for helping students learn statistics. Toward the latter goal, several pedagogical features were incorporated in the design of the package. These features were included in such a way so that they would not detract from the usefulness of the package for the non-student. The package has been used with considerable success in several courses at Dartmouth College.

First and foremost, the package is designed to be extremely easy to use so that students are encouraged to explore a set of data and to try alternative approaches to arrive at an answer. Because of its ease of use, very little of the instructor's time is required in teaching the package. For most of the descriptive statistics and tests, the formulae are shown in the analysis window, along with the values for parts of the formulae. For instance, if the mean is computed, the formula window shows the equation for the mean, the value for the sum of the scores and the value for N (the number of scores). The student is not just shown the result of a calculation, then, but the equation that was used and some of the intermediate values.

PRODUCT REVIEWS

Butler, Darrell L.. "Statistical Packages", Contemporary Psychology, pp. 485-487, (July, 1986).

TYPE OF PROGRAM
Statistical Package

PROGRAM DESIGNED FOR
Educational use

PROGRAM STYLE
Menu Driven
Integrated System

MISCELLANEOUS PROGRAM FEATURES
Copyable Disk

DOCUMENTATION
User's Manual - 8 pages, 1 technical references

DATA MANAGEMENT
Keyboard Data Entry
Data Manipulations and Transformations
Missing Values Allowed in Data

DATA EDITING
Change
Add
Delete

FOREIGN DATA ACCESS
Macintosh (Cut and Paste)

GRAPHICS FEATURES
Graphics can be Output to a Printer
Uses Pixel Graphics

GRAPHICS
Histograms
Scatter (x-y) Plots
Box Plots

PRODUCT SUPPORT
User may call at own Expense
No Classes or Instruction Available

STATISTICAL FEATURES SUPPORTED

DESCRIPTIVE STATISTICS

- Mean
- Standard Deviation or Variance
- Minimum, Maximum
- Median

t-TESTS

- One Sample t-Test
- Independent Group t-Test/Equal Variance
- Independent Group t-Test/Unequal Var
- Paired t-Test

CORRELATION AND REGRESSION

- Pearson Correlation Coefficient
- Simple Linear Regression

CATEGORICAL DATA ANALYSIS

- Chi-Square Contingency Table Analysis

ANALYSIS OF VARIANCE

- One-Way ANOVA

NONPARAMETRIC TESTS

- Wilcoxon One Sample Test
- Mann-Whitney U

DISTRIBUTION FUNCTION EVALUATION

- Normal
- t
- Chi Square
- F
- Binomial

MISCELLANEOUS

- p-Values Given With Tests

X-STAT

Wiley Professional Software
605 Third Avenue
New York, NY 10158
(212) 850 - 6788
Contact Person: D. Littwin

CONFIGURATIONS SUPPORTED

Computer	Language	Operating System	RAM	Number Drives	Cost
IBM PC	PASCAL	DOS	256K	2	$ 350

NUMBER OF CURRENT USERS 600
DATE OF FIRST RELEASE Nov 85
VERSION 1.1 RELEASED ?

PROGRAM DESCRIPTION

X-STAT is a remarkable applied statistics package for the IBM PC designed specifically for scientists and engineers who develop products and processes through laboratory research. X-STAT is primarily intended to support research where the combination of independently and continuously adjusted variables must be found in order to produce the best possible product or process. X-STAT is particularly valuable when experiments are under tight time and budget constraints and experiment runs cannot be wasted.

X-STAT provides a consistent, integrated framework for conducting experimental design, data analysis, and interpretation of the experimental results. The payoff from using X-STAT comes in reducing the number of experiments required to achieve objectives.

TYPE OF PROGRAM

Exploratory Data Analysis

PROGRAM DESIGNED FOR

Data Analysis

PROGRAM STYLE

Menu Driven
Integrated System

MISCELLANEOUS PROGRAM FEATURES

- Copyable Disk
- On Screen Help Function
- Optional Support for 80287 Mathematical Chip

DOCUMENTATION

- User's Manual - 269 pages, ? technical references
  - Table of Contents
  - Index
  - Tutorial or Example Lessons
  - Sample Runs
  - Formulas Provided
- Tutorials and Examples on Disk

DATA MANAGEMENT

- Keyboard Data Entry
- Data Manipulations and Transformations
- Missing Values Allowed in Data

DATA EDITING

- Change
- Add
- Delete

FOREIGN DATA ACCESS

- Standard Rectangular ASCII Files
- DIF Files

GRAPHICS FEATURES

- Graphics can be Output to a Printer
- Uses Pixel Graphics
- Uses Character Graphics

GRAPHICS

- Histograms
- Scatter (x-y) Plots
- Response Surface Contour Maps

PRODUCT SUPPORT

- User may call at own Expense
- Classes or Instruction Available

STATISTICAL FEATURES SUPPORTED

DESCRIPTIVE STATISTICS
- Mean
- Standard Deviation or Variance
- Standard Error of the Mean
- Coefficient of Variation
- Minimum, Maximum
- Median

CORRELATION AND REGRESSION
- Simple Linear Regression
- Non-Linear Regression
- Residuals Calculated
- Barlett's Chi Square Test
- **REGRESSION PLOTS**
  - Residuals

CONFIDENCE INTERVALS
- Means
- Difference Between Two Means
- Variances

ANALYSIS OF VARIANCE
- One-Way ANOVA
- One-Way with Repeated Measures
- Two-Way ANOVA

DISTRIBUTION FUNCTION EVALUATION
- Normal
- t
- Chi Square
- F
- Poisson

YSTAT STATISTICAL/FORECASTING PROGRAM

Ming Telecomputing Inc.
23 Oak Meadow Rd., P.O. Box 101
Lincoln Center, MA 01773
(617) 259 - 0391
Contact Person: Dr Mingche M. Li

CONFIGURATIONS SUPPORTED

Computer	Language	Operating System	RAM	Number Drives	Cost
IBM PC	C	DOS	256K	1	$ 395
HP	C	DOS	256K	1	$ 395

NUMBER OF CURRENT USERS 1000
DATE OF FIRST RELEASE July 85
VERSION 1.2 RELEASED Jan 87

PROGRAM DESCRIPTION

ySTAT integrates spreadsheet, statistics, forecasting, and graphics into one easy-to-use package. It is a general package intended for statistical, business, scientific, engineering, economic, social science, and medical applications and is ideal for research, consulting, and teaching.

ySTAT combines the best of microcomputer and mainframe statistical programs - works like Lotus 1-2-3, but has features like those found in SAS. It is the only stand-alone spreadsheet statistical program that truly integrates electronic spreadsheet with full-fledged statistical analyses of data. ySTAT adopts the menu-driven format used in standard spreadsheet programs but offers many functions that are not available even in 1-2-3, such as vector formulas, lagged variables, dummy variables, smoothing by moving averages, and interpolation or extrapolation of missing values. Ten statistical function keys let you quickly tally sums and means; subtract variable means or seasonal means; standardize the data; aggregate seasonal data; generate seasonal indicators; perform moving averages, linear-trend forecasts, and so on. The array of statistical procedures range from descriptive statistics to pooling of time-series and cross-section data. There are twelve procedures available for forecasting. With one keystroke, high-resolution chart of the actual versus forecasted values are automatically displayed.

TYPE OF PROGRAM
Statistical Package

PROGRAM DESIGNED FOR
Data Analysis

PROGRAM STYLE
Menu Driven
Integrated System

MISCELLANEOUS PROGRAM FEATURES
On Screen Help Function
Optional Support for 8087 or 80287 Mathematical Chip

DOCUMENTATION
User's Manual - 360 pages, 35 technical references
Table of Contents
Indox
Tutorial or Example Lessons
Sample Runs
Formulas Provided
Quick Reference Card
Tutorials and Examples on Disk

DATA MANAGEMENT
Keyboard Data Entry
Data Manipulations and Transformations
Missing Values Allowed in Data

DATA EDITING
Change
Add
Delete

FOREIGN DATA ACCESS
Standard Rectangular ASCII Files
dBase II Files
Lotus

GRAPHICS FEATURES
Graphics Appear in Color on the Monitor
Graphics can be Output to a Printer
Graphics can be Saved to a File
Titles and/or Labels Available
Uses Pixel Graphics
Uses Character Graphics

GRAPHICS

- Histograms
- Pie Charts
- Scatter (x-y) Plots
- Stock High-Low-Close-Volume Chart
- Area Chart
- Stacked-Bar Chart
- Line Chart
- See Time Series Plots
- SEE Regression Plots

PRODUCT SUPPORT

- User may call at own Expense
- No Classes or Instruction Available

STATISTICAL FEATURES SUPPORTED

DESCRIPTIVE STATISTICS

- Mean
- Standard Deviation or Variance
- Standard Error of the Mean
- Minimum, Maximum

t-TESTS

- One Sample t-Test
- Independent Group t-Test/Equal Variance
- Independent Group t-Test/Unequal Var
- Paired t-Test

CORRELATION AND REGRESSION

- Pearson Correlation Coefficient
- Simple Linear Regression
- Multiple Linear Regression
- Residuals Calculated
- Pooling Time Series & Cross Sectional
- Polynomial Regression
- Standardized Regression
- Weighted Least Square
- Two-Stage Least Square
- **REGRESSION PLOTS**
  - Residuals

CONFIDENCE INTERVALS

- Means

CATEGORICAL DATA ANALYSIS

- Chi-Square Contingency Table Analysis
- Multi-Dimensional Tables
- Frequencies Can be Entered Directly

ANALYSIS OF VARIANCE
- One-Way ANOVA
- Two-Way ANOVA

NONPARAMETRIC TESTS
- Sign Test (Signed Rank)
- Wilcoxon One Sample Test
- Mann-Whitney U
- Spearman or Kendall Correlation
- Run Test

DISTRIBUTION FUNCTION EVALUATION
- Normal
- t
- Chi Square
- F

TIME SERIES ANALYSIS
- Autocorrelations
- Cross Correlations
- Moving Average Smoothing
- AUTOREGRESSIVE MOVING AVERAGE
  - Parameter Estimation
- **TIME SERIES ANALYSIS - FORECASTING**
  - Exponential Smoothing
  - Double Exponential Smoothing
  - In Conjunction with Lotus 1-2-3
  - Triple Exponential Smoothing
  - Polynomial Model
  - Quadratic Trend
  - Linear Trend
  - Harmonic Exponential Smoothing
  - Exponential Smoothing/Seasonal
  - Winter's Additive Procedure
  - Winter's Multiplicative Procedure
  - Sinusoid Model
- **TIME SERIES ANALYSIS - PLOTS**
  - Time Plot

MISCELLANEOUS
- Random Number Generation
- p-Values Given With Tests

Appendices

The appendices contain additional information which you may find helpful in using this directory. A description of the contents of each appendix follows.

APPENDIX A: GLOSSARY

Appendix A is a glossary of terms used in this directory. It is included to define some of the terms used to describe the programs.

APPENDIX B: LISTING BY VENDORS

Appendix B contains a listing of the 214 programs described in this directory alphabetized by vendor. This listing should be helpful in identifying a program or programs marketed by a certain vendor.

APPENDIX C: SUMMARY TABLE - PROGRAM CAPABILITIES

Appendix C is an index to the major capabilities of the programs in this directory. It is included to facilitate locating programs which perform certain tasks. Each major group of statistical features is included. An asterisk, "*", indicates that the program is said to perform at least one procedure in the corresponding category.

APPENDIX D: SUMMARY TABLE - CONFIGURATIONS SUPPORTED

Appendix D provides an index to the computer configurations supported by the programs in the directory. The table contains those brands of computers and types of operating systems which appear most frequently in the directory as well as those which appear less frequently but are commonly used. The table is not intended to be an exhaustive summary of configurations described in this directory. An asterisk, "*", indicates that the program is said to operate on that particular brand of computer or type of operating system.

APPENDIX E: QUESTIONNAIRE

A copy of the questionnaire used to gather information for this directory is included to provide a better understanding of both the information collected and the manner in which it was collected.

APPENDIX A: GLOSSARY

Chip - (microprocessor chip) - A chip is the electronic device in a computer which holds information or performs tasks such as addition, division, etc. Different brands of microcomputers use different microprocessor chips. For example:

Microcomputer	Microprocessor
IBM P/S Series, Compaq	INTEL 8086, 80286, 80386
IBM PC, AT&T, TI Prof.	INTEL 8088, 8086, 80286
Apple II, II+, IIe	Motorola 6502
TRS 80, CP/M computers	INTEL 8080 (or Z80)
Macintosh, Lisa	Motorola 68000 series

Some microcomputers allow the use of specialty chips such as the Intel 8087 mathematical processor chip. This chip gives faster calculations and higher precision than the ordinary methods of performing mathematical calculations. Many of the FORTRAN programs listed in this directory have optional use of the 8087 chip.

The 8087 chip works as a co-processor with the 8088 or 8086. It gives greater precision and speed to microprocessor mathematical calculations. The 8087 stores numbers in an 80-bit format, more precise than most mainframes. However, installing this chip in your computer does not automatically assure faster performance. The software in which the package was written must make use of this chip before it actually provides more speed to calculations.

Command Type: Programs use two distinct methods to allow the user to specify which tasks the program should perform. These methods are (1) the command driven approach, and (2) the menu approach.

1) Command Driven Programs - A command driven program is a program which responds to commands typed onto the

keyboard. For instance to perform a One Way ANOVA with the dataset named "AFIFI", and send the output to the printer, the command expected might be:

```
1WAY DATA=AFIFI OUTPUT=PRINTER;
```

Command driven programs are often faster to operate once you master the "language", but they can be difficult to learn. Some command driven programs, such as SAS/PC offer a "mask" or menu from which you may select procedures without actually using the procedural language.

2) Menu Driven Programs - A menu driven program is one in which the user is presented with a series of options and is allowed to choose one (like a multiple choice test). This type of program often "leads" the user to the eventual result. A menu driven program is often easy to learn to use, but repeated use of menus may become irritating and laborious.

Configuration - Computers are of different brands and within brands contain different operating systems and capabilities. In order for a particular piece of software to operate correctly, the configuration of the computer must match the needs of the software. The most common considerations are the operating system, the amount of internal memory required (RAM), the number of disk drives, and the language. Some programs may require certain types of monitors, printers, or other hardware components achieve the full benefits of the program.

Copyable disk - A diskette is said to be copyable if all information (usually a program) on that disk can be readily copied to another diskette. Program diskettes provided by a vendor may or may not be copyable. If a non-copyable (copy protected) diskette is ruined or damaged, it must be replaced by the manufacturer (many times at a cost). If a diskette is copyable, backups of the disk should be made to prevent loss of the program.

Foreign Data Access - Each program generally has its own way of entering and storing information. However, in many cases, data is created outside the statistical program. Some

programs allow accessing of data from "foreign" sources. This foreign data access may be an important consideration.

Some common ways of creating files from outside sources are:

1. Mainframe statistical packages often use "rectangular", or ASCII files of information. A rectangular file typically consists of information stored casewise with variables stored in a specified format. Data may be created in this way by an editor program, or in a word processing program. Some examples are EDLIN (on the PC-DOS disk), Versatext Editor, WordPerfect, Etc.

2. Spreadsheet and database programs output special files. Some common data interchange files include DIF, SYLK, DBF, and WKS. Some of the statistical programs are able to read these "foreign files" directly giving the user direct access to the data without having to translate it through another program. A few of the programs which may be used to enter, store, and manipulate data are:

Spreadsheet Programs: Lotus 1-2-3, Supercalc, Framework, Multiplan, and others.

Database Programs: dBASE III, RBASE, VersaForm, Pfs:FILE, PC FILE III and others.

Graphics - Graphics are "pictures", designs, or charts output by a program to the screen, printer, or to a graphics plotter. There are basically two kinds of graphics: character (text) graphics and pixel graphics. Character graphics are images created using available characters from the standard character set. For example, a histogram created with character graphics might be composed of the characters "I" and "#". Pixel graphics are images created by accessing each pixel (or dot) on the computer screen or dot matrix printer. Pixel graphics are more detailed and may produce more sophisticated images than character graphics. With pixel graphics you can draw circles, diagonal lines, and more complex images.

Language - Each program is written in some computer language. A computer language is a series of commands which are translated into machine code, and direct the computer to perform tasks (adding numbers, printing to line printer, etc.). The most common languages used for statistical programs are BASIC, Pascal, FORTRAN and C.

On Screen HELP function - A convenient feature of some programs is the ability of the program to "help" you at any point in the program by displaying information about what you are doing, or what your options are. This is often implemented using a "HELP" key. When the HELP key is pressed, explanatory information appears on the screen.

Operating System - The operating system is a computer program which manages the parts of the computer to make all of them work together, e.g. reading and writing from disk, reading the keyboard, etc. Operating systems are not usually compatible from one computer brand to another. The TRSDOS (Radio Shack) operating system will not work on the APPLE, for instance. Therefore, it is necessary that you have the correct operating system (and computer) for the software package you intend to run. The most common operating systems are IBM PC-DOS (similar to and sometimes compatible with MS-DOS), TRSDOS (Radio Shack), CP/M, APPLE DOS and UNIX. You must also make sure that the version of DOS you have matches the software's needs. For example, if you are operating under IBM PC-DOS version 1.1, you may not be able to read a diskette created using IBM PC-DOS version 2.0.

Program Structure - Programs are structured in two ways, integrated or separated. An integrated program is a series of smaller programs or modules which are linked together by a command menu or access mechanism. This means that from one central menu, you may perform such tasks as ANOVA, data description, and time series analysis. The opposite programming style is separated programs. Each program in this case is fully operational in itself so that to run an ANOVA, for example, a special ANOVA program would be used.

RAM (Random Access Memory) - This is the accessible internal memory of the computer, usually specifying how much "K" the computer holds -- e.g. 64K, 128K, etc. The K stands for 1024 bytes of information, so a 64K machine has more than 64 thousand bytes of internal storage, or RAM.

Shareware or User-Supported programs are distributed in a unique way. Unlike most programs which are licensed to a single machine, "shareware" programs may be copied and given to friends and associates without violating the copyright. The user may register for the program by sending the author a (typically small) registration fee, and is usually provided with a manual, update(s), and support. Two statistical programs in this vein are KWIKSTAT and EPISTAT.

Source Code - Source Code is a copy of the program in a readable form written in the original computer language. The availability of the source code may be important if you wish to customize the program for your own particular use or run it on a computer not specifically supported by the vendor.

Statistical Package - A "package" is a program which has the capability of performing several statistical functions. In this directory we have distinguished between a "package" and a "single purpose" program.

APPENDIX B: LISTING BY VENDORS

VENDOR	PRODUCT
	LOLITA
Addison Wesley Publishing Co. Inc.	EXPLORING STATISTICS WITH THE IBM PC
Anderson-Bell Corp.	ABSTAT RELEASE 4
Applied Biostatistics	NTSYS-PC
Applied Statistics	BIOM-PC
Aptech Systems, Inc	GAUSS
Automatic Forecasting Systems Inc	BOXX
Automatic Forecasting Systems Inc	SIMBOXJ
Automatic Forecasting Systems Inc.	AUTOBOX
Automatic Forecasting Systems Inc.	AUTOBJ
Automatic Forecasting Systems Inc.	MTS
Bass Institute Inc	BASS BASE PRODUCT
BB&A	ABTAB, RELEASE 3
Belanger Research Associates	BETASTAT
BMDP Statistical Software, Inc.	BMDP STATISTICAL SOFTWARE, INC.
Brain Power, Inc.	STATVIEW
Brain Power, Inc.	STATVIEW 512+
Brooks/Cole Publishing Company	INTRODUCTORY STATISTICS

VENDOR	PRODUCT
C. ABACI	THE SCIENTIFIC DESK
Center for Statistics, QC and Design	DISTRIB/ACCEPT
Center for Statistics, QC and Design	MIPSAQ
Center for Statistics, QC and Design	RELPAK
Circle Consulting	STAT/TRANSFER
COMPress	DESCRIPTIVE STATISTICS
COMPress	FILESTAT
COMPress	STATISTICS & PROBABILITY DEMONSTRATIONS
Compumetrix Corp.	MICRO DATA ANALYZER (MDA)
Computing Resource Center	STATA AND ADD-ON MODULE STATA/GRAPHICS
Conceptual Software	PRODAS
CONDUIT, The University of Iowa	EXPLORATORY DATA ANALYSIS
CONDUIT, The University of Iowa	RESEARCH METHODS:MAIN EFFECTS/INTERACT.
CONDUIT, The University of Iowa	RESEARCH METHODS:POWER
CONDUIT, The University of Iowa	RESEARCH METHODS:SURVEY SAMPLING
Consortium Software	ABC STATISTICAL SOFTWARE
Core Analytic, Inc.	4CAST/2, 4CAST/2X

VENDOR	PRODUCT
Core Analytic, Inc.	AUTOCAST
Creative Research Systems	THE SURVEY SYSTEM
Cricket Software	STATWORKS
Crunch Software	CRISP
Cuide Systems	MAC REGRESSION
D2 Software, Inc.	MACSPIN
Data Description, Inc.	DATA DESK
Data Resourses	ECONOMIST WORKSTATION
DataMyte Corporation	DATAMYTE ATTRIBUTE SOFTWARE
DataMyte Corporation	DATAMYTE FAN II SOFTWARE
Davell Custom Software	DCS MULTISTAT
DBi Software Products	TRAJECTORIES TS
Dept. of Mathematics and Statistics	STATCALC-IBM VERSION
Dr. William H. Green	LIMDEP
DYNACOMP	DYNACOMP STATISTICAL PROGRAMS
Economic Software Inc.	RESEARCH
Ecosoft, Inc	MICROSTAT
Elsevier - Biosoft	STATSTREAM
Elsevier - Biosoft	TADPOLE
Elsevier Scientific Software	BALANCE
Elsevier Scientific Software	CLUE

VENDOR	PRODUCT
Epicenter Software	EPILOG
Epicenter Software	POWER
Epistat Services	EPISTAT STATISTICAL PACKAGE VER 3.2
Exec*U*Stat, Inc.	EXEC*U*STAT
Functional Solutions, Inc	MPSS
G. R. Technologies Inc.	QC-PRO ATTRIBUTE DATA ANALYSIS
G. R. Technologies Inc.	QC-PRO DESIGNED EXPERIMENTS
G. R. Technologies Inc.	QC-PRO GAGE CONTROL/CAPABILITY
G. R. Technologies Inc.	QC-PRO STATISTICAL PROCESS CONTROL
G. R. Technologies Inc.	QC-PRO WEIBULL RELIABILITY ANALYSIS
Gary Perlman	UNIX/STAT
Great Northern Computer Services Ltd	AURORA "STATFLOW"
Gwilym Jenkins & Partners Ltd.	CONSUMER
Gwilym Jenkins & Partners Ltd.	MICRANAL-BJ
Hewlett Packard	HP STATISTICS LIBRARY/200/300
High Technology Software Products Inc	LAB STATISTICS PACKAGE
Human Edge	FORECASTING EDGE
Human Systems Dynamics	ANOVA II
Human Systems Dynamics	CALCU-PLOT

VENDOR	PRODUCT
Human Systems Dynamics	HSD STATS
Human Systems Dynamics	PC ANOVA
Human Systems Dynamics	PC STATISTICIAN
Human Systems Dynamics	QC PLOT
Human Systems Dynamics	REGRESS II
Human Systems Dynamics	STATS PLUS
Ideal Systems	ADVANCESTAT 3.0
Ideal Systems	INTROSTAT 2.2
Ideal Systems	PASE
Ideal Systems	STUDENTSTAT
IDV Datenanalyse und Versuchsplanung	N
IDV Datenanalyse und Versuchsplanung	RANCODE
IMSL, Inc.	STAT/PC-LIBRARY
Industrial Engineering & Mgt Press	STATISTICAL ANALYSIS GROUP
Information Analysis Corporation	MEDLOG
Information Systems Corporation	P-STATISTICS
International Statistical Programs Ctr.	CENTS (CENSUS TABULATION SYSTEM)
International Statistical Programs Ctr.	CONCOR (CONSISTENCY AND CORRECTION)

VENDOR	PRODUCT
J W Loosemore	SS/SPQC
John Wiley & Sons, Inc.	STATLIB.GL: STAT GRAPHICS SUBROUTINES
John Wiley & Sons, Inc.	STATLIB.TSF: TIME SERIES LIBRARY
John Wiley & Sons, Inc.	SURVCALC: SURVIVAL ANALYSIS
Joiner Associates Inc.	JASS(TM)
Lionheart Press, Inc	BUSINESS AND ECONOMIC FORECASTING
Lionheart Press, Inc	PERT & CRITICAL PATH TECHNIQUES
Lionheart Press, Inc.	BUSINESS AND FINANCE MATH
Lionheart Press, Inc.	BUSINESS STATISTICS
Lionheart Press, Inc.	EXPERIMENTAL STAT BOOK AND 2 DISKS
Lionheart Press, Inc.	FORECASTING AND TIME SERIES BOOK & DISK
Lionheart Press, Inc.	LINEAR AND NON-LINEAR PROGRAMMING
Lionheart Press, Inc.	OPTIMIZATION BOOK AND DISK
Logical Design Corporation	QUALITY ASSURANCE/STAT PROCESS CONTROL
Marcel Dekker, Inc.	QCPAC
Marcel Dekker, Inc.	STATPAL
Mathematical Software Co.	MULTIPLE FACTOR ANALYSIS
Mercator Computer Systems Ltd.	SNAP - SURVEY ANALYSIS PACKAGE

VENDOR	PRODUCT
Micropack, Inc	QCPACK
Ming Telecomputing Inc.	YSTAT STATISTICAL/FORECASTING PROGRAM
Minitab, Inc.	MINITAB DATA ANALYSIS SOFTWARE
Minitab, Inc.	MINITAB/1-2-3 & MULTIPLAN INTERFACE
MINUTEMAN Software	GPSS/PC
Mission Technologies	KWIKSTAT
Modicom Ltd.	MODISTAT
Morgan Computing Company, Inc.	MLR
MVA Systematica	MICROSURVEY
NCSS	NUMBER CRUNCHER STATISTICAL SYSTEM
NII Analytical Software	STATISTIX
Northwest Analytical Inc.	NWA STATPAK
Northwest Analytical, Inc.	NWA QUALITY ANALYST
P-Stat, Inc	P-STAT (R)
Pacific Crest Software, Inc.	POINT FIVE tm
Paul Hertzler & Co., Inc.	GAGETROL SOFTWARE
Paul Hertzler & Co., Inc.	QA/S SYSTEM
Paul Hertzler & Co., Inc.	RHEOLOGIC SYSTEM
Penton Software, Inc	QUALITYALERT
Penton Software, Inc	STATPRO

VENDOR	PRODUCT
Persimmon Software	MODULAR STATISTICAL SYSTEM
Porter Data Systems, Inc.	STATISTICAL PROCESS CONTROL
PQ Systems	SQCPACK
PrimeSoft Corp.	THE PRIME PLOTTER
Professional Applications Development	KYPPAD
Professional Applications Development	SAMSPAD-I
Professional Applications Development	STATPAD
Programmed Press	STATISTICAL FORECASTING
Qtec Services Ltd.	PC - MATRIX
Quality America, Inc.	SPC - PC
Quality Measurement Systems, Corp.	ANSTAT - LINEAR MEASUREMENTS
Quality Resources	CHART-PAK
Quality Resources	STAT-PAK
Quality Resources	STAT-PAK II
Quant Systems	THE STATISTICIAN
Quantitative Micro Software	MICROTSP 5.0
Questionnaire Service Company	SL-MICRO
Rapid Data	LOTUS STAT
Research and Development Institute Inc	MSUSTAT

VENDOR	PRODUCT
Rosen Grandon Associates	A-STAT 83
SAS Institute Inc.	SAS SYSTEM FOR PERSONAL COMPUTERS
Scientific Systems Inc.	FORECAST MASTER
Shazam Econometrics Limited	SHAZAM: THE ECONOMETRICS COMPUTER PROG
Significant Statistics	SIGSTAT
Small Business Computers of New England	WORMSTAT
Smart Software, Inc.	SMARTFORECASTS II
Sof-ware Tools	BIOMEDICAL RESEARCH CHART TOOL KIT
Sof-ware Tools	ENGINEERING TOOL KIT
Sof-Ware Tools	PROCESS CONTROL CHART TOOL KIT
Sof-ware Tools	STATS TOOL KIT
SPSS, Inc.	SPSS/PC+
SPSS, Inc.	SPSS/PC+ ADVANCED STATISTICS
SPSS, Inc.	SPSS/PC+ TABLES
SQC Systems, Inc.	SQCS
Stat-Ease, Inc.	DESIGN-EASEtm
STATCALC Holdings Ltd.	STATCALC
Statistical Consultants, Inc.	PCNONLIN
Statistical Consultants, Inc.	STAN

VENDOR	PRODUCT
Statistical Consulting Services	INSTAT
Statistical Consulting Services	INSTAT-D:Discrete Data Analysis
Statistical Consulting Services	INSTAT-P:Poisson Regression
Statistical Consulting Services	INSTAT-QC: QUALITY CONTROL CHARTS
Statistical Consulting Services	INSTAT-QF:Quick Forecaster
Statistical Consulting Services	INSTAT-R:Multiple Regression
Statistical Consulting Services	INSTAT-SC:THE STATISTICAL CALCULATOR
Statistical Consulting Services	INSTAT-U:UTILITIES
Statistical Graphics Coroporation	STATGRAPHICS
Statistical Programs	CONTOUR - I
Statistical Programs	EXPERTIMENTAL DESIGN
Statistical Programs	REGRESSION-I
Statistical Programs	SIMPLEX-V
Statistical Programs	T-AND F-TESTS
Statsoft, Inc.	APP-STAT
Statsoft, Inc.	COMM-STAT
Statsoft, Inc.	CSS

VENDOR	PRODUCT
Statsoft, Inc.	MACSS (MACINTOSH STATISTICAL SYSTEM)
Statsoft, Inc.	PSYCHOSTAT-3
Statsoft, Inc.	STATFAST
Statsoft, Inc.	STATS-2
Stephen Computer Services, Inc	SPC DATALYZER
Stochos,Inc.	CUSTOM/QC
Stone House Systems	DAISY PROFESSIONAL STATISTICS SYSTEM
Straightforward	STATISTICS BUTTONS
Strategic Locations Planning	ATLAS
Sugar Mill Software Corp.	STAT 1 - A STATISTICAL TOOLBOX
Systat, Inc.	SYSTAT
Team	GAUSSIAN PROBABILITY PLOTTING
Technical and Engineering for Management	NORMAL PROBABILITY PLOTTING
The Center for Quality Control Training	THE CONTROLLER
The Center for Quality Control Training	THE INSPECTOR
The Center for Quality Training	THE EXPLORER
The Futures Group	STATPLAN III
The Software Hill	STATMATE/PLUS
The Winchendon Group, Inc.	ELF - THE STATISTICAL PACKAGE

VENDOR	PRODUCT
Timberlake Clark Ltd	SPP
True Basic, Inc.	TRUESTAT
VAR Econometrics, Inc.	RATS
Walonick Associates, Inc	FORECAST PLUS (TM)
Walonick Associates, Inc	STATPAC(TM)- STAT. ANALYSIS PACKAGE
Walonick Associates, Inc.	STATPAC GOLD
Westat Associates Pty.Ltd.	MASS VERSION 4
Wiley Professional Software	X-STAT
ZiaSoft, Inc.	DATASTAT

APPENDIX C: SUMMARY TABLE - PROGRAM CAPABILITIES

	Descriptive Statistics	t-Tests	Correlation and Regression	Confidence Intervals	Categorical Data Analysis	ANOVA	Nonparametric Tests	Distributions	Time Series	Exploratory Data Analysis	Quality Control	Graphics	p-values given with tests
4CAST/2, 4CAST/2X	*	*	*			*		*	*	*		*	
A-STAT 83	*	*	*		*	*			*				*
ABC STATISTICAL SOFTWARE	*		*		*								
ABSTAT RELEASE 4	*	*	*		*	*	*					*	
ABTAB, RELEASE 3	*				*							*	*
ADVANCESTAT 3.0	*	*	*			*	*					*	
ANOVA II	*					*						*	
ANSTAT - LINEAR MEASUREMENTS	*										*	*	
APP-STAT	*	*	*		*	*	*	*	*			*	*
ATLAS	*											*	
AURORA "STATFLOW"	*	*	*	*	*	*	*	*				*	
AUTOBJ	*		*						*			*	
AUTOBOX									*			*	
AUTOCAST									*	*		*	
BALANCE	*	*		*			*					*	
BASS BASE PRODUCT	*	*	*		*							*	*
BETASTAT	*	*	*		*	*	*	*	*			*	
BIOM-PC	*		*	*	*	*	*	*				*	
BIOMEDICAL RESEARCH CHART TOOL KIT	*	*	*					*				*	*
BMDP STATISTICAL SOFTWARE, INC.	*	*	*	*	*	*	*		*	*	*	*	*
BOXX									*			*	
BUSINESS AND ECONOMIC FORECASTING													
BUSINESS AND FINANCE MATH													
BUSINESS STATISTICS													
CALCU-PLOT												*	

	Descriptive Statistics	t-Tests	Correlation and Regression	Confidence Intervals	Categorical Data Analysis	ANOVA	Nonparametric Tests	Distributions	Time Series	Exploratory Data Analysis	Quality Control	Graphics	p-values given with tests
CENTS (CENSUS TABULATION SYSTEM)	*												
CHART-PAK	*										*		
CLUE	*											*	
COMM-STAT	*	*	*		*	*	*	*	*			*	*
CONCOR (CONSISTENCY AND CORRECTION)													
CONSUMER									*			*	
CONTOUR - I										*		*	
CRISP	*	*	*		*	*	*					*	*
CSS	*	*	*	*	*	*	*	*	*	*		*	*
CUSTOM/QC	*	*	*		*	*		*	*	*	*	*	*
DAISY PROFESSIONAL STATISTICS SYSTEM	*	*	*		*	*	*		*			*	
DATA DESK	*	*	*	*	*	*						*	
DATAMYTE ATTRIBUTE SOFTWARE											*	*	
DATAMYTE FAN II SOFTWARE	*							*			*	*	
DATASTAT	*	*	*		*	*						*	
DCS MULTISTAT	*	*	*	*				*	*			*	
DESCRIPTIVE STATISTICS	*												
DESIGN-EASEtm													
DISTRIB/ACCEPT								*			*	*	
DYNACOMP STATISTICAL PROGRAMS													
ECONOMIST WORKSTATION	*	*	*	*		*			*			*	
ELF - THE STATISTICAL PACKAGE	*	*	*		*	*		*				*	

	Descriptive Statistics	t-Tests	Correlation and Regression	Confidence Intervals	Categorical Data Analysis	ANOVA	Nonparametric Tests	Distributions	Time Series	Exploratory Data Analysis	Quality Control	Graphics	p-values given with tests
ENGINEERING TOOL KIT	*		*	*	*	*		*				*	
EPILOG	*	*	*		*	*	*					*	*
EPISTAT STATISTICAL PACKAGE VER 3.2	*	*	*	*	*	*	*	*				*	*
EXEC*U*STAT	*	*	*	*	*	*	*		*	*		*	*
EXPERIMENTAL STAT BOOK AND 2 DISKS													
EXPERTIMENTAL DESIGN													
EXPLORATORY DATA ANALYSIS										*		*	
EXPLORING STATISTICS WITH THE IBM PC	*	*	*		*	*		*	*	*		*	
FILESTAT	*	*	*		*	*	*					*	
FORECAST MASTER	*	*	*					*	*			*	
FORECAST PLUS (TM)			*						*	*		*	
FORECASTING AND TIME SERIES BOOK & DISK													
FORECASTING EDGE									*			*	
GAGETROL SOFTWARE	*										*	*	
GAUSS	*	*	*	*	*	*	*	*	*			*	*
GAUSSIAN PROBABILITY PLOTTING	*		*	*				*				*	
GPSS/PC	*			*								*	
HP STATISTICS LIBRARY/200/300	*	*	*	*	*	*	*	*	*			*	*
HSD STATS	*	*	*		*							*	
INSTAT	*	*	*	*	*			*				*	*
INSTAT-D:Discrete Data Analysis	*		*		*							*	
INSTAT-P:Poisson Regression	*				*			*				*	*

	Descriptive Statistics	t-Tests	Correlation and Regression	Confidence Intervals	Categorical Data Analysis	ANOVA	Nonparametric Tests	Distributions	Time Series	Exploratory Data Analysis	Quality Control	Graphics	p-values given with tests
INSTAT-QC: QUALITY CONTROL CHARTS	*										*	*	
INSTAT-QF:Quick Forecaster									*			*	
INSTAT-R:Multiple Regression	*	*	*					*	*			*	*
INSTAT-SC:THE STATISTICAL CALCULATOR	*	*	*	*	*	*		*					*
INSTAT-U:UTILITIES													
INTRODUCTORY STATISTICS	*	*	*	*	*	*	*	*				*	*
INTROSTAT 2.2	*	*	*			*	*					*	
JASS(TM)	*		*			*						*	
KWIKSTAT	*	*	*		*	*		*		*		*	*
KYPPAD	*			*				*			*	*	
LAB STATISTICS PACKAGE	*		*										
LIMDEP	*	*	*	*	*	*		*	*		*	*	*
LINEAR AND NON-LINEAR PROGRAMMING													
LOLITA													
LOTUS STAT	*	*									*	*	
MAC REGRESSION	*		*									*	
MACSPIN	*											*	
MACSS (MACINTOSH STATISTICAL SYSTEM)	*	*	*		*	*	*	*	*			*	*
MASS VERSION 4	*	*	*		*	*	*	*	*			*	*
MEDLOG	*	*	*	*	*	*	*					*	*
MICRANAL-BJ									*			*	

	Descriptive Statistics	t-Tests	Correlation and Regression	Confidence Intervals	Categorical Data Analysis	ANOVA	Nonparametric Tests	Distributions	Time Series	Exploratory Data Analysis	Quality Control	Graphics	p-values given with tests
MICRO DATA ANALYZER (MDA)	*		*		*							*	
MICROSTAT	*	*	*		*	*	*	*	*			*	*
MICROSURVEY	*		*										
MICROTSP 5.0	*		*						*	*		*	
MINITAB DATA ANALYSIS SOFTWARE	*	*	*	*	*	*	*	*	*	*		*	*
MINITAB/1-2-3 & MULTIPLAN INTERFACE													
MIPSAQ	*	*	*	*	*	*	*	*		*	*	*	*
MLR			*										
MODISTAT	*	*	*		*	*	*	*	*	*	*	*	
MODULAR STATISTICAL SYSTEM													
MPSS	*	*	*	*	*	*	*	*	*	*		*	*
MSUSTAT	*	*	*	*	*	*	*	*				*	*
MTS									*			*	
MULTIPLE FACTOR ANALYSIS	*		*									*	
N													
NORMAL PROBABILITY PLOTTING	*		*	*				*				*	
NTSYS-PC	*											*	
NUMBER CRUNCHER STATISTICAL SYSTEM	*	*	*	*	*	*	*	*	*	*		*	
NWA QUALITY ANALYST	*	*	*		*	*	*	*			*	*	
NWA STATPAK	*	*	*	*	*	*	*	*	*	*		*	*
OPTIMIZATION BOOK AND DISK													

	Descriptive Statistics	t-Tests	Correlation and Regression	Confidence Intervals	Categorical Data Analysis	ANOVA	Nonparametric Tests	Distributions	Time Series	Exploratory Data Analysis	Quality Control	Graphics	p-values given with tests
P-STAT (R)	*	*	*		*	*	*			*		*	*
P-STATISTICS	*	*	*	*	*	*	*	*					*
PASE			*										
PC - MATRIX	*	*	*	*	*	*		*	*				*
PC ANOVA						*						*	
PC STATISTICIAN	*	*	*	*	*	*	*					*	*
PCNONLIN			*									*	
PERT & CRITICAL PATH TECHNIQUES													
POINT FIVE tm	*	*					*	*	*		*	*	
POWER													
PROCESS CONTROL CHART TOOL KIT	*		*					*			*	*	
PRODAS	*	*	*	*	*	*	*	*	*	*	*	*	*
PSYCHOSTAT-3	*	*	*		*	*	*	*				*	*
QA/S SYSTEM	*	*	*		*						*	*	
QC PLOT											*	*	
QC-PRO ATTRIBUTE DATA ANALYSIS	*										*	*	
QC-PRO DESIGNED EXPERIMENTS	*	*	*	*	*	*		*				*	
QC-PRO GAGE CONTROL/CAPABILITY	*										*	*	
QC-PRO STATISTICAL PROCESS CONTROL	*							*			*	*	
QC-PRO WEIBULL RELIABILITY ANALYSIS	*		*								*	*	
QCPAC	*				*			*			*	*	
QCPACK											*		

	Descriptive Statistics	t-Tests	Correlation and Regression	Confidence Intervals	Categorical Data Analysis	ANOVA	Nonparametric Tests	Distributions	Time Series	Exploratory Data Analysis	Quality Control	Graphics	p-values given with tests
QUALITY ASSURANCE/STAT PROCE33 CONTROL	*			*	*			*			*	*	
QUALITYALERT	*							*			*	*	
RANCODE													
RATS	*		*	*				*	*			*	
REGRESS II			*									*	*
REGRESSION-I			*	*		*							*
RELPAK	*										*	*	
RESEARCH	*		*						*			*	
RESEARCH METHODS:MAIN EFFECTS/INTERACT.													
RESEARCH METHODS:POWER													
RESEARCH METHODS:SURVEY SAMPLING													
RHEOLOGIC SYSTEM	*	*	*		*						*	*	
SAMSPAD-I								*			*	*	
SAS SYSTEM FOR PERSONAL COMPUTERS	*	*	*	*	*	*	*	*		*		*	*
SHAZAM: THE ECONOMETRICS COMPUTER PROG	*	*	*			*		*	*			*	
SIGSTAT	*	*	*	*	*	*	*		*	*	*	*	*
SIMBOXJ									*			*	
SIMPLEX-V													
SL-MICRO	*		*		*	*						*	
SMARTFORECASTS II	*		*	*					*			*	*

	Descriptive Statistics	t-Tests	Correlation and Regression	Confidence Intervals	Categorical Data Analysis	ANOVA	Nonparametric Tests	Distributions	Time Series	Exploratory Data Analysis	Quality Control	Graphics	p-values given with tests
SNAP - SURVEY ANALYSIS PACKAGE	*											*	
SPC - PC	*							*			*	*	*
SPC DATALYZER	*										*	*	
SPP	*	*	*	*	*	*	*	*				*	*
SPSS/PC+	*	*	*		*	*	*	*				*	*
SPSS/PC+ ADVANCED STATISTICS													
SPSS/PC+ TABLES	*												
SQCPACK	*							*			*	*	
SQCS	*	*	*								*	*	*
SS/SPQC	*		*					*			*	*	
STAN	*	*	*	*		*			*				*
STAT 1 - A STATISTICAL TOOLBOX	*	*	*	*	*	*	*	*	*			*	*
STAT-PAK	*	*	*		*			*			*	*	
STAT-PAK II				*	*	*		*			*		
STAT/PC-LIBRARY	*	*	*	*	*	*	*	*	*	*			*
STAT/TRANSFER													
STATA AND ADD-ON MODULE STATA/GRAPHICS	*	*	*	*	*	*	*	*	*	*	*	*	*
STATCALC	*	*	*	*	*	*	*	*		*		*	*
STATCALC-IBM VERSION						*	*	*		*		*	*
STATFAST	*	*	*		*	*	*	*	*			*	*
STATGRAPHICS	*	*	*	*	*	*	*	*	*	*	*	*	*
STATISTICAL ANALYSIS GROUP	*							*				*	
STATISTICAL FORECASTING	*	*	*	*				*	*	*			

	Descriptive Statistics	t-Tests	Correlation and Regression	Confidence Intervals	Categorical Data Analysis	ANOVA	Nonparametric Tests	Distributions	Time Series	Exploratory Data Analysis	Quality Control	Graphics	p-values given with tests
STATISTICAL PROCESS CONTROL											*	*	
STATISTICS & PROBABILITY DEMONSTRATIONS					*	*						*	
STATISTICS BUTTONS	*	*	*		*	*	*	*	*				
STATISTIX	*	*	*	*	*	*	*	*	*			*	*
STATLIB.GL: STAT GRAPHICS SUBROUTINES	*							*	*	*	*	*	
STATLIB.TSF: TIME SERIES LIBRARY	*		*	*				*	*		*		
STATMATE/PLUS	*	*	*		*	*	*	*			*	*	*
STATPAC GOLD	*	*	*	*	*	*	*	*	*	*		*	*
STATPAC(TM) - STAT. ANALYSIS PACKAGE	*	*	*	*	*	*		*				*	*
STATPAD	*	*	*		*	*		*			*	*	*
STATPAL	*	*	*		*	*	*	*				*	*
STATPLAN III	*		*		*	*			*			*	
STATPRO	*	*	*	*	*	*	*	*	*	*		*	*
STATS PLUS	*	*	*		*	*	*					*	*
STATS TOOL KIT	*	*		*	*	*	*	*					
STATS-2	*	*	*		*	*	*	*	*			*	*
STATSTREAM	*	*	*	*	*	*	*					*	
STATVIEW	*	*	*		*	*	*					*	
STATVIEW 512+	*	*	*	*	*	*	*	*				*	*
STATWORKS	*	*	*			*	*	*	*			*	*
STUDENTSTAT	*	*	*		*	*	*					*	
SURVCALC: SURVIVAL ANALYSIS	*		*				*				*	*	

	Descriptive Statistics	t-Tests	Correlation and Regression	Confidence Intervals	Categorical Data Analysis	ANOVA	Nonparametric Tests	Distributions	Time Series	Exploratory Data Analysis	Quality Control	Graphics	p-values given with tests
SYSTAT	*	*	*	*	*	*	*		*	*		*	*
T-AND F-TESTS		*				*							*
TADPOLE	*	*	*	*	*	*	*						
THE CONTROLLER	*										*	*	
THE EXPLORER	*	*	*	*	*	*	*	*		*		*	*
THE INSPECTOR											*	*	
THE PRIME PLOTTER	*		*		*			*	*		*	*	
THE SCIENTIFIC DESK	*	*	*	*	*	*		*				*	
THE STATISTICIAN	*	*	*	*	*	*	*		*	*		*	
THE SURVEY SYSTEM	*	*	*		*	*						*	
TRAJECTORIES TS	*	*	*	*	*	*	*	*	*			*	
TRUESTAT	*	*	*	*				*		*		*	*
UNIX/STAT	*	*	*		*	*	*	*	*			*	*
WORMSTAT	*	*	*		*	*	*	*				*	*
X-STAT	*		*	*		*		*				*	
YSTAT STATISTICAL/FORECASTING PROGRAM	*	*	*	*	*	*	*	*	*			*	*

APPENDIX D: SUMMARY TABLE - CONFIGURATIONS SUPPORTED

	IBM PC or MS DOS	APPLE II	MACINTOSH	CP/M Based	HP	TRS DOS	P-System	UNIX	COMMODORE
4CAST/2, 4CAST/2X	*								
A-STAT 83	*	*							
ABC STATISTICAL SOFTWARE	*								
ABSTAT RELEASE 4	*								
ABTAB, RELEASE 3	*								
ADVANCESTAT 3.0	*	*							
ANOVA II		*							
ANSTAT - LINEAR MEASUREMENTS	*				*				
APP-STAT		*							
ATLAS	*								
AURORA "STATFLOW"	*			*					
AUTOBJ	*								
AUTOBOX	*								
AUTOCAST	*								
BALANCE	*	*							
BASS BASE PRODUCT	*								
BETASTAT	*	*		*		*			
BIOM-PC	*								
BIOMEDICAL RESEARCH CHART TOOL KIT			*						
BMDP STATISTICAL SOFTWARE, INC.	*								
BOXX	*								
BUSINESS AND ECONOMIC FORECASTING	*	*		*					
BUSINESS AND FINANCE MATH	*	*		*					
BUSINESS STATISTICS	*	*		*					
CALCU-PLOT		*							

	IBM PC or MS DOS	APPLE II	MACINTOSH	CP/M Based	HP	TRS DOS	P-System	UNIX	COMMODORE
CENTS (CENSUS TABULATION SYSTEM)	*								
CHART-PAK	*			*					
CLUE	*	*							
COMM-STAT									*
CONCOR (CONSISTENCY AND CORRECTION)	*								
CONSUMER	*								
CONTOUR - I	*								
CRISP	*								
CSS	*								
CUSTOM/QC	*								
DAISY PROFESSIONAL STATISTICS SYSTEM		*							
DATA DESK			*						
DATAMYTE ATTRIBUTE SOFTWARE	*								
DATAMYTE FAN II SOFTWARE	*								
DATASTAT	*								
DCS MULTISTAT	*								
DESCRIPTIVE STATISTICS		*							
DESIGN-EASEtm	*								
DISTRIB/ACCEPT	*								
DYNACOMP STATISTICAL PROGRAMS									
ECONOMIST WORKSTATION	*								
ELF - THE STATISTICAL PACKAGE	*	*							

	IBM PC or MS DOS	APPLE II	MACINTOSH	CP/M Based	HP	TRS DOS	P-System	UNIX	COMMODORE
ENGINEERING TOOL KIT	*	*	*						
EPILOG	*								
EPISTAT STATISTICAL PACKAGE VER 3.2	*								
EXEC*U*STAT	*								
EXPERIMENTAL STAT BOOK AND 2 DISKS	*	*		*					
EXPERTIMENTAL DESIGN	*								
EXPLORATORY DATA ANALYSIS		*							
EXPLORING STATISTICS WITH THE IBM PC	*								
FILESTAT		*							
FORECAST MASTER	*								
FORECAST PLUS (TM)	*								
FORECASTING AND TIME SERIES BOOK & DISK	*	*		*					
FORECASTING EDGE	*								
GAGETROL SOFTWARE	*				*				
GAUSS	*								
GAUSSIAN PROBABILITY PLOTTING	*	*		*					
GPSS/PC	*								
HP STATISTICS LIBRARY/200/300					*				
HSD STATS		*							
INSTAT	*								
INSTAT-D:Discrete Data Analysis	*								
INSTAT-P:Poisson Regression	*								

	IBM PC or MS DOS	APPLE II	MACINTOSH	CP/M Based	HP	TRS DOS	P-System	UNIX	COMMODORE
INSTAT-QC: QUALITY CONTROL CHARTS	*								
INSTAT-QF:Quick Forecaster	*								
INSTAT-R:Multiple Regression	*								
INSTAT-SC:THE STATISTICAL CALCULATOR	*								
INSTAT-U:UTILITIES	*								
INTRODUCTORY STATISTICS	*	*							
INTROSTAT 2.2	*	*							
JASS(TM)	*								
KWIKSTAT	*								
KYPPAD	*								
LAB STATISTICS PACKAGE		*							
LIMDEP	*								
LINEAR AND NON-LINEAR PROGRAMMING	*	*		*					
LOLITA				*					
LOTUS STAT	*								
MAC REGRESSION			*						
MACSPIN			*						
MACSS (MACINTOSH STATISTICAL SYSTEM)			*						
MASS VERSION 4	*		*						
MEDLOG	*								
MICRANAL-BJ	*								

	IBM PC or MS DOS	APPLE II	MACINTOSH	CP/M Based	HP	TRS DOS	P-System	UNIX	COMMODORE
MICRO DATA ANALYZER (MDA)	*								
MICROSTAT	*			*					
MICROSURVEY									
MICROTSP 5.0	*								
MINITAB DATA ANALYSIS SOFTWARE	*								
MINITAB/1-2-3 & MULTIPLAN INTERFACE	*								
MIPSAQ	*								
MLR	*								
MODISTAT	*								
MODULAR STATISTICAL SYSTEM	*								
MPSS	*	*					*		
MSUSTAT	*								
MTS	*								
MULTIPLE FACTOR ANALYSIS	*	*							
N	*								
NORMAL PROBABILITY PLOTTING	*	*		*					
NTSYS-PC	*								
NUMBER CRUNCHER STATISTICAL SYSTEM	*		*						
NWA QUALITY ANALYST	*				*				
NWA STATPAK	*				*				
OPTIMIZATION BOOK AND DISK	*	*		*					

	IBM PC or MS DOS	APPLE II	MACINTOSH	CP/M Based	HP	TRS DOS	P-System	UNIX	COMMODORE
P-STAT (R)	*								
P-STATISTICS	*								
PASE		*							
PC - MATRIX	*								
PC ANOVA	*								
PC STATISTICIAN	*								
PCNONLIN	*				*				
PERT & CRITICAL PATH TECHNIQUES	*	*		*					
POINT FIVE tm	*								
POWER	*								
PROCESS CONTROL CHART TOOL KIT	*	*	*						
PRODAS	*								
PSYCHOSTAT-3				*					
QA/S SYSTEM	*				*				
QC PLOT		*							
QC-PRO ATTRIBUTE DATA ANALYSIS	*	*							
QC-PRO DESIGNED EXPERIMENTS	*								
QC-PRO GAGE CONTROL/CAPABILITY	*	*							
QC-PRO STATISTICAL PROCESS CONTROL	*	*							
QC-PRO WEIBULL RELIABILITY ANALYSIS	*	*							
QCPAC	*								
QCPACK	*								

	IBM PC or MS DOS	APPLE II	MACINTOSH	CP/M Based	HP	TRS DOS	P-System	UNIX	COMMODORE
QUALITY ASSURANCE/STAT PROCESS CONTROL	*				*				
QUALITYALERT	*								
RANCODE	*								
RATS	*								
REGRESS II		*							
REGRESSION-I	*								
RELPAK	*								
RESEARCH	*								
RESEARCH METHODS:MAIN EFFECTS/INTERACT.	*	*							
RESEARCH METHODS:POWER	*	*							
RESEARCH METHODS:SURVEY SAMPLING	*	*							
RHEOLOGIC SYSTEM	*								
SAMSPAD-I	*								
SAS SYSTEM FOR PERSONAL COMPUTERS	*								
SHAZAM: THE ECONOMETRICS COMPUTER PROG	*								
SIGSTAT	*				*				
SIMBOXJ	*								
SIMPLEX-V	*								
SL-MICRO	*	*		*					
SMARTFORECASTS II	*								

	IBM PC or MS DOS	APPLE II	MACINTOSH	CP/M Based	HP	TRS DOS	P-System	UNIX	COMMODORE
SNAP - SURVEY ANALYSIS PACKAGE	*								
SPC - PC	*								
SPC DATALYZER	*				*				
SPP	*								
SPSS/PC+	*								
SPSS/PC+ ADVANCED STATISTICS	*								
SPSS/PC+ TABLES	*								
SQCPACK	*	*			*				
SQCS	*								
SS/SPQC		*							
STAN	*	*		*					
STAT 1 - A STATISTICAL TOOLBOX	*								
STAT-PAK	*			*		*			
STAT-PAK II	*			*					
STAT/PC-LIBRARY	*								
STAT/TRANSFER	*								
STATA AND ADD-ON MODULE STATA/GRAPHICS	*								
STATCALC	*	*							
STATCALC-IBM VERSION	*								
STATFAST			*						
STATGRAPHICS	*								
STATISTICAL ANALYSIS GROUP	*	*							
STATISTICAL FORECASTING	*	*				*			*

	IBM PC or MS DOS	APPLE II	MACINTOSH	CP/M Based	HP	TRS DOS	P-System	UNIX	COMMODORE
STATISTICAL PROCESS CONTROL					*				
STATISTICS & PROBABILITY DEMONSTRATIONS		*							
STATISTICS BUTTONS	*								
STATISTIX	*	*							
STATLIB.GL: STAT GRAPHICS SUBROUTINES	*								
STATLIB.TSF: TIME SERIES LIBRARY	*								
STATMATE/PLUS	*			*					
STATPAC GOLD	*								
STATPAC(TM)- STAT. ANALYSIS PACKAGE	*			*					
STATPAD	*								
STATPAL	*								
STATPLAN III	*								
STATPRO	*								
STATS PLUS		*							
STATS TOOL KIT			*						
STATS-2	*								
STATSTREAM		*							
STATVIEW			*						
STATVIEW 512+			*						
STATWORKS			*						
STUDENTSTAT		*							
SURVCALC: SURVIVAL ANALYSIS	*								

	IBM PC or MS DOS	APPLE II	MACINTOSH	CP/M Based	HP	TRS DOS	P-System	UNIX	COMMODORE
SYSTAT	*		*	*				*	
T-AND F-TESTS	*	*							
TADPOLE	*								
THE CONTROLLER	*								
THE EXPLORER	*								
THE INSPECTOR	*								
THE PRIME PLOTTER		*							
THE SCIENTIFIC DESK									
THE STATISTICIAN	*			*		*		*	
THE SURVEY SYSTEM	*								
TRAJECTORIES TS	*			*	*				
TRUESTAT	*		*						*
UNIX/STAT	*							*	
WORMSTAT			*						
X-STAT	*								
YSTAT STATISTICAL/FORECASTING PROGRAM	*				*				

APPENDIX E: MICROCOMPUTER STATISTICAL PROGRAM QUESTIONNAIRE

1988 Version

Return completed questionnaire to:
Dr. Wayne A. Woodward
Department of Statistics
Southern Methodist University
Dallas, TX 75275

NOTE: If you market more than one statistical program, please copy this questionnaire and complete one for each program.

NAME OF PROGRAM(S) OR PACKAGE ____________________
SUPPLIER: ____________________
____
ADDRESS: ____________________
____
PHONE: ____________________
CONTACT PERSON: ____________________
ADDRESS AND PHONE NUMBER IF DIFFERENT FROM ABOVE:
____
____

GENERAL INFORMATION

NUMBER OF CURRENT USERS ____________________
DATE OF FIRST RELEASE ____________________
SPECIFY CURRENT VERSION NUMBER ____________
RELEASE DATE OF CURRENT VERSION ____________
IS ADDITIONAL SOFTWARE REQUIRED? ____________
IF YES, LIST REQUIRED SOFTWARE ____________________

CONFIGURATIONS SUPPORTED - List the configurations supported by your program in the spaces below. If more than one configuration is supported, list the four major ones.

	CONFIGURATIONS			
	I	II	III	IV
COMPUTER(S)				
LANGUAGE(S) USED				
OPERATING SYSTEM				
RAM REQUIRED				
# DISK DRIVES				
COST OF PROGRAM (RETAIL)				

If capabilities of your program vary based on configuration or computer, please either copy the questionnaire and complete one for each version, or clarify differences as you respond.

PROGRAM DESCRIPTION - Please provide us with a brief written description (200 words or less) of your program on this sheet. In order to standardize the format of the product descriptions, your description should consist of two paragraphs, as detailed below:

Paragraph 1 - A general description of your product. For whom is the program written? What are its major uses?

Paragraph 2 - Description of what you consider to be the unique and most important features of your product, i.e. what makes it distinctive from other available programs.

PLEASE CHECK ITEMS BELOW DESCRIBING YOUR PROGRAM

GENERAL PROGRAM FEATURES
________SOURCE CODE AVAILABLE
________COPYABLE DISK
________ON SCREEN HELP FUNCTION
WHICH ONE OF THE FOLLOWING BEST DESCRIBES THE PURPOSE OF THE PROGRAM?
________EDUCATIONAL USE
________STATISTICAL ANALYSIS
WHICH ONE OF THE FOLLOWING BEST DESCRIBES "COMMAND" TYPE
________MENU/QUESTION DIRECTED?
________COMMAND DIRECTED
WHICH ONE OF THE FOLLOWING BEST DESCRIBES PROGRAM STRUCTURE?
________INTEGRATED SYSTEM (PROGRAM PERFORMS SEVERAL PROCEDURES)
________SEPARATE (UNLINKED) PROGRAMS FOR EACH PROCEDURE
________SPECIALTY CHIPS (SUCH AS 8087) SUPPORTED
IF CHECKED, WHAT CHIP(S)?____
IS SUPPORT OPTIONAL?______
HOW WOULD YOU DESCRIBE YOUR PROGRAM? (CHOOSE ONE)
________STATISTICAL PACKAGE
SPECIAL PURPOSE PROGRAM FOR
________ANOVA/GENERAL LINEAR MODELS
________REGRESSION ANALYSIS
________CATEGORICAL DATA ANALYSIS
________NONPARAMETRIC TESTS
________TIMES SERIES ANALYSIS
________EXPLORATORY DATA ANALYSIS
________GRAPHICS
________QUALITY CONTROL OR RELIABILITY
________OTHER - PLEASE SPECIFY
____

DOCUMENTATION
________USERS MANUAL
________TABLE OF CONTENTS
________INDEX
________TUTORIAL OR EXAMPLE LESSONS
________SAMPLE RUNS
________FORMULAS PROVIDED
________QUICK REFERENCE CARD
________TUTORIALS AND EXAMPLES ON DISK
NUMBER OF PAGES IN USERS MANUAL__________
NUMBER OF TECHNICAL REFERENCES IN USERS MANUAL_________

DATA MANAGEMENT

- _______KEYBOARD DATA ENTRY
- _______DATA MANIPULATION (TRANSFORMATIONS, ETC.)
- _______MISSING VALUES IN DATA ALLOWED
- DATA EDITING
  - _______CHANGE
  - _______ADD
  - _______DELETE
- FOREIGN DATA ACCESS
  - _______STANDARD RECTANGULAR ASCII FILE
  - _______DIF FILES
  - _______dBASE II FILES
  - _______OTHER - PLEASE LIST

GRAPHICS

- _______GRAPHICS APPEAR IN COLOR ON THE MONITOR
- _______GRAPHICS CAN BE OUTPUT TO A PRINTER
- _______GRAPHICS CAN BE SAVED TO A FILE
- _______TITLES AND/OR LABELS CAN BE INCLUDED ON GRAPHS
- WHAT TYPE OF GRAPHICS DOES THE PROGRAM USE?
  - _______PIXEL GRAPHICS
  - _______CHARACTER OR TEXT GRAPHICS
- WHAT GRAPHICS CAN BE CREATED?
  - _______HISTOGRAMS AND/OR BAR CHARTS
  - _______PIE CHART
  - _______SCATTER (X-Y) PLOTS
  - _______3-D PLOTTING
  - _______BOX PLOTS
  - _______OTHER GRAPHICS - PLEASE SPECIFY

PRODUCT SUPPORT

- _______CLASSES OR INSTRUCTION AVAILABLE
- _______FREE TELEPHONE SUPPORT
  - _______800 NUMBER AVAILABLE
  - _______USER MAY CALL AT OWN EXPENSE

PRODUCT REVIEW

- _______THE PRODUCT HAS BEEN REVIEWED IN THE LITERATURE

If your product has been reviewed, please provide references to any reviews which have been written about your program in the space below. In order for a review to be listed in the Directory, you must provide a full bibliographic reference including: Author(s), Title of Review Article, Name of Journal or Periodical, Page Numbers, Date. (Please attach a copy of any of these reviews which you can provide us.)

STATISTICAL PROCEDURES SUPPORTED

DESCRIPTIVE STATISTICS

________MEAN
________STANDARD DEVIATION OR VARIANCE
________STANDARD ERROR OF THE MEAN
________COEFFICIENT OF VARIATION
________MINIMUM, MAXIMUM
________MEDIAN
________PERCENTILES
________SKEWNESS
________KURTOSIS
________OTHERS - PLEASE LIST

T-TESTS

________ONE-SAMPLE T-TEST
________INDEPENDENT GROUP T-TEST WITH EQUAL VARIANCES
________INDEPENDENT GROUP T-TEST WITH UNEQUAL VARIANCES
________PAIRED T-TEST
________OTHER - PLEASE LIST

CORRELATION AND REGRESSION

________PEARSON CORRELATION COEFFICIENT
________SIMPLE LINEAR REGRESSION
________MULTIPLE LINEAR REGRESSION
________STEPWISE MULTIPLE LINEAR REGRESSION
________NON-LINEAR REGRESSION
________RESIDUALS CALCULATED
________RESIDUALS PLOTTED
________OTHER - PLEASE LIST

CONFIDENCE INTERVALS

________MEANS
________DIFFERENCE BETWEEN TWO MEANS
________PROPORTIONS
________DIFFERENCE BETWEEN TWO PROPORTIONS
________VARIANCES
________RATIO OF VARIANCES
________OTHER - PLEASE LIST

CATEGORICAL DATA ANALYSIS

_______CHI-SQUARE CONTINGENCY TABLE ANALYSIS
_______MULTI-DIMENSIONAL TABLES
_______FISHER'S EXACT TEST
_______GOODNESS-OF-FIT TESTS
_______FREQUENCIES CAN BE ENTERED DIRECTLY
_______OTHER - PLEASE LIST

ANALYSIS OF VARIANCE (ANOVA)

_______ONE WAY ANOVA
_______REPEATED MEASURES ONE WAY ANOVA
_______TWO-WAY ANALYSIS OF VARIANCE
 _______UNEQUAL CELL SIZES ALLOWED
_______MULTIPLE COMPARISON TESTS - PLEASE LIST
_______ANALYSIS OF COVARIANCE
_______OTHER ANOVAS - PLEASE LIST

NONPARAMETRIC TESTS

_______SIGN TEST (SIGNED-RANK)
_______WILCOXON ONE SAMPLE TEST
_______MANN-WHITNEY U
_______KRUSKAL-WALLIS TEST
_______FRIEDMAN CHI-SQUARE TEST
_______SPEARMAN OR KENDALL CORRELATION COEFFICIENT
_______OTHERS - PLEASE LIST

DISTRIBUTION FUNCTION EVALUATION

_______NORMAL
_______T
_______CHI-SQUARE
_______F
_______BINOMIAL
_______HYPERGEOMETRIC
_______POISSON
_______OTHERS - PLEASE LIST

TIME SERIES ANALYSIS
- ______AUTOCORRELATIONS
- ______CROSS CORRELATIONS
- ______PLOTS - WHAT PLOTS ARE AVAILABLE?______
- ______MOVING AVERAGE SMOOTHING
- ______AUTOREGRESSIVE MOVING AVERAGE (ARMA AND ARIMA)
  - ______MODEL IDENTIFICATION
  - ______PARAMETER ESTIMATION
- ______FORECASTING - WHAT METHODS?______
- ______SPECTRAL ESTIMATES - WHICH METHODS?______

EXPLORATORY DATA ANALYSIS
- ______STEM-AND-LEAF DISPLAYS
- ______LETTER-VALUE DISPLAYS
- ______RESISTANT LINE
- ______SMOOTHING TECHNIQUES
- ______MEDIAN POLISH
- ______ROOTOGRAMS
- ______OTHER - PLEASE LIST

QUALITY CONTROL OR RELIABILITY

CONTROL CHARTS FOR
- ______$\bar{X}$
- ______S
- ______PROPORTIONS
- ______NUMBER OF DEFECTS
- ______NUMBER OF DEFECTIVES

ACCEPTANCE SAMPLING BY
- ______ATTRIBUTES
- ______VARIABLES

RELIABILITY BASED ON
- ______EXPONENTIAL
- ______WEIBULL
- ______GAMMA
- ______LOGISTIC
- ______OTHER - PLEASE LIST

OTHER - PLEASE LIST

MISCELLANEOUS
- ______CLUSTER ANALYSIS
- ______LIFE TABLE ANALYSIS
- ______RANDOM NUMBER GENERATION
- ______TEST FOR NORMALITY OF DATA
- ______TEST FOR EQUALITY OF VARIANCES
- ______LINEAR DISCRIMINANT FUNCTION CALCULATION
- ______SAMPLE SIZE ESTIMATION
- ______P-VALUES GIVEN WITH TESTS
- ______OTHER - PLEASE LIST

PROGRAM DESIGNED FOR
Data Analysis

PROGRAM STYLE
Menu Driven
Integrated System

MISCELLANEOUS PROGRAM FEATURES
On Screen Help Function

DOCUMENTATION
User's Manual - ? pages, ? technical references
Table of Contents
Index
Tutorial or Example Lessons
Sample Runs
Tutorials and Examples on Disk

DATA MANAGEMENT
Keyboard Data Entry

DATA EDITING
Change
Add
Delete

GRAPHICS FEATURES
Graphics can be Output to a Printer
Graphics can be Saved to a File

GRAPHICS
Histograms

PRODUCT SUPPORT
User may call at own Expense
Classes or Instruction Available

STATISTICAL FEATURES SUPPORTED

DESCRIPTIVE STATISTICS
- Mean
- Standard Deviation or Variance
- Minimum, Maximum
- Percentiles
- Skewness
- Kurtosis
- Capability Ratio
- Capability Index
- ZU
- ZL

CONFIDENCE INTERVALS
- Means

CATEGORICAL DATA ANALYSIS
- Frequencies Can be Entered Directly

DISTRIBUTION FUNCTION EVALUATION
- Normal

CONTROL CHARTS
- X-Bar
- s
- Proportions
- Number of Defects
- Number of Defectives
- Pareto Charts
- U
- C
- NP
- P
- R

QUALITYALERT

Penton Software, Inc
420 Lexington Ave., Suite 2846
New York, NY 10017
(212) 878 - 9600
Contact Person: Christine Curtin

CONFIGURATIONS SUPPORTED

Computer	Language	Operating System	RAM	Number Drives	Cost
IBM PC	BASIC	DOS	256K	2	$ 795

NUMBER OF CURRENT USERS 4000
DATE OF FIRST RELEASE Jul 83
CURRENT VERSION RELEASED Sept 86

PROGRAM DESCRIPTION

QUALITYALERT is a general purpose statistical quality control program designed primarily for the purpose of process control based upon sample data using a microcomputer. This is accomplished by means of 8 control charts that consider different aspects of variable and attribute data. The system may also be used for process monitoring, pattern detection, and to some extent, lot acceptance and monitoring. Three data simulators are included which can be used to generate normal and binomial samples and Poisson data. The latter are useful for developing data files easily within the system as well as understanding how the system responds to variation of input parameters. Output of the system consists of numeric and graphic information. QUALITYALERT embodies a point of view, concepts and approaches for identifying process problems and for correcting them.

Error trap routines are embedded through the program to catch inconsistencies and incorrectly imputted responses. These are accompanied by prompted retry options. The program is accompanied by a user's manual and an extensive set of tutorials that can be used to learn the system easily and thoroughly. For most, working through one tutorial is sufficient to learn the system. Versions of QUALITYALERT have been installed in more than 4000 organizations throughout the United States and Canada. On the basis of that experience QUALITYALERT has been changed to better fulfill end user requirements.

PRODUCT REVIEWS

"Keeping Current", Production Engineering Magazine, (May 1984).

Computer Aided Engineering, pp. 22, (Mar/Apr 1984).

Interface Age Magazine, pp. 111, (March 1984).

"Software for Quality Control", Chemical Engineering, (May 1985).

"PC's and Software Chart Quality Control", Design News, (February 1986).

Stoll, Marilyn. "Software has Special Stat. Functions for Quality Control", PC Week, (December 1985).

TYPE OF PROGRAM

Quality Control or Reliability

PROGRAM DESIGNED FOR

Data Analysis

PROGRAM STYLE

Menu Driven
Integrated System

DOCUMENTATION

User's Manual - 100 pages, ? technical references
- Table of Contents
- Index
- Tutorial or Example Lessons
- Sample Runs
- Formulas Provided

DATA MANAGEMENT

Keyboard Data Entry

DATA EDITING

Change
Add
Delete

FOREIGN DATA ACCESS

DIF Files
dBase II Files
Gage Talker OS-4 Interface
Datamyte Interface
Symphony
dBASE III Files
Lotus 1-2-3
ASCII

GRAPHICS FEATURES

Graphics can be Output to a Printer
Graphics can be Saved to a File
Titles and/or Labels Available

GRAPHICS

Histograms
Control Charts
Process Capability
Descriptive Statistics

PRODUCT SUPPORT

Free Phone Support Available
Classes or Instruction Available

STATISTICAL FEATURES SUPPORTED

DESCRIPTIVE STATISTICS

Mean
Standard Deviation or Variance
Standard Error of the Mean
Minimum, Maximum
Median
Skewness
Kurtosis

DISTRIBUTION FUNCTION EVALUATION

Normal
Binomial
Poisson

CONTROL CHARTS

- Number of Defects
- Number of Defectives
- CuSum Chart
- c-Chart
- Chart of Individual Values
- Moving Range Chart
- Moving Average Chart
- P(%) for % Defective/Variable N
- P(%) for % Defective/Constant N
- X-Bar/SD
- X-Bar/Range

OTHER QUALITY CONTROL PROCEDURES

- Acceptance Sampling by Attributes
- Acceptance Sampling by Variables
- Process Capability for Variable Data
- Process Capability Index
- Z-Values Based on Tolerance Limits
- Transformations to Normality
- Others

RANCODE

IDV Datenanalyse und Versuchsppplanung
Wessobrunner Str. 6
8035 Gauting, W. GERMANY
089/850-8001
Contact Person: Dr. V.W. Rahlfs

CONFIGURATIONS SUPPORTED

Computer	Language	Operating System	RAM	Number Drives	Cost
IBM PC		DOS	192K	1	$750

NUMBER OF CURRENT USERS 65
DATE OF FIRST RELEASE 1984
VERSION 2.2 RELEASED JUN 86

PROGRAM DESCRIPTION

RANCODE is a program designed to carry out a fully automatic randomizing for experimental design, i.e. production of random code lists, identification cards, printing of labels for packaging, etc.

RANCODE creates random code lists for the planning of randomized experiments according to a simple randomization scheme or a random permuted block scheme. (In the latter, the treatment groups are balanced concerning the number of experimental units after each "block" of a user defined size: e.g. each "block" of four subjects contains exactly two subjects with treatment A, and two subjects with treatment B). In a single execution you can create up to 20 random code lists, each with up to twenty treatment groups; one code list may contain up to 800 units. The program dialog with the user is very simple and well structured, and it should take a novice no more than 15 minutes to comprehend its operation.

TYPE OF PROGRAM

Experimental Design Randomizing

PROGRAM DESIGNED FOR

Data Analysis

PROGRAM STYLE
Menu Driven
Integrated System

MISCELLANEOUS PROGRAM FEATURES
Copyable Disk

DOCUMENTATION
User's Manual - 14 pages, technical references

PRODUCT SUPPORT
User may call at own Expense
No Classes or Instruction Available

STATISTICAL FEATURES SUPPORTED

MISCELLANEOUS
Random Number Generation

RATS

VAR Econometrics, Inc.
PO Box 19334
Minneapolis, MN 55418
(612) 789 - 9020
Contact Person: John Smach

CONFIGURATIONS SUPPORTED

Computer	Language	Operating System	RAM	Number Drives	Cost
IBM PC		DOS	256K	2	$ 200

NUMBER OF CURRENT USERS 4000
DATE OF FIRST RELEASE JUN 84
VERSION 2.1 RELEASED JUL 86

ADDITIONAL SOFTWARE REQUIRED

Wordprocessing Software for Batch

PROGRAM DESCRIPTION

RATS is a command driven package that can perform every task one is likely to encounter in a first year graduate econometrics course at a leading university. RATS is a serious econometrics package that was developed for main frame computers and has been used in Economics Departments at leading universities, government agencies and businesses for the past six years. RATS now comes with a menu driven program, E-Z-RATS that makes it easily accessible to new users.

RATS handles Bayesian Vector Autoregressions and other time series problems very easily. RATS performs the standard OLS, ARIMA, BVAR's time varying coefficients, probit and logit, two and three stage least squares, weighted least squares, instrumental variables, seemingly unrelated regression, nonlinear least squares, Cochrane-Orcutt, the Kalman filter, ridge regression, polynomial distributed lags, Shiller Smoothness prior, and principal components analysis.

PRODUCT REVIEWS

Bryan, Marvin. "Business Forecasting: 16 Ways to Predict the Future", PC Magazine, Vol. 5, No. 14, pp. 211-234.

TYPE OF PROGRAM
Statistical Package

PROGRAM DESIGNED FOR
Data Analysis

PROGRAM STYLE
Menu Driven
Command Driven
Integrated System

MISCELLANEOUS PROGRAM FEATURES
Copyable Disk
On Screen Help Function
Optional Support for 8087, 80287 Mathematical Chip

DOCUMENTATION
User's Manual - 500 pages, ? technical references
Table of Contents
Index
Tutorial or Example Lessons
Sample Runs
Formulas Provided
Quick Reference Card
Tutorials and Examples on Disk

DATA MANAGEMENT
Keyboard Data Entry
Data Manipulations and Transformations
Missing Values Allowed in Data

DATA EDITING
Change
Add
Delete

FOREIGN DATA ACCESS
Standard Rectangular ASCII Files
DIF Files
WKS Files
Citibase Mini

GRAPHICS FEATURES
Graphics Appear in Color on the Monitor
Graphics can be Output to a Printer
Graphics can be Saved to a File
Titles and/or Labels Available
Uses Pixel Graphics

GRAPHICS
- Histograms
- Box Plots

PRODUCT SUPPORT
- User may call at own Expense
- No Classes or Instruction Available

STATISTICAL FEATURES SUPPORTED

DESCRIPTIVE STATISTICS
- Mean
- Standard Deviation or Variance
- Standard Error of the Mean
- Coefficient of Variation
- Minimum, Maximum
- Skewness
- Kurtosis

CORRELATION AND REGRESSION
- Simple Linear Regression
- Multiple Linear Regression
- Non-Linear Regression
- Residuals Calculated
- **REGRESSION PLOTS**
  - Residuals

CONFIDENCE INTERVALS
- Means

DISTRIBUTION FUNCTION EVALUATION
- Normal
- t
- Chi Square
- F

TIME SERIES ANALYSIS
- Autocorrelations
- Cross Correlations
- Moving Average Smoothing
- AUTOREGRESSIVE MOVING AVERAGE
  - Model Identification
  - Parameter Estimation
- Spectral Estimation
- **TIME SERIES ANALYSIS - FORECASTING**
  - ARIMA
  - Regression
  - VAR

MISCELLANEOUS

Random Number Generation

REGRESS II

Human Systems Dynamics
9010 Reseda Blvd, Suite 222
Northridge, CA 91324
(818) 993 - 8536
Contact Person: Merideth Wiberg

CONFIGURATIONS SUPPORTED

Computer	Language	Operating System	RAM	Number Drives	Cost
APPLE II	BASIC	DOS	48K	1	$ 150

NUMBER OF CURRENT USERS 1000
DATE OF FIRST RELEASE Jul 83
VERSION 1 RELEASED Jan 85

PROGRAM DESCRIPTION

REGRESS II an integrated set of programs for the analysis of multiple correlation and regression. The package provides professionals with a research database and five full multiple regression solution methods. With REGRESS II the user can obtain correlation and covariance matrices along with descriptive statistics, multiple and partial correlations and serial correlation of residuals. Data can be entered from other HSD programs or from VISICALC or entered by keyboard and saved or analyzed directly.

REGRESS II includes data file creation and maintenance programs with search and select and data transformation abilities. The program is very easy to use. It is almost entirely menu-driven, guiding problem definition and data entry with ease. The highly comprehensive documentation leads the user step-by-step through each type of analysis.

PRODUCT REVIEWS

"Psychotherapy in Practice", Popular Computing, (Oct 1983).

TYPE OF PROGRAM

Statistical Package

PROGRAM DESIGNED FOR
Data Analysis

PROGRAM STYLE
Menu Driven
Integrated System

DOCUMENTATION
User's Manual - 83 pages, 7 technical references
Index
Sample Runs

DATA MANAGEMENT
Keyboard Data Entry
Data Manipulations and Transformations

FOREIGN DATA ACCESS
VisiCalc

GRAPHICS FEATURES
Graphics can be Saved to a File
Titles and/or Labels Available
Uses Pixel Graphics

GRAPHICS
Scatter (x-y) Plots

PRODUCT SUPPORT
Free Phone Support Available
No Classes or Instruction Available

STATISTICAL FEATURES SUPPORTED

CORRELATION AND REGRESSION
Multiple Linear Regression
Stepwise Multiple Linear Regression
Non-Linear Regression
Residuals Calculated
Partial Correlation
Correlation Matrices
Cp Statistic
Logarithmic Regression
Multiple Correlation

MISCELLANEOUS
p-Values Given With Tests

REGRESSION-I

Statistical Programs
9941 Rowlett, Suite 6
Houston, TX 77075
(713) 947 - 1551
Contact Person: Bonnie Deming

CONFIGURATIONS SUPPORTED

Computer	Language	Operating System	RAM	Number Drives	Cost
IBM PC	BASIC	DOS	256K	1	$150

NUMBER OF CURRENT USERS ?
DATE OF FIRST RELEASE 1985
CURRENT VERSION RELEASED ?

PROGRAM DESCRIPTION

REGRESSION-I is a computer program for scientists and engineers involved in Research and Development. It is used for fitting linear models to data.

With REGRESSION-I the user must first supply the data set and model through two BASIC language subprograms. These programs are then merged with REGRESSION-I and the complete program is then run. Several models may be fit to a single data set or a single model may be fit sequentially to several data sets, because, once entered, the data and model are present on the diskette. Great flexibility is allowed, because the user is able to create the subprogram containing the model. The only requirement is that the model be linear in the parameters (i.e., any one term in the model may contain one and only one multiplicative parameter).

TYPE OF PROGRAM

Regression Analysis

PROGRAM DESIGNED FOR

Data Analysis
Educational use

PROGRAM STYLE

Command Driven
Integrated System

MISCELLANEOUS PROGRAM FEATURES
Source Code Available
Copyable Disk

DOCUMENTATION
User's Manual - 25 pages, 5 technical references
Table of Contents
Tutorial or Example Lessons
Tutorials and Examples on Disk

DATA MANAGEMENT
Keyboard Data Entry

DATA EDITING
Change
Add
Delete

PRODUCT SUPPORT
User may call at own Expense
No Classes or Instruction Available

STATISTICAL FEATURES SUPPORTED

CORRELATION AND REGRESSION
Simple Linear Regression
Multiple Linear Regression
Residuals Calculated

CONFIDENCE INTERVALS
Variances
Ratio of Variances

ANALYSIS OF VARIANCE
For Linear Models

MISCELLANEOUS
Test for Equality of Variances
p-Values Given With Tests

RELPAK

Center for Statistics, QC and Design
SUNY - Binghamton
Binghamton, NY 13901
(607) 777 - 2619
Contact Person: Ellen Tattenbaum

CONFIGURATIONS SUPPORTED

Computer	Language	Operating System	RAM	Number Drives	Cost
IBM PC	BASIC	MS-DOS	64K	2	$ 100

NUMBER OF CURRENT USERS 120
DATE OF FIRST RELEASE Jan 84
CURRENT VERSION RELEASED Jan 84

PROGRAM DESCRIPTION

RELPAK is a menu-driven package specifically designed for reliability analysis of failure data. Its main feature is its high-resolution probability plotting capability for graphical fitting of failure data to a variety of standard life distributions. In addition, it does high-resolution plots of histograms and empirical CDF's and calculates the usual descriptive statistics. Data can be entered from the keyboard, from an external data disk, or can be simulated from a variety of distributions.

RELPAK has undergone thousands of hours of user testing in an industrial workshop on reliability analysis.

TYPE OF PROGRAM
Statistical Package

PROGRAM DESIGNED FOR
Data Analysis

PROGRAM STYLE
Menu Driven
Integrated System

MISCELLANEOUS PROGRAM FEATURES
Copyable Disk

DOCUMENTATION
User's Manual - 0 pages, 0 technical references
Table of Contents
Index
Tutorial or Example Lessons
Sample Runs
Formulas Provided
Tutorials and Examples on Disk

DATA MANAGEMENT
Keyboard Data Entry

GRAPHICS FEATURES
Graphics can be Output to a Printer
Uses Pixel Graphics

GRAPHICS
Histograms
Probability Plots
Empirical CDF

PRODUCT SUPPORT
User may call at own Expense
No Classes or Instruction Available

STATISTICAL FEATURES SUPPORTED

DESCRIPTIVE STATISTICS
Mean
Standard Deviation or Variance
Minimum, Maximum
Median
Percentiles

RELIABILITY
Exponential
Weibull
Normal
Log-normal
Extreme Value

MISCELLANEOUS
Random Number Generation

RESEARCH
Economic Software Inc.
P.O. Box 10925
Eugene, OR 97440
(503) 686 - 8807
Contact Person: Jay Wilson

CONFIGURATIONS SUPPORTED

Computer	Language	Operating System	RAM	Number Drives	Cost
IBM PC		DOS	192K		$424

NUMBER OF CURRENT USERS ?
DATE OF FIRST RELEASE 1983
VERSION 2.0 RELEASED 1985

PROGRAM DESCRIPTION

RESEARCH is a time-series analysis program designed for two applications. First, to support classroom instruction in micro and macroeconomics. Secondly, to help persons analyze investments. RESEARCH helps you manage, analyze, and forecast daily, weekly, monthly, quarterly, and annually, data using graphics, statistics and forecasting designed for business and economic analysis. RESEARCH is simple and easy to use. Descriptive statistics, plus multiple and stepwise regression. Excellent reviews. Database management routines create and combine databases, transform data, and conveniently take care of dates using seven built-in calendars. Compatible with 1-2-3, the IBM PC, IBM XT, and IBM AT.

RESEARCH has unique features. (1) Its graphics and statistics are fast, easy-to-use, and colorful. RESEARCH turns the keyboard over to you. Type any words or draw symbols on your graphs, add boxes and lines, change colors. Automatically graph percent changes, moving averages, moving sums, trends and growth rates. (2) Use ten forecasting methods to forecast up to 750 datapoints. Forecasting contains a Tournament of Methods to show you the best method to use with your data. (3) Screen displays can be saved for permanent reuse. A "storyboard" feature helps you link displays to one another for presentation to groups or classes. (4) Finally, RESEARCH comes with ten years of data on 40 major economic series and 35 years of data on another 60 series.

PRODUCT REVIEWS

Business Software.

Lynott, William J.. "Research Economic Database Manager", Online Today, pp. 39.

Swearingen, D.. "Economic Software's Research", PC Products, pp. 79-82, (July 1985).

Mullins, N.. "Powerful Package Evaluates Economic Trends", PC Week.

Social Science Micro Review.

TYPE OF PROGRAM

Regression Analysis

PROGRAM DESIGNED FOR

Educational use

PROGRAM STYLE

Menu Driven
Integrated System

MISCELLANEOUS PROGRAM FEATURES

Copyable Disk
On Screen Help Function

DOCUMENTATION

User's Manual - 260 pages, ? technical references
- Table of Contents
- Index
- Tutorial or Example Lessons
- Formulas Provided

Tutorials and Examples on Disk

DATA MANAGEMENT

Keyboard Data Entry
Data Manipulations and Transformations
Missing Values Allowed in Data

DATA EDITING

Change
Add
Delete

FOREIGN DATA ACCESS
- Standard Rectangular ASCII Files
- DIF Files

GRAPHICS FEATURES
- Graphics Appear in Color on the Monitor
- Graphics can be Output to a Printer
- Graphics can be Saved to a File
- Titles and/or Labels Available
- Uses Pixel Graphics
- Uses Character Graphics

GRAPHICS
- Histograms
- Scatter (x-y) Plots
- Line Charts
- Growth Curves

PRODUCT SUPPORT
- User may call at own Expense
- No Classes or Instruction Available

STATISTICAL FEATURES SUPPORTED

DESCRIPTIVE STATISTICS
- Mean
- Standard Deviation or Variance
- Standard Error of the Mean
- Minimum, Maximum
- Median
- Percentiles

CORRELATION AND REGRESSION
- Pearson Correlation Coefficient
- Simple Linear Regression
- Multiple Linear Regression
- Stepwise Multiple Linear Regression
- Residuals Calculated

TIME SERIES ANALYSIS
- Autocorrelations
- Moving Average Smoothing
- **TIME SERIES ANALYSIS - FORECASTING**
  - Exponential Smoothing
  - Double Exponential Smoothing
  - Search Procedures to Find Coefficients
  - Regression Trend Analysis
  - Adaptive-Rate-Response
  - Moving Averages
  - Holt's Smoothing with Trend
  - Compares Forecasting Methods
  - Winter's Seasonal

RESEARCH METHODS:MAIN EFFECTS/INTERACT.
CONDUIT, The University of Iowa
Oakdale Campus
Iowa City, Iowa 52242
(319) 353 - 5789
Contact Person: Jim Leaven

CONFIGURATIONS SUPPORTED

Computer	Language	Operating System	RAM	Number Drives	Cost
APPLE II	BASIC	DOS	48K	1	$ 50
IBM PC	BASIC	DOS	128K	1	$ 50

NUMBER OF CURRENT USERS ?
DATE OF FIRST RELEASE 1984
CURRENT VERSION RELEASED ?

PROGRAM DESCRIPTION

This package helps students discern whether independent variables in an experiment are exerting main and/or interactive effects on the dependent variable. The program first describes 2X2 and 2X2X2 designs and design notation. Through a series of exercises and graphs, it then explains the variety of main effects and interactions tested in each design. After running this program students will be able to examine a table or graph of means and, without formal statistical analysis, decide which effects are suggested by the data.

PRODUCT REVIEWS

Rushton, Brian S.. "Topics in Research Methods: Main Effects and Tnteractions", Science Software Quarterly, pp. 42-44, (Fall 1984).

Andree, R V. "Topics in Research Methods: Main Effects and Interactions", Choice, pp. 677-678, (Feb 1985).

"Topics in Research Methods: Main Effects and Interactions", Software Reports, pp. 233, (April 30, 1985).

TYPE OF PROGRAM
UNKNOWN

PROGRAM DESIGNED FOR
Educational use

PROGRAM STYLE
Menu Driven
Separate Programs for each Procedure

DOCUMENTATION
User's Manual - 16 pages, ? technical references
Tutorials and Examples on Disk

DATA MANAGEMENT
Keyboard Data Entry

GRAPHICS FEATURES
Graphics Appear in Color on the Monitor
Uses Pixel Graphics

PRODUCT SUPPORT
User may call at own Expense
No Classes or Instruction Available

RESEARCH METHODS:POWER

CONDUIT, The University of Iowa
Oakdale Campus
Iowa City, Iowa 52242
(319) 353 - 5789
Contact Person: Jim Leaven

CONFIGURATIONS SUPPORTED

Computer	Language	Operating System	RAM	Number Drives	Cost
APPLE II	BASIC	DOS	48K	1	$ 50
IBM PC	BASIC	DOS	128K	1	$ 50

NUMBER OF CURRENT USERS ?
DATE OF FIRST RELEASE 1984
CURRENT VERSION RELEASED ?

PROGRAM DESCRIPTION

This package uses simulated experiments to acquaint the students with the concepts of power and error variance. The program is based on an experiment testing a signaling device for home cooling and allows students to run a variety of experiments comparing electrical consumption in homes with and without the device. Students can compare the results of the original experiment to (a) an experiment involving a larger sample size: (b) an experiment that attempts to improve the reliability of the measures by lengthening the period of observation; (c) an experiment that increases the homogeneity of the sample by selecting only houses with the same number of bedrooms; (d) an experiment that included an important source of variation (two, three, or four bedroom houses) as an additional factor in the design; (e) an experiment involving matched pairs (based on insulation levels) and (f) an experiment that uses repeated measures by obtaining a pretreatment consumption level for each home.

PRODUCT REVIEWS

Cook, Tony. "Topics in Research Methods: Power", Science Software Quarterly, pp. 39-41, (Fall 1984).

Andree, R V. "Topics in Research Methods: Power",

Choice, pp. 677-678, (Feb 1985).

"Power: Topics in Research Methods", Software Reports, pp. 313, (April 30, 1985).

TYPE OF PROGRAM
UNKNOWN

PROGRAM DESIGNED FOR
Educational use

PROGRAM STYLE
Menu Driven
Separate Programs for each Procedure

DOCUMENTATION
User's Manual - 9 pages, ? technical references
Tutorials and Examples on Disk

DATA MANAGEMENT
Keyboard Data Entry

GRAPHICS FEATURES
Graphics Appear in Color on the Monitor
Uses Pixel Graphics

PRODUCT SUPPORT
User may call at own Expense
No Classes or Instruction Available

RESEARCH METHODS:SURVEY SAMPLING
Conduit, The University of Iowa
Oakdale Campus
Iowa City, Iowa 52242
(319) 353 - 5789
Contact Person: Jim Leaven

CONFIGURATIONS SUPPORTED

Computer	Language	Operating System	RAM	Number Drives	Cost
APPLE II	BASIC	DOS	48K	1	$ 50
IBM PC	BASIC	DOS	128K	1	$ 50

NUMBER OF CURRENT USERS ?
DATE OF FIRST RELEASE 1984
CURRENT VERSION RELEASED ?

PROGRAM DESCRIPTION

This simulation program introduces students to surveys and sampling procedures. The package shows that any sample estimate has an assosciated error rate and that the precision of the estimate varies as a function of sample size.

To begin the program, students select a question from such topics as nuclear power, school busing, and government spending. They specify two sample sizes, and the program selects two random samples. Alternatively, students can request one stratified random sample. The program then conducts the polls and displays the proportion of respondents selecting each alternative along with the confidence interval. Students can then compare the precision of the estimates across two samples.

PRODUCT REVIEWS

Cook, Tony and Rushton, Brian S.. "Topics in Research Methods: Survey Sampling", Science Software Quarterly, pp. 45-46, (Fall 1984).

Rennert, R. A.. "Topics in Research Methods: Survey Sampling", Choice, pp. 654, (Jan 1985).

"Topics in Research Methods: Survey Sampling",

Software Reports, pp. 392, (April 30, 1985).

TYPE OF PROGRAM
UNKNOWN

PROGRAM DESIGNED FOR
Educational use

PROGRAM STYLE
Menu Driven
Separate Programs for each Procedure

DOCUMENTATION
User's Manual - 8 pages, ? technical references
Tutorials and Examples on Disk

DATA MANAGEMENT
Keyboard Data Entry

GRAPHICS FEATURES
Graphics Appear in Color on the Monitor
Uses Pixel Graphics

PRODUCT SUPPORT
User may call at own Expense
No Classes or Instruction Available

RHEOLOGIC SYSTEM

Paul Hertzler & Co., Inc.
P.O. Box 578
Gochen, IN 46526
(219) 533- 0571
Contact Person: Thomas Capps

CONFIGURATIONS SUPPORTED

Computer	Language	Operating System	RAM	Number Drives	Cost
IBM PC	PASCAL ASSEMBLY	DOS	640K	1	CALL

NUMBER OF CURRENT USERS 22
DATE OF FIRST RELEASE Mar 83
VERSION 2.20 RELEASED July 86

PROGRAM DESCRIPTION

The RheoLogic System is designed for statistical process control in rubber laboratories. The software acquires data automatically from a Monsanto R-100 Rheometer during a Rheometer test. Sixteen curve-defining data points and six other Rheometer values are computed and stored for each test. Up to 10 physical property test results may be entered in the database manually.

Standard test conditions, customer specifications and fixed control limits are recorded. Rheometer curves for any time period may be reconstructed. Statistical summaries, histograms, and control charts for any or all of the 32 data points may be produced at any time. RheoLogic features a sophisticated data base. Data may be retrieved and sorted by compound, date, lot, mixer and so forth.

TYPE OF PROGRAM

Quality Control or Reliability

PROGRAM DESIGNED FOR

Data Analysis

PROGRAM STYLE

Menu Driven
Integrated System

MISCELLANEOUS PROGRAM FEATURES
Copyable Disk

DOCUMENTATION
User's Manual - 200 pages, ? technical references
Table of Contents
Formulas Provided

DATA MANAGEMENT
Keyboard Data Entry
Data Manipulations and Transformations
Missing Values Allowed in Data

DATA EDITING
Change
Add
Delete

FOREIGN DATA ACCESS
Properly Formatted 1-2-3 PRN Files
Direct from Monsanto R-100 Rheometer

GRAPHICS FEATURES
Graphics can be Output to a Printer
Titles and/or Labels Available
Uses Pixel Graphics

GRAPHICS
Histograms
Scatter (x-y) Plots
Rheometer Redraw
Control Charts
Chi-Square Analysis

PRODUCT SUPPORT
User may call at own Expense
Classes or Instruction Available

STATISTICAL FEATURES SUPPORTED

DESCRIPTIVE STATISTICS

- Mean
- Standard Deviation or Variance
- Minimum, Maximum
- Percentiles
- Skewness
- Kurtosis
- Actual and Predicted Out-Of-Spec

t-TESTS

- Independent Group t-Test/Equal Variance
- Independent Group t-Test/Unequal Var
- Paired t-Test

CORRELATION AND REGRESSION

- Pearson Correlation Coefficient
- Simple Linear Regression

CATEGORICAL DATA ANALYSIS

- Chi-Square Contingency Table Analysis

CONTROL CHARTS

- X-Bar
- Control Limits based on A2 Factor
- Cp
- R-Bar
- Cpk
- Actual and Predicted Out-of-Spec
- **OTHER QUALITY CONTROL PROCEDURES**
    - Acceptance Sampling by Variables

SAMSPAD-I

Professional Applications Development
12 Sandy Way
Weymouth, MA 02191
(617) 331 - 4062
Contact Person: John A Clements

CONFIGURATIONS SUPPORTED

Computer	Language	Operating System	RAM	Number Drives	Cost
IBM PC	LOTUS 1-2-3	DOS	192K	1	$ 65

NUMBER OF CURRENT USERS 105
DATE OF FIRST RELEASE Mar 86
VERSION 1.1 RELEASED July 86

ADDITIONAL SOFTWARE REQUIRED
Lotus 1-2-3

PROGRAM DESCRIPTION

SAMSPAD is a library of 1-2-3 templates for the design and analysis of sampling plans used in quality control and research. It provides sampling plans and curves for a wide variation of input parameters which are not contained in published tables. It makes effective use of Lotus 1-2-3 menu and graphic capilities.

SAMSPAD enables quality control and research workers to design and analyse sampling plans for percent nonconforming, nonconformities per hundred units, means and standard deviations. Fixed sample and sequential sample plans may be produced from input of acceptable and rejectable quality levels (AQL/RQL) and producer and consumer risks. The Operating characteristics (OC) and power curves of each plan are plotted, as well as the average number (ASN), average outgoing quality (AOQ) and average total inspection (ATI) curves where appropriate. Sequential analysis charts may be plotted, and these can be used for multiple sampling. Attribute inspection by variables plans are provided. These templates provide far greater flexibility and ease of use than conventional sampling tables and other methods of designing sampling plans. ASQC sponsored workshops are offered.

TYPE OF PROGRAM
Quality Control or Reliability

PROGRAM DESIGNED FOR
Data Analysis

PROGRAM STYLE
Menu Driven
Separate Programs for each Procedure

MISCELLANEOUS PROGRAM FEATURES
Source Code Available
Copyable Disk

DOCUMENTATION
User's Manual - 93 pages, 0 technical references
Table of Contents
Sample Runs

DATA MANAGEMENT
Keyboard Data Entry

DATA EDITING
Change

GRAPHICS FEATURES
Graphics Appear in Color on the Monitor
Graphics can be Output to a Printer
Graphics can be Saved to a File
Titles and/or Labels Available
Uses Pixel Graphics

GRAPHICS
OC Curves
Power curves,AOQ,ASN,ATI curves
Sequential Charts

PRODUCT SUPPORT
User may call at own Expense
Classes or Instruction Available

STATISTICAL FEATURES SUPPORTED

DISTRIBUTION FUNCTION EVALUATION
- Normal
- Binomial
- Poisson

CONTROL CHARTS
- **OTHER QUALITY CONTROL PROCEDURES**
  - Acceptance Sampling by Attributes
  - Acceptance Sampling by Variables

MISCELLANEOUS
- Sample Size Estimation

SAS SYSTEM FOR PERSONAL COMPUTERS
SAS Institute Inc.
Box 8000, SAS Circle
Cary, NC 27511-8000
(919) 467 - 8000
Contact Person: Sally Roberson

CONFIGURATIONS SUPPORTED

Computer	Language	Operating System	RAM	Number Drives	Cost
IBM PC	C	DOS	512K		

NUMBER OF CURRENT USERS 950
DATE OF FIRST RELEASE OCT 85
VERSION 6.02 RELEASED APR 86

PROGRAM DESCRIPTION

The SAS System is an integrated data analysis system and fourth generation language that can be used for a wide variety of application. The SAS System for personal computers includes base SAS software, for data management, descriptive statistical analysis, and report writing; and SAS/STATtm software, for full-function statistical analysis; and SAS/IMLtm software, for interactive matrix programming. Additional products are under development. The SAS System runs on mainframes, minicomputers, and personal computers and includes a micro-to-host link. The software is widely installed in corporations, universities, and government agencies. To use any product in the SAS System, sites first need base SAS software.

The SAS System for PC's is available only under a site licensing policy. Fees are based on the number of workstations supported. This site licensing policy includes enhancements and technical support. The institute also offers instructor-based and video-based training for the SAS System for PC's.

TYPE OF PROGRAM

Statistical Package

PROGRAM DESIGNED FOR

Data Analysis

PROGRAM STYLE
- Command Driven
- Integrated System

MISCELLANEOUS PROGRAM FEATURES
- Copyable Disk
- On Screen Help Function
- Supports 8087, 8287 Mathematical Chip

DOCUMENTATION
- User's Manual - ? pages, ? technical references
  - Table of Contents
  - Index
  - Tutorial or Example Lessons
  - Sample Runs
  - Formulas Provided
- Quick Reference Card

DATA MANAGEMENT
- Keyboard Data Entry
- Data Manipulations and Transformations

DATA EDITING
- Change
- Add
- Delete

FOREIGN DATA ACCESS
- Standard Rectangular ASCII Files
- DIF Files
- dBase II Files

GRAPHICS FEATURES
- Graphics can be Output to a Printer
- Titles and/or Labels Available
- Uses Character Graphics

GRAPHICS
- Histograms
- Pie Charts
- Scatter (x-y) Plots
- Box Plots
- Probability Plots
- Stem and Leaf

PRODUCT SUPPORT
- User may call at own Expense
- Classes or Instruction Available

STATISTICAL FEATURES SUPPORTED

DESCRIPTIVE STATISTICS
- Mean
- Standard Deviation or Variance
- Standard Error of the Mean
- Coefficient of Variation
- Minimum, Maximum
- Median
- Percentiles
- Skewness
- Kurtosis
- Frequencies
- Range

t-TESTS
- One Sample t-Test
- Independent Group t-Test/Equal Variance
- Independent Group t-Test/Unequal Var
- Paired t-Test

CORRELATION AND REGRESSION
- Pearson Correlation Coefficient
- Simple Linear Regression
- Multiple Linear Regression
- Stepwise Multiple Linear Regression
- Residuals Calculated
- **REGRESSION PLOTS**
  - Residuals

CONFIDENCE INTERVALS
- Means
- Difference Between Two Means
- Proportions
- Difference Between Two Proportions
- Variances
- Ratio of Variances

CATEGORICAL DATA ANALYSIS
- Chi-Square Contingency Table Analysis
- Multi-Dimensional Tables
- Fisher's Exact Test
- Goodness-of-Fit Tests
- Frequencies Can be Entered Directly

ANALYSIS OF VARIANCE
- One-Way ANOVA
- One-Way with Repeated Measures
- Two-Way ANOVA
- Two-Way Unequal Cell Sizes Allowed
- Analysis of Covariance

NONPARAMETRIC TESTS
- Sign Test (Signed Rank)
- Wilcoxon One Sample Test
- Mann-Whitney U
- Kruskal-Wallis Test
- Friedman Chi-Square Test

DISTRIBUTION FUNCTION EVALUATION
- Normal
- t
- Chi Square
- F
- Binomial
- Hypergeometric
- Poisson

EXPLORATORY DATA ANALYSIS
- Stem-and-Leaf Displays
- Smoothing Techniques

MISCELLANEOUS
- Cluster Analysis
- Random Number Generation
- Test for Normality of Data
- Test for Equality of Variances
- Linear Discriminant Function Calculation
- p-Values Given With Tests

SHAZAM: THE ECONOMETRICS COMPUTER PROG

Shazam Econometrics Limited
12 Varsdale Place NW
Calgary, Alberta, CANADA T3A OG7
(403) 220 - 4096
Contact Person: Robert McRae

CONFIGURATIONS SUPPORTED

Computer	Language	Operating System	RAM	Number Drives	Cost
IBM PC		DOS	512K	HD	$250

NUMBER OF CURRENT USERS 200+
DATE OF FIRST RELEASE 1974
VERSION 5.1 RELEASED Oct 86

PROGRAM DESCRIPTION

The much improved SHAZAM Version 5 Computer Program is now available for the IBM PC, XT, AT, and compatible machines. SHAZAM is now easier to use, more comprehensive and has capabilities above and beyond those offered by earlier versions. An on-line HELP command and Tutorial are now available. SHAZAM Version 5 makes data manipulation simple. Data can be manipulated as matrices, vectors, or as single observations all within the same SHAZAM run. It is even possible to program in SHAZAM using the many techniques now incorporated. Programming with matrices is as simple as B=INV(X'X)*X'Y. The regression analysis available is more extensive than ever. For instance, the Ordinary Least Squares Regression command permits you to obtain exact Durbin-Watson Statistics, Ridge Regression, Weighted Least Squares Regressions amd Stepwise Regressions. Linear and Nonlinear Hypothesis Testing and Linear Restrictions are available on most regression commands. Systems of Equations, Two and Three Stage Least squares, Probit, Logit, Tobit, Autoregressive, Box-Cox, Distributed Lags, Pooled Cross Section - Time Series, and Nonlinear models are easy. Regression results can be saved and made available for your use in future calculations. This version of SHAZAM also introduces a new regression command to do Maximum Likelihood Estimation of Non-normal Models.

TYPE OF PROGRAM
Statistical Package

PROGRAM DESIGNED FOR
Data Analysis

PROGRAM STYLE
Command Driven
Integrated System

MISCELLANEOUS PROGRAM FEATURES
Copyable Disk
On Screen Help Function
Supports 8087, 80287 Mathematical Chip

DOCUMENTATION
User's Manual - 291 pages, 100 technical references
Table of Contents
Index
Tutorial or Example Lessons
Sample Runs
Tutorials and Examples on Disk

DATA MANAGEMENT
Keyboard Data Entry
Data Manipulations and Transformations

FOREIGN DATA ACCESS
Standard Rectangular ASCII Files

GRAPHICS FEATURES
Graphics can be Output to a Printer

GRAPHICS
Histograms
Scatter (x-y) Plots
SEE Regression Plots

PRODUCT SUPPORT
User may call at own Expense
No Classes or Instruction Available

STATISTICAL FEATURES SUPPORTED

DESCRIPTIVE STATISTICS
- Mean
- Standard Deviation or Variance
- Standard Error of the Mean
- Coefficient of Variation
- Minimum, Maximum
- Median
- Kurtosis

t-TESTS
- One Sample t-Test
- Independent Group t-Test/Equal Variance

CORRELATION AND REGRESSION
- Simple Linear Regression
- Multiple Linear Regression
- Stepwise Multiple Linear Regression
- Non-Linear Regression
- Residuals Calculated
- Two-Stage Least Squares
- Cochrane-Orcutt & Hildreth-Lu
- Generalized Least Squares
- Maximum Likelihood
- **REGRESSION PLOTS**
  - Residuals

ANALYSIS OF VARIANCE
- One-Way ANOVA

DISTRIBUTION FUNCTION EVALUATION
- Normal
- t
- Chi Square
- F

TIME SERIES ANALYSIS
- Autocorrelations
- Plots
- Pooled Cross Section

MISCELLANEOUS

Random Number Generation
Index Numbers
Logit Analysis
Matrix Operations
Probability Calculations
Data Sorting
Principal Components Analysis
Factor Analysis

SIGSTAT

Significant Statistics
3336 North Canyon Road
Provo, UT 84604
(801) 377 - 4860
Contact Person: Richard C Galbraith, Ph. D.

CONFIGURATIONS SUPPORTED

Computer	Language	Operating System	RAM	Number Drives	Cost
IBM PC		DOS	256K	1	$ 595
HP 110 150		DOS	256K	1	$ 595

NUMBER OF CURRENT USERS 500+
DATE OF FIRST RELEASE Oct 83
CURRENT VERSION RELEASED May 86

ADDITIONAL SOFTWARE REQUIRED
Microsoft FORTRAN

PROGRAM DESCRIPTION

SIGSTAT is a statistical analysis package allowing mainframecapability for the IBM PC/PCjr/XT/AT and compatibles. SIGSTAT is a modernized version of the BMD statistical package and provides a wide array of statistical procedures for data presentation and analysis. It is intended for the intermediate to advanced statistician having beginning to advanced computer skills.

SIGSTAT'S 77 programs include univariate and multivariate analysis of variance and covariance (including repeated measures), general linear models, regression (multiple, stepwise, best subset, ridge, polynomial, periodic and harmonic, maximum likelihood, logistic, probit, non-linear least squares), factor analysis (3 rotations, produces factor scores), canonical correlations (produces canonical variables), discriminant analysis (multi group, stepwise). Cluster analysis life table power spectral analysis), linear programming, quality control, histograms, scatter plots, and data transformations. SIGSTAT handles up to 80 variables on 100 million cases, including pairwise and listwise deletion options for missing variables. 8087 support is also available.

TYPE OF PROGRAM
Statistical Package

PROGRAM DESIGNED FOR
Data Analysis

PROGRAM STYLE
Menu Driven
Separate Programs for each Procedure

MISCELLANEOUS PROGRAM FEATURES
Copyable Disk
Optional Support for 8087 Mathematical Chip

DOCUMENTATION
User's Manual - 300 pages, 100 technical references
Index
Tutorial or Example Lessons
Sample Runs
Formulas Provided
Tutorials and Examples on Disk

DATA MANAGEMENT
Keyboard Data Entry
Data Manipulations and Transformations
Missing Values Allowed in Data

FOREIGN DATA ACCESS
Standard Rectangular ASCII Files

GRAPHICS FEATURES
Titles and/or Labels Available

GRAPHICS
Histograms
Scatter (x-y) Plots

PRODUCT SUPPORT
User may call at own Expense
No Classes or Instruction Available

STATISTICAL FEATURES SUPPORTED

DESCRIPTIVE STATISTICS

- Mean
- Standard Deviation or Variance
- Coefficient of Variation
- Minimum, Maximum
- Median
- Skewness
- Kurtosis
- Quartiles

t-TESTS

- One Sample t-Test
- Independent Group t-Test/Equal Variance
- Independent Group t-Test/Unequal Var
- Paired t-Test

CORRELATION AND REGRESSION

- Pearson Correlation Coefficient
- Simple Linear Regression
- Multiple Linear Regression
- Stepwise Multiple Linear Regression
- Non-Linear Regression
- Residuals Calculated
- Estimate Asymptotic Standard Errors
- Ridge Regression
- Polynomial Regression
- Inverse Regression
- Periodic and Harmonic
- Logistic Regression
- Maximum Likelihood
- **REGRESSION PLOTS**
    - Residuals

CONFIDENCE INTERVALS

- Means
- Time Series Forecasts

CATEGORICAL DATA ANALYSIS

- Chi-Square Contingency Table Analysis
- Multi-Dimensional Tables
- Goodness-of-Fit Tests
- Full Log-linear Model Fitting

ANALYSIS OF VARIANCE

- One-Way ANOVA
- One-Way with Repeated Measures
- Two-Way ANOVA
- Two-Way Unequal Cell Sizes Allowed
- Analysis of Covariance
- Univariate or Multivariate ANOVA/ANCOVA
- Full or Reduced Model
- Eight-Way Unequal Cell Sizes Allowed
- Eight-Way with Repeated Measures
- Multi-Way ANCOVA
- **MULTIPLE COMPARISONS**
  - Newman-Keuls
  - Tukey
  - Post-Hoc Comparisons

NONPARAMETRIC TESTS

- Sign Test (Signed Rank)
- Wilcoxon One Sample Test
- Mann-Whitney U
- Kruskal-Wallis Test
- Spearman or Kendall Correlation
- Conover-Friedman F Approximation
- Kendall's Coefficient of Concordance
- Friedman's Two-Way ANOVA
- Kolmogorov-Smirnov Goodness of Fit
- Yule's Q, Y and Cross-Product Ratio
- Stewart-Maxwell Test for Category Change
- Cochran's Q
- Tetrachoric Correlation
- Phi (and Maximum Phi) Coefficient
- McNemar's Test
- Others

EXPLORATORY DATA ANALYSIS

- Stem-and-Leaf Displays
- Smoothing Techniques
- Box Plots

TIME SERIES ANALYSIS

- Autocorrelations
- Cross Correlations
- AUTOREGRESSIVE MOVING AVERAGE
  - Model Identification
  - Parameter Estimation
- **TIME SERIES ANALYSIS - FORECASTING**
  - ARIMA
  - Time Series Smoothing
  - Winter's 3 Parameter Exp. Smoothing
  - Holt's 2 Parameter Exponential Smoothing
  - Exp. Smoothing (Single, Double, Triple)
  - Single and Linear Moving Average
  - Linear Regression/Fixed Periods
- **TIME SERIES ANALYSIS - PLOTS**
  - Autocorrelations
  - Partial Autocorrelations
  - Residuals
  - Power Spectrum
  - Autocovariances

CONTROL CHARTS

- X-Bar
- R
- p-Chart
- c-Chart
- u-Chart
- **RELIABILITY**
  - Cronbach's Alpha

MISCELLANEOUS

- Cluster Analysis
- Life Table Analysis
- Random Number Generation
- Linear Discriminant Function Calculation
- p-Values Given With Tests
- Multidimensional Scaling
- Stepwise Discriminant Analysis
- Canonical Correlation
- Crosstabs
- Probit Analysis
- Exploratory Data Analysis
- Linear Programming

SIMBOXJ
Automatic Forecasting Systems Inc
PO Box 563
Hatboro, PA 19040
(215) 675 - 0652
Contact Person: David P. Reilly

CONFIGURATIONS SUPPORTED

Computer	Language	Operating System	RAM	Number Drives	Cost
IBM PC	FORTRAN	DOS	256K	2	$ 195

NUMBER OF CURRENT USERS 20
DATE OF FIRST RELEASE Jul 84
CURRENT VERSION RELEASED Mar 86

PROGRAM DESCRIPTION

AFS's products for time series analysis were designed to meet all your software needs pertaining to Box-Jenkins or ARIMA model building. If you are new to Box-Jenkins modeling, you can use SIMBOXJ not only in generating forecasts quickly, but also as a computer-assisted learning device to further your understanding of the modeling process.

The SIMBOXJ program generates from 1 to 5 discrete time series. Starting with a set of random numbers, the program computes data by multiplying the random numbers by the user specified Box-Jenkins equation. This program handles univariate, transfer function, single intervention and Vector ARMA models. The SIMBOXJ program provides a convenient way to generate time series for research purposes. The SIMBOXJ is a handy tool for both teachers and students of time series analysis.

TYPE OF PROGRAM

Statistical Package

PROGRAM DESIGNED FOR

Educational use

PROGRAM STYLE
Menu Driven
Integrated System

MISCELLANEOUS PROGRAM FEATURES
On Screen Help Function
Supports 8087 Mathematical Chip

DOCUMENTATION
User's Manual - 30 pages, 3 technical references
Table of Contents
Index
Tutorial or Example Lessons
Sample Runs
Formulas Provided
Tutorials and Examples on Disk

DATA MANAGEMENT
Keyboard Data Entry
Data Manipulations and Transformations

DATA EDITING
Change
Add
Delete

FOREIGN DATA ACCESS
Standard Rectangular ASCII Files

GRAPHICS FEATURES
Graphics can be Output to a Printer
Graphics can be Saved to a File
Titles and/or Labels Available

GRAPHICS
Scatter (x-y) Plots

PRODUCT SUPPORT
User may call at own Expense
Classes or Instruction Available

STATISTICAL FEATURES SUPPORTED

TIME SERIES ANALYSIS

Autocorrelations
Cross Correlations
Transfer Function Simulation
Intervention Simulation
ARIMA Simulation

SIMPLEX-V

Statistical Programs
9941 Rowlett, Suite 6
Houston, TX 77075
(713) 947 - 1551
Contact Person: Bonnie Deming

CONFIGURATIONS SUPPORTED

Computer	Language	Operating System	RAM	Number Drives	Cost
IBM PC	PASCAL	DOS	256K	1	$150

NUMBER OF CURRENT USERS ?
DATE OF FIRST RELEASE Aug 85
CURRENT VERSION RELEASED ?

PROGRAM DESCRIPTION

SIMPLEX-V is an interactive menu-driven computer program aimed at scientists and engineers involved in R & D. It is used for the rapid experimental optimization of up to twelve continuous variables that can be ajusted simultaneously using a modified sequential simplex algorithm. Typical applications include increasing the yield of a synthetic reaction, improving the efficiency of an extraction process, and reducing the cost of an existing reaction or process.

An initial dialog requests information about the experimental system. SIMPLEX-V then displays a set of experiments to be performed. The user carries out the requested experiments and inputs the results to the program. SIMPLEX-V evaluates the results and tells the user what experiment to perform next to move toward optimum conditions. At any time the program can display (or print) various tabular or graphic summaries of the experimental progress. The program may be halted and re-entered at a later time after additional experimentation has been carried out.

TYPE OF PROGRAM

Optimization Package

PROGRAM DESIGNED FOR
Data Analysis

PROGRAM STYLE
Menu Driven
Integrated System

MISCELLANEOUS PROGRAM FEATURES
Copyable Disk
On Screen Help Function

DOCUMENTATION
User's Manual - 33 pages, 6 technical references
Table of Contents
Tutorial or Example Lessons
Formulas Provided
Tutorials and Examples on Disk

DATA MANAGEMENT
Keyboard Data Entry

PRODUCT SUPPORT
User may call at own Expense
No Classes or Instruction Available

STATISTICAL FEATURES SUPPORTED

MISCELLANEOUS
Sequential-Simplex Method

SL-MICRO
Questionnaire Service Company
Box 778
East Lansing, MI 48823
(517) 641 - 4428
Contact Person: Ray or Alice Kalush

CONFIGURATIONS SUPPORTED

Computer	Language	Operating System	RAM	Number Drives	Cost
IBM PC		DOS	128K	2	$ 250
KAYPRO APPLE OSBORNE		CP/M	48K	2	$ 250
8 INCH		CP/M	128K	2	$ 250

NUMBER OF CURRENT USERS 450
DATE OF FIRST RELEASE Jan 82
VERSION 2.1 RELEASED July 85

PROGRAM DESCRIPTION

SL-MICRO is a statistical language for microcomputers. It can quickly process up to 32,600 cases with 200 variables and produce professional results. SL-MICRO includes the procedures Frequencies, Crosstabs, Condescriptive, Pearson Correlation and Multiple Regression, Anova, and Breakdown.

SL-MICRO has variable and value labels, long variable names, missing values and English error messages. SL-MICRO has its own data editor and is also compatible with database systems. Data transformations can be used to produce new variables or select a subset of the data for compatibility with most database systems. Data transformations can be used to produce new variables or select a subset of the data for processing.

TYPE OF PROGRAM

Statistical Package

PROGRAM DESIGNED FOR
Data Analysis

PROGRAM STYLE
Command Driven
Integrated System

MISCELLANEOUS PROGRAM FEATURES
Copyable Disk

DOCUMENTATION
User's Manual - 150 pages, 3 technical references
Table of Contents
Index
Tutorial or Example Lessons
Sample Runs
Formulas Provided
Quick Reference Card
Tutorials and Examples on Disk

DATA MANAGEMENT
Keyboard Data Entry
Data Manipulations and Transformations
Missing Values Allowed in Data

DATA EDITING
Change
Add
Delete

FOREIGN DATA ACCESS
Standard Rectangular ASCII Files
Comma Delimited ASCII Files

GRAPHICS FEATURES
Graphics can be Output to a Printer
Graphics can be Saved to a File
Titles and/or Labels Available
Uses Character Graphics

GRAPHICS
Histograms

PRODUCT SUPPORT
User may call at own Expense
No Classes or Instruction Available

STATISTICAL FEATURES SUPPORTED

DESCRIPTIVE STATISTICS

- Mean
- Standard Deviation or Variance
- Standard Error of the Mean
- Minimum, Maximum
- Median
- Skewness
- Kurtosis
- Mode
- Sum

CORRELATION AND REGRESSION

- Pearson Correlation Coefficient
- Simple Linear Regression
- Multiple Linear Regression
- Stepwise Multiple Linear Regression

CATEGORICAL DATA ANALYSIS

- Chi-Square Contingency Table Analysis

ANALYSIS OF VARIANCE

- One-Way ANOVA
- Two-Way ANOVA

SMARTFORECASTS II

Smart Software, Inc.
392 Concord Ave.
Belmont, MA 02178
(617) 489 - 2743
Contact Person: Dr. Nelson S. Hartunian

CONFIGURATIONS SUPPORTED

Computer	Language	Operating System	RAM	Number Drives	Cost
IBM PC	PASCAL	DOS	256K	2	$ 695

NUMBER OF CURRENT USERS 1000
DATE OF FIRST RELEASE Aug 84
VERSION 2.0 RELEASED Feb 86

PROGRAM DESCRIPTION

SmartForecasts II is an all-purpose business forecasting program designed to forecast key business variables, such as sales, revenues, costs, inventory, industry trends and market share. The program is aimed at managers and business analysts in sales/marketing, finance, planning, inventory control and general management. Users do not need extensive training in statistics or expertise with personal computers. Reviewers confirm that Smartforecasts II is unusually easy to learn and use.

Smartforecasts II is the first software to successfully combine the two best approaches to forecasting: statistical analysis based on company data and subjective analysis based on the user's EXPERT SYSTEM technology to select and use the right time-series forecasting method for your data, make your forecasts, and show the range of forecast reliability, all with only a few strokes. The EYEBALL Forecasting feature makes maximum use of your business knowledge and judgement. Its built-in statistical functions and easy interactive graphics let you quickly make and adjust trend projection directly on-screen. The MULTISERIES Forecasting feature extends both AUTOMATIC and EYEBALL Forecasting to the simultaneous forecasting of up to 45 related variables, such as sales of items in the same product line. Other forecasting features include exponential smoothing, moving averages, linear and exponential trend projections, multivariate regression and seasonal adjustment. A number of statistical data analysis and color graphics features support the forecasting functions.

PRODUCT REVIEWS

Byramji, Homi M.. "Handy Tool for Forecasting Future Values of Firm Data", Wall Street Computer Review, pp. 61, (April 1985).

Bryan, Shawn W.. "Smart Software Inc.'s SmartForecasts", PC Products, pp. 95, (June 1985).

Quinn, Elizabeth. "SmartForecasts by Smart Software", PC Software & Hardware Evaluation Newsletter, (Oct 1985).

Zachmann, William F.. "Pick-of-the- Month", Software News, pp. 33, (Dec 1985).

Fersko-Weiss, Henry. "Business Forecasts that are Automated", Personal Computing, pp. 168, (June 1986).

Bryan, Marvin. "Business Forecasting: 16 Ways to Predict the Future", PC Magazine, pp. 211, (Aug 1986).

Forrest, N. B.. "Heavy Duty PC Forecasting", PC Magazine, pp. 231, (July 1985).

TYPE OF PROGRAM

Regression Analysis

PROGRAM DESIGNED FOR

Data Analysis

PROGRAM STYLE

Command Driven
Integrated System

MISCELLANEOUS PROGRAM FEATURES

Copyable Disk
On Screen Help Function

DOCUMENTATION

User's Manual - 295 pages, 10 technical references
- Table of Contents
- Index
- Tutorial or Example Lessons
- Sample Runs
- Formulas Provided

Quick Reference Card
Tutorials and Examples on Disk

DATA MANAGEMENT
Keyboard Data Entry
Data Manipulations and Transformations
Missing Values Allowed in Data

DATA EDITING
Change
Add
Delete

FOREIGN DATA ACCESS
DIF Files
Fixed and Variable Format ASCII Files
Lotus PRN Files

GRAPHICS FEATURES
Graphics Appear in Color on the Monitor
Graphics can be Output to a Printer
Titles and/or Labels Available
Uses Pixel Graphics

GRAPHICS
Histograms
Scatter (x-y) Plots
SEE Time Series Plots

PRODUCT SUPPORT
User may call at own Expense
Classes or Instruction Available

STATISTICAL FEATURES SUPPORTED

DESCRIPTIVE STATISTICS
Mean
Standard Deviation or Variance
Minimum, Maximum
Median
Count of cases

CORRELATION AND REGRESSION
Simple Linear Regression
Multiple Linear Regression
Residuals Calculated
REGRESSION PLOTS
Residuals

CONFIDENCE INTERVALS
Forecast error

TIME SERIES ANALYSIS
- Autocorrelations
- Cross Correlations
- Moving Average Smoothing
- **TIME SERIES ANALYSIS - FORECASTING**
  - Automatic Forecasting
  - Eyeball(Interactive Graphical)
  - Multivariate Regression
  - Multiseries (Product Line) Forecasting
  - Linear and Exponential Trend Projections
  - Exponential Smoothing (Winters, Brown)
- **TIME SERIES ANALYSIS - PLOTS**
  - Forecasts
  - Seasonal Adjustment
  - Time Series Decompostion
  - Correlation
  - Multiple Timeplots

MISCELLANEOUS
- p-Values Given With Tests
- Seasonal Adjustment
- Trainer Version of Program is Available

SNAP - SURVEY ANALYSIS PACKAGE

Mercator Computer Systems Ltd.
9 Elmdale Road, Clifton
Bristol, England BS8 1SL
(0272) 293 - 231
Contact Person: Suzanne Wembridge

CONFIGURATIONS SUPPORTED

Computer	Language	Operating System	RAM	Number Drives	Cost
IBM PC	BASIC	DOS	128K	2	645
SIRUS	BASIC	DOS	128K	2	645
APRICOT	BASIC	DOS	128K	2	645

NUMBER OF CURRENT USERS 550
DATE OF FIRST RELEASE Jun 81
VERSION 6 RELEASED Mar 86

PROGRAM DESCRIPTION

SNAP - Market Survey Analysis and General Data Analyser Package: SNAP is a survey analysis package designed to analyse the results from any type of market survey from political opinion polls to transportation studies.

SNAP is easy to use for researchers with no previous computer experience. The programs have been written to provide all the facilities required for definition, collection, validation, correction, and subsequent analysis of such data. Various methods are available to handle each of these tasks. Data can be collected either directly through the keyboard, via diskettes from Mercator's compatible data prep bureau or transmitted via British Telecom from other computer systems. The analysis is in terms of holecounts or cross tabulations with filtering and weighting. Graphs and histograms are available. Descriptive statistics include mean, mode, standard deviation and variance. SNAP is now widely established in the industry.

PRODUCT REVIEWS

Micro Decisions, (July 1982).

Practical Computing, (Jan 1983).

TYPE OF PROGRAM
Statistical Package

PROGRAM DESIGNED FOR
Data Analysis
Educational use

PROGRAM STYLE
Menu Driven
Integrated System

MISCELLANEOUS PROGRAM FEATURES
Copyable Disk
On Screen Help Function

DOCUMENTATION
User's Manual - 170 pages, 0 technical references
Index
Tutorial or Example Lessons
Sample Runs
Formulas Provided
Tutorials and Examples on Disk

DATA MANAGEMENT
Keyboard Data Entry
Missing Values Allowed in Data

DATA EDITING
Change
Add
Delete

FOREIGN DATA ACCESS
DIF Files
dBase II Files

GRAPHICS FEATURES
Graphics can be Output to a Printer
Graphics can be Saved to a File
Titles and/or Labels Available

GRAPHICS
Histograms

PRODUCT SUPPORT
User may call at own Expense
Classes or Instruction Available

STATISTICAL FEATURES SUPPORTED

DESCRIPTIVE STATISTICS

- Mean
- Standard Deviation or Variance
- Standard Error of the Mean
- Minimum, Maximum
- Median

MISCELLANEOUS

- Survey Analysis Package/Market Surveys

SPC - PC
Quality America, Inc.
5430 S. 12th Avenue, Ste C
Tuscon, AZ 85706
(602) 294 - 1188
Contact Person: Tom Pyzdek

CONFIGURATIONS SUPPORTED

Computer	Language	Operating System	RAM	Number Drives	Cost
IBM PC	Compiled BASIC	DOS	256K	2	$ 795

NUMBER OF CURRENT USERS 100
DATE OF FIRST RELEASE Mar 86
CURRENT VERSION RELEASED Aug 86

PROGRAM DESCRIPTION

SPC-PC performs 10 separate SPC functions: Xbar and R charts, XBar and Sigma Charts, X charts, P charts, NP charts, W charts, U charts, Histograms, Scatter Plots, and Pareto diagrams. The program is completely menu driven and user friendly (honest!). All graphics are high resolution and the user can choose his colors. Nearly all printers, plotters, displays, and film recorders are supported. SPC-PC supports the VDI/CGI graphics standards. The program includes a simple dBASE III/Lotus 1-2-3 interface.

TYPE OF PROGRAM

Statistical Process Control

PROGRAM DESIGNED FOR

Data Analysis

PROGRAM STYLE

Menu Driven
Integrated System

DOCUMENTATION

User's Manual - 245 pages, 8 technical references

Table of Contents

Index

Tutorial or Example Lessons

Sample Runs

Formulas Provided

Tutorials and Examples on Disk

DATA MANAGEMENT

Keyboard Data Entry

FOREIGN DATA ACCESS

Standard Rectangular ASCII Files

Lotus 1-2-3

dBASE III

GRAPHICS FEATURES

Graphics Appear in Color on the Monitor

Graphics can be Output to a Printer

Uses Pixel Graphics

GRAPHICS

Control Charts

PRODUCT SUPPORT

No Classes or Instruction Available

STATISTICAL FEATURES SUPPORTED

DESCRIPTIVE STATISTICS

Mean

Standard Deviation or Variance

Standard Error of the Mean

Minimum, Maximum

Median

Percentiles

Skewness

Kurtosis

Coefficient of Excess

Modules of Precision

Mode

DISTRIBUTION FUNCTION EVALUATION

Normal
Binomial
Poisson
Skewed Folded Normal

CONTROL CHARTS

X-Bar
s
Proportions
Number of Defects
Number of Defectives
R
Pareto Analysis and Diagrams
Process Capability Ratios
% Above/Below Specs.
Histograms With Spec. Lines

MISCELLANEOUS

p-Values Given With Tests

SPC DATALYZER

Stephen Computer Services, Inc
34700 Grand River Avenue
Farmington Hills, MI 48024
(313) 478 - 1868
Contact Person: W.R Stephen, Craig Stephen

CONFIGURATIONS SUPPORTED

Computer	Language	Operating System	RAM	Number Drives	Cost
HP 86A	BASIC	HP	128K	2	$ 995
HP 86B	BASIC	HP	128K	2	$ 995
IBM PC	COMPILED	DOS	384K	1	$ 799

NUMBER OF CURRENT USERS 800
DATE OF FIRST RELEASE 1981
VERSION 1.4 RELEASED June 84

PROGRAM DESCRIPTION

The SPC Datalyzer is made up of four individual programs:
1. Variables-To collect and store process control data for X-bar-R,X bar-S, and individuals charts.
2. Attributes -To collect and store attribute data for p, np, CU and pareto charts.
3. Capability - To collect and store data for capability analysis charts on probability paper.
4. Gage Validation -a. Measuring system gage repeatability and reproducibility studies for variable and attribute gage -b. Gage performance curves for variables and attribute gages.
c. Gage surveillance data storage and retrieval.

The Datalyzer is a computer stand alone package to automate statistical process control in a manufacturing environment, with the ability to interface to gages, download from satellite collector or keyboard entry. Charts can be output to the CRT or hardcopy produced from a multi-color plotter or dot matrix printer. The package is designed for use by a computer novice after approximately two hours of training. While designed to automotive industry specifications, it is applicable to all industrial processes. Customization is available for special requirement.

PRODUCT REVIEWS
Quality Progress Buyer's Guide.

TYPE OF PROGRAM
Quality Control or Reliability

PROGRAM DESIGNED FOR
Data Analysis

PROGRAM STYLE
Menu Driven
Integrated System

DOCUMENTATION
User's Manual - 130 pages, technical references
Table of Contents
Index
Sample Runs
Formulas Provided
Tutorials and Examples on Disk

DATA MANAGEMENT
Keyboard Data Entry
Data Manipulations and Transformations

DATA EDITING
Change
Add
Delete

FOREIGN DATA ACCESS
Standard Rectangular ASCII Files

GRAPHICS FEATURES
Graphics can be Output to a Printer
Graphics can be Saved to a File
Titles and/or Labels Available
Uses Pixel Graphics
Uses Character Graphics

GRAPHICS
- Histograms
- Control Charts

PRODUCT SUPPORT
- User may call at own Expense
- Classes or Instruction Available

STATISTICAL FEATURES SUPPORTED

DESCRIPTIVE STATISTICS
- Mean
- Standard Deviation or Variance
- Coefficient of Variation
- Minimum, Maximum
- Median
- Percentiles
- Skewness
- Kurtosis

CONTROL CHARTS
- X-Bar
- s
- Number of Defects
- Number of Defectives
- **OTHER QUALITY CONTROL PROCEDURES**
    - Acceptance Sampling by Attributes
    - Acceptance Sampling by Variables

SPP

Timberlake Clark Ltd
40B Royal Hill, Greenwich
London SE 10, U.K.
01 (692) 6636
Contact Person: Janet Donbavand

CONFIGURATIONS SUPPORTED

Computer	Language	Operating System	RAM	Number Drives	Cost
IBM PC	BASIC	DOS	128K	1	450
PET/64	BASIC	COMMODORE	32K	1	260

NUMBER OF CURRENT USERS 150
DATE OF FIRST RELEASE Jun 83
VERSION 5.2 RELEASED May 86

PROGRAM DESCRIPTION

SPP is a general purpose statistics and survey package suitable for scientific, professional, commercial and educational users. It provides the usual statistical facilities, but in addition is a powerful tool that may be applied to data of any kind, and so has wide applicability -- for example, for storing and retrieving scientific references.

SPP is fast and can handle large sets efficiently, the only effective limitation is disk space. Tests of statistical assumptions are a consistent feature; equality of variances in ANOVA, tests of normality of residuals, histograms. Numeric, alphanumeric and missing data are fully catered. In non-parametric testing, the program selects the appropriate analysis according to the structure of the data. Results of analysis can be printed or saved to a file for later incorporation in reports. Some powerful data management features are available, for example, flexible file join or split, sorting of large data sets.

TYPE OF PROGRAM

Statistical Package

PROGRAM DESIGNED FOR
Data Analysis

PROGRAM STYLE
Menu Driven
Integrated System

MISCELLANEOUS PROGRAM FEATURES
Copyable Disk
On Screen Help Function

DOCUMENTATION
User's Manual - 135 pages, 6 technical references
Table of Contents
Index
Tutorial or Example Lessons
Sample Runs
Formulas Provided
Tutorials and Examples on Disk

DATA MANAGEMENT
Keyboard Data Entry
Data Manipulations and Transformations
Missing Values Allowed in Data

DATA EDITING
Change
Add
Delete

FOREIGN DATA ACCESS
Standard Rectangular ASCII Files
DIF Files
dBase II Files

GRAPHICS FEATURES
Graphics can be Output to a Printer
Graphics can be Saved to a File
Titles and/or Labels Available

GRAPHICS
Histograms
Scatter (x-y) Plots
Box Plots

PRODUCT SUPPORT
Free Phone Support Available
Classes or Instruction Available

STATISTICAL FEATURES SUPPORTED

DESCRIPTIVE STATISTICS
- Mean
- Standard Deviation or Variance
- Standard Error of the Mean
- Coefficient of Variation
- Minimum, Maximum
- Median
- Quartiles

t-TESTS
- Independent Group t-Test/Equal Variance
- Paired t-Test

CORRELATION AND REGRESSION
- Pearson Correlation Coefficient
- Simple Linear Regression
- Multiple Linear Regression
- Stepwise Multiple Linear Regression
- Residuals Calculated
- Estimate Asymptotic Standard Errors
- Partial Correlation
- Polynomial Regression

CONFIDENCE INTERVALS
- Difference Between Two Means
- Confidence Limits on Predicted Values

CATEGORICAL DATA ANALYSIS
- Chi-Square Contingency Table Analysis
- Multi-Dimensional Tables
- Frequencies Can be Entered Directly
- Trend and Contrast Chi-square

ANALYSIS OF VARIANCE
- One-Way ANOVA
- Two-Way ANOVA
- Two-Way Unequal Cell Sizes Allowed
- **MULTIPLE COMPARISONS**
  - Scheffe
  - Treatment Contrasts

NONPARAMETRIC TESTS

Sign Test (Signed Rank)
Mann-Whitney U
Kruskal-Wallis Test
Friedman Chi-Square Test
Spearman or Kendall Correlation
Wilcoxon Stratified
Two-way Unbalanced ANOVA

DISTRIBUTION FUNCTION EVALUATION

Normal
t
Chi Square
F

MISCELLANEOUS

Random Number Generation
Test for Normality of Data
Test for Equality of Variances
p-Values Given With Tests
Principal Components Analysis
Select If
Data Sorting
Merge Files

SPSS/PC+

SPSS, Inc.
444 North Michigan Avenue
Chicago, IL 60611
(312) 329 - 3500
Contact Person: Marketing Dept.

CONFIGURATIONS SUPPORTED

Computer	Language	Operating System	RAM	Number Drives	Cost
IBM PC	FORTRAN	DOS	384K	HD	

NUMBER OF CURRENT USERS 15,000
DATE OF FIRST RELEASE July 84
VERSION 2.0 RELEASED SEP 85

PROGRAM DESCRIPTION

SPSS/PC+ is an interactive data analysis package. SPSS/PC+ contains data and file handling routines, basic descriptive, categorical, correlational and regression procedures, and report writing, graphing and plotting functions. It is a much enhanced version of the highly successful SPSS/PC data analysis product introduced in July 1984.

SPSS/PC+ has been used in areas of Quality Control, Personnel, Market Research, Health Care, Government and many others. SPSS/PC+ is the package to make your data analysis simple.

PRODUCT REVIEWS

Barcikowski, Robert S.. "SPSS/PC+", American Statistician, pp. 225-227, (August 1986).

TYPE OF PROGRAM

Statistical Package

PROGRAM DESIGNED FOR

Data Analysis

PROGRAM STYLE
- Command Driven
- Integrated System

MISCELLANEOUS PROGRAM FEATURES
- On Screen Help Function
- Optional Support for 8087 Mathematical Chip

DOCUMENTATION
- User's Manual - 631 pages, 54 technical references
  - Table of Contents
  - Index
  - Tutorial or Example Lessons
  - Sample Runs
  - Formulas Provided
- Quick Reference Card
- Tutorials and Examples on Disk

DATA MANAGEMENT
- Keyboard Data Entry
- Data Manipulations and Transformations
- Missing Values Allowed in Data

DATA EDITING
- Change
- Add
- Delete

FOREIGN DATA ACCESS
- Standard Rectangular ASCII Files
- SPSS Portable File

GRAPHICS FEATURES
- Graphics can be Output to a Printer
- Graphics can be Saved to a File
- Titles and/or Labels Available
- Uses Character Graphics

GRAPHICS
- Histograms
- Scatter (x-y) Plots
- Contour Plots

PRODUCT SUPPORT
- User may call at own Expense
- Classes or Instruction Available

STATISTICAL FEATURES SUPPORTED

DESCRIPTIVE STATISTICS

- Mean
- Standard Deviation or Variance
- Standard Error of the Mean
- Minimum, Maximum
- Median
- Percentiles
- Skewness
- Kurtosis
- Sum of Values
- N-tiles

t-TESTS

- One Sample t-Test
- Independent Group t-Test/Equal Variance
- Independent Group t-Test/Unequal Var
- Paired t-Test

CORRELATION AND REGRESSION

- Pearson Correlation Coefficient
- Simple Linear Regression
- Multiple Linear Regression
- Stepwise Multiple Linear Regression
- Residuals Calculated
- **REGRESSION PLOTS**
  - Residuals

CATEGORICAL DATA ANALYSIS

- Chi-Square Contingency Table Analysis
- Multi-Dimensional Tables
- Fisher's Exact Test
- Goodness-of-Fit Tests
- Frequencies Can be Entered Directly
- Phi Statistic
- Cramer's V
- Contingency Coefficient
- Lambda
- Uncertainty Coefficient
- Gamma
- Tau C
- Somer's D
- Tau b

ANALYSIS OF VARIANCE
- One-Way ANOVA
- Two-Way ANOVA
- Two-Way Unequal Cell Sizes Allowed
- Analysis of Covariance
- **MULTIPLE COMPARISONS**
  - Scheffe
  - Student-Newman-Keuls
  - Dawson
  - Leon Sie Diff
  - Modified Leon Sie Diff

NONPARAMETRIC TESTS
- Sign Test (Signed Rank)
- Wilcoxon One Sample Test
- Mann-Whitney U
- Kruskal-Wallis Test
- Friedman Chi-Square Test
- Spearman or Kendall Correlation
- Cochran Q-test
- McNemar Test for Correlated Proportions

DISTRIBUTION FUNCTION EVALUATION
- Normal
- Chi Square
- Binomial
- Poisson

MISCELLANEOUS
- Random Number Generation
- Test for Normality of Data
- Test for Equality of Variances
- p-Values Given With Tests

SPSS/PC+ ADVANCED STATISTICS
SPSS, Inc.
444 No Michigan Avenue
Chicago, IL 60611
(312) 329 - 3500
Contact Person: Marketing Department

CONFIGURATIONS SUPPORTED

Computer	Language	Operating System	RAM	Number Drives	Cost
IBM PC	FORTRAN	DOS	448K	HD	CALL

NUMBER OF CURRENT USERS 3000
DATE OF FIRST RELEASE Sep 85
VERSION 1.0 RELEASED Sep 85

ADDITIONAL SOFTWARE REQUIRED
SPSS/PC+

PROGRAM DESCRIPTION
SPSS/PC+ Advanced Statistics is an optional module to the SPSS/PC+ base system for performing sophisticated analyses. Procedures included are MANOVA, discriminant, factor, hiloglinear, cluster and quickcluster. Cluster memberships as well as factor and discriminant scores can be saved and added to a file. Analytical plots and the ability to read and write matrix material also available.

TYPE OF PROGRAM
Statistical Package

PROGRAM DESIGNED FOR
Data Analysis

PROGRAM STYLE
Command Driven
Integrated System

MISCELLANEOUS PROGRAM FEATURES

On Screen Help Function
Optional Support for 8087 Mathematical Chip

DOCUMENTATION

User's Manual - 332 pages, ? technical references
- Table of Contents
- Index
- Tutorial or Example Lessons
- Sample Runs
- Formulas Provided

Quick Reference Card
Tutorials and Examples on Disk

DATA MANAGEMENT

Keyboard Data Entry
Data Manipulations and Transformations
Missing Values Allowed in Data

DATA EDITING

Change
Add
Delete

FOREIGN DATA ACCESS

Standard Rectangular ASCII Files
dBase II Files
Lotus 1-2-3

PRODUCT SUPPORT

User may call at own Expense
Classes or Instruction Available

STATISTICAL FEATURES SUPPORTED

MISCELLANEOUS

- Cluster Analysis
- Factor Analysis
- Discriminant Analysis
- Multivariate Analysis of Variance
- Log Linear Analysis

SPSS/PC+ TABLES
SPSS, Inc.
444 No. Michigan Avenue
Chicago, IL 60611
(312) 329 - 3500
Contact Person: Marketing Department

CONFIGURATIONS SUPPORTED

Computer	Language	Operating System	RAM	Number Drives	Cost
IBM PC	FORTRAN	DOS	448K	HD	?

NUMBER OF CURRENT USERS ?
DATE OF FIRST RELEASE Sep 85
VERSION 1.0 RELEASED Sep 85

ADDITIONAL SOFTWARE REQUIRED
SPSS/PC+

PROGRAM DESCRIPTION
SPSS/PC+ Tables is an optional module to the SPSS/PC+ base system for producing publication-ready stub and banner tables. Provides for easy handling of multiple response data; presenting multiple tables in one display; and nesting multiple subtables in any dimension. Default formatting, statistics, labeling and titling can be overridden giving the user complete control over the layout and content of a table. Allows for any combination of table, column, row, or subtable summary statistics including percentages, totals and means. There is no restriction on the number of cases nor on the physical size of a table.

SPSS/PC+ Tables allows you to use special characters on your printer. Virtually all IBM, Epson and Okidata printers are supported, as well as the Hewlett Packard Lasrjet. Contact SPSS, Inc. for the latest information of supported printers.

TYPE OF PROGRAM
Presentation Quality Tables

PROGRAM DESIGNED FOR
Data Analysis

PROGRAM STYLE
- Command Driven
- Integrated System

MISCELLANEOUS PROGRAM FEATURES
- On Screen Help Function
- Optional Support for 8087 Mathematical Chip

DOCUMENTATION
- User's Manual - 274 pages, 0 technical references
  - Table of Contents
  - Index
  - Tutorial or Example Lessons
  - Sample Runs
- Quick Reference Card
- Tutorials and Examples on Disk

DATA MANAGEMENT
- Keyboard Data Entry
- Data Manipulations and Transformations
- Missing Values Allowed in Data

DATA EDITING
- Change
- Add
- Delete

FOREIGN DATA ACCESS
- Standard Rectangular ASCII Files
- SPSS Portable File
- Freefield Input

PRODUCT SUPPORT
- User may call at own Expense
- Classes or Instruction Available

STATISTICAL FEATURES SUPPORTED

DESCRIPTIVE STATISTICS

- Mean
- Standard Deviation or Variance
- Standard Error of the Mean
- Minimum, Maximum
- Median
- Percentiles
- Sum
- N-tiles

SQCPACK

PQ Systems
470 Windsor Park Drive
Dayton, OH 45459
(800) 547 - 1565
Contact Person: In Ohio Call 513-435-9717 Ken Reed

CONFIGURATIONS SUPPORTED

Computer	Language	Operating System	RAM	Number Drives	Cost
IBM PC	COMPILED BASIC	DOS	256K	2	$ 695
HP-150	COMPILED BASIC	DOS	256K	2	$ 595
TI PC	COMPILED BASIC	DOS	256K	2	$ 595
APPLE	APPLESOFT	DOS	48K	2	$ 495

NUMBER OF CURRENT USERS 3000
DATE OF FIRST RELEASE Oct 81
VERSION 3.0 RELEASED Sept 86

PROGRAM DESCRIPTION

The SQCpack is a general-purpose statistical quality control package. The system's written for the quality control professional and is user friendly and menu driven for operational ease of entry and data manipulation. The SQCPACK also features a powerful "JOB PROCESSING" MODE. Accompanied by documentation and a demonstration data diskette, the SQCpack is a self contained package. Techniques include descriptive statistics, frequency distributions and histograms, capabilities analysis and both variable and attribute control charts. In addition, the package includes PARETO analysis and cause and effect diagrams.

The package displays high resolution screens which can be dumped to the printer. It produces a high quality output to a dot matrix printer. Technical support is available via an 800 hot line number and includes support on statistical quality control techniques.

PRODUCT REVIEWS
Quality Progress, (1984).

TYPE OF PROGRAM
Quality Control or Reliability

PROGRAM DESIGNED FOR
Data Analysis

PROGRAM STYLE
Menu Driven
Integrated System

MISCELLANEOUS PROGRAM FEATURES
Copyable Disk

DOCUMENTATION
User's Manual - 90 pages, 1 technical references
Table of Contents
Index
Tutorial or Example Lessons
Sample Runs
Formulas Provided
Tutorials and Examples on Disk

DATA MANAGEMENT
Keyboard Data Entry
Missing Values Allowed in Data

DATA EDITING
Change
Add
Delete

FOREIGN DATA ACCESS
Standard Rectangular ASCII Files
DIF Files
dBase II Files

GRAPHICS FEATURES
Graphics Appear in Color on the Monitor
Graphics can be Output to a Printer
Uses Pixel Graphics

GRAPHICS
Histograms
Control Charts
Pareto Cause and Effect Diagram

PRODUCT SUPPORT

Free Phone Support Available
Classes or Instruction Available

STATISTICAL FEATURES SUPPORTED

DESCRIPTIVE STATISTICS

Mean
Standard Deviation or Variance
Coefficient of Variation
Minimum, Maximum
Median
Skewness
Kurtosis

DISTRIBUTION FUNCTION EVALUATION

Chi Square

CONTROL CHARTS

X-Bar
s
Number of Defects
Number of Defectives
p-Chart
np-Chart
c-Chart
u-Chart
Test for Out-Of-Control Conditions
Individuals
Range

SQCS

SQC Systems, Inc.
2351 College Station Road, Suite 475
Athens, GA 30605
(404) 546 - 8141
Contact Person: R.S. Parrish, T.P. Ryan

CONFIGURATIONS SUPPORTED

Computer	Language	Operating System	RAM	Number Drives	Cost
IBM PC	COMPILED	DOS	128K	2	$ 595

NUMBER OF CURRENT USERS ?
DATE OF FIRST RELEASE Jan 85
VERSION 2.0 RELEASED Feb 86

PROGRAM DESCRIPTION

SQCS is a fully integrated system for producing control charts, and contains several related statistical procedures. Specifically designed for the IBM Personal Computer as an interactive system, SQCS takes advantage of many features of the PC. It is being used by manufacturing companies in several diverse fields mainly for process control, but it also has value for other applications such as lab analyses and as an instructional aid.

SQCS incorporates the latest developments in control-chart methodology, especially in the areas of CUSUM and multivariate procedures. As part of the data management capabilities, a full-screen text editor provides a convenient mechanism for entering and editing data sets while remaining within the SQCS environoment. Built-in data input flexibility provides the ability to interface between procedures using the same data file. SQCS contains extensive tutorials designed to help the first-time user quickly develop a sound working knowledge of the system. The user has control throughout all stages of the procedures including the output phase where, by simple one-touch keystrokes, any of several screens may be immediately displayed. Additional features: graphics displays, provisions for hardcopy output, extensive error handling, on-line HELP facility. SQCS may be operated as either a menu-driven or a command-oriented system. In addition, SQCS contains a macro-programming facility for batch-style usage. Planned for future release.

PRODUCT REVIEWS

Berger, Roger W.. "Recent Advances in Computer Software for Quality", ASQC Quality Congress Transactions, pp. 269-273, (1986).

TYPE OF PROGRAM

Quality Control or Reliability

PROGRAM DESIGNED FOR

Data Analysis

PROGRAM STYLE

Menu Driven
Command Driven
Integrated System

MISCELLANEOUS PROGRAM FEATURES

Copyable Disk
On Screen Help Function

DOCUMENTATION

User's Manual - 350 pages, 14 technical references
- Table of Contents
- Index
- Tutorial or Example Lessons
- Sample Runs
- Formulas Provided

Tutorials and Examples on Disk

DATA MANAGEMENT

Keyboard Data Entry

DATA EDITING

Change
Add
Delete

FOREIGN DATA ACCESS

Standard Rectangular ASCII Files

GRAPHICS FEATURES

Graphics Appear in Color on the Monitor
Graphics can be Output to a Printer
Graphics can be Saved to a File
Titles and/or Labels Available
Uses Pixel Graphics
Uses Character Graphics

GRAPHICS

Histograms
Scatter (x-y) Plots
Pareto Analysis
SEE QC Plots
Normal Probability Plot
Time-Sequence Plots

PRODUCT SUPPORT

User may call at own Expense
Classes or Instruction Available

STATISTICAL FEATURES SUPPORTED

DESCRIPTIVE STATISTICS

Mean
Standard Deviation or Variance
Standard Error of the Mean
Coefficient of Variation
Minimum, Maximum
Skewness
Kurtosis
Range
Sum
Sample Size

t-TESTS

On Simple Linear Regression Parameters

CORRELATION AND REGRESSION

Pearson Correlation Coefficient
Simple Linear Regression

CONTROL CHARTS

X-Bar
s
Proportions
Number of Defects
Number of Defectives
R
Individual Values
Moving Average and Range
Acceptance
CuSum for Averages
CuSum for Individuals
Multivariate for Averages
Difference for Grouped Data
Multivariate for Individuals
Acceptance Control Chart
Difference for Paired Data
p
np
ku
u
c

MISCELLANEOUS

p-Values Given With Tests
User-Tested on: AT&T6300, Compaq, Epson
Specification Limits
CuSum with FIR (Fast Initial Response)
User-Selectable K-Sigma Control Limits
Process Capability - Cpk, Cp, Zmin
Full Screen Editor
Macro Programming Facility

SS/SPQC

J W Loosemore
150 N Bailey Dr.
Porter, IN 46304
(219) 926 - 6825
Contact Person: Jack Loosemore

CONFIGURATIONS SUPPORTED

Computer	Language	Operating System	RAM	Number Drives	Cost
APPLE II	BASIC	DOS	64K	2	$ 250
QUADLINK	BASIC	DOS	64K	2	$ 250

NUMBER OF CURRENT USERS ?
DATE OF FIRST RELEASE Mar 85
VERSION IV RELEASED Sept 86

PROGRAM DESCRIPTION

SS/SPQC is an integrated set of statistical process control programs. Free format record design allows 60 data fields per record, typically 500-2000 records per file. SS/SPQC assumes little knowledge of computers to use effectively. However, some familiarity with methods of statistical process control is assummed. A 200+ page user manual and demo data disk are provided.

For variables type data, SS/SPQC will construct x-bar and Range charts, moving x-bar and moving Range, individuals and moving Range charts, time sequence plot of individuals against sigma or spec. limits, histograms, and x-y regression residual plots. Auto-plot functions can improve productivity. For attributes type data, SS/SPQC will construct p charts, np charts, c charts, and u charts. Print any SS/SPQC data file subset. Data base management activities include: file search and copy, file restructure, data entry error detection, and data import/export from DIF and ASCII files.

TYPE OF PROGRAM

Quality Control or Reliability

PROGRAM DESIGNED FOR
Data Analysis

PROGRAM STYLE
Menu Driven
Integrated System

MISCELLANEOUS PROGRAM FEATURES
Source Code Available
Copyable Disk

DOCUMENTATION
User's Manual - 200+ pages, ? technical references
Table of Contents
Tutorial or Example Lessons
Sample Runs
Formulas Provided
Tutorials and Examples on Disk

DATA MANAGEMENT
Keyboard Data Entry
Data Manipulations and Transformations
Missing Values Allowed in Data

DATA EDITING
Change
Add
Delete

FOREIGN DATA ACCESS
Standard Rectangular ASCII Files
DIF Files

GRAPHICS FEATURES
Graphics can be Output to a Printer
Graphics can be Saved to a File
Titles and/or Labels Available
Uses Pixel Graphics

GRAPHICS
Histograms
Scatter (x-y) Plots
Control Charts

PRODUCT SUPPORT
User may call at own Expense
No Classes or Instruction Available

STATISTICAL FEATURES SUPPORTED

DESCRIPTIVE STATISTICS
- Mean
- Standard Deviation or Variance
- Minimum, Maximum
- Skewness
- Kurtosis

CORRELATION AND REGRESSION
- Simple Linear Regression
- Residuals Calculated
- **REGRESSION PLOTS**
  - Residuals

DISTRIBUTION FUNCTION EVALUATION
- Normal

CONTROL CHARTS
- X-Bar
- Proportions
- Number of Defects
- Number of Defectives
- Moving Range
- Moving X-Bar
- Individuals
- Range
- Time Sequence Plot

STAN

Statistical Consultants, Inc
462 East High Street
Lexington, KY 40508
(606) 252 - 3890
Contact Person: Susan Williams

CONFIGURATIONS SUPPORTED

Computer	Language	Operating System	RAM	Number Drives	Cost
IBM PC	PASCAL	DOS	128K	2	$ 95
N* ADVANTAGE S100	PASCAL	CP/M	64K	2	$ 95
N*HORIZON APPLE OSBORNE	PASCAL	CP/M	56K	2	$ 95
APPLE II	PASCAL	UCSD-P	64K	2	$ 95

NUMBER OF CURRENT USERS 100+
DATE OF FIRST RELEASE Fall 82
VERSION 2.0 RELEASED May 84

PROGRAM DESCRIPTION

STAN is an interactive statistical analysis system for microcomputers. Considerable effort was made to make STAN easy to use. Prompts are given at every stage to show possible options. Variables are referenced by mnemonic names given by the user and not by their positions in the data set or a model. STAN tries to recover from input errors. Should a variable be specified that is not in a data set, then the names of the legal variables are displayed so that a substitute may be entered. Illegal characters in numeric input are detected, and the user may then enter the proper values. Since the results of a statistical analysis is usually presented in a report or paper, STAN has a text formatting procedure to merge discussion and selected tables and graphs.

STAN includes extensive Data Management, Data Description, Linear Models, Graphics and Report Writing capabilities not found in many other packages.

PRODUCT REVIEWS

Carpenter, James et al.. "Statistical Software Available for Microcomputers", BYTE, pp. 234-264, (April 19, 1984).

"A Software Review", Journal of Pascal and ADA, (May/June, 1983).

TYPE OF PROGRAM

Statistical Package

PROGRAM DESIGNED FOR

Data Analysis

PROGRAM STYLE

Menu Driven
Integrated System

MISCELLANEOUS PROGRAM FEATURES

Copyable Disk
On Screen Help Function
Supports 8087 Mathematical Chip

DOCUMENTATION

User's Manual - 129 pages, 9 technical references
- Table of Contents
- Index
- Tutorial or Example Lessons
- Sample Runs
- Formulas Provided

Tutorials and Examples on Disk

DATA MANAGEMENT

Data Manipulations and Transformations
Missing Values Allowed in Data

FOREIGN DATA ACCESS

Standard Rectangular ASCII Files

GRAPHICS FEATURES

Graphics can be Output to a Printer
Graphics can be Saved to a File
Titles and/or Labels Available
Uses Pixel Graphics

PRODUCT SUPPORT

User may call at own Expense
No Classes or Instruction Available

STATISTICAL FEATURES SUPPORTED

DESCRIPTIVE STATISTICS

- Mean
- Standard Deviation or Variance
- Standard Error of the Mean
- Minimum, Maximum
- Median
- Percentiles

t-TESTS

- One Sample t-Test
- Independent Group t-Test/Equal Variance
- Independent Group t-Test/Unequal Var
- Paired t-Test

CORRELATION AND REGRESSION

- Simple Linear Regression
- Multiple Linear Regression
- Residuals Calculated
- Estimate Asymptotic Standard Errors

CONFIDENCE INTERVALS

- Confidence Limits on Predicted Values

ANALYSIS OF VARIANCE

- One-Way ANOVA
- One-Way with Repeated Measures
- Two-Way ANOVA
- Two-Way Unequal Cell Sizes Allowed
- Analysis of Covariance
- Nested Factors
- Multi-way ANOVA
- Split Plot
- Cell Means Estimates -Unbalanced Design

TIME SERIES ANALYSIS

- Autocorrelations
- Durbin Watson Exponential Smoothing

MISCELLANEOUS

- Random Number Generation
- Test for Normality of Data
- p-Values Given With Tests
- Output Data-Predicted & Redidual Values
- Linear Restrictions on Model Coefficient

STAT 1 - A STATISTICAL TOOLBOX

Sugar Mill Software Corp.
1180 Kika Place
Kailua, Hawaii 96734
(808) 261 - 7536
Contact Person: Dr. Lawrence H. Nitz, Dr. Jerry Brennan

CONFIGURATIONS SUPPORTED

Computer	Language	Operating System	RAM	Number Drives	Cost
IBM PC		DOS	256K	1	$130

NUMBER OF CURRENT USERS ?
DATE OF FIRST RELEASE Feb 85
VERSION 3.1 RELEASED Sept 86

PROGRAM DESCRIPTION

Stat 1 is a menu-driven statistics package designed for business, medical research, the social sciences, the health professions, social service agencies, research bureaus, policy and planning offices, and both applied subject matter and statistics and research methods courses in colleges and universities. It provides a set of research tools that are easy to use. The Stat 1 Manual applies each statistical technique to elementary and to more advanced research problems from various fields.

The features of Stat 1 are as follows. (a) Data entry and management-full screen editor and file import; (b) variable handling-interactive recode, fixed transformations, formula transformations, winsorize, truncate, and lag variables, and generate distributions; (c) descriptive statistics; (d) crosstabs -n-dimensional tables and chi-square; (e) t test- one or two groups, paired or unpaired observations, parametric and nonparametric test statistics; (f) correlaltion-Pearson, Spearman, Gamma, Tau-a, Tau-b, Sommers'D; (g) regression-OLS (hierarchical and simultaneous), ANCOVA and Unequal-n ANOVA, general linear model (multiple dependent variables), automatic dummy variable and interaction coding, robust regression on ranks; (h) smallest space analysis.

PRODUCT REVIEWS

Stall, Marilyn. "Sugar Mill Offers Tutorial Tool Kit For Statisticians", PC WEEK, pp. 97, (August 20, 1985).

Wiswell, Phil. "Analyzing and Reporting Statistics on the PC", PC MAGAZINE, pp. 283, (March 11, 1986).

Brettschneider, Stuart. "Stat 1", Social Science Microcomputer Review, V.4, # 2, pp. 241-244, (Summer 1986).

TYPE OF PROGRAM
Statistical Package

PROGRAM DESIGNED FOR
Data Analysis

PROGRAM STYLE
Menu Driven
Integrated System

MISCELLANEOUS PROGRAM FEATURES
Copyable Disk
On Screen Help Function
Optional Support for 8087, 80287 Mathematical Chip

DOCUMENTATION
User's Manual - 224 pages, ? technical references
- Table of Contents
- Index
- Tutorial or Example Lessons
- Sample Runs
- Formulas Provided

Quick Reference Card
Tutorials and Examples on Disk

DATA MANAGEMENT
Keyboard Data Entry
Data Manipulations and Transformations
Missing Values Allowed in Data

DATA EDITING
Change
Add
Delete

FOREIGN DATA ACCESS
Standard Rectangular ASCII Files

GRAPHICS FEATURES
Graphics can be Output to a Printer
Graphics can be Saved to a File
Titles and/or Labels Available
Uses Character Graphics

GRAPHICS
Histograms
Scatter (x-y) Plots
3-D Plotting

PRODUCT SUPPORT
Free Phone Support Available
No Classes or Instruction Available

STATISTICAL FEATURES SUPPORTED

DESCRIPTIVE STATISTICS
Mean
Standard Deviation or Variance
Standard Error of the Mean
Minimum, Maximum
Median
Percentiles
Skewness
Kurtosis

t-TESTS
One Sample t-Test
Independent Group t-Test/Equal Variance
Independent Group t-Test/Unequal Var
Paired t-Test

CORRELATION AND REGRESSION
Pearson Correlation Coefficient
Simple Linear Regression
Multiple Linear Regression
Stepwise Multiple Linear Regression
Residuals Calculated
Hierarchical
Multiple Dependent Variables

CONFIDENCE INTERVALS
Means
Difference Between Two Means

CATEGORICAL DATA ANALYSIS

Chi-Square Contingency Table Analysis
Multi-Dimensional Tables
Goodness-of-Fit Tests
Frequencies Can be Entered Directly
Collapse and Delete Rows/Columns

ANALYSIS OF VARIANCE

One-Way ANOVA
Two-Way ANOVA
Two-Way Unequal Cell Sizes Allowed
Analysis of Covariance
General Linear Model
MANOVA

NONPARAMETRIC TESTS

Wilcoxon One Sample Test
Mann-Whitney U
Kruskal-Wallis Test
Friedman Chi-Square Test
Spearman or Kendall Correlation
Sommers D
Tau-b
Gamma

DISTRIBUTION FUNCTION EVALUATION

Chi Square
Binomial
Poisson

TIME SERIES ANALYSIS

Autocorrelations
Moving Average Smoothing
TIME SERIES ANALYSIS - PLOTS
Original Data

MISCELLANEOUS

Cluster Analysis
Random Number Generation
p-Values Given With Tests

STAT-PAK

Quality Resources
840 McKinley
Plymouth, MI 48170
(313) 453 - 4616
Contact Person: W.A. Loesch

CONFIGURATIONS SUPPORTED

Computer	Language	Operating System	RAM	Number Drives	Cost
IBM PC	BASIC	DOS	64K	2	$100
TANDY	BASIC	TRS-DOS	16K	2	$100
KAYPRO	BASIC	CP/M	64K	2	$100

NUMBER OF CURRENT USERS ?
DATE OF FIRST RELEASE Jan 81
VERSION 1.3 RELEASED Jun 86

PROGRAM DESCRIPTION

STAT-PAK is a set of (8) statistical programs. The programs were selected as being the most commonly used for basic SPC work. It is intended for the QC analyst or engineer in determining capability or trouble-shooting a process.

The SIGMA program in the set, in addition to providing a histogram and calculated statistics, provides an optional correction for skewness, based upon the "mirror image" algorithm. The ZSCORES program provides a method of determining capability for short runs, before sufficient data is available for charting.

PROGRAM LIST:
SIGMA (Single Sample Statistics)
LINEAR CORRELATION (Pearson)
F & T Tests
BIVARIATE REGRESSION (w. Transforms)
PARETO ANALYSIS
MULTIPLE REGRESSION
CHI-SQUARE CONTINGENCY (Attribute Data)
Z-SCORES (Short Run Capability)

TYPE OF PROGRAM
Statistical Package

PROGRAM DESIGNED FOR
Data Analysis

PROGRAM STYLE
Menu Driven
Separate Programs for each Procedure

MISCELLANEOUS PROGRAM FEATURES
Copyable Disk
On Screen Help Function

DOCUMENTATION
User's Manual - 2 pages, 0 technical references
Index
Tutorial or Example Lessons
Sample Runs

DATA MANAGEMENT
Keyboard Data Entry

DATA EDITING
Change
Add
Delete

GRAPHICS FEATURES
Titles and/or Labels Available
Uses Character Graphics

GRAPHICS
Histograms

PRODUCT SUPPORT
User may call at own Expense
Classes or Instruction Available

STATISTICAL FEATURES SUPPORTED

DESCRIPTIVE STATISTICS
- Mean
- Standard Deviation or Variance
- Minimum, Maximum
- Skewness
- Kurtosis
- Z
- T
- F
- R

t-TESTS
- Independent Group t-Test/Equal Variance

CORRELATION AND REGRESSION
- Pearson Correlation Coefficient
- Simple Linear Regression
- Multiple Linear Regression
- Non-Linear Regression

CATEGORICAL DATA ANALYSIS
- Chi-Square Contingency Table Analysis

DISTRIBUTION FUNCTION EVALUATION
- Normal
- t
- Chi Square
- F

CONTROL CHARTS
- **OTHER QUALITY CONTROL PROCEDURES**
  - Acceptance Sampling by Variables

MISCELLANEOUS
- Test for Normality of Data
- Acceptance Sampling by Variables

STAT-PAK II

Quality Resources
840 McKinley
Plymouth, MI 48170
(313) 453 - 4616
Contact Person: W.A. Loesch

CONFIGURATIONS SUPPORTED

Computer	Language	Operating System	RAM	Number Drives	Cost
IBM PC	BASIC	DOS	64K	2	$100
TANDY	BASIC	DOS	16K	2	$100
KAYPRO	BASIC	CP/M	64K	2	$100

NUMBER OF CURRENT USERS ?
DATE OF FIRST RELEASE Jan 86
VERSION 1.2 RELEASED June 86

PROGRAM DESCRIPTION

STAT-PAK II is a set of (10) statistical programs developed for the more advanced QC Analyst or Engineer engaged in SPC capability, product improvement and/or trouble shooting.

The set of programs contains a choice of (6) ANOVA programs, depending on the nature of the data or experiment. Included is an ANOVA program for attribute data, gage reliability and reproductive (GRR) OC & and AOQ curve development.

TYPE OF PROGRAM
Statistical Package

PROGRAM DESIGNED FOR
Data Analysis

PROGRAM STYLE
Menu Driven
Separate Programs for each Procedure

MISCELLANEOUS PROGRAM FEATURES
Copyable Disk
On Screen Help Function

DOCUMENTATION
User's Manual - 2 pages, ? technical references
Index
Tutorial or Example Lessons
Sample Runs

DATA MANAGEMENT
Keyboard Data Entry

DATA EDITING
Change
Add
Delete

PRODUCT SUPPORT
User may call at own Expense
Classes or Instruction Available

STATISTICAL FEATURES SUPPORTED

CONFIDENCE INTERVALS
Ratio of Variances

CATEGORICAL DATA ANALYSIS
Chi-Square Contingency Table Analysis
Up to 6x6

ANALYSIS OF VARIANCE
One-Way ANOVA
Two-Way ANOVA
Attributes
Two-Level Factorial
Randomized Block
Latin Square
Three-Way ANOVA

DISTRIBUTION FUNCTION EVALUATION
Chi Square
F
Hypergeometric

CONTROL CHARTS
OTHER QUALITY CONTROL PROCEDURES
Acceptance Sampling by Attributes

STAT/PC-LIBRARY
IMSL, Inc.
2500 Parkwest Tower One
Houston, TX 77042
(713) 782 - 6060
Contact Person: IMSL Sales Division

CONFIGURATIONS SUPPORTED

Computer	Language	Operating System	RAM	Number Drives	Cost
IBM PC	FORTRAN	DOS	192K	2	$ 420

NUMBER OF CURRENT USERS 158
DATE OF FIRST RELEASE Aug 84
CURRENT VERSION RELEASED Feb 85

ADDITIONAL SOFTWARE REQUIRED
IBM Professional Fortran 1.0
Microsoft FORTRAN 3.2 Compiler

PROGRAM DESCRIPTION

The IMSL STAT/PC-LIBRARY system offers a selection of the most frequently-used statistical FORTRAN subroutines from the widely respected IMSL Library. This "subset" system is designed to meet the increasing demand for advanced statistical problem-solving software for a new generation of powerful desk-top computers.

By allowing the user to select complete, fully tested subroutines, rather than writing them, the STAT/PC-LIBRARY system can eliminate much of the time and expense involved in developing application programs. With users in more than 50 countries, the IMSL Library contains over 500 FORTRAN subroutines. To make this widely used software resource affordable and manageable for the microcomputer user, IMSL has developed the powerful STAT/PC-LIBRARY.

TYPE OF PROGRAM
Statistical Package

PROGRAM DESIGNED FOR
Data Analysis

PROGRAM STYLE
Command Driven
Separate Programs for each Procedure

MISCELLANEOUS PROGRAM FEATURES
On Screen Help Function
Optional Support for 8087 Mathematical Chip

DOCUMENTATION
User's Manual - 300 pages, 0 technical references
Table of Contents
Index
Tutorial or Example Lessons
Sample Runs
Formulas Provided
Tutorials and Examples on Disk

DATA MANAGEMENT
Keyboard Data Entry

PRODUCT SUPPORT
Free Phone Support Available
Classes or Instruction Available

STATISTICAL FEATURES SUPPORTED

DESCRIPTIVE STATISTICS
Mean
Standard Deviation or Variance
Coefficient of Variation
Minimum, Maximum
Skewness
Kurtosis
Mean and Variance for Grouped Data

t-TESTS
One Sample t-Test
Independent Group t-Test/Equal Variance
Independent Group t-Test/Unequal Var
Paired t-Test

CORRELATION AND REGRESSION
- Pearson Correlation Coefficient
- Simple Linear Regression
- Multiple Linear Regression
- Stepwise Multiple Linear Regression
- Non-Linear Regression
- Polynomial Regression
- Inverse Regression
- Transformations

CONFIDENCE INTERVALS
- Means
- Difference Between Two Means
- Variances
- Ratio of Variances
- Regression Coefficients

CATEGORICAL DATA ANALYSIS
- Chi-Square Contingency Table Analysis
- Goodness-of-Fit Tests
- Frequencies Can be Entered Directly

ANALYSIS OF VARIANCE
- One-Way ANOVA
- One-Way with Repeated Measures
- Two-Way ANOVA
- Two-Way Unequal Cell Sizes Allowed
- Analysis of Covariance
- Factorial Designs
- General Linear Models
- **MULTIPLE COMPARISONS**
  - Newman-Keuls

NONPARAMETRIC TESTS
- Sign Test (Signed Rank)
- Mann-Whitney U
- Kruskal-Wallis Test

DISTRIBUTION FUNCTION EVALUATION
- Normal
- t
- Chi Square
- F
- Beta
- Asymptotic Kolmogorov-Smirnov

EXPLORATORY DATA ANALYSIS
- Box Plots

TIME SERIES ANALYSIS

- Autocorrelations
- Cross Correlations
- AUTOREGRESSIVE MOVING AVERAGE
  - Model Identification
  - Parameter Estimation
- **TIME SERIES ANALYSIS - FORECASTING**
  - ARIMA
- **TIME SERIES ANALYSIS - SPECTRAL ESTIMATE**
  - FFT with Parzen Window

MISCELLANEOUS

- Random Number Generation
- Test for Equality of Variances
- Linear Discriminant Function Calculation
- p-Values Given With Tests

STAT/TRANSFER

Circle Consulting
10 Arnold Circle
Cambridge, MA 02139
(617) 491 - 4511
Contact Person: Steven Dubnoff

CONFIGURATIONS SUPPORTED

Computer	Language	Operating System	RAM	Number Drives	Cost
IBM PC	C	DOS	128K	1	$95

NUMBER OF CURRENT USERS 500
DATE OF FIRST RELEASE Jan 86
VERSION 1.1 RELEASED May 86

ADDITIONAL SOFTWARE REQUIRED

PROGRAM DESCRIPTION

STAT/TRANSFER moves statistical data between programs automatically, accurately, the first time. STAT/TRANSFER will read and write: LOTUS worksheets (it will read 1-2-3 versions 1A, 2 and SYMPHONY files and write worksheets which can be read by any of these); dBase II, III, and III+ files; GAUSS files; SPSS Export files (you can move your data to and from mainframe SPSS); STATA files; and SYSTAT files.

STAT/TRANSFER has a consistent Lotus-like user interface and enough intelligence to transfer as much of the information as is possible and necessary from one format to another. It will handle a large number of variables, multiple missing values, and, when the target program permit it, value and variable labels. Variables, files, and formats can be selected by simply pointing with the cursor. We are planning to add support for other systems. Please call or write for the latest list.

TYPE OF PROGRAM

File Transfer

PROGRAM DESIGNED FOR

Data Analysis

PROGRAM STYLE
Menu Driven
Integrated System

MISCELLANEOUS PROGRAM FEATURES
Source Code Available
Copyable Disk
Optional Support for 80871, 80287 Mathematical Chip

DOCUMENTATION
User's Manual - 16 pages, 0 technical references
Tutorials and Examples on Disk

DATA MANAGEMENT
Missing Values Allowed in Data

FOREIGN DATA ACCESS
SYSTAT
SPSS EXPORT (PFF)
GAUSS
Symphony
dBase II & III Files
Lotus

PRODUCT SUPPORT
User may call at own Expense
No Classes or Instruction Available

STATA AND ADD-ON MODULE STATA/GRAPHICS

Computing Resource Center
10801 National Blvd., 3rd Floor
Los Angeles, CA 90064
1-(800)- STATAPC
Contact Person: G.E. (Ted) Anderson, Marketing Director

CONFIGURATIONS SUPPORTED

Computer	Language	Operating System	RAM	Number Drives	Cost
IBM PC	C	DOS	256K	2	$ 395

NUMBER OF CURRENT USERS 1000+
DATE OF FIRST RELEASE Dec 86
VERSION 1.4 RELEASED July 86

PROGRAM DESCRIPTION

STATA is an integrated package for managing, displaying and analyzing data. It is designed to be used by both data professionals and novices. Users can choose either a command-driven mode with complete macro and programming facilities or a full-screen menu system. STATA is expandable through the purchase of additional integrated modules. STATA/Graphics, the first of those modules to be released, provides sophisticated presentation and analysis graphics including box plots, one-way scatterplots, scatterplots matrices, bar and pie charts.

STATA is notable for its flexibility, speed and compactness. Rather than limiting users to a collection of canned procedures. STATA's tool kit approach makes it possible to calculate almost any statistic. STATA's speed makes it practical to analyze data interactively. STATA processes data sets containing up to 246,000 elements on a 640K PC (63,000 on a 256K PC). STATA's moment matrix capabilities make it possible to analyze data sets containing an unlimited number of observations. A student edition of STATA is also available.

PRODUCT REVIEWS

Siegal, Jay. Statistical Software for Microcomputers:Guide to 40 Programs.

Petzold, Charles. "Turning Data Into Information", PC Magazine, Vol. 4, No. 23, pp. 155, (Nov 12, 1985).

Bengston, William. "Stata", Social Science Microcomputer Review, Vol. 3, No. 4, pp. 394, (Winter 85).

Rycroft, Robert. "Econometric and Forecasting Software for the IBM PC", Journal Of Economic Education.

Turner, David. "Review of Stata", The American Statistician.

TYPE OF PROGRAM
Statistical Package

PROGRAM DESIGNED FOR
Data Analysis

PROGRAM STYLE
Menu Driven
Command Driven
Integrated System

MISCELLANEOUS PROGRAM FEATURES
Copyable Disk
On Screen Help Function
Optional Support for 8087 Mathematical Chip

DOCUMENTATION
User's Manual - 413 pages, 100+ technical references
Table of Contents
Index
Tutorial or Example Lessons
Sample Runs
Formulas Provided
Tutorials and Examples on Disk

DATA MANAGEMENT
Keyboard Data Entry
Data Manipulations and Transformations
Missing Values Allowed in Data

DATA EDITING
Change
Add
Delete

FOREIGN DATA ACCESS
Standard Rectangular ASCII Files

GRAPHICS FEATURES

Graphics can be Output to a Printer
Graphics can be Saved to a File
Titles and/or Labels Available
Uses Pixel Graphics
Uses Character Graphics

GRAPHICS

Histograms
Pie Charts
Scatter (x-y) Plots
Box Plots
Standard Error Bar Charts
Partial Leverage Plots
Scatterplot Matrices
SEE EDA Plots

PRODUCT SUPPORT

Free Phone Support Available
Classes or Instruction Available

STATISTICAL FEATURES SUPPORTED

DESCRIPTIVE STATISTICS

Mean
Standard Deviation or Variance
Standard Error of the Mean
Minimum, Maximum
Median
Percentiles
Skewness
Kurtosis
Sum of Values

t-TESTS

One Sample t-Test
Independent Group t-Test/Equal Variance
Independent Group t-Test/Unequal Var
Paired t-Test

CORRELATION AND REGRESSION

Pearson Correlation Coefficient
Simple Linear Regression
Multiple Linear Regression
Residuals Calculated

REGRESSION PLOTS

Residuals

CONFIDENCE INTERVALS
- Means
- Difference Between Two Means
- Proportions
- Difference Between Two Proportions
- Variances

CATEGORICAL DATA ANALYSIS
- Chi-Square Contingency Table Analysis
- Multi-Dimensional Tables
- Frequencies Can be Entered Directly

ANALYSIS OF VARIANCE
- One-Way ANOVA
- One-Way with Repeated Measures
- Two-Way ANOVA
- Two-Way Unequal Cell Sizes Allowed
- Analysis of Covariance
- Nested Effects
- Random Effects
- Missing Cells Allowed
- N-Way ANCOVA
- **MULTIPLE COMPARISONS**
    - Duncan's Multiple Range
    - Scheffe
    - Bonferroni
    - Tukey
    - Contrasts

NONPARAMETRIC TESTS
- Sign Test (Signed Rank)
- Wilcoxon One Sample Test
- Mann-Whitney U
- Kruskal-Wallis Test
- Spearman or Kendall Correlation
- Rank-Sum Test

DISTRIBUTION FUNCTION EVALUATION
- Normal
- t
- Chi Square
- F
- Inverse Normal

EXPLORATORY DATA ANALYSIS
- Symmetry Plots
- Quantile-Quantile Plots
- Quantile Normal Plots
- Leverage Plots

TIME SERIES ANALYSIS
- Autocorrelations
- Cross Correlations
- Moving Average Smoothing
- **TIME SERIES ANALYSIS - PLOTS**
  - Autocorrelations
  - Partial Autocorrelations

CONTROL CHARTS
- X-Bar
- s
- Proportions
- Number of Defects
- Number of Defectives
- Cumsum Charts
- **OTHER QUALITY CONTROL PROCEDURES**
  - Acceptance Sampling by Attributes
  - Acceptance Sampling by Variables

MISCELLANEOUS
- Random Number Generation
- Test for Equality of Variances
- p-Values Given With Tests

STATCALC

STATCALC Holdings Ltd.
120 Rangatira Rd., Birkenhead
Auckland 10, New Zealnd
437283
Contact Person: Peter Mullins

CONFIGURATIONS SUPPORTED

Computer	Language	Operating System	RAM	Number Drives	Cost
APPLE II	BASIC/ ASSEMBLER	DOS	64K	1	
IBM PC	COMPILED BASIC	DOS	256K	1	

NUMBER OF CURRENT USERS 400
DATE OF FIRST RELEASE May 84
VERSION 1.5 RELEASED June 85

PROGRAM DESCRIPTION

STATCALC is an integrated package for performing statistical analyses on the Apple and IBM computers. Its design emphasises interactive use and user friendliness; on the Apple, data sets of up to 2000 numbers can be analyzed; on the IBM PC, data sets of up to 12000 numbers can analyzed. The program is aimed at two markets: It is an excellent educational tool for teaching undergraduate applied statistics, and it is a useful statistical tool for researchers with small to medium size data sets.

Specific features of the program include plotting and storing residuals, extensive use of high resolution graphics (Apple), capability of dumping the screen to a printer when desired, for easy hard copies of both text and graphic output, easy data entry and editing, fast loading and saving of data files, and fully documented file format so that files may be created by external programs or externally converted into STATCALC format. The simple but powerful command driven language makes this package unique among microcomputer statistical software that we have seen.

TYPE OF PROGRAM

Statistical Package

PROGRAM DESIGNED FOR
Educational use

PROGRAM STYLE
Command Driven
Integrated System

MISCELLANEOUS PROGRAM FEATURES
Copyable Disk
On Screen Help Function

DOCUMENTATION
User's Manual - 148 pages, 31 technical references
Table of Contents
Index
Tutorial or Example Lessons
Sample Runs
Formulas Provided
Quick Reference Card
Tutorials and Examples on Disk

DATA MANAGEMENT
Keyboard Data Entry
Data Manipulations and Transformations

DATA EDITING
Change
Add
Delete

FOREIGN DATA ACCESS
Standard Rectangular ASCII Files

GRAPHICS FEATURES
Graphics can be Output to a Printer
Graphics can be Saved to a File
Uses Pixel Graphics
Uses Character Graphics

GRAPHICS
Histograms
Scatter (x-y) Plots
3-D Plotting
Box Plots
Least Significant Difference Plots
Coded Residual Plots

PRODUCT SUPPORT
User may call at own Expense
Classes or Instruction Available

STATISTICAL FEATURES SUPPORTED

DESCRIPTIVE STATISTICS
- Mean
- Standard Deviation or Variance
- Standard Error of the Mean
- Coefficient of Variation
- Minimum, Maximum
- Median
- Percentiles
- Midspread

t-TESTS
- One Sample t-Test
- Independent Group t-Test/Equal Variance
- Independent Group t-Test/Unequal Var
- Paired t-Test
- t-Tests for Regression Coefficients

CORRELATION AND REGRESSION
- Pearson Correlation Coefficient
- Simple Linear Regression
- Multiple Linear Regression
- Residuals Calculated
- Matrix of Regression Coeff. Estimates
- Hat Matrix Diagonals
- Variance Inflation Factors
- Standarized Residuals
- Cook's D
- Robust Regression
- **REGRESSION PLOTS**
  - Residuals
  - Partial Regression Plots

CONFIDENCE INTERVALS
- Means
- Difference Between Two Means
- Proportions
- Difference Between Two Proportions
- Regression Coefficients

CATEGORICAL DATA ANALYSIS
- Chi-Square Contingency Table Analysis
- Multi-Dimensional Tables
- Goodness-of-Fit Tests
- Frequencies Can be Entered Directly

ANALYSIS OF VARIANCE
- One-Way ANOVA
- One-Way with Repeated Measures
- Two-Way ANOVA
- Two-Way Unequal Cell Sizes Allowed
- Analysis of Covariance
- **MULTIPLE COMPARISONS**
  - Bonferroni

NONPARAMETRIC TESTS
- Sign Test (Signed Rank)
- Wilcoxon One Sample Test
- Mann-Whitney U
- Kruskal-Wallis Test
- Spearman or Kendall Correlation

DISTRIBUTION FUNCTION EVALUATION
- Normal
- t
- Chi Square
- F

EXPLORATORY DATA ANALYSIS
- Stem-and-Leaf Displays
- Resistant Line
- Median Polish

MISCELLANEOUS
- Life Table Analysis
- Random Number Generation
- Test for Normality of Data
- p-Values Given With Tests

STATCALC-IBM VERSION

Dept. of Mathematics and Statistics
University of Auckland, Private Bag
Auckland, New Zealand

CONFIGURATIONS SUPPORTED

Computer	Language	Operating System	RAM	Number Drives	Cost
IBM PC	COMPILED BASIC	DOS	128K	1	$ 225

NUMBER OF CURRENT USERS 400
DATE OF FIRST RELEASE Mar 85
VERSION 2.0 RELEASED Aug 85

PROGRAM DESCRIPTION

STATCALC is an integrated system for performing statistical analysis on data sets of up to 12,000 observations. It features simple commands which the user can combine to build an analysis. The design emphasises interactive use and user friendliness, and is intended for use by non-specialists. Most standard analyses can be performed directly, and many others by judicious combinations of commands.

The program has been designed to function as a statistical calculator, so many analyses not directly included can be performed by a combination of commands. For example, the RANK command coupled with the LET command (transformations) and some of the standard analyses allow a wide range of non-parametric procedures to be carried out. More complicated ANOVA procedures than those listed below may likewise be performed. Special features of the program include plotting and storing of residuals, extensive use of character graphics (high resolution graphics are not required) fast loading and saving of data files, easy data entry from the keyboard or from existing ASCII files, an on-line HELP facility, and extensive use of model checking diagnostics. Hard copies of all output are obtained by directly dumping the screen to a printer, or alternatively to a disk file for later editing using an editor or word processor. A macro facility is available: a sequence of commands may be saved as a macro and executed with a single invocation.

TYPE OF PROGRAM
Statistical Package

PROGRAM DESIGNED FOR
Educational use

PROGRAM STYLE
Command Driven
Integrated System

MISCELLANEOUS PROGRAM FEATURES
Copyable Disk

DOCUMENTATION
User's Manual - 190 pages, 31 technical references
Index
Tutorial or Example Lessons
Sample Runs
Formulas Provided

DATA MANAGEMENT
Keyboard Data Entry
Data Manipulations and Transformations

DATA EDITING
Change
Add
Delete

FOREIGN DATA ACCESS
Standard Rectangular ASCII Files

GRAPHICS FEATURES
Graphics can be Output to a Printer
Graphics can be Saved to a File
Titles and/or Labels Available
Uses Character Graphics

GRAPHICS
Histograms
Scatter (x-y) Plots
3-D Plotting
Box Plots
SEE Regression Plots
Least Significant Different Plots
Coded Residual Plots From Median Polish
Coded Residual Plots From Two Way Anova

PRODUCT SUPPORT
No Classes or Instruction Available

STATISTICAL FEATURES SUPPORTED

ANALYSIS OF VARIANCE
- One-Way ANOVA
- One-Way with Repeated Measures
- Two-Way ANOVA
- Two-Way Unequal Cell Sizes Allowed
- Analysis of Covariance
- **MULTIPLE COMPARISONS**
  - Bonferroni

NONPARAMETRIC TESTS
- Sign Test (Signed Rank)
- Wilcoxon One Sample Test
- Mann-Whitney U
- Kruskal-Wallis Test
- Spearman or Kendall Correlation

DISTRIBUTION FUNCTION EVALUATION
- Normal
- t
- Chi Square
- F

EXPLORATORY DATA ANALYSIS
- Stem-and-Leaf Displays
- Resistant Line
- Median Polish

MISCELLANEOUS
- Random Number Generation
- Test for Normality of Data
- p-Values Given With Tests
- Mantel-Haenzel Test
- Kaplan Meier Estimates

STATFAST

Statsoft, Inc.
2832 East 10th, Suite 4
Tulsa, OK 74104
(918) 583 - 4149
Contact Person: Sales Office

CONFIGURATIONS SUPPORTED

Computer	Language	Operating System	RAM	Number Drives	Cost
MACINTOSH	FORTRAN		128K	1	$119
MACINTOSH	FORTRAN		512K	1	$119

NUMBER OF CURRENT USERS 5000
DATE OF FIRST RELEASE 1985
VERSION 2.1 RELEASED 1985

PROGRAM DESCRIPTION

STATFAST is a general purpose statistical package (basic statistics, nonparametric statistics, multivariarte statistics) with graphics and statistical database management functions.

The program is super fast, takes full advantage of 32-bit arithmetic of the 68000 processor. Two data editors are included: Command driven and mouse driven.

TYPE OF PROGRAM

Statistical Package

PROGRAM DESIGNED FOR

Data Analysis
Educational use

PROGRAM STYLE

Menu Driven
Integrated System

MISCELLANEOUS PROGRAM FEATURES

Copyable Disk

DOCUMENTATION

User's Manual - 180 pages, 20 technical references
- Table of Contents
- Tutorial or Example Lessons
- Sample Runs
- Formulas Provided

DATA MANAGEMENT
- Keyboard Data Entry
- Data Manipulations and Transformations
- Missing Values Allowed in Data

DATA EDITING
- Change
- Add
- Delete

FOREIGN DATA ACCESS
- Standard Rectangular ASCII Files
- Any Text Files
- Clipboard or Scrapbook Files

GRAPHICS FEATURES
- Graphics can be Output to a Printer
- Graphics can be Saved to a File
- Titles and/or Labels Available
- Uses Pixel Graphics

GRAPHICS
- Histograms
- Scatter (x-y) Plots

PRODUCT SUPPORT
- User may call at own Expense
- No Classes or Instruction Available

STATISTICAL FEATURES SUPPORTED

DESCRIPTIVE STATISTICS
- Mean
- Standard Deviation or Variance
- Standard Error of the Mean
- Coefficient of Variation
- Minimum, Maximum
- Median
- Skewness
- Kurtosis

t-TESTS
- One Sample t-Test
- Independent Group t-Test/Equal Variance
- Independent Group t-Test/Unequal Var
- Paired t-Test

CORRELATION AND REGRESSION
- Pearson Correlation Coefficient
- Simple Linear Regression
- Multiple Linear Regression
- Residuals Calculated
- Autocorrelation of Residuals
- Durbin Watson Statistic
- **REGRESSION PLOTS**
  - Residuals

CATEGORICAL DATA ANALYSIS
- Chi-Square Contingency Table Analysis
- Frequencies Can be Entered Directly

ANALYSIS OF VARIANCE
- One-Way ANOVA
- One-Way with Repeated Measures
- Two-Way ANOVA
- Two-Way Unequal Cell Sizes Allowed
- Analysis of Covariance
- Repeated Measures
- General ANOVA/ANCOVA
- Up to 5 Way
- Incomplete/Unbalanced Designs
- **MULTIPLE COMPARISONS**
  - Planned Comparisons

NONPARAMETRIC TESTS

Wilcoxon One Sample Test
Mann-Whitney U
Kruskal-Wallis Test
Spearman or Kendall Correlation
Phi-Square
Nu-Square

DISTRIBUTION FUNCTION EVALUATION

Normal
t
Chi Square
F

TIME SERIES ANALYSIS

Autocorrelations of Residuals

TIME SERIES ANALYSIS - FORECASTING

Regression Methods

MISCELLANEOUS

p-Values Given With Tests

STATGRAPHICS
Statistical Graphics Coroporation
5 Independence Way, Princeton Corp. Ctr.
Princeton, NJ 08540
(609) 924 - 9374
Contact Person: Grace Polhemus

CONFIGURATIONS SUPPORTED

Computer	Language	Operating System	RAM	Number Drives	Cost
IBM PC	APL	DOS	512K	2	$ 795

NUMBER OF CURRENT USERS 6000
DATE OF FIRST RELEASE Mar 83
VERSION 2.1 RELEASED ?

PROGRAM DESCRIPTION

STATGRAPHICS is an integrated system for interactive data analysis, data management and statistical graphics. It is designed to provide a flexible user-friendly environment for serious statistical computing, covering all major areas of statistical analysis. STATGRAPHICS is characterized by extensive integration of graphics directly into the statistical procedures. Graphical output may be generated by simply pressing selected function keys. Graphics displayed on the screen may be easily dumped to attached printers or routed to pen plotters. Selection of variables, transformations, and other options is accomplished by direct editing on fullscreen panels, rather than through sequences of complicated commands.

TYPE OF PROGRAM

Statistical Package

PROGRAM DESIGNED FOR

Data Analysis

PROGRAM STYLE
Menu Driven
Integrated System

MISCELLANEOUS PROGRAM FEATURES
Copyable Disk
On Screen Help Function
Optional Support for 8087 Mathematical Chip

DOCUMENTATION
User's Manual - 800 pages, ? technical references
Table of Contents
Index
Sample Runs
Formulas Provided
Tutorials and Examples on Disk

DATA MANAGEMENT
Keyboard Data Entry
Data Manipulations and Transformations
Missing Values Allowed in Data

DATA EDITING
Change
Add
Delete

FOREIGN DATA ACCESS
Standard Rectangular ASCII Files
DIF Files
Lotus
dBASE II and III Files

GRAPHICS FEATURES
Graphics Appear in Color on the Monitor
Graphics can be Output to a Printer
Graphics can be Saved to a File
Titles and/or Labels Available

GRAPHICS
Histograms
Pie Charts
Scatter (x-y) Plots
3-D Plotting
SEE Time Series Plots
SEE Regression Plots
SEE EDA Plots
Multiple Overlay Plots

PRODUCT SUPPORT
- User may call at own Expense
- Classes or Instruction Available

STATISTICAL FEATURES SUPPORTED

DESCRIPTIVE STATISTICS
- Mean
- Standard Deviation or Variance
- Standard Error of the Mean
- Coefficient of Variation
- Minimum, Maximum
- Median
- Percentiles
- Skewness
- Kurtosis

t-TESTS
- One Sample t-Test
- Independent Group t-Test/Equal Variance
- Independent Group t-Test/Unequal Var
- Paired t-Test

CORRELATION AND REGRESSION
- Pearson Correlation Coefficient
- Simple Linear Regression
- Multiple Linear Regression
- Stepwise Multiple Linear Regression
- Non-Linear Regression
- Residuals Calculated
- Ridge Regression
- Polynomial Regression
- **REGRESSION PLOTS**
  - Residuals

CONFIDENCE INTERVALS
- Means
- Difference Between Two Means
- Variances
- Ratio of Variances

CATEGORICAL DATA ANALYSIS
- Chi-Square Contingency Table Analysis
- Multi-Dimensional Tables
- Goodness-of-Fit Tests
- Frequencies Can be Entered Directly

ANALYSIS OF VARIANCE
- One-Way ANOVA
- One-Way with Repeated Measures
- Two-Way ANOVA
- Two-Way Unequal Cell Sizes Allowed
- Analysis of Covariance
- Hierarchical ANOVAs
- **MULTIPLE COMPARISONS**
    - ANOVA Post-Hoc Tests
    - Tukey

NONPARAMETRIC TESTS
- Sign Test (Signed Rank)
- Wilcoxon One Sample Test
- Mann-Whitney U
- Kruskal-Wallis Test
- Friedman Chi-Square Test
- Spearman or Kendall Correlation
- Kolmogorov-Smirnov Test

DISTRIBUTION FUNCTION EVALUATION
- Normal
- t
- Chi Square
- F
- Binomial
- Hypergeometric
- Poisson

EXPLORATORY DATA ANALYSIS
- Stem-and-Leaf Displays
- Resistant Line
- Smoothing Techniques
- Median Polish
- Rootograms
- Notched Box Plots

TIME SERIES ANALYSIS

- Autocorrelations
- Cross Correlations
- Moving Average Smoothing
- AUTOREGRESSIVE MOVING AVERAGE
  - Model Identification
  - Parameter Estimation
- Exp. Smoothing (Holt's, Winter, Brown)
- **TIME SERIES ANALYSIS - FORECASTING**
  - Exponential Smoothing
  - Polynomial Curves
- **TIME SERIES ANALYSIS - PLOTS**
  - Autocorrelations
  - Partial Autocorrelations
  - Cross Correlation
  - Periodogram
- **TIME SERIES ANALYSIS - SPECTRAL ESTIMATE**
  - Periodogram

CONTROL CHARTS

- X-Bar
- s
- Proportions
- Number of Defects
- Number of Defectives
- u-Chart
- **OTHER QUALITY CONTROL PROCEDURES**
  - Acceptance Sampling by Attributes
  - Acceptance Sampling by Variables

MISCELLANEOUS

- Cluster Analysis
- Random Number Generation
- Test for Normality of Data
- Test for Equality of Variances
- Linear Discriminant Function Calculation
- Sample Size Estimation
- p-Values Given With Tests
- Zoom in on a Portion of a Plot
- Variable Text Size for Plot Titles

STATISTICAL ANALYSIS GROUP

Industrial Engineering & Mgt Press
25 Technology Pk/Atlanta
Norcross, GA 30092
(404) 449 - 0460
Contact Person: Tom Johnson

CONFIGURATIONS SUPPORTED

Computer	Language	Operating System	RAM	Number Drives	Cost
IBM PC	BASIC	DOS	128K	1	$175
APPLE II	BASIC	DOS	48K	1	$175

NUMBER OF CURRENT USERS 1500+
DATE OF FIRST RELEASE 1981
VERSION 1A RELEASED 1986

PROGRAM DESCRIPTION

Statistical Analysis is intended for engineers and managers to help improve productivity and profits by simplifying repetitive tasks and decreasing timely manual calculations. This package includes four programs written in BASIC and includes step-by-step documentation, practical case examples, frequent menu prompts for entering, changing, and storing data, plus complete source codes for each program and a 5 1/4" diskette.

Programs included in this package are as follows: The Mann-Whitney Test analyzes given data to determine if two different samples come from the same populations, Statistical Data Analysis calculates several standard statistical descriptions of a given set of data such as the mean, median, variance, and standard deviation, Polynomial Curve Fit calculates the "best" least square polynomial curve fit for a series of data supplied, Distribution Fitting uses the Kolmogorov-Smirnov Statistical Test to determine whether a given set of data is from a certain distribution.

TYPE OF PROGRAM

Statistical Package

PROGRAM DESIGNED FOR
Data Analysis

PROGRAM STYLE
Menu Driven
Integrated System

MISCELLANEOUS PROGRAM FEATURES
Source Code Available
Copyable Disk

DOCUMENTATION
User's Manual - 100 pages, 25 technical references
Table of Contents
Index
Tutorial or Example Lessons
Sample Runs

DATA MANAGEMENT
Keyboard Data Entry
Missing Values Allowed in Data

DATA EDITING
Change
Add
Delete

FOREIGN DATA ACCESS
Can be Linked by User

GRAPHICS
Histograms

PRODUCT SUPPORT
User may call at own Expense
No Classes or Instruction Available

STATISTICAL FEATURES SUPPORTED

DESCRIPTIVE STATISTICS

Mean
Standard Deviation or Variance
Minimum, Maximum
Median
Skewness
Kurtosis

DISTRIBUTION FUNCTION EVALUATION

Normal
Binomial
Poisson
Exponential

STATISTICAL FORECASTING

Programmed Press
2301 Baylis Avenue
Elmont, NY 11003
(516) 775 - 0933
Contact Person: Dr. A. Bookbinder

CONFIGURATIONS SUPPORTED

Computer	Language	Operating System	RAM	Number Drives	Cost
IBM PC	BASIC	DOS	64K	1	$ 120
APPLE	BASIC	DOS	48K	1	$ 120
TRS-80	BASIC	TRS DOS	48K	1	$ 120
COMMODORE	BASIC	COMMODORE	64K	1	$ 120

NUMBER OF CURRENT USERS 5000
DATE OF FIRST RELEASE 83
VERSION 1.2 RELEASED 85

PROGRAM DESCRIPTION

Investment-Oriented Statistical Software Package of 50 programs. Statistical forecasting for STOCK, BONDS and INTEREST RATES, OPTIONS and ARBITRAGE, COMMODITIES and FUTURES and FOREIGN EXCHANGE. The 50 statistical programs are as follows: 1.Average2.Median 3.Geometric Mean 4.Harmonic Mean 5.Mean Deviation 6.Standard Deviation 7.Variation Coefficient 8.Range 9.Moving Average 10.Exponential Moving Average 11.Exponential Smoothing for Forecasting 12.Trend Projection 13.Growth Rate & Projection 14.Monthly Seasonal Index 15.Quarterly Seasonal 16. Month Link Relative 17.Quarter Link Relative 18.Time Series Decomposition 19.Quarter Time Series Decomposition 20.Multiple Correlation and Coefficient-up to 10 Variable 21.Treasury Bill Value 22.91-Day Treasury Bill Yield 23.6-Month TB Yield 24.One Year Treasury Bill Yield 25.Compound Interest 26.Yield on Bonds 27. High Coupon Bond Yield Tables-prints whole Bond Yield Book-up to 20% 28.Mortgage Payments 29.Annuity Present Value 30.Lump Sum Present Value 31.Return from Investment 32.After Tax Bond Yield 33.Soybean Crush Speed 34.Soybean Crush Contact Values 35.Multilateral Foreign Value 36.Bilateral Exchange

37.Interest Rates and Foreign Exchange Forecasting 38.Arbitrage-Option Conversion 39.Arbitrage-Reverse Option Conversion 40.Black-Scholes Option Model 41.Stoll put Model 42.Bookbinder Put Model 43.Bookbinder Option Model 44.Stock Index Futures 45.Projecting Dow Jones 46.Forecasting Dow Changes 47.Break-Even Volumn 48.Earnings Forecasting 49.Projecting Earnings Growth 50.Price-Earnings Ratio and Dividend Yield.

PRODUCT REVIEWS

"Investment-Oriented Statistical Software", American Statistician, pp. 224, (Aug 84).

Roosma, Dr. H. Journal of Finance, pp. 1259-1261, (Sept 1985).

American Statistician, (1985).

New York Times, (1983).

Publishers Weekly, (1983).

TYPE OF PROGRAM

Statistical Package

PROGRAM DESIGNED FOR

Data Analysis

PROGRAM STYLE

Menu Driven
Separate Programs for each Procedure

MISCELLANEOUS PROGRAM FEATURES

Source Code Available
Copyable Disk
On Screen Help Function

DOCUMENTATION

User's Manual - 220 pages, technical references
- Table of Contents
- Index
- Tutorial or Example Lessons
- Sample Runs
- Formulas Provided

Quick Reference Card

DATA MANAGEMENT

Keyboard Data Entry

FOREIGN DATA ACCESS
Standard Rectangular ASCII Files

PRODUCT SUPPORT
User may call at own Expense
No Classes or Instruction Available

STATISTICAL FEATURES SUPPORTED

DESCRIPTIVE STATISTICS
Mean
Standard Deviation or Variance
Coefficient of Variation
Median
Harmonic Mean
Geometric Mean

t-TESTS
One Sample t-Test

CORRELATION AND REGRESSION
Pearson Correlation Coefficient
Simple Linear Regression
Multiple Linear Regression
Stepwise Multiple Linear Regression
Forecasting

CONFIDENCE INTERVALS
Means

DISTRIBUTION FUNCTION EVALUATION
Normal

EXPLORATORY DATA ANALYSIS
Smoothing Techniques

TIME SERIES ANALYSIS
Autocorrelations
Cross Correlations
Moving Average Smoothing
AUTOREGRESSIVE MOVING AVERAGE
Exp Smoothing(Holts, Winters, Browns)
TIME SERIES ANALYSIS - FORECASTING
Exponential Smoothing

STATISTICAL PROCESS CONTROL

Porter Data Systems, Inc.
470 Buckeye Dr.
Colorado Springs, CO 80919
(303) 599 - 5548
Contact Person: Fred Porter

CONFIGURATIONS SUPPORTED

Computer	Language	Operating System	RAM	Number Drives	Cost
HP 200	BASIC	BASIC	768K	1	
HP 300	BASIC	BASIC	1M	1	

NUMBER OF CURRENT USERS 200
DATE OF FIRST RELEASE 1982
CURRENT VERSION RELEASED Sept 85

PROGRAM DESCRIPTION

Written for industrial quality control and real-time monitoring or analysis, this software generates standard Shewart control charts.

This system runs stand-alone as shipped with its own data base. It is easily modified to interface directly to sensors in a process or to other computers.

TYPE OF PROGRAM

Quality Control or Reliability

PROGRAM DESIGNED FOR

Data Analysis

PROGRAM STYLE

Menu Driven
Integrated System

MISCELLANEOUS PROGRAM FEATURES

Copyable Disk
On Screen Help Function

DOCUMENTATION

User's Manual - 70 pages, 10 technical references
- Table of Contents
- Index
- Tutorial or Example Lessons
- Sample Runs
- Formulas Provided

Quick Reference Card
Tutorials and Examples on Disk

DATA MANAGEMENT

Keyboard Data Entry
Data Manipulations and Transformations
Missing Values Allowed in Data

DATA EDITING

Change
Add
Delete

GRAPHICS FEATURES

Graphics Appear in Color on the Monitor
Graphics can be Output to a Printer
Graphics can be Saved to a File
Titles and/or Labels Available
Uses Pixel Graphics

GRAPHICS

Histograms
SEE QC Plots

PRODUCT SUPPORT

User may call at own Expense
Classes or Instruction Available

STATISTICAL FEATURES SUPPORTED

CONTROL CHARTS
- X-Bar
- Number of Defects
- Number of Defectives
- Pareto Diagrams
- Process Capability

STATISTICS & PROBABILITY DEMONSTRATIONS

COMPress
P.O. Box 102
Wentworth, NH 03282
(603) 764 - 5831
Contact Person: Ellen Young

CONFIGURATIONS SUPPORTED

Computer	Language	Operating System	RAM	Number Drives	Cost
APPLE II	BASIC	DOS	48K	1	$ 475

NUMBER OF CURRENT USERS ?
DATE OF FIRST RELEASE 1983
VERSION 2 RELEASED 1985

PROGRAM DESCRIPTION

Statistics and Probability Demonstrations and Tutorials were written by Professor Bruce E. Trumbo of California State University, Hayward. These programs can be used with any standard statistics/probability text, and they are useful for both classroom demonstrations and individual study.

Key features include interactive demonstrations which are better than a blackboard sketch and live simulations which are more extensive than ever possible in the classroom and more convincing than any textbook description. Additionally, the user has access to a variety of computational methods for statistical analysis, hidden control options for the instructor, and flexibility in data entry.

PRODUCT REVIEWS

Druva, Cindy. "Statistics Demonstration", The Courseware Critique, pp. 13-14, (May 1985).

Software Reports, (Apr 30, 1985).

TYPE OF PROGRAM

Statistical Package

PROGRAM DESIGNED FOR
Educational use

PROGRAM STYLE
Menu Driven
Separate Programs for each Procedure

DOCUMENTATION
User's Manual - ? pages, ? technical references
Table of Contents
Tutorial or Example Lessons
Sample Runs
Tutorials and Examples on Disk

DATA MANAGEMENT
Keyboard Data Entry
Data Manipulations and Transformations

DATA EDITING
Change
Add
Delete

GRAPHICS
Histograms
Pie Charts

PRODUCT SUPPORT
Free Phone Support Available
No Classes or Instruction Available

STATISTICAL FEATURES SUPPORTED

CATEGORICAL DATA ANALYSIS
Chi-Square Contingency Table Analysis

ANALYSIS OF VARIANCE
One-Way ANOVA
MULTIPLE COMPARISONS
Fisher's LSD
Duncan's Multiple Range
Scheffe
Newman-Keuls

STATISTICS BUTTONS
Straightforward
15000 Halldale Ave.,Suite 115
Gardena, CA 90247
(213) 324 - 8827
Contact Person: Yates J. Canipe

CONFIGURATIONS SUPPORTED

Computer	Language	Operating System	RAM	Number Drives	Cost
IBM PC	FORTH/HP41	DOS	128K	1	$40

NUMBER OF CURRENT USERS 1000
DATE OF FIRST RELEASE Nov 85
VERSION 1.1 RELEASED July 86

PROGRAM DESCRIPTION

Statistics Buttons is a series of independent yet compatible programs to perform a wide variety of statistical functions. The programs are written for the user with some statistics knowledge. They are most popular in research (including marketing research) and educational situations. The objective is to provide fundamental statistical functions at the touch of a button.

These programs are simple to use, fast, inexpensive and have a common interface. They were derived from HP41 programs. Source code can be modified with the Straightforward Forty one and emulator of the HP41 which runs on the IBM PC.

TYPE OF PROGRAM

Statistical Package

PROGRAM DESIGNED FOR

Data Analysis

PROGRAM STYLE

Menu Driven
Separate Programs for each Procedure

MISCELLANEOUS PROGRAM FEATURES
Source Code Available
Copyable Disk
On Screen Help Function
Optional Support for 8087 Mathematical Chip

DOCUMENTATION
User's Manual - ? pages, ? technical references
Tutorial or Example Lessons
Formulas Provided
Tutorials and Examples on Disk

DATA MANAGEMENT
Keyboard Data Entry
Missing Values Allowed in Data

DATA EDITING
Change
Add
Delete

FOREIGN DATA ACCESS
Standard Rectangular ASCII Files
DIF Files

PRODUCT SUPPORT
User may call at own Expense
No Classes or Instruction Available

STATISTICAL FEATURES SUPPORTED

DESCRIPTIVE STATISTICS
Mean
Standard Deviation or Variance
Standard Error of the Mean
Coefficient of Variation
Skewness
Kurtosis

t-TESTS
Paired t-Test

CORRELATION AND REGRESSION
Simple Linear Regression
Multiple Linear Regression
Non-Linear Regression

CATEGORICAL DATA ANALYSIS

Chi-Square Contingency Table Analysis
Multi-Dimensional Tables
Goodness-of-Fit Tests

ANALYSIS OF VARIANCE

One-Way ANOVA
Two-Way ANOVA
Analysis of Covariance

NONPARAMETRIC TESTS

Spearman or Kendall Correlation

DISTRIBUTION FUNCTION EVALUATION

Normal
t
Chi Square
F

TIME SERIES ANALYSIS

Moving Average Smoothing

STATISTIX

NH Analytical Software
801 West Iowa Avenue
St. Paul, MN 55117
(612) 488 - 4436
Contact Person: Gerard Nimis

CONFIGURATIONS SUPPORTED

Computer	Language	Operating System	RAM	Number Drives	Cost
IBM PC	COMPILED	DOS	128K	1	$75
APPLE II	COMPILED	SUPPLIED	64K	1	$75

NUMBER OF CURRENT USERS ?
DATE OF FIRST RELEASE July 85
VERSION 1.1 RELEASED May 86

PROGRAM DESCRIPTION

STATISTIX is a powerful yet very easy-to-use interactive statistical analysis system for microcomputers. STATISTIX is a general purpose system; it was designed to take maximum advantage of the personal and interactive nature of the microcomputer. Its power and sophistication met most of the analytical needs of research professional, while its ease-of-use and flexibility make it readily available to the student. STATISTIX is widely used for research and instruction in academia, business, government and medicine.

STATISTIX has outstanding data manipulation abilities, including user-specified arithmetic transformations, conditional transformations, missing value recognition, editing, and analyses by subsets. Data entry from keyboard or text files is allowed, permitting compatibility with most other popular programs. Many statistical analyses can be performed, including almost any nearly balanced complete analysis of variance or covariance (crossed, nested, split-plot, etc.) with up to five factors and five covariates, multiple, logistic and Poisson regression, eigensystem analysis, most standard one and two sample parametric and nonparametric tests, goodness-of-fit tests including log-linear models, probability values for nine distributions, summmary statistics, histograms, scatterplots, and much more. A 200 page manual with numerous examples is included. STATISTIX is available for the IBM

PC's and compatibles, MS DOS machines and Apple II's with at least 64K. The program comes on two diskettes, and is not copy-protected. Regular updates will be provided, and phone support is available for users.

PRODUCT REVIEWS

Russek-Cohen, Estelle. "Statistical Package for Microcomputers: STATISTIX 1.0", Bulletin of the Ecological Society of America, Vol. 67 No. 2, pp. 194-196, (1986).

TYPE OF PROGRAM

Statistical Package

PROGRAM DESIGNED FOR

Data Analysis
Educational use

PROGRAM STYLE

Menu Driven
Integrated System

MISCELLANEOUS PROGRAM FEATURES

Copyable Disk
Optional Support for 8087, 80287 Mathematical Chip

DOCUMENTATION

User's Manual - 224 pages, 65 technical references
- Table of Contents
- Index
- Tutorial or Example Lessons
- Sample Runs
- Formulas Provided

DATA MANAGEMENT

Keyboard Data Entry
Data Manipulations and Transformations
Missing Values Allowed in Data

DATA EDITING

Change
Add
Delete

FOREIGN DATA ACCESS

Standard Rectangular ASCII Files

GRAPHICS FEATURES
Graphics can be Output to a Printer
Titles and/or Labels Available
Uses Character Graphics

GRAPHICS
Histograms
Scatter (x-y) Plots

PRODUCT SUPPORT
User may call at own Expense
No Classes or Instruction Available

STATISTICAL FEATURES SUPPORTED

DESCRIPTIVE STATISTICS
Mean
Standard Deviation or Variance
Standard Error of the Mean
Minimum, Maximum
Median
Percentiles
Skewness
Kurtosis

t-TESTS
One Sample t-Test
Independent Group t-Test/Equal Variance
Independent Group t-Test/Unequal Var
Paired t-Test

CORRELATION AND REGRESSION
Pearson Correlation Coefficient
Simple Linear Regression
Multiple Linear Regression
Residuals Calculated
REGRESSION PLOTS
Residuals

CONFIDENCE INTERVALS
Means
Difference Between Two Means
Multiple Linear Regression

CATEGORICAL DATA ANALYSIS
- Chi-Square Contingency Table Analysis
- Multi-Dimensional Tables
- Fisher's Exact Test
- Goodness-of-Fit Tests
- Frequencies Can be Entered Directly
- McNemar's Symmetry Test
- Logistic and Poisson Regression
- Log Linear Models

ANALYSIS OF VARIANCE
- One-Way ANOVA
- One-Way with Repeated Measures
- Two-Way ANOVA
- Two-Way Unequal Cell Sizes Allowed
- Analysis of Covariance
- Nested
- Split-Plot
- Up to 5 Factors
- Partially Crossed and Nested
- **MULTIPLE COMPARISONS**
    - Scheffe
    - Bonferroni
    - Tukey's (HSD)
    - Sidak
    - LSD

NONPARAMETRIC TESTS
- Sign Test (Signed Rank)
- Wilcoxon One Sample Test
- Mann-Whitney U
- Kruskal-Wallis Test
- Friedman Chi-Square Test
- Spearman or Kendall Correlation
- Kolmogorov-Smirnoff 2 Sample Test
- Median Test
- Runs Test
- Kruskal-Wallis 1-Way

DISTRIBUTION FUNCTION EVALUATION
- Normal
- t
- Chi Square
- F
- Binomial
- Hypergeometric
- Poisson
- Negative Binomial
- Beta

TIME SERIES ANALYSIS

TIME SERIES ANALYSIS - PLOTS

Up to 5 X-Y Pairs Superimposed

Scatterplots

MISCELLANEOUS

Random Number Generation

Test for Normality of Data

Test for Equality of Variances

p-Values Given With Tests

STATLIB.GL: STAT GRAPHICS SUBROUTINES

John Wiley & Sons, Inc.
605 3rd Avenue
New York, NY 10158
(212) 850 - 6788
Contact Person: Dianne Littwin

CONFIGURATIONS SUPPORTED

Computer	Language	Operating System	RAM	Number Drives	Cost
IBM PC	FORTRAN	DOS	512K	2	$295
IBM PC	FORTRAN	DOS	512K	2	$295

NUMBER OF CURRENT USERS ?
DATE OF FIRST RELEASE Jan 87
CURRENT VERSION RELEASED Jan 87

PROGRAM DESCRIPTION

This is a most powerful collection of statistical graphical subroutines supplied on disk, as a linkable library and as a source code. The package includes appropriate pieces of the GSS GKS Toolkit. The subroutines allow the user the following graphical representations of data: scatter plots with log & linear axes; bar charts and histograms; curvefit graphs; descriptive statistics graphs; normality (Q-Q) plots; Box Jenkins Identification; relationships and clusters in multivariate data; contour map and axonometric plots for representations of 3 dimensional data in two dimensional form; and a non-parametric technique known as stem and leaf display used for exploratory data analysis of numbers.

This subroutine library gives you all the benefits of a complete package and the added advantage of allowing you to quickly and easily customize your program for your needs.

TYPE OF PROGRAM

Subroutine Library - Statistics

PROGRAM DESIGNED FOR

Data Analysis
Educational use

PROGRAM STYLE

Separate Programs for each Procedure

MISCELLANEOUS PROGRAM FEATURES

Source Code Available
Copyable Disk
Optional Support for 8087, 80287 Mathematical Chip

DOCUMENTATION

User's Manual - 250 pages, 20 technical references
- Table of Contents
- Index
- Tutorial or Example Lessons
- Sample Runs
- Formulas Provided

Tutorials and Examples on Disk

GRAPHICS FEATURES

Graphics Appear in Color on the Monitor
Graphics can be Output to a Printer
Titles and/or Labels Available
Uses Pixel Graphics

GRAPHICS

Histograms
Scatter (x-y) Plots
3-D Plotting
Contour Maps
Variance Bar Plots
Triangular Scatter Plots
Stem & Leaf Cluster Analysis
Dendrograms
SEE Time Series Plots

PRODUCT SUPPORT

User may call at own Expense
No Classes or Instruction Available

STATISTICAL FEATURES SUPPORTED

DESCRIPTIVE STATISTICS
- Mean
- Standard Deviation or Variance
- Standard Error of the Mean
- Quartiles
- Range Bar

DISTRIBUTION FUNCTION EVALUATION
- Normal

EXPLORATORY DATA ANALYSIS
- Resistant Line

TIME SERIES ANALYSIS
- Autocorrelations
- **TIME SERIES ANALYSIS - PLOTS**
  - Autocorrelations
  - Partial Autocorrelations

CONTROL CHARTS
- X-Bar

MISCELLANEOUS
- Cluster Analysis
- Life Table Analysis

STATLIB.TSF: TIME SERIES LIBRARY

John Wiley & Sons, Inc.
605 3rd Avenue
New York, NY 10158
(212) 850 - 6788
Contact Person: Dianne Littwin

CONFIGURATIONS SUPPORTED

Computer	Language	Operating System	RAM	Number Drives	Cost
IBM PC	FORTRAN	DOS	512K	2	$295

NUMBER OF CURRENT USERS ?
DATE OF FIRST RELEASE Jan 87
CURRENT VERSION RELEASED Jan 87

PROGRAM DESCRIPTION

This is a subroutine library with applicationa in a variety of disciplines. The subroutines are supplied on disk, as a linkable library and as source code. Some of the specific applications are as follows: moving averages and variances; linear regression models of time series in which regression has been implemented using singular value decomposition; exponential forecasting in non-seasonal and seasonal models which give short term projections; ARIMA models which implements the univariate Box-Jenkins method for forecasting; spectral analysis implements the FTT & several windowing techniques; and survival analysis describes lifetime distributions which are of interest to reliability engineers, actuaries and biostatisticians.

The manual lists the source code of each subroutine in both single precision and double precision forms. The source code of the test program for the single precision version is also listed in the manual. Double precision test programs, while not listed in the manual, are included on diskette. This library gives you all the benefits of a complete package and the added advantage of allowing you to quickly and easily customize your program for your needs. Also see the directory listing under STATLIB. GL.

TYPE OF PROGRAM

Time Series Analysis

PROGRAM DESIGNED FOR
Data Analysis
Educational use

PROGRAM STYLE
Separate Programs for each Procedure

MISCELLANEOUS PROGRAM FEATURES
Source Code Available
Copyable Disk
Supports 80287, 8087 Mathematical Chip

DOCUMENTATION
User's Manual - 250 pages, ? technical references
Table of Contents
Index
Tutorial or Example Lessons
Sample Runs
Formulas Provided
Tutorials and Examples on Disk

PRODUCT SUPPORT
User may call at own Expense
No Classes or Instruction Available

STATISTICAL FEATURES SUPPORTED

DESCRIPTIVE STATISTICS
Mean
Standard Deviation or Variance

CORRELATION AND REGRESSION
Multiple Linear Regression

CONFIDENCE INTERVALS
Estimates for Survival Distributions

DISTRIBUTION FUNCTION EVALUATION
Chi Square
Gamma

TIME SERIES ANALYSIS
Autocorrelations
Moving Average Smoothing
AUTOREGRESSIVE MOVING AVERAGE
TIME SERIES ANALYSIS - FORECASTING
ARIMA: Exponential
TIME SERIES ANALYSIS - SPECTRAL ESTIMATE
Windowing: FFT

RELIABILITY

Exponential
Weibull
Cox Regression
Weibull Regression
Log Normal

MISCELLANEOUS

Life Table Analysis
Mixed Estimation
Durbin-Watson Statistic
Influential Data Identification

STATMATE/PLUS
The Software Hill
1857 Apple Tree Lane
Mountain View, CA 94040
(415) 969 - 4233
Contact Person: Wayne Watson

CONFIGURATIONS SUPPORTED

Computer	Language	Operating System	RAM	Number Drives	Cost
CP/M BASED	PL/I-80	CP/M	64K	2	$ 149
IBM PC	PL/I-86	DOS	128K	2	$ 149

NUMBER OF CURRENT USERS ?
DATE OF FIRST RELEASE May 84
VERSION 1.2 RELEASED Mar 85

PROGRAM DESCRIPTION

STATMATE/PLUS is the advanced version of the STATMATE family of statistcal packages designed for use on CP/M based or IBM PC compatible microcomputers. It is designed for use by engineers, scientists, statisticians, businessmen, QC engineers and social scientists. STATMATE/PLUS provides a variety of methods including non-linear regression, multiple regression, scatter plots, ANOVA, nonparametric analyses, cross tabulations and a number of basic statistical capabilities.

The program was designed to provide a complete set of methods which operate together to form a cohesive system. Missing data allowances, 'if-like' data selection, data transformations and editing are among its many features. Analyses are provided for both numeric and character data. Data may be entered from ASCII files or directly through the keyboard. Large problem sizes are permitted.

PRODUCT REVIEWS

American Statistician, (1983).

American Statistician, (Late 1986).

The Seybold Report on Professional Computing, pp. 11, (November 26, 1984).

TYPE OF PROGRAM
Statistical Package

PROGRAM DESIGNED FOR
Data Analysis

PROGRAM STYLE
Command Driven
Integrated System

MISCELLANEOUS PROGRAM FEATURES
Copyable Disk
On Screen Help Function

DOCUMENTATION
User's Manual - 145 pages, 16 technical references
Table of Contents
Index
Sample Runs
Formulas Provided
Tutorials and Examples on Disk

DATA MANAGEMENT
Keyboard Data Entry
Data Manipulations and Transformations
Missing Values Allowed in Data

DATA EDITING
Change
Add
Delete

FOREIGN DATA ACCESS
Standard Rectangular ASCII Files

GRAPHICS FEATURES
Graphics can be Output to a Printer
Graphics can be Saved to a File
Titles and/or Labels Available
Uses Character Graphics

GRAPHICS
Histograms
Scatter (x-y) Plots
SEE Regression Plots

PRODUCT SUPPORT
User may call at own Expense
No Classes or Instruction Available

STATISTICAL FEATURES SUPPORTED

DESCRIPTIVE STATISTICS
Mean
Standard Deviation or Variance
Minimum, Maximum
Median
Percentiles
Skewness
Kurtosis
Mid-mean
Trimmed Mean
Tri-mean

t-TESTS
One Sample t-Test
Independent Group t-Test/Equal Variance
Independent Group t-Test/Unequal Var

CORRELATION AND REGRESSION
Pearson Correlation Coefficient
Simple Linear Regression
Multiple Linear Regression
Stepwise Multiple Linear Regression
Non-Linear Regression
Residuals Calculated
Prediction
REGRESSION PLOTS
Residuals

CATEGORICAL DATA ANALYSIS
Chi-Square Contingency Table Analysis
Fisher's Exact Test
Goodness-of-Fit Tests

ANALYSIS OF VARIANCE
- One-Way ANOVA
- Two-Way ANOVA
- Two-Way Unequal Cell Sizes Allowed
- **MULTIPLE COMPARISONS**
  - Fisher's LSD
  - Duncan's Multiple Range

NONPARAMETRIC TESTS
- Mann-Whitney U
- Kruskal-Wallis Test
- Spearman or Kendall Correlation
- Friedman 2-way ANOVA
- Cochran Q-test

DISTRIBUTION FUNCTION EVALUATION
- Normal
- t
- Chi Square
- F
- Exponential
- Weibull
- Cauchy

CONTROL CHARTS
- X-Bar
- R

MISCELLANEOUS
- Random Number Generation
- Test for Normality of Data
- p-Values Given With Tests
- Select If

STATPAC GOLD

Walonick Associates, Inc.
6500 Nicollet Ave. S
Minneapolis, MN 55423
(800) 328 - 4907
Contact Person: David Walonick

CONFIGURATIONS SUPPORTED

Computer	Language	Operating System	RAM	Number Drives	Cost
IBM PC	COMPILED	DOS	192K	H	$595

NUMBER OF CURRENT USERS 1000
DATE OF FIRST RELEASE Mar 86
VERSION V 2.0 RELEASED Mar 87

PROGRAM DESCRIPTION

StatPac Gold is an enhanced statistical analysis package for professional resarchers. It is designed primarily for advanced researchers requiring sophisticated multivariate analysis.

It features interactive and batch processing, frequencies, descriptive statistics, breakdown, crosstabs and banners, correlation and regression, stepwise multiple regression, probit regression, principal components and multicollinearity analyses, factor analysis, t-tests, eleven ANOVA techniques and multiple variable response. A quality control and forecasting module is also available that includes an exploratory package and a dozen forecasting techniques. Many printing options, including high resolution graphics, are available on all analyses. Data manipulation includes writing, listing, weighting, sorting and aggregating cases; also select-if, recode, recode-if, compute, compute-if, sum, lag, difference, dummy and normalize. Data files may contain 32,767 records and 500 variables of alpha or numeric information. StatPac Gold can be run using menus or commands. It contains a complete data manager including three different data entry and editing techniques. The program reads fixed or free format ASCII files allowing compatability with mainframe files and other microcomputer programs.

TYPE OF PROGRAM
Statistical Package

PROGRAM DESIGNED FOR
Data Analysis

PROGRAM STYLE
Menu Driven
Command Driven
Integrated System

MISCELLANEOUS PROGRAM FEATURES
Copyable Disk
On Screen Help Function

DOCUMENTATION
User's Manual - 500 pages, 36 technical references
Table of Contents
Index
Tutorial or Example Lessons
Sample Runs
Formulas Provided
Tutorials and Examples on Disk

DATA MANAGEMENT
Keyboard Data Entry
Data Manipulations and Transformations
Missing Values Allowed in Data

DATA EDITING
Change
Add
Delete

FOREIGN DATA ACCESS
Standard Rectangular ASCII Files
DIF Files
dBase II Files
Any Fixed or Comma Delimited ASCII File

GRAPHICS FEATURES
Graphics can be Output to a Printer
Graphics can be Saved to a File
Titles and/or Labels Available
Uses Pixel Graphics
Uses Character Graphics

GRAPHICS

- Histograms
- Bar Graphs
- Pie Charts
- Scatter (x-y) Plots
- Time Plots
- SEE Regression Plots
- SEE Time Series Plots
- SEE EDA Plots

PRODUCT SUPPORT

- User may call at own Expense
- No Classes or Instruction Available

STATISTICAL FEATURES SUPPORTED

DESCRIPTIVE STATISTICS

- Mean
- Standard Deviation or Variance
- Standard Error of the Mean
- Coefficient of Variation
- Minimum, Maximum
- Median
- Skewness
- Kurtosis
- Kolmogorov - Smirnov Statistic
- Confidence Intervals
- Mode(s)
- Sum

t-TESTS

- Independent Group t-Test/Equal Variance
- Independent Group t-Test/Unequal Var
- Paired t-Test
- Post Hoc LSD after ANOVA

CORRELATION AND REGRESSION

- Pearson Correlation Coefficient
- Simple Linear Regression
- Multiple Linear Regression
- Stepwise Multiple Linear Regression
- Non-Linear Regression
- Residuals Calculated
- **REGRESSION PLOTS**
    - Residuals

CONFIDENCE INTERVALS

- Means

CATEGORICAL DATA ANALYSIS

Chi-Square Contingency Table Analysis
Multi-Dimensional Tables
Goodness-of-Fit Tests
Interaction Analysis
Residual Analysis

ANALYSIS OF VARIANCE

One-Way ANOVA
One-Way with Repeated Measures
Two-Way ANOVA
Two-Way Unequal Cell Sizes Allowed
Factorial Designs
Latin Square
Split-Plot
Up to 3 Factors-30 Levels Each

NONPARAMETRIC TESTS

Wilcoxon One Sample Test
Mann-Whitney U
Kruskal-Wallis Test
Spearman or Kendall Correlation

DISTRIBUTION FUNCTION EVALUATION

Normal
t
Chi Square
F

EXPLORATORY DATA ANALYSIS

Smoothing Techniques
Aggregate Box Plots
Box Plots
Spread vs. Level Plots
ACF Plots
Time Plots

TIME SERIES ANALYSIS
- Autocorrelations
- Moving Average Smoothing
- AUTOREGRESSIVE MOVING AVERAGE
  - Model Identification
  - Parameter Estimation
- **TIME SERIES ANALYSIS - FORECASTING**
  - Exponential Smoothing
  - Double Exponential Smoothing
  - Regression
  - Adaptive Filtering
  - SABL Decomposition
  - Census X-11 Decomposition
  - Winter's Seasonal Smoothing
  - Harrison's Harmonic Smoothing
  - Holt's Two Parameter Smoothing
  - Triple Exponential Smoothing
  - Box-Jenkins
  - Moving Average
- **TIME SERIES ANALYSIS - PLOTS**
  - Spread vs Level Plots
  - O, E, and Error
  - Seasonal Component by Month Plots
  - Box Plots
  - ACF Plots
  - Decomposition Plots
  - Smoothed Data Plots
  - Time

MISCELLANEOUS
- Random Number Generation
- Test for Normality of Data
- Sample Size Estimation
- p-Values Given With Tests

STATPAC(TM)- STAT. ANALYSIS PACKAGE

Walonick Associates, Inc
6500 Nicollet, Ave. S
Minneapolis, MN 55423
(800) 328 - 4907
Contact Person: David Walonick

CONFIGURATIONS SUPPORTED

Computer	Language	Operating System	RAM	Number Drives	Cost
IBM PC	COMPILED	DOS	192K	2	$ 495
CP/M FORMAT	COMPILED	CP/M	64K	2	$ 495

NUMBER OF CURRENT USERS 5500
DATE OF FIRST RELEASE 1980
CURRENT VERSION RELEASED May 86

PROGRAM DESCRIPTION

StatPac is a general purpose statistical analysis package for professional researchers. The primary users of Statpac are universities, medical researchers, marketing researchers, and large corporations.

It features batch processing, frequencies, descriptive statistics, breakdown, crosstabs, banners, correlation & regression, stepwise multiple regression, t-tests, one and two way ANOVA, factor analysis, principal components analysis, and multiple variable response. Many printing options, including graphics, are available on all analyses, Data manipulation includes writing, listing, weighting, sorting and aggregating cases; also select if, recode, recode-if, compute, and comute-if. Data files may contain 5000 records and 254 columns of alpha or numeric information. StatPac is menu driven and contains a complete data manager including a built in word processor for file editing. The program reads fixed or free format ASCII files allowing compatibility with mainframe files and/or other microcomputer programs.

PRODUCT REVIEWS

Lee, Robert S.. "Adding it Up with StatPac", PC Magazine, (Jan 24, 1984).

Foxwell, Harry. "StatPac - Software Review", Capital PC User's Group Publication.

Carpenter, James et. al.. "Statistical Software for Microcomputers", Byte Magazine, pp. 234-264, (April 1984).

Judd, Robert. "The Impact of Personal Computers on Marketing Research", Governor's State Univ - Dept of Business Administration, (1983).

Pettibone, Dr. Tim. "StatPac", The Software Critic, pp. Vol 2, #1, (1982).

Siegel, Dr. Jay. "Econometric Report 83", Quantitative Software Reports, (Nov 1983).

Good, Phillip. "Statistical Software for All Applications", Software Retailing, (Aug 1983).

Good, Phillip I. "A Critics Guide to Software for the IBM PC and Compatibles", Chilton Publishing Company, (1983).

TYPE OF PROGRAM

Statistical Package

PROGRAM DESIGNED FOR

Data Analysis

PROGRAM STYLE

Menu Driven
Integrated System

MISCELLANEOUS PROGRAM FEATURES

Copyable Disk
On Screen Help Function

DOCUMENTATION

User's Manual - 298 pages, 14 technical references
- Table of Contents
- Index
- Tutorial or Example Lessons
- Sample Runs
- Formulas Provided

Tutorials and Examples on Disk

DATA MANAGEMENT
- Keyboard Data Entry
- Data Manipulations and Transformations
- Missing Values Allowed in Data

DATA EDITING
- Change
- Add
- Delete

FOREIGN DATA ACCESS
- Standard Rectangular ASCII Files
- dBase II Files
- 1-2-3 PRN Format
- RBASE Files
- Condor Files

GRAPHICS FEATURES
- Graphics can be Output to a Printer
- Graphics can be Saved to a File
- Titles and/or Labels Available

GRAPHICS
- Histograms
- Pie Charts
- Scatter (x-y) Plots
- Bar Charts
- Residual Plots
- Autocorrelation Function Plots
- Observed/Expected Data Plots

PRODUCT SUPPORT
- Free Phone Support Available
- No Classes or Instruction Available

STATISTICAL FEATURES SUPPORTED

DESCRIPTIVE STATISTICS

Mean
Standard Deviation or Variance
Standard Error of the Mean
Minimum, Maximum
Median
Skewness
Kurtosis
Range
Mode
Sum
Kolmogorov-Smirnov

t-TESTS

Independent Group t-Test/Equal Variance
Paired t-Test

CORRELATION AND REGRESSION

Pearson Correlation Coefficient
Simple Linear Regression
Multiple Linear Regression
Non-Linear Regression
Residuals Calculated
Covariance Matrices
Spearmans rho

CONFIDENCE INTERVALS

Means

CATEGORICAL DATA ANALYSIS

Chi-Square Contingency Table Analysis
Phi Statistic
Cramer's V
Contingency Coefficient
Distribution Index
Entropy
Lambda
Gamma
Somers D (X indep, Y indep, Sym)
Equiweight Data
Residual Analysis
Interaction Analysis
TAU A, B, & C

ANALYSIS OF VARIANCE
- One-Way ANOVA
- One-Way with Repeated Measures
- Two-Way ANOVA
- Two-Way Unequal Cell Sizes Allowed

DISTRIBUTION FUNCTION EVALUATION
- Normal
- t
- Chi Square
- F

MISCELLANEOUS
- Random Number Generation
- Sample Size Estimation
- p-Values Given With Tests
- Frequencies
- Multiple Variable Response
- Breakdown
- Aggregate(True & Compositional)
- File Format Conversion
- Restructure Files
- Merge Files

STATPAD

Professional Applications Development
12 Sandy Way
Weymouth, MA 02191
(617) 331 - 4062
Contact Person: John A Clements

CONFIGURATIONS SUPPORTED

Computer	Language	Operating System	RAM	Number Drives	Cost
IBM PC	LOTUS 1-2-3	DOS	192K	2	$ 65

NUMBER OF CURRENT USERS 600
DATE OF FIRST RELEASE Mar 85
VERSION A-1.1 RELEASED Oct 85

ADDITIONAL SOFTWARE REQUIRED
LOTUS 1-2-3

PROGRAM DESCRIPTION

STATPAD is a system of menu driven Lotus 1-2-3 templates (automatic worksheets) for quality control and other statistical applications. It is easy to use by novices in quality control and/or computers and introduces the more experienced user to a valuable resource for producing customized applications. The comprehensive 93 page manual contains examples on running each template and advice on making statistical worksheets.

STATPAD makes effective use of the data handling and graphical utilities of Lotus 1-2-3. It not only provides the user with ready to use programs in most of the important statistical quality control techniques, but also demonstrates how Lotus 1-2-3 can be used as a powerful tool for producing customized applications. By following its example the user who is not a programming expert could produce worksheets for many of the new methods which appear in the literature and for which programs are rarely available. Workshops on using Lotus 1-2-3 for statistical quality control are available to divisions and sections of the American Society for Quality Control. STATPAD is provided as course material for these workshops.

TYPE OF PROGRAM
Quality Control or Reliability

PROGRAM DESIGNED FOR
Data Analysis

PROGRAM STYLE
Menu Driven
Separate Programs for each Procedure

MISCELLANEOUS PROGRAM FEATURES
Source Code Available
Copyable Disk

DOCUMENTATION
User's Manual - 93 pages, 10 technical references
Table of Contents
Tutorial or Example Lessons
Sample Runs
Example Data on Disk

DATA MANAGEMENT
Keyboard Data Entry
Data Manipulations and Transformations
Missing Values Allowed in Data

DATA EDITING
Change
Add
Delete

FOREIGN DATA ACCESS
Standard Rectangular ASCII Files
DIF Files
dBase II Files

GRAPHICS FEATURES
Graphics Appear in Color on the Monitor
Graphics can be Output to a Printer
Graphics can be Saved to a File
Titles and/or Labels Available
Uses Pixel Graphics

GRAPHICS
Histograms
Scatter (x-y) Plots
Control Charts
Normal Distribution Plot

PRODUCT SUPPORT
User may call at own Expense
Classes or Instruction Available

STATISTICAL FEATURES SUPPORTED

DESCRIPTIVE STATISTICS
Mean
Standard Deviation or Variance
Standard Error of the Mean
Minimum, Maximum
Percentiles

t-TESTS
One Sample t-Test
Independent Group t-Test/Equal Variance
Paired t-Test

CORRELATION AND REGRESSION
Pearson Correlation Coefficient
Simple Linear Regression
Multiple Linear Regression
Non-Linear Regression
Residuals Calculated
Estimate Asymptotic Standard Errors

CATEGORICAL DATA ANALYSIS
Chi-Square Contingency Table Analysis
Frequencies Can be Entered Directly

ANALYSIS OF VARIANCE
One-Way ANOVA

DISTRIBUTION FUNCTION EVALUATION
t
Chi Square
F

CONTROL CHARTS
X-Bar
s
Proportions
Number of Defects
Number of Defectives

MISCELLANEOUS
p-Values Given With Tests

STATPAL

Marcel Dekker, Inc.
270 Madison Ave
New York, NY 10016
(212) 696 - 9000
Contact Person: Bruce J. Chalmer, PhD

CONFIGURATIONS SUPPORTED

Computer	Language	Operating System	RAM	Number Drives	Cost
IBM PC		DOS	128K	2	$40

NUMBER OF CURRENT USERS 350
DATE OF FIRST RELEASE July 84
VERSION 5.0 RELEASED Oct 86

PROGRAM DESCRIPTION

STATPAL is a general-purpose statistical package for both researcher and students. It is packaged with the textbook Understanding Statistics by Bruce J. Chalmer, which includes exercises using STATPAL. STATPAL is easy to learn and use, yet provides the power and sophistication needed by professionals working in the real world.

STATPAL is an exceptional value. For under $40, a researcher receives a comprehensive introductory statistics textbook, a complete user's guide to the software, and a statistical package featuring extraordinary accuracy, speed, convenience, and ease of use.

TYPE OF PROGRAM

Statistical Package

PROGRAM DESIGNED FOR

Data Analysis

PROGRAM STYLE

Menu Driven
Integrated System

MISCELLANEOUS PROGRAM FEATURES

Copyable Disk
On Screen Help Function

DOCUMENTATION

User's Manual - ? pages, ? technical references
- Table of Contents
- Index
- Tutorial or Example Lessons
- Sample Runs
- Formulas Provided

Tutorials and Examples on Disk

DATA MANAGEMENT

Keyboard Data Entry
Data Manipulations and Transformations
Missing Values Allowed in Data

DATA EDITING

Change
Add
Delete

FOREIGN DATA ACCESS

Standard Rectangular ASCII Files
DIF Files

GRAPHICS FEATURES

Graphics can be Output to a Printer
Graphics can be Saved to a File
Titles and/or Labels Available
Uses Character Graphics

GRAPHICS

Histograms
Scatter (x-y) Plots

PRODUCT SUPPORT

User may call at own Expense
Classes or Instruction Available

STATISTICAL FEATURES SUPPORTED

DESCRIPTIVE STATISTICS
- Mean
- Standard Deviation or Variance
- Standard Error of the Mean
- Minimum, Maximum

t-TESTS
- One Sample t-Test
- Independent Group t-Test/Equal Variance
- Independent Group t-Test/Unequal Var
- Paired t-Test

CORRELATION AND REGRESSION
- Pearson Correlation Coefficient
- Simple Linear Regression
- Multiple Linear Regression
- Stepwise Multiple Linear Regression
- Residuals Calculated
- **REGRESSION PLOTS**
  - Residuals

CATEGORICAL DATA ANALYSIS
- Chi-Square Contingency Table Analysis

ANALYSIS OF VARIANCE
- One-Way ANOVA
- Two-Way ANOVA
- Two-Way Unequal Cell Sizes Allowed
- Analysis of Covariance
- Up to 5-Way Factorial Design/Covariates

NONPARAMETRIC TESTS
- Sign Test (Signed Rank)
- Wilcoxon One Sample Test
- Mann-Whitney U
- Kruskal-Wallis Test
- Friedman Chi-Square Test
- Spearman or Kendall Correlation

DISTRIBUTION FUNCTION EVALUATION
- Normal
- t
- Chi Square
- F
- Binomial

MISCELLANEOUS

Test for Equality of Variances
p-Values Given With Tests

STATPLAN III
The Futures Group
76 Eastern Blvd
Glastonbury, CT 06033
(203) 633 - 3501
Contact Person: Ed Abel

CONFIGURATIONS SUPPORTED

Computer	Language	Operating System	RAM	Number Drives	Cost
IBM PC	PASCAL	DOS	256K	1	$179

NUMBER OF CURRENT USERS 1200
DATE OF FIRST RELEASE Nov 83
VERSION 4.0 RELEASED Sept 86

PROGRAM DESCRIPTION

STATPLAN is a statistical analysis package designed for the non-statistician. It is extremely easy to use. The program is designed for managers, researchers, teachers and analysts who want quick easy access to statistical analysis. Its on screen menus and HELP functions guide the user quickly through the statistical procedures.

STATPLAN provides a wealth of statistical procedures at considerably less cost than other complete packages. It provides a full screen editor for data entry and editing and easily exchanges data with popular spreadsheet programs (such as LOTUS 1-2-3 and VISICALC) and with data base and other programs through rectangular ASCII files (for exchange with dBASEII and dBASEIII, for example). In addition HELP screens and an easy to use manual are available to help the beginning user.

PRODUCT REVIEWS

Gray, Irwin. Engineering Management Newsletter, (June 1984).

PC Week, (forthcoming).

Minor, Michael. "PC Statistician and Statplan II", PC Week, pp. 91-94, (Oct 9, 1984).

TYPE OF PROGRAM
Statistical Package

PROGRAM DESIGNED FOR
Data Analysis

PROGRAM STYLE
Menu Driven
Integrated System

MISCELLANEOUS PROGRAM FEATURES
Copyable Disk
On Screen Help Function
Optional Support for 8087 Mathematical Chip

DOCUMENTATION
User's Manual - 120 pages, 0 technical references
Table of Contents
Index
Tutorial or Example Lessons
Sample Runs
Formulas Provided
Tutorials and Examples on Disk

DATA MANAGEMENT
Keyboard Data Entry
Data Manipulations and Transformations
Missing Values Allowed in Data

DATA EDITING
Change
Add
Delete

FOREIGN DATA ACCESS
Standard Rectangular ASCII Files
DIF Files
Lotus 1-2-3 Files

GRAPHICS FEATURES
Graphics can be Output to a Printer
Graphics can be Saved to a File
Titles and/or Labels Available
Uses Pixel Graphics

GRAPHICS
- Histograms
- Scatter (x-y) Plots
- SEE Time Series Plots
- Actual vs Calculated Values
- SEE Regression Plots

PRODUCT SUPPORT
- User may call at own Expense
- No Classes or Instruction Available

STATISTICAL FEATURES SUPPORTED

DESCRIPTIVE STATISTICS
- Mean
- Standard Deviation or Variance
- Coefficient of Variation
- Minimum, Maximum
- Median
- Skewness
- Kurtosis
- Range

CORRELATION AND REGRESSION
- Simple Linear Regression
- Multiple Linear Regression
- Residuals Calculated
- Estimate Asymptotic Standard Errors
- **REGRESSION PLOTS**
  - Residuals

CATEGORICAL DATA ANALYSIS
- Chi-Square Contingency Table Analysis

ANALYSIS OF VARIANCE
- One-Way ANOVA

TIME SERIES ANALYSIS
- Autocorrelations
- Cross Correlations
- **TIME SERIES ANALYSIS - FORECASTING**
  - Exponential Smoothing
- **TIME SERIES ANALYSIS - PLOTS**
  - Autocorrelations
  - Residuals
  - Time Series

MISCELLANEOUS

Random Number Generation

Seasonality and Cycle Analysis

STATPRO

Penton Software, Inc
420 Lexington Avenue, Suite 2846
New York, NY 10017

Contact Person: Christine Curtin

CONFIGURATIONS SUPPORTED

Computer	Language	Operating System	RAM	Number Drives	Cost
IBM PC	PASCAL	DOS	256K	2	$ 795

NUMBER OF CURRENT USERS 1000
DATE OF FIRST RELEASE JUN 83
CURRENT VERSION RELEASED NOV 85

PROGRAM DESCRIPTION

Penton Software, Inc. has developed STATPRO: The statistics and Graphics Database workstation for the professional data analyst. STATPRO allows individuals to do data analysis once limited to the maninframe. Primary users of STATPRO can be found in the academic, corporate, and government markets. In academia STATPRO is used for teaching statistics as well as advanced research. Corporate managers use the product for market research, long-range planning, quality control, etc. Government applications include forecasting, budgeting, census analysis etc.

STATPRO is an integrated statistical package offering more statistical and graphic analyses than any other according to BYTE magazine. Distinct modules include a database manager with extensive data editing capabilities, the most comprehensive statistical routines available for a personal computer and a graphics module which generates customized graphs in color.

PRODUCT REVIEWS

Bryan, W Shawn. "A Peek at Statpro", Microcomputing Magazine, (March 1984).

Carpenter, James et al.. "Statistical Software Available for Microcomputers", BYTE, pp. 234-264, (April 19, 1984).

Boehmer, Richard. Boston Computer Society, (1983).

Katz, A. Jerome. "Statistical Programs for Apple Computers", University of Michigan.

Morganstein, David. "STATPRO, A Statistical Workstation", Incider Magazine.

Siegal, B Jay. "Quantitive Software Reports", Econometric Report, (1983).

Cable, David and Rowe, Beverly SGCSA Committee. "Software for Statistical and Survey Analysis", Study Group on Computers and Survey Analysis.

"Micros in Big Business", Computerworld.

Bryan, W Shawn. "Statpro Brings Serious Statistical Tool to Micros", Business Computer Systems, (Jan 1985).

Bryan, Marvin. "Painless and Powerful; Statistics with Statpro", Business Software, (December 1986).

Bryan, Marvin. "Business Forecasting: 16 Ways to Predict the Future", PC Magazine, (August 1986).

TYPE OF PROGRAM
Statistical Package

PROGRAM DESIGNED FOR
Data Analysis

PROGRAM STYLE
Menu Driven
Integrated System

MISCELLANEOUS PROGRAM FEATURES
Copyable Disk
On Screen Help Function

DOCUMENTATION
User's Manual - 400 pages, 9 technical references
Table of Contents
Index
Tutorial or Example Lessons
Sample Runs
Formulas Provided
Quick Reference Card
Tutorials and Examples on Disk

DATA MANAGEMENT
Keyboard Data Entry
Data Manipulations and Transformations
Missing Values Allowed in Data

DATA EDITING
Change
Add
Delete

FOREIGN DATA ACCESS
Standard Rectangular ASCII Files
DIF Files
dBase II Files
SYLK
1-2-3 PRN Format
P-system Text Files

GRAPHICS FEATURES
Graphics Appear in Color on the Monitor
Graphics can be Output to a Printer
Graphics can be Saved to a File
Titles and/or Labels Available
Uses Pixel Graphics

GRAPHICS
Histograms
Pie Charts
Scatter (x-y) Plots
Box Plots
Empirical CDF
Triangular Scatter Plots
Plots of Bivariate Means
Interval Plots
Directional Scatter Plots
User Defined Functions
Function Overlay on Scatter Plots
Variance Bar Plots
Range Bar Plots
Sampling Cost Efficiency Plots
Normality (Q-Q) Plots
Circular Star Plots
Andrew's Fourier Plots
Cluster Analysis Dendrograms
SEE Time Series Plots
SEE Regression Plots
SEE EDA Plots
Multivariate Plots

PRODUCT SUPPORT

Free Phone Support Available
Classes or Instruction Available

STATISTICAL FEATURES SUPPORTED

DESCRIPTIVE STATISTICS

Mean
Standard Deviation or Variance
Standard Error of the Mean
Coefficient of Variation
Minimum, Maximum
Median
Percentiles
Skewness
Kurtosis
Moments (2nd,3rd,4th)
Sum of Values
Sum of Squares of Values
Harmonic Mean
Geometric Mean

t-TESTS

Independent Group t-Test/Equal Variance
Independent Group t-Test/Unequal Var
Paired t-Test

CORRELATION AND REGRESSION

Pearson Correlation Coefficient
Simple Linear Regression
Multiple Linear Regression
Stepwise Multiple Linear Regression
Non-Linear Regression
Residuals Calculated
Residual Sum of Squares
Multi-Stage Least Squares
Standard Error of the Estimate
Functional Regression Coefficients
Covariance
Adjusted R-squared
Durbin-Watson

REGRESSION PLOTS

Residuals

CONFIDENCE INTERVALS

Variances
Ratio of Variances

CATEGORICAL DATA ANALYSIS
- Chi-Square Contingency Table Analysis
- Frequencies Can be Entered Directly
- G Statistic
- Phi Statistic
- Multiple Contingency Table Analysis
- Uncertainty Coefficient
- Lambda
- Contingency Coefficient
- Cramer's V

ANALYSIS OF VARIANCE
- One-Way ANOVA
- Two-Way ANOVA
- Two-Way Unequal Cell Sizes Allowed
- Three-Way ANOVA
- Nested Factors

NONPARAMETRIC TESTS
- Sign Test (Signed Rank)
- Mann-Whitney U
- Kruskal-Wallis Test
- Spearman or Kendall Correlation
- Wald-Wolfowitz Runs Test
- Kolmogorov-Smirnov Test
- Kruskal-Wallis ANOVA
- Runs Tests

DISTRIBUTION FUNCTION EVALUATION
- Normal
- t
- Chi Square
- F

EXPLORATORY DATA ANALYSIS
- Stem-and-Leaf Displays
- Letter-Value Displays
- Box Plots

TIME SERIES ANALYSIS
- Autocorrelations
- Moving Average Smoothing
- AUTOREGRESSIVE MOVING AVERAGE
  - Model Identification
- **TIME SERIES ANALYSIS - FORECASTING**
  - Additive
  - Multiplicative
  - Exponential
- **TIME SERIES ANALYSIS - PLOTS**
  - Autocorrelations
  - Partial Autocorrelations
  - Moving Average with Error Bars
  - Data, First or Second Differences

MISCELLANEOUS
- Cluster Analysis
- Random Number Generation
- Test for Normality of Data
- Test for Equality of Variances
- Linear Discriminant Function Calculation
- p-Values Given With Tests
- Critical Values Given with Statistics
- Euclidean Distance Matrix
- Positive Definite Matrix Inverse/Det
- Canonical Correlation
- Principal Axes Factor Analysis
- Principal Components Analysis

STATS PLUS
Human Systems Dynamics
9010 Reseda Blvd, Suite 222
Northridge, CA 91324
(818) 993 - 8563
Contact Person: Merideth Wiberg

CONFIGURATIONS SUPPORTED

Computer	Language	Operating System	RAM	Number Drives	Cost
APPLE II APPLE III	BASIC	DOS 3.3	48K	1	$ 200

NUMBER OF CURRENT USERS 2000
DATE OF FIRST RELEASE Dec 82
VERSION 1.0 RELEASED Jun 85

PROGRAM DESCRIPTION

STATS PLUS is a complete general statistics package with database management. It provides almost all the statistical analyses required by the professional researcher. The user needs no previous computer experience. By following documentation examples the user can start analyzing experiment or survey data immediately. The program is menu driven, so no commands are necessary.

STATS PLUS has a research database for up to twenty fields or variables. The program can review/edit, merge files, create subfiles, search and select records on up to 4 variables, delete records and delete files.

PRODUCT REVIEWS

Popular Computing, (Oct 1983).

TYPE OF PROGRAM

Statistical Package

PROGRAM DESIGNED FOR

Data Analysis

PROGRAM STYLE
Menu Driven
Integrated System

DOCUMENTATION
User's Manual - 104 pages, 5 technical references
Index
Sample Runs

DATA MANAGEMENT
Keyboard Data Entry
Data Manipulations and Transformations
Missing Values Allowed in Data

DATA EDITING
Change
Add
Delete

FOREIGN DATA ACCESS
VisiCalc

GRAPHICS FEATURES
Graphics can be Saved to a File
Titles and/or Labels Available
Uses Pixel Graphics

GRAPHICS
Histograms
Scatter (x-y) Plots

PRODUCT SUPPORT
Free Phone Support Available
No Classes or Instruction Available

STATISTICAL FEATURES SUPPORTED

DESCRIPTIVE STATISTICS
- Mean
- Standard Deviation or Variance
- Standard Error of the Mean
- Minimum, Maximum
- Median
- Percentiles

t-TESTS
- One Sample t-Test
- Independent Group t-Test/Equal Variance
- Independent Group t-Test/Unequal Var
- Paired t-Test

CORRELATION AND REGRESSION
- Simple Linear Regression
- Multiple Linear Regression

CATEGORICAL DATA ANALYSIS
- Chi-Square Contingency Table Analysis
- Fisher's Exact Test

ANALYSIS OF VARIANCE
- One-Way ANOVA
- Two-Way ANOVA
- Two-Way Unequal Cell Sizes Allowed

NONPARAMETRIC TESTS
- Sign Test (Signed Rank)
- Wilcoxon One Sample Test
- Mann-Whitney U
- Kruskal-Wallis Test
- Spearman or Kendall Correlation
- Friedman 2-way ANOVA

MISCELLANEOUS
- Test for Equality of Variances
- p-Values Given With Tests
- Crosstabs
- Merge Files
- Frequency Distribution

STATS TOOL KIT
Sof-ware Tools
P.O. Box 8751
Boise, Idaho 83707
(208) 343 - 1437
Contact Person: Joan Heitzeberg

CONFIGURATIONS SUPPORTED

Computer	Language	Operating System	RAM	Number Drives	Cost
MACINTOSH	BASIC	DOS	128K	1	$99

NUMBER OF CURRENT USERS 20
DATE OF FIRST RELEASE June 85
VERSION 1.61 RELEASED June 85

PROGRAM DESCRIPTION

STATS TOOL KIT is a statistical analysis software package that provides a variety of statistical tests and analysis reports for physicians, scientists, researchers, professors, students, engineers and technicians.

The statistical tests include: ANOVA (One-way, Two-Way with repetitions and without repetions), Student's t Test, Chi-Square Contigency Test, Wilcoxon's Signed Rank Test, Distribution tests (Binomial, Poisson, F, and Chi-square), Mann-Whitney U Test, Kendall's Tau, and a variety of statistical comparisons for one and two variables grouped and ungrouped. It provides the most popular statistical tests in one user-friendly package.

TYPE OF PROGRAM

Statistical Package

PROGRAM DESIGNED FOR

Data Analysis
Educational use

PROGRAM STYLE

Menu Driven
Integrated System

DOCUMENTATION

User's Manual - 60 pages, 26 technical references

- Table of Contents
- Index
- Sample Runs
- Formulas Provided

DATA MANAGEMENT

- Keyboard Data Entry
- Data Manipulations and Transformations

DATA EDITING

- Change
- Add
- Delete

FOREIGN DATA ACCESS

- Standard Rectangular ASCII Files
- Read Clipboard Data - Multiplan, Excel

PRODUCT SUPPORT

- User may call at own Expense
- No Classes or Instruction Available

STATISTICAL FEATURES SUPPORTED

DESCRIPTIVE STATISTICS

- Mean
- Standard Deviation or Variance
- Standard Error of the Mean
- Coefficient of Variation
- Minimum, Maximum
- Skewness
- Kurtosis

t-TESTS

- One Sample t-Test
- Independent Group t-Test/Equal Variance
- Independent Group t-Test/Unequal Var
- Paired t-Test

CONFIDENCE INTERVALS

- Means
- Difference Between Two Means
- Difference Between Two Proportions
- Variances
- Ratio of Variances

CATEGORICAL DATA ANALYSIS
- Chi-Square Contingency Table Analysis

ANALYSIS OF VARIANCE
- One-Way ANOVA
- One-Way with Repeated Measures
- Two-Way ANOVA

NONPARAMETRIC TESTS
- Sign Test (Signed Rank)
- Wilcoxon One Sample Test
- Mann-Whitney U
- Spearman or Kendall Correlation

DISTRIBUTION FUNCTION EVALUATION
- t
- Chi Square
- F
- Binomial
- Poisson

MISCELLANEOUS
- Random Number Generation

STATS-2

Statsoft, Inc.
2832 East 10th, Suite 4
Tulsa, OK 74104
(918) 583 - 4149
Contact Person: Sales Office

CONFIGURATIONS SUPPORTED

Computer	Language	Operating System	RAM	Number Drives	Cost
IBM PC	FORTRAN	DOS	256K	2	$149

NUMBER OF CURRENT USERS 5000
DATE OF FIRST RELEASE 1985
VERSION 2.1 RELEASED 1985

PROGRAM DESCRIPTION

A general purpose statistical package (basic statistics, nonparametric statistics, multivariate statistics) with presentation quality graphics and tables, and complete database management functions.

STATS-2 is superfast (8087 support), very easy to use (completely menu driven), presentation quality graphs and tables (over 80 printers supported), can be used as a statistical supplement to spreadsheets and database management programs (easy access to Lotus 1-2-3, and dB III files).

TYPE OF PROGRAM
Statistical Package

PROGRAM DESIGNED FOR
Data Analysis
Educational use

PROGRAM STYLE
Menu Driven
Integrated System

MISCELLANEOUS PROGRAM FEATURES
Copyable Disk
Supports 8087, 80287 Mathematical Chip

DOCUMENTATION
User's Manual - 185 pages, 20 technical references
Table of Contents
Index
Tutorial or Example Lessons
Sample Runs
Formulas Provided

DATA MANAGEMENT
Keyboard Data Entry
Data Manipulations and Transformations
Missing Values Allowed in Data

DATA EDITING
Change
Add
Delete

FOREIGN DATA ACCESS
Standard Rectangular ASCII Files
Any Text or ASCII File

GRAPHICS FEATURES
Graphics Appear in Color on the Monitor
Graphics can be Output to a Printer
Titles and/or Labels Available
Uses Pixel Graphics

GRAPHICS
Histograms
Scatter (x-y) Plots

PRODUCT SUPPORT
User may call at own Expense
No Classes or Instruction Available

STATISTICAL FEATURES SUPPORTED

DESCRIPTIVE STATISTICS

- Mean
- Standard Deviation or Variance
- Standard Error of the Mean
- Coefficient of Variation
- Minimum, Maximum
- Median
- Percentiles
- Skewness
- Kurtosis

t-TESTS

- One Sample t-Test
- Independent Group t-Test/Equal Variance
- Independent Group t-Test/Unequal Var
- Paired t-Test

CORRELATION AND REGRESSION

- Pearson Correlation Coefficient
- Simple Linear Regression
- Multiple Linear Regression
- Residuals Calculated
- Autocorrelation of Residuals
- Durbin Watson Statistic
- Regression Forecasting
- **REGRESSION PLOTS**
  - Residuals

CATEGORICAL DATA ANALYSIS

- Chi-Square Contingency Table Analysis
- Frequencies Can be Entered Directly

ANALYSIS OF VARIANCE

- One-Way ANOVA
- One-Way with Repeated Measures
- Two-Way ANOVA
- Two-Way Unequal Cell Sizes Allowed
- Analysis of Covariance
- Repeated Measures
- Up to 5-Way including a Covariate
- General Multifactor ANOVA/ANCOVA
- Incomplete/Unbalanced Designs
- **MULTIPLE COMPARISONS**
  - Planned Comparisons

NONPARAMETRIC TESTS

- Wilcoxon One Sample Test
- Mann-Whitney U
- Kruskal-Wallis Test
- Spearman or Kendall Correlation
- Phi-Square
- Nu-Square

DISTRIBUTION FUNCTION EVALUATION

- Normal
- t
- Chi Square
- F

TIME SERIES ANALYSIS

- Autocorrelation of Residuals
- **TIME SERIES ANALYSIS - FORECASTING**
  - Regression Methods

MISCELLANEOUS

- p-Values Given With Tests

STATSTREAM

Elsevier - Biosoft
68 Hills Road
Cambridge, ENGLAND CB2 ILA
(44) 223-668622
Contact Person: Dr. J. Lamble

CONFIGURATIONS SUPPORTED

Computer	Language	Operating System	RAM	Number Drives	Cost
APPLE II	BASIC	DOS	48K	1	$140

NUMBER OF CURRENT USERS 250
DATE OF FIRST RELEASE Mar 84
VERSION 1.0 RELEASED Mar 84

PROGRAM DESCRIPTION

STATSTREAM includes 76 procedures for numerical, graphical and statistical analysis. They are accessed either from a menu-driven statpack or directly from the keyboard or by incorporating a single-line instruction in a basic program. Powerful data editing and storage facilities are incorporated. STATSTREAM is based on structured basic. This extends APPLESOFT to allow structuring commands such as repeat-until and also procedures. Many example programs are incorporated. STATSTREAM consists of two packed 5 1/4 inch floppies plus manual. Procedures interact with the user through windows i.e., they are overlaid, then once used can be forgotten.

STATSTREAM was designed for scientific and educational use. It is also applicable to economics and business. Its main strength is its great flexibility, since users can easily customise it to their own requirements.

PRODUCT REVIEWS

Times Higher Educational Supplement No. 712, pp. 27, (June 27, 1986).

TYPE OF PROGRAM

Statistical Package

PROGRAM DESIGNED FOR
Data Analysis

PROGRAM STYLE
Menu Driven
Command Driven
Integrated System

MISCELLANEOUS PROGRAM FEATURES
Source Code Available
Copyable Disk
On Screen Help Function

DOCUMENTATION
User's Manual - 96 pages, 10 technical references
Index
Tutorial or Example Lessons
Sample Runs
Tutorials and Examples on Disk

DATA MANAGEMENT
Keyboard Data Entry
Data Manipulations and Transformations

DATA EDITING
Change
Add
Delete

FOREIGN DATA ACCESS
Standard Rectangular ASCII Files
DIF Files
Visicalc
Most Apple II Files

GRAPHICS FEATURES
Graphics can be Output to a Printer
Graphics can be Saved to a File
Titles and/or Labels Available
Uses Character Graphics

GRAPHICS
Histograms
Scatter (x-y) Plots

PRODUCT SUPPORT
User may call at own Expense
No Classes or Instruction Available

STATISTICAL FEATURES SUPPORTED

DESCRIPTIVE STATISTICS
- Mean
- Standard Deviation or Variance
- Standard Error of the Mean
- Coefficient of Variation
- Minimum, Maximum
- Median

t-TESTS
- Independent Group t-Test/Equal Variance
- Paired t-Test

CORRELATION AND REGRESSION
- Pearson Correlation Coefficient
- Simple Linear Regression
- Multiple Linear Regression
- Stepwise Multiple Linear Regression
- Non-Linear Regression
- Residuals Calculated
- **REGRESSION PLOTS**
  - Residuals

CONFIDENCE INTERVALS
- Means

CATEGORICAL DATA ANALYSIS
- Chi-Square Contingency Table Analysis
- Frequencies Can be Entered Directly

ANALYSIS OF VARIANCE
- One-Way ANOVA
- Two-Way ANOVA

NONPARAMETRIC TESTS
- Sign Test (Signed Rank)
- Wilcoxon One Sample Test
- Mann-Whitney U
- Kruskal-Wallis Test
- Friedman Chi-Square Test
- Spearman or Kendall Correlation

MISCELLANEOUS
- Random Number Generation

STATVIEW
Brain Power, Inc.
24009 Ventura Blvd.
Calabasas, CA 91302
(818) 884 - 6911
Contact Person: Michael Cuneo

CONFIGURATIONS SUPPORTED

Computer	Language	Operating System	RAM	Number Drives	Cost
MACINTOSH	PASCAL	MACINTOSH	128K	1	$100
XL	PASCAL	MACINTOSH	128K	1	$100

NUMBER OF CURRENT USERS 4,000
DATE OF FIRST RELEASE Apr 85
VERSION 1.0 RELEASED Apr 85

PROGRAM DESCRIPTION

StatView is a general purpose statistical analysis package that offers descriptive, comparative, and nonparametric analyses; graphic and table views of analysis results; and transformations, range setting capabilities, recode capabilities, and general data handling capabilities. StatView's 18 significant figure accuracy allows it to out perform many mainframe packages in this area.

StatView (and its counterpart, StatView 512+) are the only Macintosh statistics programs that utilize that computer's interface and graphics, and offer significant computational and data collection power. Both StatView's feature interactive analysis capabilities which allow users to see instantly the affects of alterations to ranges, variables, or analysis specifications. StatView, at $99.95, is also one of the least expensive statistics packages.

PRODUCT REVIEWS

Sidel, Philip. "STATVIEW 1.0", Social Science Microcomputer Review, Volume 4 #2, pp. 232-237, (Summer 1986).

Chial, Michael. "STATVIEW", Journal of the American Speech-Language Hearing Association, pp. 73-74.

TYPE OF PROGRAM
Statistical Package

PROGRAM DESIGNED FOR
Data Analysis

PROGRAM STYLE
Menu Driven
Integrated System

MISCELLANEOUS PROGRAM FEATURES
Copyable Disk
Optional Support for 68020, 68881 Mathematical Chip

DOCUMENTATION
User's Manual - ? pages, ? technical references
Table of Contents
Tutorial or Example Lessons
Sample Runs
Formulas Provided
Tutorials and Examples on Disk

DATA MANAGEMENT
Keyboard Data Entry
Data Manipulations and Transformations
Missing Values Allowed in Data

DATA EDITING
Change
Add
Delete

FOREIGN DATA ACCESS
Standard Rectangular ASCII Files

GRAPHICS FEATURES
Graphics can be Output to a Printer
Titles and/or Labels Available
Uses Pixel Graphics

GRAPHICS
Histograms
Pie Charts
Scatter (x-y) Plots

PRODUCT SUPPORT
User may call at own Expense
No Classes or Instruction Available

STATISTICAL FEATURES SUPPORTED

DESCRIPTIVE STATISTICS
- Mean
- Standard Deviation or Variance
- Standard Error of the Mean
- Coefficient of Variation
- Minimum, Maximum
- Median
- Skewness
- Kurtosis
- Frequency Distribution

t-TESTS
- One Sample t-Test
- Paired t-Test
- Unpaired t-Test

CORRELATION AND REGRESSION
- Pearson Correlation Coefficient
- Simple Linear Regression
- Multiple Linear Regression
- Non-Linear Regression
- Residuals Calculated
- **REGRESSION PLOTS**
    - Residuals

CATEGORICAL DATA ANALYSIS
- Chi-Square Contingency Table Analysis

ANALYSIS OF VARIANCE
- One-Way ANOVA
- One-Way with Repeated Measures
- Two-Way ANOVA
- Two-Way Unequal Cell Sizes Allowed

NONPARAMETRIC TESTS
- Wilcoxon One Sample Test
- Mann-Whitney U
- Kruskal-Wallis Test
- Friedman Chi-Square Test
- Spearman or Kendall Correlation

STATVIEW 512+

Brain Power, Inc.
24009 Ventura Blvd.
Calabasas, CA 91302
(818) 884 - 6911
Contact Person: Michael Cuneo

CONFIGURATIONS SUPPORTED

Computer	Language	Operating System	RAM	Number Drives	Cost
MACINTOSH	PASCAL	MACINTOSH	512K	1	$400
XL	PASCAL	MACINTOSH	1024	2	$350

NUMBER OF CURRENT USERS 2,000
DATE OF FIRST RELEASE June 86
VERSION 1.1 RELEASED Sept 86

PROGRAM DESCRIPTION

StatView 512+ offers the professional statistics user the same features as StatView, but with major enchancements in the number and power of analyses offered, the graphic analysis result views, and the data handling capabilities offered. StatView 512+ adds stepwise regression, 1600 cell contingency tables, 1-16 way ANOVAs, multivariate factor analysis, composite graphics, and more to the original StatView's power. StatView's 18 significant figure accuracy allows it to out perform many mainframe packages in this area.

StatView (and its counterpart, StatView 512+) are the only Macintosh statistics programs that utilize that computer's interface and graphics, and offer significant computational and data collection power. Both StatView's feature interactive analysis capabilities which allow users to see instantly the affects of alterations to ranges, variables, or analysis specifications.

PRODUCT REVIEWS

MacWorld, (December 1986).

MacUser, (December 1986).

TYPE OF PROGRAM
Statistical Package

PROGRAM DESIGNED FOR
Data Analysis

PROGRAM STYLE
Menu Driven
Integrated System

MISCELLANEOUS PROGRAM FEATURES
Copyable Disk
Optional Support for 68020, 68881 Mathematical Chip

DOCUMENTATION
User's Manual - 180 pages, 35 technical references
Table of Contents
Index
Tutorial or Example Lessons
Sample Runs
Formulas Provided
Tutorials and Examples on Disk

DATA MANAGEMENT
Keyboard Data Entry
Data Manipulations and Transformations
Missing Values Allowed in Data

DATA EDITING
Change
Add
Delete

FOREIGN DATA ACCESS
Standard Rectangular ASCII Files

GRAPHICS FEATURES
Graphics can be Output to a Printer
Titles and/or Labels Available
Uses Pixel Graphics

GRAPHICS
Histograms
Pie Charts
Scatter (x-y) Plots
Box Plots

PRODUCT SUPPORT
User may call at own Expense
No Classes or Instruction Available

STATISTICAL FEATURES SUPPORTED

DESCRIPTIVE STATISTICS
- Mean
- Standard Deviation or Variance
- Standard Error of the Mean
- Coefficient of Variation
- Minimum, Maximum
- Median
- Percentiles
- Skewness
- Kurtosis
- Frequency Distribution

t-TESTS
- One Sample t-Test
- Paired t-Test
- Unpaired t-Test

CORRELATION AND REGRESSION
- Pearson Correlation Coefficient
- Simple Linear Regression
- Multiple Linear Regression
- Stepwise Multiple Linear Regression
- Non-Linear Regression
- Residuals Calculated
- **REGRESSION PLOTS**
  - Residuals

CONFIDENCE INTERVALS
- Means

CATEGORICAL DATA ANALYSIS
- Chi-Square Contingency Table Analysis
- Fisher's PLSD Test

ANALYSIS OF VARIANCE
- One-Way ANOVA
- One-Way with Repeated Measures
- Two-Way ANOVA
- Two-Way Unequal Cell Sizes Allowed
- Up to 16-Way ANOVA
- Multiple Comparisons

NONPARAMETRIC TESTS

Wilcoxon One Sample Test
Mann-Whitney U
Kruskal-Wallis Test
Friedman Chi-Square Test
Spearman or Kendall Correlation

DISTRIBUTION FUNCTION EVALUATION

Normal
t

MISCELLANEOUS

p-Values Given With Tests
Multivariate Factor Analysis

STATWORKS
Cricket Software
3508 Market St., Ste # 206
Philadelphia, PA 19104
(215) 387 - 7955
Contact Person: Doug Seward, Jan Deruiter

CONFIGURATIONS SUPPORTED

Computer	Language	Operating System	RAM	Number Drives	Cost
MACINTOSH	PASCAL	MFS or HFS	128K	1	$125

NUMBER OF CURRENT USERS 10,000
DATE OF FIRST RELEASE June 85
VERSION 1.2 RELEASED Aug 86

PROGRAM DESCRIPTION
None Provided

TYPE OF PROGRAM
Statistical Package

PROGRAM DESIGNED FOR
Data Analysis

PROGRAM STYLE
Menu Driven
Integrated System

MISCELLANEOUS PROGRAM FEATURES
Copyable Disk

DOCUMENTATION
User's Manual - 98 pages, 15 technical references
Table of Contents
Index
Tutorial or Example Lessons
Sample Runs
Formulas Provided
Tutorials and Examples on Disk

DATA MANAGEMENT
- Keyboard Data Entry
- Data Manipulations and Transformations
- Missing Values Allowed in Data

DATA EDITING
- Change
- Add
- Delete

FOREIGN DATA ACCESS
- Standard Rectangular ASCII Files
- DIF Files
- TEXT files
- SYLK format

GRAPHICS FEATURES
- Graphics can be Output to a Printer
- Graphics can be Saved to a File
- Uses Pixel Graphics
- Uses Character Graphics

GRAPHICS
- Histograms
- Scatter (x-y) Plots
- Box Plots
- 3-D Histogram
- 3-D Scatter Diagram
- Line Plots

PRODUCT SUPPORT
- User may call at own Expense
- No Classes or Instruction Available

STATISTICAL FEATURES SUPPORTED

DESCRIPTIVE STATISTICS
- Mean
- Standard Deviation or Variance
- Standard Error of the Mean
- Coefficient of Variation
- Minimum, Maximum
- Median
- Skewness
- Kurtosis

t-TESTS
- One Sample t-Test
- Independent Group t-Test/Equal Variance
- Paired t-Test

CORRELATION AND REGRESSION
- Pearson Correlation Coefficient
- Simple Linear Regression
- Multiple Linear Regression
- Residuals Calculated
- Correlation Matrix
- ANOVA Table
- Durbin Watson
- Residuals Saved
- Regression through Origin
- **REGRESSION PLOTS**
  - Residuals
  - Regression Line

ANALYSIS OF VARIANCE
- One-Way ANOVA
- Two-Way ANOVA

NONPARAMETRIC TESTS
- Wilcoxon One Sample Test
- Mann-Whitney U
- Kruskal-Wallis Test
- Friedman Chi-Square Test
- Spearman or Kendall Correlation

DISTRIBUTION FUNCTION EVALUATION
- Normal
- t
- Chi Square
- F
- Binomial

TIME SERIES ANALYSIS
Moving Average Smoothing

MISCELLANEOUS
p-Values Given With Tests

STUDENTSTAT
Ideal Systems
P.O. Box 681
Fairfield, Iowa 52556
(515) 472 - 4507
Contact Person: Christopher Dennen

CONFIGURATIONS SUPPORTED

Computer	Language	Operating System	RAM	Number Drives	Cost
APPLE II	BASIC	DOS	64K	1	$ 30

NUMBER OF CURRENT USERS ?
DATE OF FIRST RELEASE SEP 85
VERSION 1.0 RELEASED SEP 85

PROGRAM DESCRIPTION

When Dr. Christopher Dennen recently acquired Ideal Systems he brought with him both a background in computer marketing and professional training as a science educator. His expertise in the educational computer market and his special understanding of the needs of teachers and students has lead to our development of STUDENTSTAT. This program meets the needs of the statistics educator at an affordable price for both schools and students.

We started by taking all the tests in ADVANCESTAT, our full featured statistical package, and incorporating them in a program that is easy to operate. All of the user friendly features in INTROSTAT and ADVANCESTAT have been retained, but the maximum number of cases has been limited to 25 with up to 12 variables per case. We compiled the program to speed it up. There are enough tests here to provide material for 3 or more courses. But, the really amazing thing about STUDENTSTAT is the price. Over 275 universities, colleges, and school districts in 12 countries have purchased INTROSTAT and ADVANCEMENT.

TYPE OF PROGRAM

Statistical Package

PROGRAM DESIGNED FOR
- Data Analysis
- Educational use

PROGRAM STYLE
- Menu Driven
- Integrated System

MISCELLANEOUS PROGRAM FEATURES
- Source Code Available
- Copyable Disk

DOCUMENTATION
- User's Manual - 60 pages, technical references
  - Table of Contents
  - Index
  - Tutorial or Example Lessons
  - Sample Runs

DATA MANAGEMENT
- Keyboard Data Entry
- Data Manipulations and Transformations
- Missing Values Allowed in Data

DATA EDITING
- Change
- Add
- Delete

GRAPHICS FEATURES
- Uses Pixel Graphics

GRAPHICS
- Scatter (x-y) Plots
- SEE Regression Plots

PRODUCT SUPPORT
- User may call at own Expense
- No Classes or Instruction Available

STATISTICAL FEATURES SUPPORTED

DESCRIPTIVE STATISTICS
- Mean
- Standard Deviation or Variance
- Standard Error of the Mean
- Coefficient of Variation
- Minimum, Maximum
- Median
- Frequency Table

t-TESTS
- One Sample t-Test
- Independent Group t-Test/Equal Variance
- Paired t-Test

CORRELATION AND REGRESSION
- Pearson Correlation Coefficient
- Simple Linear Regression
- Multiple Linear Regression
- **REGRESSION PLOTS**
  - Regression Line

CATEGORICAL DATA ANALYSIS
- Chi-Square Contingency Table Analysis

ANALYSIS OF VARIANCE
- One-Way ANOVA
- Two-Way ANOVA

NONPARAMETRIC TESTS
- Wilcoxon One Sample Test
- Mann-Whitney U

MISCELLANEOUS
- Crosstabs

SURVCALC: SURVIVAL ANALYSIS

John Wiley & Sons, Inc.
605 3rd Ave.
New York, NY 10158
(212) 850 - 6788
Contact Person: Dianne Littwin

CONFIGURATIONS SUPPORTED

Computer	Language	Operating System	RAM	Number Drives	Cost
IBM PC	COMPILED BASIC	DOS	256K	2	$125

NUMBER OF CURRENT USERS 52
DATE OF FIRST RELEASE June 86
VERSION 1.0 RELEASED June 86

PROGRAM DESCRIPTION

This is an indespensible statistics package for application in medicine, environmental and social sciences and industry, which employs survival analysis/reliability theory methods. Specific applications include: predicting life expectancy of machinery; projecting time-change spans for equipment parts; calculating life table or define mortality curves in demography; and studying enviromental hazards (both actual and potential).

Survcalc permits the user to analyze survival data via both parametric and nonparametric models. Additional features include: extensive graphic output for each type of analysis, detailed user's guide, with a tutorial and sample screens, test models and menu-driven customizations of survival distributions.

TYPE OF PROGRAM

Survival Analysis

PROGRAM DESIGNED FOR

Data Analysis

PROGRAM STYLE

Command Driven
Integrated System

MISCELLANEOUS PROGRAM FEATURES
- Source Code Available
- Copyable Disk
- On Screen Help Function

DOCUMENTATION
- User's Manual - 86 pages, 10 technical references
  - Table of Contents
  - Index
  - Tutorial or Example Lessons
  - Sample Runs
  - Formulas Provided
- Tutorials and Examples on Disk

DATA MANAGEMENT
- Keyboard Data Entry
- Data Manipulations and Transformations
- Missing Values Allowed in Data

DATA EDITING
- Change
- Add
- Delete

FOREIGN DATA ACCESS
- Standard Rectangular ASCII Files
- DIF Files

GRAPHICS FEATURES
- Graphics can be Output to a Printer
- Uses Pixel Graphics

GRAPHICS
- Scatter (x-y) Plots
- Product Limit Curves
- Survival Distributions

PRODUCT SUPPORT
- User may call at own Expense
- No Classes or Instruction Available

STATISTICAL FEATURES SUPPORTED

DESCRIPTIVE STATISTICS
- Mean
- Standard Deviation or Variance
- Minimum, Maximum
- Skewness
- Kurtosis

CORRELATION AND REGRESSION
- Residuals Calculated
- **REGRESSION PLOTS**
  - Residuals

NONPARAMETRIC TESTS
- Fleming-Harrington G
- Gehan-Wilcoxon
- Peto-Peto-Wilcoxon
- Log Rank

RELIABILITY
- Weibull
- Gamma
- Logistic
- Gompertz

MISCELLANEOUS
- Life Table Analysis
- Simplex-(Nelder-Mead) Likelihood
- Newton-Raphson Likelihood

SYSTAT

Systat, Inc.
2902 Central St.
Evanston, IL 60201
(312) 864 - 5670
Contact Person: Eve Goldman

CONFIGURATIONS SUPPORTED

Computer	Language	Operating System	RAM	Number Drives	Cost
IBM PC	FORTRAN	MS-DOS	256K	2	$ 595
CP/M BASED	FORTRAN	CP/M	64K	2	$ 620
UNIX BASED	FORTRAN	UNIX	500K	2	$ 850
MACINTOSH	FORTRAN	MACINTOSH	512K	1	$ 595

NUMBER OF CURRENT USERS 8000
DATE OF FIRST RELEASE Jan 84
VERSION 3.0 RELEASED May 86

PROGRAM DESCRIPTION

SYSTAT is a comprehensive statistics, graphics, and data management package. The star of its statistical capabilities is a general linear model module which can do simple multiple and stepwise regression, ANOVA, ANOCOVA, MANOVA (including unbalanced, nested, missing cells or repeated measures designs) and discriminant analysis. Other modules within SYSTAT produce descriptive statistics, t-tests, correlation matrices, non-parametric statistics, cross-tabulations, PRE statistics, log linear models, time-series analysis, factor analysis, multi-dimensional scaling, cluster analysis, and nonlinear estimation. Graphics include scatterplots, histograms, box plots, stem-and-leaf plots and probability plots. A full-screen data editor simplifies data entry and editing. Supplementary modules will perform scoring and item analysis, logit, probit, and report writing.

SYSTAT can merge files, sort files, maintain a relational database, transpose a file and read or write triangular files among other data management capabilities. SYSTAT has an easy-to-use command language with programming capabilities. Context-sensitive HELP files are available at any time. Tutorials and sample runs are included and the user manual is indexed and includes extensive technical references.

PRODUCT REVIEWS

BYTE, (April 1984).

PC World, (August 1984).

The ICPSR Micro News, (February 1984).

The Washington DC PC User's Group. Special Interest Group in Statistics Newsletter, (June 1984).

Infoworld, (September 1, 1986).

TYPE OF PROGRAM

Statistical Package

PROGRAM DESIGNED FOR

Data Analysis

PROGRAM STYLE

Command Driven
Integrated System

MISCELLANEOUS PROGRAM FEATURES

Copyable Disk
On Screen Help Function
Optional Support for 8087 Mathematical Chip

DOCUMENTATION

User's Manual - 548 pages, 169 technical references
- Table of Contents
- Index
- Tutorial or Example Lessons
- Sample Runs
- Formulas Provided

Quick Reference Card

DATA MANAGEMENT

Keyboard Data Entry
Data Manipulations and Transformations
Missing Values Allowed in Data

DATA EDITING

Change
Add
Delete

FOREIGN DATA ACCESS

Standard Rectangular ASCII Files
Non-rectangular ASCII Files
SPSS-PC
Lotus 1-2-3
Gauss
dBase Files

GRAPHICS FEATURES

Graphics can be Output to a Printer
Graphics can be Saved to a File
Titles and/or Labels Available
Uses Character Graphics

GRAPHICS

Histograms
Scatter (x-y) Plots
Box Plots
Contour Plots
Probability Plots
Quantile Plots
Bar Charts
Stem and Leaf
SEE Regression Plots

PRODUCT SUPPORT

User may call at own Expense
No Classes or Instruction Available

STATISTICAL FEATURES SUPPORTED

DESCRIPTIVE STATISTICS

Mean
Standard Deviation or Variance
Standard Error of the Mean
Coefficient of Variation
Minimum, Maximum
Median
Percentiles
Skewness
Kurtosis
Sum of Values
Trimmed Mean

t-TESTS

One Sample t-Test
Independent Group t-Test/Equal Variance
Independent Group t-Test/Unequal Var
Paired t-Test

CORRELATION AND REGRESSION

- Pearson Correlation Coefficient
- Simple Linear Regression
- Multiple Linear Regression
- Stepwise Multiple Linear Regression
- Non-Linear Regression
- Residuals Calculated
- **REGRESSION PLOTS**
    - Residuals

CONFIDENCE INTERVALS

- Means
- Difference Between Two Means
- Proportions
- Difference Between Two Proportions

CATEGORICAL DATA ANALYSIS

- Chi-Square Contingency Table Analysis
- Multi-Dimensional Tables
- Goodness-of-Fit Tests
- Frequencies Can be Entered Directly
- Residuals & Fitted Frequencies - Saved
- Pre Statistics

ANALYSIS OF VARIANCE

- One-Way ANOVA
- One-Way with Repeated Measures
- Two-Way ANOVA
- Two-Way Unequal Cell Sizes Allowed
- Analysis of Covariance
- Nested Factors
- Multi-way ANOVA
- Post Hoc Tests
- Mixed Models
- Complete Block
- Randomized Block
- Split Plot
- Latin Squares
- **MULTIPLE COMPARISONS**
    - Scheffe
    - Bonferroni

NONPARAMETRIC TESTS

Sign Test (Signed Rank)
Wilcoxon One Sample Test
Mann-Whitney U
Kruskal-Wallis Test
Friedman Chi-Square Test
Spearman or Kendall Correlation
Friedman 2-way ANOVA
Goodman Kruskal Gamma
Kolomogorov 1 and 2-sample tests
Lilliefors

EXPLORATORY DATA ANALYSIS

Stem-and-Leaf Displays
Smoothing Techniques
Box Plots

TIME SERIES ANALYSIS

Autocorrelations
Cross Correlations
Moving Average Smoothing
AUTOREGRESSIVE MOVING AVERAGE
Lowess Smoothing
ARIMA
Box Jenkins
Fourier Analysis
Forecasting
Transformations
Partial Correlation Function

MISCELLANEOUS

Cluster Analysis
Random Number Generation
Test for Normality of Data
Linear Discriminant Function Calculation
p-Values Given With Tests
Multidimensional Scaling
Factor Analysis
Report Writing
Classical & Latent Trait Analysis-Tests
Logistic Regression
Probit Analysis

T- AND F-TESTS

Statistical Programs
9941 Rowlett, Suite 6
Houston, TX 77075
(713) 947 - 1551
Contact Person: Bonnie Deming

CONFIGURATIONS SUPPORTED

Computer	Language	Operating System	RAM	Number Drives	Cost
IBM PC	BASIC	DOS	256K	1	$150
APPLE	BASIC	DOS	128K	1	$150

NUMBER OF CURRENT USERS ?
DATE OF FIRST RELEASE 1985
CURRENT VERSION RELEASED ?

PROGRAM DESCRIPTION

T-AND F-TESTS is a computer program aimed at scientists and engineers involved in R & D. It is used to help an experimenter decide if a measured difference between two quantities is probably real or if it might have simply occurred by chance.

T- AND F-TESTS accepts a calculated value of Student's of Fisher's F statistic and returns the exact level of confidence at which the null hypothesis can be rejected.

TYPE OF PROGRAM
Statistical Package

PROGRAM DESIGNED FOR
Data Analysis
Educational use

PROGRAM STYLE
Command Driven
Integrated System

MISCELLANEOUS PROGRAM FEATURES
Source Code Available
Copyable Disk

PRODUCT SUPPORT
No Classes or Instruction Available

STATISTICAL FEATURES SUPPORTED

t-TESTS
One Sample t-Test
Independent Group t-Test/Equal Variance
Independent Group t-Test/Unequal Var
Paired t-Test

ANALYSIS OF VARIANCE
One-Way ANOVA
Finds Exact Level of Confidence for F

MISCELLANEOUS
p-Values Given With Tests

TADPOLE
Elsevier - Biosoft
68 Hills Road
Cambridge, ENGLAND CB2ILA
(44) 223-68622
Contact Person: Dr. John Lamble

CONFIGURATIONS SUPPORTED

Computer	Language	Operating System	RAM	Number Drives	Cost
IBM PC	BASIC	DOS	128K	1	$140

NUMBER OF CURRENT USERS 200
DATE OF FIRST RELEASE Oct 85
VERSION 1.0 RELEASED Sept 86

PROGRAM DESCRIPTION

General purpose numeric database with built-in statistics package can contain up to 9999 records each with up to 60 fields; each field is a real number with up to 6 significant figures. Statistics files can be created by sorting selected fields from database or entered direct from keyboard. TADPOLE can convert PRN files from Lotus 1-2-3 into data or statistics file format. Statistical tests include all common descriptive, parametric and non-parametric tests, plus Mantel-Haenzel survivorship (logrank) test.

TADPOLE was created for clinical trial and biological research. It is especially useful for storing experimental or trial data, then selecting subsets for analysis using the powerful sorting routines.

PRODUCT REVIEWS

Prichard, Dr. P.J.. British Medical Journal, pp. 128, (1986).

TYPE OF PROGRAM

Statistical Package

PROGRAM DESIGNED FOR

Data Analysis

PROGRAM STYLE
- Menu Driven
- Integrated System

MISCELLANEOUS PROGRAM FEATURES
- Source Code Available
- Copyable Disk
- On Screen Help Function

DOCUMENTATION
- User's Manual - 49 pages, ? technical references
  - Table of Contents
  - Index
  - Tutorial or Example Lessons
  - Sample Runs
- Tutorials and Examples on Disk

DATA MANAGEMENT
- Keyboard Data Entry
- Data Manipulations and Transformations
- Missing Values Allowed in Data

DATA EDITING
- Change
- Add
- Delete

FOREIGN DATA ACCESS
- Lotus 1-2-3

PRODUCT SUPPORT
- User may call at own Expense
- No Classes or Instruction Available

STATISTICAL FEATURES SUPPORTED

DESCRIPTIVE STATISTICS
- Mean
- Standard Deviation or Variance
- Standard Error of the Mean
- Minimum, Maximum
- Median
- Skewness
- Kurtosis
- Frequency Analysis with Bar Diagrams

t-TESTS
- One Sample t-Test
- Independent Group t-Test/Equal Variance
- Paired t-Test

CORRELATION AND REGRESSION
- Pearson Correlation Coefficient
- Simple Linear Regression
- Multiple Linear Regression

CONFIDENCE INTERVALS
- Means

CATEGORICAL DATA ANALYSIS
- Chi-Square Contingency Table Analysis
- Fisher's Exact Test

ANALYSIS OF VARIANCE
- One-Way ANOVA
- Two-Way ANOVA
- Two-Way Unequal Cell Sizes Allowed

NONPARAMETRIC TESTS
- Sign Test (Signed Rank)
- Wilcoxon One Sample Test
- Mann-Whitney U
- Kruskal-Wallis Test
- Friedman Chi-Square Test
- Spearman or Kendall Correlation
- Log Rank Test
- Mantel Haenzel Survivorship
- Kendall's Coefficient of Concordance
- McNemars Test
- Fishers Exact Test
- Contingency Tables

THE CONTROLLER

The Center for Quality Control Training
P.O.Box 713
LaGrange, IL 60525
(312) 579 - 1488
Contact Person: John Blazejak

CONFIGURATIONS SUPPORTED

Computer	Language	Operating System	RAM	Number Drives	Cost
IBM PC	BASIC COMPILED	DOS	256K	1	$ 425

NUMBER OF CURRENT USERS 600
DATE OF FIRST RELEASE June 83
VERSION 2.1 RELEASED May 86

PROGRAM DESCRIPTION

The Controller is a program to perform Statistical Process Control. The Controller makes it easy to apply SPC to any or all of your processes. It is equally at home on the shop floor or in the production or quality control office. It is intended for use by production personnel, and production engineering.

The Controller is menu-driven for ease of use. Control charts for average, range, defects, defectives, defects per unit, and individuals are available. Process capability studies are also performed by The Controller. Data can be input from other programs as well as dumped to other programs such as 1-2-3, dBase III, etc. In addition, comments about materials, operators, machine settings, etc., can be entered in a special comment section in order to determine why your process is out-of-control. The Controller accepts sample sizes from 2 to 50 for x-bar and R charts and stores data for up to 32,000 time periods.

TYPE OF PROGRAM

Statistical Package

PROGRAM DESIGNED FOR

Data Analysis

PROGRAM STYLE
- Menu Driven
- Integrated System

MISCELLANEOUS PROGRAM FEATURES
- Copyable Disk

DOCUMENTATION
- User's Manual - 55 pages, 6 technical references
  - Table of Contents
  - Index
  - Tutorial or Example Lessons
  - Sample Runs
  - Formulas Provided

DATA MANAGEMENT
- Keyboard Data Entry

DATA EDITING
- Change
- Add
- Delete

FOREIGN DATA ACCESS
- Standard Rectangular ASCII Files

GRAPHICS FEATURES
- Graphics Appear in Color on the Monitor
- Graphics can be Output to a Printer
- Titles and/or Labels Available
- Uses Pixel Graphics
- Uses Character Graphics

GRAPHICS
- Histograms
- Control Charts

PRODUCT SUPPORT
- User may call at own Expense
- Classes or Instruction Available

STATISTICAL FEATURES SUPPORTED

DESCRIPTIVE STATISTICS

- Mean
- Standard Deviation or Variance
- Minimum, Maximum

CONTROL CHARTS

- X-Bar
- Proportions
- Number of Defects
- Number of Defectives
- R
- Individuals

THE EXPLORER

The Center for Quality Training
P.O. Box 713
LaGrange, IL 60525
(312) 579 - 1488
Contact Person: John Blazejak

CONFIGURATIONS SUPPORTED

Computer	Language	Operating System	RAM	Number Drives	Cost
IBM PC	COMPILED BASIC	DOS	192K	1	$ 175

NUMBER OF CURRENT USERS 278
DATE OF FIRST RELEASE Sep 83
VERSION 1.1 RELEASED Mar 85

PROGRAM DESCRIPTION

The Explorer is a powerful, yet easy to use, Software package for statistical analysis on the IBM PC. It is intended for use by quality control specialists, engineers, R.D scientists, statisticians, or anyone who wants to analyze data quickly, easily and inexpensively.

The Explorer includes procedures for most standard statistical procedures, such as t-tests, ANOVA, multiple regression, etc., as well as the more recently developed tools of Exploratory Data Analysis. The Explorer can handle up to 5000 data points and 100 variables. Data can be exchanged easily between the The Explorer and most other programs, such as 1-2-3, dBase III, etc. Also, regression analysis results can be viewed with response surface contour plots.

TYPE OF PROGRAM

Statistical Package

PROGRAM DESIGNED FOR

Data Analysis

PROGRAM STYLE
Menu Driven
Integrated System

MISCELLANEOUS PROGRAM FEATURES
Copyable Disk

DOCUMENTATION
User's Manual - 65 pages, 8 technical references
Table of Contents
Index
Tutorial or Example Lessons
Sample Runs

DATA MANAGEMENT
Keyboard Data Entry
Data Manipulations and Transformations
Missing Values Allowed in Data

DATA EDITING
Change
Add
Delete

FOREIGN DATA ACCESS
Standard Rectangular ASCII Files

GRAPHICS FEATURES
Graphics Appear in Color on the Monitor
Uses Character Graphics

GRAPHICS
Histograms
Scatter (x-y) Plots
Box Plots

PRODUCT SUPPORT
User may call at own Expense
Classes or Instruction Available

STATISTICAL FEATURES SUPPORTED

DESCRIPTIVE STATISTICS
- Mean
- Standard Deviation or Variance
- Minimum, Maximum
- Median

t-TESTS
- One Sample t-Test
- Independent Group t-Test/Equal Variance
- Independent Group t-Test/Unequal Var
- Paired t-Test

CORRELATION AND REGRESSION
- Pearson Correlation Coefficient
- Simple Linear Regression
- Multiple Linear Regression
- Residuals Calculated
- **REGRESSION PLOTS**
  - Residuals

CONFIDENCE INTERVALS
- Means
- Difference Between Two Means
- Proportions
- Difference Between Two Proportions
- Variances
- Ratio of Variances

CATEGORICAL DATA ANALYSIS
- Chi-Square Contingency Table Analysis
- Fisher's Exact Test

ANALYSIS OF VARIANCE
- One-Way ANOVA
- Two-Way ANOVA
- Two-Way Unequal Cell Sizes Allowed

NONPARAMETRIC TESTS
- Sign Test (Signed Rank)
- Wilcoxon One Sample Test
- Mann-Whitney U

DISTRIBUTION FUNCTION EVALUATION

- Normal
- t
- Chi Square
- F
- Binomial
- Hypergeometric
- Poisson

EXPLORATORY DATA ANALYSIS

- Stem-and-Leaf Displays
- Letter-Value Displays
- Resistant Line
- Smoothing Techniques
- Box Plots

MISCELLANEOUS

- Test for Normality of Data
- Test for Equality of Variances
- p-Values Given With Tests

THE INSPECTOR

The Center for Quality Control Training
P.O. Box 713
LaGrange, IL 60525
(312) 579 - 1488
Contact Person: John Blazejak

CONFIGURATIONS SUPPORTED

Computer	Language	Operating System	RAM	Number Drives	Cost
IBM PC	COMPILED BASIC	DOS	128K	1	$ 95

NUMBER OF CURRENT USERS 305
DATE OF FIRST RELEASE June 83
VERSION 1.3 RELEASED July 85

PROGRAM DESCRIPTION

The Inspector is an easy to use computer program developed to help determine and evaluate attribute sampling plans. Many companies are finding that the widely used published sampling plans, such as Mil-Std-1050, do not meet their special needs or are not economical. You can use the Inspector to develop economical attribites sampling plans tailored to your exact needs.

The Inspector calculates and plots the operating characteristic curves for any single or double sampling plan. Probabilities of acceptance can be specified and the Inspector will calculate the corresponding proportion defective. Specify any proportion defective and the probability of acceptance is calculated. The Inspector also allows you to specify any AQL or RQL and appropriate sampling plans are calculated.

TYPE OF PROGRAM
Sampling Plan Analysis

PROGRAM DESIGNED FOR
Data Analysis

PROGRAM STYLE
Menu Driven
Integrated System

MISCELLANEOUS PROGRAM FEATURES
Copyable Disk

DOCUMENTATION
User's Manual - 20 pages, 2 technical references
Table of Contents
Index
Tutorial or Example Lessons

DATA MANAGEMENT
Keyboard Data Entry

GRAPHICS FEATURES
Graphics Appear in Color on the Monitor
Graphics can be Output to a Printer
Uses Character Graphics

GRAPHICS
OC Curves

PRODUCT SUPPORT
User may call at own Expense
Classes or Instruction Available

STATISTICAL FEATURES SUPPORTED

CONTROL CHARTS
OTHER QUALITY CONTROL PROCEDURES
Acceptance Sampling by Attributes

MISCELLANEOUS
Sample Size Estimation

THE PRIME PLOTTER
PrimeSoft Corp.
P.O. Box 30
Cabin John, MD 20818
(301) 229 - 4229
Contact Person: Ron Zahavi

CONFIGURATIONS SUPPORTED

Computer	Language	Operating System	RAM	Number Drives	Cost
APPLE II	BASIC/ ASSEMBLY	DOS	64K	1	$240

NUMBER OF CURRENT USERS 1000+
DATE OF FIRST RELEASE 1982
VERSION 1.1 RELEASED 1984

PROGRAM DESCRIPTION

This is a comprehensive graphics and statistics package, suitable for business, technical and scientific applications. Statistics and data management: On-line statistical modules provide more than 16 curve fit regressions and distributions, as well as averaging, smoothing, and conversion through user-defined functions. The program can read/write DIF files used by VisiCalc. X-Y and pie charts: You can choose unlimited combinations and overlays of scatter, lines, area fill, bars, multiple bars, 3-D bars, hi-lo charts, error bars, and log scales. Also choose from pies in 3-D perspective, pushed and/or exploded pieces, and an endless variety of fillings. Labeling and graphics- Your choices include: automatic or manual labeling, placement on any screen location, eight directions, and superscripts and subscripts. More than 20 letter types are available. Character sets include uppercase and lowercase, small letters, Greek alphabet, and a set of symbols. More sets can be added. Graphics routine include free-draw, fill, frames, copy, and shape manipulation.

The program is modular, allowing expansion and customization through add-on modules. It is menu-driven (with default settings that the user can change), and includes on-line help. A unique replay feature allows you to design an hour-long, multi-screen presentation of both text and graphics. When plotted, the graphics are ideal for reports and presentations. Plotter software interfaces allow the user to interface with the plotter directly, from within the program. The user can specify the area of the paper to which the screen is translated, communicate directly with the plotter through a user like option and have manual or automatic pen selection.

PRODUCT REVIEWS

Business Software, Vol. 1, No. 5 (Software Profile), (Sept-Oct 1983).

Morgenstein, David. Washington Apple Pi, Vol. 5, No, 5, (May 83).

Williams, Chris. Micro, No. 63, pp. 126.

MacNicol, Gregory. InfoWorld.

Burlbaw, Edward. Peelings II, Vol. 4, No, 4, pp. 13-15, 29, (1983).

Softalk, pp. 175, (Sept 83).

TYPE OF PROGRAM
Graphics

PROGRAM DESIGNED FOR
Data Analysis

PROGRAM STYLE
Menu Driven
Integrated System

MISCELLANEOUS PROGRAM FEATURES
On Screen Help Function

DOCUMENTATION
User's Manual - 250 pages, ? technical references
- Table of Contents
- Tutorial or Example Lessons
- Sample Runs
- Formulas Provided

Quick Reference Card
Tutorials and Examples on Disk

DATA MANAGEMENT
Keyboard Data Entry
Data Manipulations and Transformations
Missing Values Allowed in Data

DATA EDITING
- Change
- Add
- Delete

FOREIGN DATA ACCESS
- Standard Rectangular ASCII Files
- DIF Files

GRAPHICS FEATURES
- Graphics Appear in Color on the Monitor
- Graphics can be Output to a Printer
- Graphics can be Saved to a File
- Titles and/or Labels Available
- Uses Pixel Graphics
- Uses Character Graphics

GRAPHICS
- Histograms
- Pie Charts
- Scatter (x-y) Plots
- 3-D Plotting
- Box Plots
- 3-D Pie

PRODUCT SUPPORT
- User may call at own Expense
- No Classes or Instruction Available

STATISTICAL FEATURES SUPPORTED

DESCRIPTIVE STATISTICS
- Mean
- Standard Deviation or Variance
- Standard Error of the Mean
- Coefficient of Variation
- Minimum, Maximum
- Median
- Percentiles

CORRELATION AND REGRESSION
- Simple Linear Regression
- Nth Order
- Spillman
- Inverse Log
- Exponential
- Inverse
- Geometric
- Logarithmic

CATEGORICAL DATA ANALYSIS
- Chi-Square Contingency Table Analysis
- Goodness-of-Fit Tests
- Frequencies Can be Entered Directly

DISTRIBUTION FUNCTION EVALUATION
- Normal
- Chi Square
- Gamma

TIME SERIES ANALYSIS
- Moving Average Smoothing
- **TIME SERIES ANALYSIS - FORECASTING**
  - Growth Rate

RELIABILITY
- Exponential
- Gamma
- Logistic

THE SCIENTIFIC DESK

C. ABACI
208 St. Mary's Street
Raleigh, NC 27605
(919) 832 - 4847
Contact Person: Dr. Edward Battiste

CONFIGURATIONS SUPPORTED

Computer	Language	Operating System	RAM	Number Drives	Cost
	FORTRAN	DOS AIX	256K	1	$1320

NUMBER OF CURRENT USERS 350
DATE OF FIRST RELEASE May 84
VERSION 2 RELEASED May 86

ADDITIONAL SOFTWARE REQUIRED
FORTRAN Compiler (needed for library)

PROGRAM DESCRIPTION

"THE SCIENTIFIC DESK" is a problem solving environment for scientific users of computers. It contains a large tool set consisting of (1) a user interface in which programs, documentation, tutorials, and examples are integrated in a scope-oriented, menu-driven (interactive) form. This interface is oriented toward leading the user from problem to tools for use in solutions. The tools are a large library of functions and subroutines which cover the areas of arithmetic, error analysis, elementary and special functions of mathematical physics, linear algebra, interpolation, solution of nonlinear equations, optimization, differentiation and integration, differential equations, integral transforms (ffts), approximation and data fitting, statistics and probability.

In addition to the library, the DESK includes a large number of problem solvers, which require no programming. These cover approximation, eigensystem analysis, zeroes of polynomials, generation and testing of random deviates, linear algebraic equations, vector/matrix arithmetic, multiple linear regression, constrained least squares, ordinary differential equations solving, over-determined system solving, plotting (and fitting) histograms, scatterplots, quadrature (user defined functions or tabled data) and statistical inference and estimation. Leaders in the evolution of numerical techniques for application on computers aid C. Abaci in building the DESK. THE SCIENTIFIC DESK operates on IMB PC, AT, XT, and RT PC and large scale VAX and compatible machines.

TYPE OF PROGRAM
Mathematical/Statistical Problem Solving

PROGRAM DESIGNED FOR
Data Analysis
Educational use

PROGRAM STYLE
Command Driven
Integrated System

MISCELLANEOUS PROGRAM FEATURES
Source Code Available
Copyable Disk
On Screen Help Function

DOCUMENTATION
User's Manual - ? pages, 100 technical references
Table of Contents
Tutorial or Example Lessons
Sample Runs
Tutorials and Examples on Disk

DATA MANAGEMENT
Keyboard Data Entry
Data Manipulations and Transformations

DATA EDITING
Change
Add
Delete

GRAPHICS FEATURES
Graphics can be Output to a Printer
Graphics can be Saved to a File
Titles and/or Labels Available
Uses Pixel Graphics

GRAPHICS
Histograms
Scatter (x-y) Plots

PRODUCT SUPPORT
User may call at own Expense
No Classes or Instruction Available

STATISTICAL FEATURES SUPPORTED

DESCRIPTIVE STATISTICS

- Mean
- Standard Deviation or Variance
- Standard Error of the Mean
- Coefficient of Variation
- Minimum, Maximum
- Median
- Percentiles
- Skewness
- Kurtosis

t-TESTS

- One Sample t-Test
- Independent Group t-Test/Equal Variance
- Independent Group t-Test/Unequal Var
- Paired t-Test

CORRELATION AND REGRESSION

- Pearson Correlation Coefficient
- Simple Linear Regression
- Multiple Linear Regression
- Non-Linear Regression
- Residuals Calculated
- **REGRESSION PLOTS**
  - Residuals

CONFIDENCE INTERVALS

- Means
- Difference Between Two Means
- Variances
- Ratio of Variances

CATEGORICAL DATA ANALYSIS

- Goodness-of-Fit Tests

ANALYSIS OF VARIANCE

- One-Way ANOVA

DISTRIBUTION FUNCTION EVALUATION

- Normal
- t
- Chi Square
- F
- Binomial
- Hypergeometric
- Poisson

MISCELLANEOUS

Random Number Generation
Test for Normality of Data
Test for Equality of Variances
Sample Size Estimation